WITCHCRAFT AND
IN ENGLAND AND AMERICA, 1550-1750

WITCHCRAFT AND SOCIETY IN ENGLAND AND AMERICA, 1550–1750

Edited by Marion Gibson

Cornell University Press

Ithaca, New York

This selection and introductory material
© Marion Gibson 2003.

First published 2003 by Cornell University Press.

ISBN cloth 0-8014-4224-9
ISBN paper 0-8014-8874-5

Printed in Great Britain.

Librarians: Library of Congress Cataloging-in-Publication
Data are available.

CONTENTS

ACKNOWLEDGEMENTS

Many thanks to Manchester University Press, the Peabody Essex Museum, Cambridge University Press, Penguin Books, Professors A. R. Braunmuller, Peter Corbin and Douglas Sedge for their permission to quote or otherwise make use of materials in this edition. Thanks also to the British Library, Bodleian Library, Huntington Library, Folger Shakespeare Library, Devon Record Office, the Public Record Office and Exeter University Library, and their helpful staffs. An especial thank you to those who conceived and made available 'Early English Books Online' and 'UMI microfilms of Early English Books', and to Exeter University for allowing me access to these resources.

Thanks as always to Mum and Dad, and thanks to Dr Adeline Johns-Putra and Dr Ella Westland for being superb and supportive new colleagues. This book is for Dr Harry Bennett, with love.

INTRODUCTION

The documents and extracts chosen for this edited collection are intended to give a picture of how diversely witchcraft was understood by a wide range of people in, to use George Lyman Kittredge's phrase, 'Old and New England' in the sixteenth, seventeenth and early eighteenth centuries.[1]

English witchcraft has often been perceived as special, different from 'Continental' (including, apparently, Scottish) witchcraft, which was characterized by un-English orgies of sex with Satan, followed by equally foreign orgies of witch-burning. English witches were seen as more likely to be solitary practitioners, accompanied by animal familiars, who died neatly and in restricted numbers on the gallows. American witchcraft was different again, the story of the Salem witches being told and retold with increasing emphasis on un-American voodoo in the forest, puritan repression and chauvinism in the New World. But in the 1990s, further research established that there were more similarities between the witch-beliefs and prosecuting activities of different cultures than had been supposed. England was seen to be rather like the Nordic and Baltic states, whilst the traditional 'Continental' stereotype of witch-hunting was a phenomenon mainly confined to France, Germany and Italy – a heartland surrounded by a periphery of less lurid histories, which nevertheless shared important assumptions about what witches did.[2] In scholarship, American witchcraft still tends to stand apart from these European histories, but it can be seen here that there is a further continuum – between such writers as, say, the Englishman George Gifford and the Anglo-American Increase Mather – which suggests a shared history as well as a divergent one. In societies across Europe and America, witchcraft was seen as a problematic menace: a phenomenon on the one hand obviously at work within the community but, on the other, extremely hard to define, and riddled with theological traps. No amount of exegesis of biblical texts, testing of suspects or logical argument could satisfy the urge to pin witchcraft down, to define it correctly on a permanent basis. The central place that the Salem witch trials

---

1. G. L. Kittredge, *Witchcraft in Old and New England* (Cambridge, MA: Harvard University Press, 1929).
2. Bengt Ankarloo and Gustav Henningsen, eds, *Early Modern European Witchcraft: Centres and Peripheries* (Oxford: Clarendon, 1993).

have been assigned within the teaching of American history and literature shows how a mistaken definition of witchcraft could scar a culture, and English history also demonstrates that the definition of witchcraft could become central to the affirmation of a national myth. In the sixteenth and seventeenth centuries, the witchcraft menace was defined against English Protestant divine right, but by the mid–eighteenth century that belief itself stood condemned as an embarrassment to national, rational progress. In the twentieth century, the reinvention of witchcraft as Wicca in England and as feminist Witchcraft in America, with emphasis on mythic Celtic and Druid influences and the powers of sexuality and the mind, confirms its ongoing importance in the histories discussed in this book.

Indeed, as this volume hopes to show, histories are made up of stories: myths, opinions and anecdotes that may tell a coherent tale or that may disintegrate on closer inspection into contradictions, qualifications and general subtlety. There is thus no insistence on any particular version of the story of English and American witchcraft in this volume, but there are many fascinating stories to be read and interpreted as part of a bigger, infinitely complex picture. The accounts reproduced here come from as far apart as Salem and East Anglia, Yorkshire and Devon, and range from the 1550s to the 1730s. Represented are the words of housewives, conjurors, farmers, possession victims, lawyers, nurses, churchmen, physicians, exorcists, poets and a famous novelist.

The collection begins with the definition of witchcraft in English law, which set the parameters for the detection and prosecution of the crime in territories under England's control, including her American colonies (although Scotland had her own witchcraft laws). Witches are shown to be those who afflict their neighbours and others with misfortune, sickness and death, and who also practise a range of ungodly magical rites in the community. Later, in Chapters 1, 2 and 8, the collection gives examples of legal documents produced in England and in her colony of Massachusetts in the process of prosecuting such witches, and it adds an example from a church court, for comparison with informations (accusations), examinations (of suspects) and indictments (formal charges) from the Assizes (secular, criminal courts). Chapter 2 looks at how witchcraft was perceived by observers, as opposed to participants in cases, with a pamphlet produced with the guidance of a magistrate who had examined witches, and a descriptive manuscript written by someone attending a witch trial.

Chapter 3 continues the theme of scholarly observation of witchcraft, giving three examples of attempts to theorize it. English writers did not invent demonology, the study of devils and witches, and so each writer was reacting to previous Classical and European writers, who form a great, unrepresented bulk outside the scope of this collection. The best study of demonology is Stuart Clark's *Thinking with Demons: The Idea of Witchcraft in Early Modern Europe* (Oxford: Clarendon, 1997) and readers who want to know more about the context in which these English writers formulated their theories should refer to it. But each writer chosen here has something to say about the theorists who informed his viewpoint, and makes a distinctive contribution to the debate about what witchcraft was (and was not) in his experience, and how it might best be dealt with. There are a further three examples of demonological writing in Chapter 8, on American witchcraft.

Demonologists studied witchcraft because they believed that in and alongside a proper understanding of the devil and the supernatural lay a proper understanding of God and the natural world. Their tone, therefore, is earnest, angry, engaged. Contrastingly, Chapter 4 introduces representations of witchcraft produced by writers intent on the entertainment of their audience. Comic (*The Witch*) and tragic (*Macbeth*) representations of the figure of the witch are followed by arguably the most interesting witchcraft play from the English Renaissance (*The Witch of Edmonton*), which attempted to reproduce on stage elements of a real-life occurrence in Jacobean Middlesex. The dramatists' fiction raises questions about reality, illusion and moral responsibility, which were often left unexplored in actual prosecutions. An extract from a sixteenth-century epic poem (*The Faerie Queene*) shows us a fantasy witch-figure, a powerful and seductive woman very unlike her real-life counterparts, whilst an extract from a Jacobean masque (*The Masque of Queenes*) displays the witch as demonologists saw her: a hideous, disruptive female with roots in classical culture. Finally, a late-seventeenth- or eighteenth-century poem by a churchman gives moral guidance on witchcraft. Needless to say, most modern readers will find elements of the fictional in all the accounts of witchcraft offered in this book.

Chapter 5 looks at the victims of witchcraft, in particular those said to be possessed by the devil, or obsessed – a form of control exercised by the devil from outside the victim's body rather than within. Possession and obsession were usually thought to be caused by a witch sending the devil to or into the victim as an additionally unpleasant way of punishing that individual for causing offence. Chapter 6 moves on from the debates about malefic (harmful) witchcraft, its practitioners and its consequences, to introduce representations of those who believed they practised magic for higher ends. This chapter concentrates on male conjurors: men whose study of magic, and contact with the devil, was intended to bring them closer to an understanding of the secrets of spirits and nature, and keep them free from accusations of devil-worship.

Christopher Marlowe's tragic play *Dr Faustus* raises many of the questions sixteenth-century people posed about the practice of magic, and the relationship between man, God and the devil (or devils). Was magic inherently anti-Christian? Could it not be used for good? Did its practice lead straight to damnation? Was a pact with the devil necessary? How did such a pact work? The anonymous play *The Merry Devil of Edmonton*, conversely, brushes aside such questions in the pursuit of a good joke. Like Thomas Middleton's *The Witch*, it finds black comedy in even the most devilish darkness, as the conjuror outwits his demon. Chapter 7 continues the theme of crowd-pleasing tricksters with extracts from two early-seventeenth-century comedies based on the characters of pseudo-scientific quacks. The idea that most 'magic' was simply a con-trick was to become increasingly important in seventeenth-century debate on witches, and was to triumph completely (officially, at least) in the eighteenth.

However, increasing scepticism in some quarters was balanced by fervent belief in others. Chapter 8 looks at witchcraft in colonial America, taking the most famous New England case as its example, and Chapter 9 ends the collection with a series of extracts from the works of later seventeenth- and eighteenth-century writers, whose demonological speculations were becoming increasingly heated and party-political. Taking up the arguments of earlier demonologists from Chapter 3, Joseph Glanvill, Francis Hutchinson and Daniel Defoe (among many others) debated the contemporary relevance of witchcraft, and set some of the parameters for future theorists, dramatists and lawmakers. For Glanvill, witchcraft was as concrete a reality as it had ever been at a sixteenth-century Assize, but for Hutchinson witchcraft prosecution was itself a socio-cultural phenomenon, and for Defoe the whole vexed hell-brew was mostly a metaphor for human vice and ignorance. Belief in witchcraft certainly did not die in the eighteenth century, but it entered several new phases as it ceased to be a crime.[3]

Editorial Note

All prose texts are presented with original spelling, punctuation (or lack of it) and paragraphing, but play and poem texts have been modernized. This is because many plays and poems, especially very well-known texts such as *Dr Faustus*, *The Faerie Queene* and *Macbeth*, have been edited and re-edited over several centuries, and much valuable scholarship must be discarded, unpicked and redone if they are to be returned to their original published form. All have been re-edited from original printed versions, however, and as much original punctuation as is practical has been retained. Secondly, lengthy pieces of verse are traditionally more intimidating to readers than prose, and so by modernizing poems' and plays' texts, the editor hopes to make them more recognizable and accessible. They can also be cross-referenced with existing modern editions very easily. In several cases, readers are referred to an excellent existing edition, the editorial practice and notes of which have been particularly useful guides in the present edition. Where surviving printed versions of a text are sufficiently various, the edition, and/or library owning the copy consulted, is given.

---

3. For witchcraft after 1750, see Owen Davies, *Witchcraft, Magic and Culture 1736–1951* (Manchester: Manchester University Press, 1999), and Ronald Hutton, *The Triumph of the Moon: A History of Modern Pagan Witchcraft* (Oxford: Oxford University Press, 1999).

Early modern texts, especially in manuscript form, often use a large number of abbreviations, which can add both difficulty and flavour to an old text. Here, contractions have almost always been noted where they are longer than one letter, with the word as it originally appears left in the main text and the full form appearing in a footnote. Where only one letter is to be added, using a very common contraction, it has usually been added without comment. 'Ye' and other archaisms are left untouched, although their sense as abbreviations is obvious. The intention throughout has been to give the reader a sense of what the text looks like in its original form without making it unreadable.

Other editorial conventions (the use of curly brackets to indicate erasures, the use of square brackets for all stage directions, and so forth) are explained in the first footnote to deal with a particular form – say, manuscript or drama – so that they can be easily found. The footnotes offer a glossary, explanations of difficult syntax, extra information and comment on textual problems such as illegibility or mistranscription. Where a text is reproduced incomplete, readers are referred to a complete edition or facsimile (usually a fairly accessible one, where possible; see the 'Select bibliography and further reading' at the back of the volume).

Each text is introduced with a discussion of its origin and context. The texts in the volume should be read more or less in the order in which they appear, as the introductions build on one another to give a picture of the range and development of views on English and American witchcraft.

This book is dedicated to Harry Bennett
and to the memory of Chris Brooks

ONE

WITCHCRAFT IN THE COURTS

1. Acts: how was witchcraft defined?

An Act against Conjurations, Witchcrafts, Sorcery, and Enchantments 1541/2
33 Hen. VIII c. 8[1]

Henry VIII's Act, the eighth of the thirty-third year of his reign, was the first to define witchcraft as a felony, a serious crime. It was concerned with all manner of magical activity, from magical harming (maleficium) to treasure-hunting, and imposed the death penalty for all of these. It was repealed in general (that is, along with other old legislation) by an Act of Edward VI, so that by Elizabeth I's time there was no Act imposing penalties for witchcraft, as 5 Eliz. I c. 16 (below) notes.

Where dyvers and sundrie persones unlawfully have devised and practised Invocacons[2] and conjuracons of Sprites, ptendyng[3] by such meanes to understande and get Knowlege for their own lucre in what place treasure of golde and Silver shulde or mought be founde or had in the earthe or other secrete places, and also have used and occupied wichecraftes inchauntement and sorceries to the distruccon of their neighbours persones and goodes, And for execucon of their said falce devyses and practises have made or caused to be made dyvers Images and pictures of men women childrene

---

1. Statutes of the Realm have a life beyond their original form: retranscribed, retitled and modernized in standard reference works and legal textbooks, the witchcraft Acts are still usable in court, as evidenced in the Appeal of Helen Duncan against her conviction under the 1735 Act on 8–19 June 1944 (see Malcolm Gaskill, *Hellish Nell: Last of Britain's Witches* (London: Fourth Estate, 2001), pp. 315–20. The texts here use the original spelling with editorial structuring, titling and occasional repunctuation, as in most 'modern' textbooks (here, as in John Raithby, ed., *The Statutes at Large of England and of Great Britain* (London, 1811) and *A Collection of Public General Statutes* (London, 1824)).
2. The spelling is abbreviated: '-cons' is accompanied by a contraction mark to indicate '-cions' throughout. In this edition, common contractions (per, par, pro, and so forth) are noted where the word makes no sense without them.
3. With contraction: 'pretending'.

Angelles or develles beastes or fowles, and have also made Crownes Septures Swordes rynges glasses and other thinges, and gyving faithe & credit to suche fantasticall practises have dygged up and pulled downe an infinite nombre of Crosses wtin[4] this Realme, and taken upon them to declare and tell where thinges lost or stollen shulde be become; wiche thinges cannot be used and excersised but to the great offence of Godes lawe, hurt and damage of the Kinges Subjectes, and losse of the sowles of such Offenders, to the greate dishonor of God, Infamy and disquyetnes of the Realme:

For Reformacon wherof be it enacted by the Kyng oure Soveraigne Lorde wt thassent[5] of the Lordes spuall[6] and temporall and the Comons in this psent[7] Parliament assembled and by auctoritie of the same, that yf any persone or persones, after the first daye of Maye next comyng, use devise practise or exercise, or cause to be used devysed practised or exercised, any Invocacons or conjuracons of Sprites wichecraftes enchauntmentes or sorceries, to thentent to get or fynde money or treasure, or to waste consume or destroy any persone in his bodie membres or goodes, or to pvoke[8] any persone to unlawfull love, or for any other unlawfull intente or purpose, or by occacon or color of suche thinges or any of them, or for dispite of Cryste, or for lucre of money, dygge up or pull downe any Crosse or Crosses, or by suche Invocacons or conjuracons of Sprites wichecraftes enchauntementes or sorcerie or any of them take upon them to tell or declare where goodes stollen or lost shall become, That then all and evy[9] suche Offence and Offences, frome the saide first day of May next comyng, shalbe demyde[10] accepted and adjuged Felonye; And that all and evy persone and persones offendyng as is abovesaide their Councellors Abettors and Procurors and evy of them from the saide first day of Maye shallbe demyde accepted and adjuged a Felon and felones; And thoffender and offenders contrarie to this Acte, being therof lawfullie convicte before suche as shall have power and auctoritie to here and determyn felonyes,[11] shall have and suffre such paynes of deathe losse and forfaytures of their lands tentes[12] goodes and Catalles[13] as in cases of felonie by the course of the Comon lawes of this Realme, And also shall lose privilege of Clergie and Sayntuarie.[14]

---

4. Within.
5. The assent; 'the' was often merged with the word following it.
6. Spiritual.
7. Present.
8. Provoke.
9. Every.
10. Deemed.
11. Courts of Oyer and Terminer, Assizes.
12. Tenements.
13. Chattels.
14. Benefit of clergy was a legal loophole which would save literate persons from hanging if they could read a passage from the Bible. Sanctuary was the protection from secular justice offered by churches if the offender could reach a church before his or her pursuers.

An Act against Conjurations, Enchantments and Witchcrafts 1563
5 Eliz. I c. 16

In 1558 one of Henry VIII's daughters, the Protestant Queen Elizabeth, succeeded another, her Catholic sister Mary, and the resurgence and consolidation of Protestant government is an important context for understanding the Elizabethan Witchcraft Act. Scholars, with few records of the private deliberations of government to help them, have struggled to identify particular individuals who may have promoted legislation against witchcraft, but it is likely that the return of the Marian exiles, Protestants who had fled abroad to escape persecution by Mary, was an important factor. Returnee John Jewel, later Bishop of Salisbury, preached to the Queen in the second year of her reign on the horrors of witchcraft rampant in England. Jewel's emphasis was on the physical harm that witches caused their victims, and the Act's stress reflects his concern. More 'godly', puritan-leaning, churchmen would probably have preferred greater emphasis on the wickedness of compact with Satan, but instead the Act stressed supposedly verifiable, material grounds for conviction. It was more merciful than the previous Act, imposing a prison term (then an unusual penalty) rather than execution for offences causing harm short of death. Nevertheless, the Act also prohibited non-harmful magical activities such as treasure-hunting and was accompanied by An Act against fond and fantastical Prophesies, especially those of a political nature. Magical knowledge could, after all, be turned to seditious purposes.

Where at this present there ys no ordinarye ne condigne Punishement provided agaynst the Practisers of the wicked Offences of Conjuracons and Invocacons of evill Spirites, and of Sorceries Enchauntementes Charmes and Witchecraftes, the wch[15] Offences, by force of a Statute made in the xxxiii. yere of the Reigne of the late King Henry the Eyghthe were made to bee Felonye, and so continued untill the sayd Statute was repealed by Thacte and Statute of Repeale made in the first yere of the Reigne of the late King Edwarde the VIth; sythens the Repeale wherof many fantasticall and devilishe psons[16] have devised and practised Invocacons and Conjuracons of evill and wicked Spirites, and have used and practised Wytchecraftes Enchantementes Charms and Sorceries, to the Destruccoon of the Psons and Goodes of their Neighebours, and other Subjectes of this Realme, and for other lewde Intentes and Purposes, contrarye to the Lawes of Almighty God, to the Perill of theyr owne Soules, and to the great Infamye and Disquietnes of this Realme: For Reformacon wherof, be it enacted by the Quenes Matie[17] wth thassent of the Lordes Spuall and

---

15. Which.
16. Since the repeal ... persons.
17. Majesty.

Temporall and the Comons, in this pnte Pliament[18] assembled, and by thaucthoritee of the same, That yf any pson or psons, after the first daye of June nexte comming, use practise or exersise any Invocacons or Conjuracons of evill and wicked Spirites, to or for any Intent or Purpose; or els if any pson or psons after the said first daye of June shall use practise or exercise any Witchecrafte Enchantment Charme or Sorcerie, wherby any pson shall happen to be killed or destroyed, that then aswell every suche offendor or offendors in Invocacons or Conjuracons as ys aforesayd, their Concellors & Aidours, as also every suche offendor or offendors in Witchecrafte Enchantement Charme or Sorcerie wherby the Deathe of any pson dothe ensue, their Aidours and Concellors, being of either of the said Offences laufully convicted and attainted, shall suffer paynes of Deathe as a Felon or Felons, and shall lose the Priviledg and Benefite of Sanctuarie & Clergie: Saving to the Wief of such parsone[19] her Title of Dower, and also to the Heyre and Successour of such pson his or theyr Tytles of Inheritaunce Succession and other Rightes, as thoughe no suche Attayndour of the Auncestour or Predecessour had been hadd or made.

II. And further bee yt enacted by thaucthoritee aforesayd, That if any pson or psons, after the saide first daye of June nexte commyng, shall use practise or exercyse any Wytchecrafte Enchauntement Charme or Sorcerie, wherby any pon[20] shall happen to bee wasted consumed or lamed in his or her Bodye or Member, or wherby any Goodes or Cattelles of any pson shalbee destroyed wasted or impayred, then every suche offendour or Offendours their Councelloures and Aydoures, being therof laufully convicted, shall for his or their first Offence or Offences, suffer Imprisonment by the Space of one whole Yere, wthout Bayle or Mayneprise, and once in every Quarter of the said Yere, shall in some Market Towne, upon the Market Daye or at such tyme as any Fayer shallbee kepte there, stande openly upon the Pillorie, by the Space of Syxe Houres, and there shall openly confesse his or her Erroure and Offence; and for the Seconde offence, being as ys aforesayd laufully convicted or attaynted, shall suffer Deathe as a Felon, and shall lose the Privilege of Clergie and Sanctuarye ...

The same provisions are made for the wife and heir of a person so convicted. Section III provided for the trial of a peer accused of witchcraft. As was usual, he would be tried by the House of Lords.

IV. And further to thintent that all maner of practise use or exercise of Witchecrafte Enchantement Charme or Sorcerye shoulde bee from hensforthe utterly avoyded, abolished and taken awaye; Bee it enacted by

---

18. Present Parliament.
19. Person.
20. Person.

thaucthoritee of this pnte Pliament, That yf any pson or psons shall from and after the sayd first daye of June nexte comming, take upon him or them, by Witchecrafte Enchantement Charme or Sorcerie, to tell or declare in what Place any Treasure of Golde or Sylver shoulde or might bee founde or had in the Earthe or other secret Places, or where Goodes or Thinges lost or stollen should bee founde or becume, or shall use or practise anye Sorcerye Enchantement Charme or Witchcrafte, to thintent to provoke any pson to unlaufull love, or to hurte or destroye any pson in his or her Body, Member or Goodes; that then every suche pson or psons so offending, and being therof laufully convicted, shall for the said offence suffer Imprysonement by the space of One whole yere, wthout Bayle or Mayneprise, and once in every Quarter of the said yere shall in some Market Towne, upon the Marcket day or at suche tyme as any Fayer shall bee kept there, stande openly upon the Pillorie by the space of Sixe Houres, and there shall openly confesse his or her Error and Offence; And yf anye pson or psons, beyng once convicted of the same Offences as ys aforesayd, doo eftesones ppetrate[21] and committ the lyke Offence, that then every suche Offendour beyng thereof the seconde tyme convicted as ys aforesaid, shall forfaitee unto the Quenes Majesty, her heires and successoures, all his Goodes and Cattelles and suffer Imprysonement during Lyef.

An Act against Conjuration, Witchcraft and dealing with evil and wicked Spirits 1604
1 Jas. I c. 12

The 1604 Act, one of the first pieces of legislation in the reign of James I, changed the definition of witchcraft substantially. James, the author of a book on conjuration and witchcraft (*Daemonologie*, 1597), had a known interest in prosecuting witches (although this later developed into an interest in investigating fraudulent claims of bewitchment), and the new Act was harsher than Elizabeth's though less so than Henry's. It extended the death penalty to acts of witchcraft causing harm short of death to a victim, and prescribed death for all second offences whatsoever. It also added provisions against the keeping of evil spirits, as opposed to merely conjuring them, and the use of dead bodies in magic. Maleficium was no longer the only concern, and the tools and materials of the supposed trade of the witch received more attention. It was easier to prosecute witches, since theoretically all that was needed was a witness to assert that the witch kept spirits or the suspect to confess that s/he did so. Witches were also more likely to die for their offences. There was, however, no rush to prosecute and execute more witches. If anything, surviving records show a continued decline in prosecutions from a peak in the 1580s; a

---

21. Perpetrate.

trend that would not be reversed until the Civil War (see legal documents, Suffolk 1645 below) and which resumed thereafter.

Be it enacted by the King our Sovaigne[22] Lorde the Lordes Spirituall and Temporall and the Comons, in the psent Parliament assembled, and by the authoritie of the same, That the Statute made in the fifte yeere of the Raigne of our late Sovaigne Ladie of moste famous and happie memorie Queene Elizabeth, intituled An Acte againste Conjurations Inchantmentes and Witchcraftes, be from the Feaste of Saint Michaell the Archangell nexte comminge, for and concerninge all Offences to be committed after the same Feaste, utterlie repealed.

II. And for the better restrayninge of the saide Offenses, and more severe punishinge the same, be it further enacted by the authoritie aforesaide, That if any pson or persons, after the saide Feaste of Saint Michaell the Archangell next comminge, shall use practise or exercise any Invocation or Conjuration of any evill and wicked Spirit, or shall consult covenant with entertaine employ feede or rewarde any evill and wicked Spirit to or for any intent or purpose; or take up any dead man woman or child out of his her or theire grave, or any other place where the dead bodie resteth, or the skin bone or any other parte of any dead person, to be imployed or used in any manner of Witchcrafte Sorcerie Charme or Inchantment; or shall use practise or exercise any Witchcrafte Inchantment Charme or Sorcerie, wherebie any pson shalbe killed destroyed wasted consumed pined or lamed in his or her bodie, or any parte thereof; that then everie such offendor or offendors, theire Ayders Abettors and Counsellors, being of any the said Offences dulie and lawfullie convicted and attainted, shall suffer pains of deathe as a Felon or Felons, and shall loose the priviledge and Benefit of Cleargie and Sanctuarie.

III. And further, to the intent that all manner of practise use or exercise of Witchcrafte Inchantment Charme or Sorcerie should be from henceforth utterly avoyded abolished and taken away, Be it enacted by the authoritie of this psent Parliament, That if any pson or psons shall from and after the saide Feaste of Saint Michaell the Archangell next comminge, take upon him or them by Witchcrafte Inchantment Charme or Sorcerie to tell or declare in what place any treasure of Golde or Silver should or might be founde or had in the earth or other secret places, or where Goodes or Thinges loste or stollen should be founde or become; or to the intent to pvoke any person to unlawfull love or wherebie any Cattel or Goods of any pson shall be destroyed wasted or impaired, or to hurt or destroy any pson in his or her bodie, although the same be not effected and done; that then all and everie such pson or psons so offendinge, and beinge thereof lawfullie convicted, shall for the

---

22. Soveraigne.

said Offence suffer Imprisonment by the space of one whole yeere, without baile or maineprise, and once in everie quarter of the said yere, shall in some Markett Towne, upon the Markett Day, or at suche tyme as any Faire shalbe kepte there, stande openlie upon the Pillorie by the space of sixe houres, and there shall openlie confesse his or her error and offence.

IV. And if any pson or psons beinge once convicted of the same offences as is aforesaide, doe eftsones ppetrate and commit the like offence, that then everie such Offender, beinge of any the saide offences the second tyme lawfullie and duelie convicted and attainted as is aforesaide, shall suffer paines of death as a Felon or Felons, and shall loose the benefitt and priviledge of Clergie and Sanctuarie ...

The same provisions were made for wives and heirs as above, and the same provision made for the trial of peers.

The Witchcraft Act 1735
9 Geo. II c. 5

By 1735 there was enough influential weight behind the opinion that witchcraft, as traditionally constituted, did not exist, for an Act to be passed repealing the Witchcraft Act of 1604 as well as its Scottish counterpart. The new Act by its very existence redefined starkly what was and was not considered to be humanly possible: it replaced penalties for the actual practice of witchcraft with penalties for the pretence of witchcraft. People who claimed to be conjurors, dealers with spirits and so on would be prosecuted solely for their pretence and for the financial fraud usually believed to be involved, and not because they were believed to have real powers or traffic with Satan. Those who still believed that witches did have such powers, and that the Act was misguided, were forced to accept its provisions. The Act was still being used in the 1940s, when a number of people, from spiritualist mediums to gypsy diviners, were prosecuted under its terms. It was repealed in 1951.

An Act to repeal the Statute made in the First Year of the Reign of King James the First, intituled, An Act against Conjuration, Witchcraft, and dealing with evil and wicked Spirits, except so much thereof as repeals an Act of the Fifth Year of the Reign of Queen Elizabeth, against Conjurations, Inchantments, and Witchcrafts, and to repeal an Act passed in the Parliament of Scotland in the Ninth Parliament of Queen Mary, intituled, Anentis Witchcrafts,[23] and

---

23. For the text of the 1563 Scottish Act, see Lawrence Normand and Gareth Roberts, eds, *Witchcraft in Early Modern Scotland* (Exeter: Exeter University Press, 2000), p. 89. The Act prohibited the consultation of witches as well as magical activity and the penalty for all of these crimes was death.

for punishing such Persons as pretend to exercise or use any Kind of Witchcraft, Sorcery, Inchantment, or Conjuration.

Be it enacted by the King's most Excellent Majesty, by and with the Advice and Consent of the Lords Spiritual and Temporal, and Commons, in this present Parliament assembled, and by the Authority of the same, That the Statute made in the first Year of the Reign of King James the First, intituled, An Act against Conjuration, Witchcraft, and dealing with evil and wicked Spirits, shall, from the Twenty-fourth Day of June next, be repealed and utterly void and of none Effect (except so much thereof as repeals the Statute made in the Fifth Year of the Reign of Queen Elizabeth, intituled, An Act against Conjurations, Inchantments and Witchcrafts).

Section II repeated the previous repealing of the Scottish Act.

III. And be it further enacted, That from and after the said Twenty-fourth Day of June, no Prosecution, Suit, or Proceeding, shall be commenced or carried on against any Person or Persons for Witchcraft, Sorcery, Inchantment or Conjuration, or for charging another with any such Offence,[24] in any Court whatsoever in Great Britain.

IV. And for the more effectual preventing and punishing of any Pretences to such Arts or Powers as are before mentioned, whereby ignorant Persons are frequently deluded and defrauded; be it further enacted by the Authority aforesaid, That if any Person shall, from and after the said Twenty-fourth Day of June, pretend to exercise or use any kind of Witchcraft, Sorcery, Inchantment or Conjuration, or undertake to tell Fortunes, or pretend from his or her Skill or Knowledge in any occult or crafty Science, to discover where or in what Manner any Goods or Chattels, supposed to have been stolen or lost, may be found, every Person so offending, being thereof lawfully convicted on Indictment or Information in that part of Great Britain called England, or on Indictment or Libel in that part of Great Britain called Scotland, shall for every such offence suffer Imprisonment by the Space of one whole Year without Bail or Mainprize, and once in every Quarter of the said Year in some Market Town of the proper County, upon the Market Day, there stand openly on the Pillory by the Space of One Hour, and also shall (if the Court by which such Judgement shall be given shall think fit) be obliged to give Sureties for his or her good Behaviour, in such Sum, and for such Time, as the said Court shall judge proper according to the Circumstances of the Offence, and in such case shall be further imprisoned until such Sureties be given.

---

24. Accusers were sometimes themselves brought to trial for wrongful accusation.

2. Legal documents: how was witchcraft prosecuted?

Information, Examinations and Indictments

When a person was suspected of witchcraft, the first officially documented evidence of the suspicion was an 'information', a formal accusation made by the victim to a Justice of the Peace, a local magistrate. The information could be given on the victim's behalf if, for example, the victim was a child, very sick or had died. On this evidence, the magistrate was duty bound to call in the suspected witch and question him or her, producing a documentary record of what the suspect had said: this was an 'examination', sometimes referred to as a confession. The suspect, because they had been accused of a felony or serious crime, would then be committed for trial at the Assizes, the criminal court which dealt with felonies.

The charge against the suspect would be recorded in an 'indictment', written mostly in heavily abbreviated, formulaic Latin, unlike the pre-trial documents. The indictment might first go to the Quarter Sessions, where groups of local magistrates dealt with minor crimes and processed any outstanding felonies for the Assize Court. The Quarter Sessions grand jury would be asked to look at the evidence and decide whether there seemed to be a case to answer. If there was, the case would be passed to the Assizes. More usually, the case went straight to the Assizes where it would be scrutinized by the Assize grand jury. Like the alternative Quarter Sessions grand jury, they would decide whether there seemed to be a case to answer. If they thought there was not, the indictment would be marked 'ignoramus' and no further action would be taken. If they thought there was, it would be marked 'billa vera', a true bill. It would then be passed to the court itself, where at least one eminent judge (there were supposed to be two) would be presiding. The judge and a petty jury of 12 men would hear statements from the parties involved in the supposed crime, and the jury would (very quickly by modern standards) at once find the accused either guilty or not guilty. This verdict would be recorded on the indictment, which would then be filed with the records of the court.

Large numbers of indictments survive, therefore, but almost no pre-trial documents, as these were discarded after the trial. However, if someone involved in the trial process as a participant or spectator was interested in the evidence, it would sometimes be copied out by hand, and sometimes printed in a pamphlet account of the case. Other documents also survive in this way, most notably private accounts of witches' confessions and accusers' stories, by the accuser themselves, or do-it-yourself interrogators, or observers. The selection of pre-trial and trial documents below suggests the range of different materials available and includes a private record of materials containing accusers' informations and witches' confessions, an information and an examination from a printed pamphlet, and a translation of an indictment relating to a pamphlet of 1579, which incorporates some of the pre-trial evidence about the case.

1. Information and Examination: Suffolk 1645
From British Library Additional Manuscript 27402 (ff. 104–21)

In 1645, three years into England's Civil War, a gentleman from Manningtree in Essex named Matthew Hopkins began to interrogate people in his neighbour-hood who were suspected of witchcraft. Normally, suspects would simply be questioned by a Justice of the Peace and then imprisoned to await trial, although sometimes they had to endure lengthy and repeated testing (such as being thrown into water to see if they floated magically, or repeating the Lord's Prayer) by their supposed victims and interested magistrates. But Hopkins and his associates went much further than this: they introduced a complete system of interrogation which avoided the need for some of the more frequently discredited tests, and they put huge numbers of suspects through it. They decided that witches might more easily be brought to confess the truth if they were kept under guard, kept awake, searched for witches' teats, from which familiar spirits were supposed to suck blood, and watched. The reason for this watching was to see if familiar spirits came to the suspect but, as surviving documents make clear, there was a link between the sleep deprivation and subsequent confessions. Other pressures were also brought to bear: one text in this manuscript speaks candidly of 'violence, watchinge, or other threts'. With his psychologically corrosive combination of watching, searching and ques-tioning, Hopkins has become one of the great villains of English witchcraft history, portrayals of his activities in older history books, literature and films such as *Witchfinder General* depicting him as a deranged sadist.[25] But Hopkins' preoccupations were widely shared and his methods were approved of: witchfinding activities spread over England's eastern counties, and over 250 people were tried, most of them in 1645. Hopkins and others were often called in by communities to test and interrogate those they suspected locally. A Special Commission was appointed to try suspects identified in this way. Trials associated with Hopkins continued until 1647 (when he probably died) and somewhere between 100 and 200 people were probably hanged, although records are patchy and it is hard to be sure.

The confessions contained in surviving documents were untypical for their time, as was the vast number of the accusations and executions. Suspects routinely described meetings with the devil himself, having sex and covenanting with him, rather than simply the more usual contacts with ambiguously demonic familiars. It seems likely that the ideologically motivated Civil War, with its increased puritan activity, dislocation of local governmental and social structures, and the temporary absence of the usual Assize system, helped create conditions in which accusations spread very quickly and particular local people had great influence over forms of questioning and thus over answers given. After 1645, English witchcraft was perceived differently, both by fervent

---

25. *Witchfinder General* (dir. Michael Reeves, Salvation Films, 1968).

believers in demonic pact and by those who began to see witch-hunting as a flawed and repugnant activity.

The manuscript from which these texts are taken is a compilation: a mixture of notes taken by those watching the accused, informations by accusers and records of jury verdicts. It is in inconsistently spelled, abbreviated English with Latin phrases, and the syntax is often disrupted and confusing. The creator of the compilation, Thomas Martin of Palgrave (a village near Diss, Norfolk), stated that he had received the 'examinations', as he called them, from John Thruston or Thurston, a gentleman of Hoxne (4 miles to the east) whose ancestors were magistrates. He thought that one of those ancestors might have taken 'these Depositions'. But the documents seem like rough notes rather than word for word transcripts of formal informations and examinations. One says that the same confession was made 'again ... beefor the Justices', implying that the text which survives is part of unofficial interrogations by Hopkins and others, which later provided a basis for (lost) indictments.

Information of William Wels and others against Margaret Legate[26]

Margaret Legat de Playford,[27] Will Wels testatur.[28] that about 7 years since he fallinge out wth ye sone of Mar. Legate, his child fell sick. and askeinge the devise[29] of a Physitian in ipswitch cold find no cause of the desease, the child still continueinge sick. Cryed out it thought it was stunge wth wasps, soone after this Legate came to this informants howse upon[30] he thretened if she came there any more he wold through her in to ye river he beeinge a miller, yet after this she came to his howse, and {he} although he reviled her yet she came into his howse and sate upon his bed, and after he forced her out of his howse she fell downe and asked him[31] forgivenes,

Eadem[32] testatur Clerke that she sd to this infor.[33] that she was a damned creature and if she had not beene taken[34] she shold have done much harme. Alicia Fayth[35] testatur idem ut ante.[36]

Mar. Jason[37] sayth that whilst {she} this accusant[38] was watchinge one of her imps {came} like a mowle came to her and sucked her in ye secret pts.[39]

---

26. Words within curly brackets indicate intended erasures in the original manuscript.
27. Of Playford, near Ipswich, nearly 20 miles south of Hoxne.
28. Gives evidence.
29. Advice.
30. Upon which?
31. 'Him' is substituted for the erased 'her'.
32. The same (that is, against Margaret Legate).
33. Informant.
34. Arrested.
35. A difficult word to read. Cecil L'Estrange Ewen's transcript in *Witch Hunting and Witch Trials* (London: Kegan Paul, Trench, Trubner, 1929), pp. 294–5, suggests 'Eayth'.
36. The same as before.
37. The first letter here is obscured. Ewen suggests 'Jason'.
38. Jason.
39. Parts.

John Wilkinson testatur that she after 3 days watchinge sd that she had a thinge laiyd[40] by her like a child and cried but she never saw it nor never heard it speake, Ignoramus,[41]

Examination of Briget Bigsby

This examination-like text is in fact an account of what the suspect said to Richard Glamfield or Glanfield, one of those involved in watching the accused. In an examination under usual circumstances, the suspect spoke directly to the questioning magistrate.

Briget Bigsby. de eade.[42] testatur Rich. Glamfield, that she confessed freely wthout watchinge, ye first day. that she was a witch & that her grandmother had made her so, and that about 3 weeks after the last sessions there came 2 mise as she lay by the fier and scratched her by the foote & drew blood on her & that she was affraid and told her grandmother of it who bad her not be affraid but enteine[43] them and she shold be avenged of all her enemies, and upon the Thursday after the[44] came againe and drew tokens wch weare found about her[45] and at that time she heard a voyce speake to her wch bad her denie god &. Ch.[46] and he wold be a husband to her but she denied it, and saw not who it was that spake it, her imps told her theyr names Joweare John & naturall,[47] and have sucked 5 times since she had them, they told if she wold grant to theyr covenant she shold never rest day nor night.[48] billa: vera:

2. Printed Information and Examination: Devon 1682
From *A True and Impartial Relation of the Informations Against Three Witches* (London, 1682)

The writer of this pamphlet, describing the accusation and conviction of Temperance Lloyd, Mary Trembles and Susanna Edwards of Bideford, a small town in north Devon, states that 'this Relation was written by a faithful

---

40. Again, semi-legible. Ewen suggests 'livyd' but he has left out 'and cried' later in the sentence, which might suggest a different, more time-specific reading.
41. Despite this evidence, this annotation suggests that the lost bill of indictment was rejected.
42. Of the same: here, Hintlesham, 5 miles south-west of Playford.
43. Entertain.
44. *Sic.*
45. They drew (blood), evidence of which was found.
46. Christ.
47. Since she has only two imps earlier in the examination, this may be an error: perhaps it should read '{Jo} weare John and naturall', with the writer beginning to write 'John', then stopping and forgetting to erase it before writing 'weare' (were) and completing two names.
48. This seems to be a reference to the sleep deprivation to be expected.

and able Hand, employed in taking the Examinations and Confessions', alleging that 'it is the onely True, Authentick, and Exact Account'. This 'Hand' seems likely to be that of John Hill, the Town Clerk, whose name appears in the pamphlet certifying that he had examined at least one transcription with reference to the original, and that the copy was a true one. But in any process of transcription there are likely to be some errors, and when one adds the process of transferring a manuscript account to print, the risks that the original document will be altered, however subtly, increase. Nevertheless, all the informations and examinations reproduced in print (see also *A true and just Recorde* (London, 1582) below, pp. 24–52) are extremely important as a record of documents now lost, and/or as a demonstration of the value pre-trial documents had in seeming to provide an original, irrefutably true account of what had happened.

Information of Grace Barnes

Devon Ss. Biddiford Ss.[49] The Information of Grace Barnes, the Wife of John Barnes of Biddiford in the County aforesaid Yeoman, taken upon her Oath before Thomas Gift Mayor of the Burrough, Town, and Mannor of Biddiford aforesaid, and John Davie Alderman, two of his Majesties Justices of the Peace within the same Burrough, &c. the 2d day of August, Anno Dom. 1682.

The said Informant upon her Oath saith, That she hath been very much pain'd and tormented in her Body these many years last past, insomuch that she hath sought out for Remedy far and neer, and never had any suspition that she had had any Magical Art or Witchcraft used upon her Body, until it was about a year and a half ago, that she was informed by some Physicians that it was so.

And further saith, That thereupon she this Informant had some suspition of one Susanna Edwards of Biddiford aforesaid Widow, because that she the said Susanna would oftentimes repair unto this Informants Husband's house upon frivolous or no occasions at all.

And further saith, That about the middle of the month of May last past, she was taken with very great pains of sticking and pricking in her Arms, Breasts, and Heart, as though divers Awls had been pricked or stuck into her Body, and was in great tormenting pain for many days and nights together, with a very little intermission.

And saith, That upon Sunday the 16th day of July last, she was taken in a very grievous and tormenting manner; at which instant of time one Agnes Whitefield, the Wife of John Whitefield of Biddiford; was in this Informants Husband's house, who opening the Door, and looking out, found one Mary Trembles of Biddiford Single woman, standing before the Door. And thereupon this Informant did ask of the said Agnes Whitefield who it was that stood in the Door; who answered, that it was the said Mary Trembles. Upon which this Informant was fully assured, that the said Mary Trembles, together with the said Susanna Edwards, were the very persons that had tormented her, by using some Magical Art or Witchcraft upon her said Body as aforesaid.

Thomas Gift Mayor.
John Davie Alderman.

This information, which seems straightforward at first sight, is, however, probably a formal record drawn up for the 14 August Assizes in Exeter, rather than the first record of the accuser complaining of the suspected witch. This raises a variety of issues, most obviously the question 'has the original story been changed or become neater with retelling?' It cannot be the original complaint, for on 18 July Barnes and the women she had already accused were all brought to the Town Hall in Bideford, and Mary Trembles confessed:

Examination of Mary Trembles

Devon Ss. Biddiford Ss. The Examination of Mary Trembles of Biddiford in the County aforesaid Single woman, taken before Thomas Gift Mayor of the Burrough, Town, and Mannor of Biddiford aforesaid, and John Davie Alderman, two of his Majesties Justices of the Peace within the same Burrough, &c. the 18 day of July, Anno Dom. 1682.

The said Examinant being brought before us, and accused for practising of Witchcraft upon the Body of Grace Barnes the Wife of John Barnes of Biddiford aforesaid Yeoman, was demanded by us how long she had practised Witchcraft,[50] said and confessed, That about three years last past, one Susanna Edwards of Biddiford aforesaid Widow, did inform her, that if she would do as she the said Susanna did, that this Examinant should do very well. Whereupon this Examinant did yield unto the said Susanna Edwards, and said she would do as the said Susanna did.

And this Examinant further confessed, that the said Susanna Edwards did promise that she this Examinant should neither want for Money, Meat, Drink, nor Clothes.

And further confesseth, That after she had made this Bargain with the said Susanna Edwards, that the Devil in the shape of a Lyon (as she conceived) did come to this Examinant, and lay with her, and had carnal knowledge of her Body. And that after the Devil had had knowledge of her Body, that he did suck her in her Secret parts, and that his sucking was so hard, which caused her to cry out for the pain thereof.[51]

And further confesseth, That on Tuesday in Easter-week, which was the 18th day of May last past, she this Examinant did go about the Town of

---

50. Apparently a common opening question and one hard to answer safely.
51. *Sic.*

Biddiford to beg some Bread, and in her walk she did meet with the said Susanna Edwards, who asked of this Examinant where she had been. Unto whom this Examinant answered, That she had been about the Town, and had begged some Meat, but could get none. Whereupon this Examinant, together with the said Susanna Edwards, did go to the said John Barnes' house, in hope that there they should have some Meat. But the said John Barnes not being within his house, they could get no Meat or Bread, being denied by the said Grace Barnes and her Servant, who would not give them any Meat. Whereupon the said Susanna Edwards and this Informant[52] went away from the said John Barnes his house. And afterwards on the same day the said Susanna Edwards did bid this Examinant to go to the said John Barnes his house again for a Farthings worth of Tobacco. Whereupon this Examinant did go, but could not have any; whereof this Examinant did acquaint the said Susanna Edwards, who then said that it should be better for her the said Grace if that she had let this said Examinant to have had some Tobacco.

And further confesseth, That on the 16th day of this instant month of July, she this Examinant, with the said Susanna, did go to the said John Barnes his house in Biddiford aforesaid, and went at the Fore-door invisibly into the Room, where they did pinch and prick the said Grace Barnes almost unto death; and that she saw the said John Barnes in bed with his Wife on the inner-side of the Bed.

The said Examinant being further demanded how many times the Devil had had the carnal knowledge of her Body besides the time above-mentioned; She saith and confesseth, That the Devil hath had the carnal knowledge of her Body three other times; and that the last of the said three times, was upon the said 16th day of July as she was going towards the common Bakehouse. And that at the time she, with the help of the Devil, would have killed the said Grace Barnes, if that she the said Examinant had not spilt some of the Meat she was then carrying unto the said Bakehouse.

John Barnes said in his information that Trembles appeared to be going to the bakehouse when she was seen outside his door. Susanna Edwards also confessed to taking part in the attack on Grace Barnes. Edwards was also accused of harming others, as was another woman, Temperance Lloyd. All three women were convicted and hanged.

These examples illustrate both the value of pre-trial documents and the difficulties of interpreting the information contained in them. Itself a product of the dynamics of question and answer, experiment and rhetoric, the information often provokes more questions than it answers but it does tell us something of what witches were thought to have done and what suspects were prepared to admit. But there are almost always further problems of

---

52. A mistake, although Trembles is informing against Edwards.

transmission with these fragile accounts: mistranscription, eyeskip, torn or missing pages, and the difficulties of reading the secretary hand in which such documents were written.

3. Indictment: Essex 1579

Elena Smythe's indictment (below) survives among Assize records at the Public Record Office. We also know more about this woman: a contemporary pamphlet, *A Detection of damnable driftes* (London, 1579) includes material on one Ellein or Ellen Smithe, from Maldon in Essex, whose mother had been executed for witchcraft. A falling out with her stepfather, and the begging activities of Ellein's 13-year-old son caused accusations of witchcraft, the pamphlet suggests, whilst the accusation detailed here came after Ellein had hit the daughter of Widow Webbe. The child died two days later, and the mother 'fell distraught of her wittes'.[53]

Indictment of Elena Smythe

Essex Ss. The Jurors for our lady the Queen do present that Elena Smythe of Maldon in the county aforesaid, spynster, being a common witch and enchantress,[54] not having God before her eyes but seduced by the instigation of the devil, of her malice aforethought, on the seventh day of March in the twenty first year of the reign of our lady Queen Elizabeth[55] by the grace of God queen of England, France and Ireland defender of the faith, at Maldon aforesaid in the county aforesaid, a certain Susanna Webbe, an infant of four years or thereabouts, impiously, devilishly and feloniously did bewitch and enchant by reason of which bewitchment and enchantment the same Susanna on the said seventh day of March in the twenty first year abovesaid, and up to the eighth day of the month of March next following, at Maldon aforesaid did vehemently languish, upon which eighth day of March the same Susanna at Maldon aforesaid of the enchantment and bewitchment aforesaid died. And so the jurors aforesaid say upon their oaths that the said Elena Smythe did feloniously kill and murder the said Susanna Webbe by her enchantment and witchcraft aforesaid, against the peace of the said lady the Queen, her

---

53. For the pamphlet's account, see Marion Gibson, ed., *Early Modern Witches: Witchcraft Cases in Contemporary Writing* (London and New York: Routledge, 2000), pp. 44–5. It is interesting that a charge of murder by witchcraft was preferred to the more straightforward one of murder by physical assault, which the evidence (as we have it) would seem to support.

54. 'Fascinatrix et incantatrix', the female forms of 'fascinater' and 'enchanter'. Fascination was a classical idea analogous to the 'evil eye'. My translation preserves any English words in the indictment and adopts the usual legal equivalents for Latin terms.

55. The Assizes were on 2 April 1579, and Queen Elizabeth acceded to the throne in November 1558.

crown and dignity, and against the form of the statute in this case made and provided &c.[56]

The plea of the accused, together with the verdict, financial status of the accused and the carrying out of sentence were all recorded: *po se cul ca null Judic.* 'Po se' means 'ponit se super patriam' – the accused put herself (that is, her case) to the country. This shows that Ellein Smithe pleaded 'not guilty'. People who pleaded guilty were not tried, since they had confessed, so anyone pleading not guilty was in effect asking for a trial and judgement by their fellow countrymen. 'Cul' means 'culpabilis', guilty – Ellein was convicted of the crime. 'Ca null' indicates that she had 'catalla nulla', no chattels to be seized or left to others (almost all indictments say this, so although it does appear from other evidence that Ellein was poor, this annotation is not sufficient on its own to indicate this). The sentence for this crime was death, and 'Judic' records that 'judicium secundum formam statuti', the sentence was carried out according to the form of the statute.

56. PRO ASSI/35/21/4.

TWO

WITCHCRAFT IN ELIZABETHAN AND JACOBEAN ENGLAND

1. A cunning man in a church court

The examination of John Walsh or Welshe, 1566

In 1566 a Dorset man named John Walsh or Welshe was questioned in a church court, by the Commissary to the Bishop of Exeter, about his supposed practising of witchcraft. Commissary courts, like other church courts, were empowered to investigate suspected witchcraft but Walsh's alleged crimes could instead have been reported to a magistrate and he could have been sent to the Assizes. Clearly the new Witchcraft Act of 1563 did not spring to the minds of his accusers, perhaps because whilst Walsh was accused by his questioners of matters mentioned by the Act (conjuring evil spirits, especially for the finding of stolen goods) he was not questioned about harming specific goods or killing specific animals or persons. The 1563 Act concentrated upon these crimes of maleficium, and almost all Assize indictments were for maleficial acts rather than invocation. Walsh was fortunate that he was sent to a church court rather than a secular one, as the penalties imposed by ecclesiastical courts for crimes such as witchcraft were much less severe than secular sentences. If found guilty (and we do not know the court's judgment) Walsh would have been told to do penance rather than suffering a heavier penalty: he might well have been sentenced to death by an Assize court.

Because of the nature of the remaining records, it seems likely that the case against Walsh was brought by private persons. We do not know anything of them, and the record is very brief: a list of questions (known in this court as interrogatories) about particular charges (known as articles) with answers by Walsh himself (responsiones). Unlike the secular courts, these church courts operated a kind of adversarial system, with proctors making and rebutting the case against a suspect, each using a list of questions. But there is little evidence in this record of how the case was argued, and it seems likely that, as often happened, Walsh was asked to speak for himself. What is fascinating about the document is that its recorder has made modifications to his account of the case as he wrote, with additions, scribblings out and marginal comments that cast light on the way the questioners were thinking, and on Walsh himself.

There is another sidelight on the document, since it found its way into print in 1566. How this happened is unclear. Perhaps an official from Exeter went to London with the document (but why?) and found an interested publisher, or sent it to a friend who thought it worthy of wider readership? The publisher, John Awdeley, apparently found the chief interest of the document to be in its potential for anti-Catholic rhetoric, emphasizing for the reader the very brief mentions of Walsh's employer, Sir Robert of Drayton, as well as his reliance on the Catholic paternoster and 'hallowed' magical substances. The publisher wrote or commissioned a preface denouncing Catholic sorcery, and printed the document practically unchanged, except that he altered references to the protective power of the paternoster to the Protestant Lord's Prayer.[1] It seems likely, from this context, that the court may have been interested in Walsh as a Catholic, although his traditional understanding of religion may well have been simply the habit of a lifetime rather than deliberate recusancy.

This document is in the Devon Record Office, Chanter MSS 855B (f. 310–312v).

Res[2] die martis[3] xxmo die mensis Augustii[4] Ao[5] 1566.
{John Welshe}[6]

there was examynyd by m[7] williams Comissary to the byshop of Exon John walshe {was examynyd} certein inter[8] upon wiche[9] craft in the howse of Mr Tho[10] Sinkler keper of the Shereve[11] warde in the presences of jo[12] butler and Robert buller william blacheford and Jo bordfyld gentelmen[13]

John welshe beinge demondyd of his habitacion, he saythe that he dwellythe in a pishe[14] callyd netherberry in dosett shere.[15]

Ad secund[16] beinge demondyd whether he were ever Sr[17] Robert of

---

1. The pamphlet's text is available in Gibson, ed., *Early Modern Witches*, pp. 25–32.
2. Responsiones.
3. Tuesday.
4. The twentieth of the month of August.
5. Anno.
6. As before, words within curly brackets indicate intended erasures in the original manuscript.
7. Master.
8. Interrogatories.
9. Here there is a marginal note 'L yere or there about', suggesting that Walsh/Welshe was about 50 years old.
10. Thomas.
11. Sheriff's.
12. John.
13. Another marginal note 'he is L yeres old or there about'.
14. Parish.
15. Netherbury is a Dorsetshire village about 35 miles east of Exeter.
16. Ad secundum (secondly).
17. Sir (here, a title given to Catholic priests).

dreatons[18] man he saythe that he was reteininge to hem by the space of vii yeres.

Ad iii[19] he beinge demondyd whether he do practyse any fisike or surgerye he saythe that he do practyse bothe for the Tisikes and the agues[20] and that he hathe practysed this fisike by the space of vii yeres sithens his mr[21] dyed Sr Robert of dreaton died for the sayde cases only

Ad iiii beinge demondyd of home[22] he larnyd his fisike and surgery he answeryd that he larnyd yt[23] of his m Robert of dreaton.

Ad v he beinge demondyd whether he doth yt by arte naturally or else {by any familiar}[24] by any other secreat or pryvy meane use this fisike or surgery he answeryd yt he dothe yt by arte naturally practysed as he saythe and not by any other yll or secreat meanes and yt he beinge demondyd whether he knewe the naturall operacion of the herbes as whether they were whot or cold[25] and in what degre they were so he answeryd he cold not tell

Ad vi he beinge demondyd whether he had a ffamiliar or not he answeryd utterly that he hathe none aboute hem nether in any other place of the woreld ether above grounde or under the grounde ether in {ay} any place secreat or open.

Ad vii he beinge demondyd howe he knowth {whether any} when any man ys wiched he saythe that he knewe yt partlye by the feres[26] and that there be iii kindes of ferises whit[27] grene and blacke wch when he is disposid to use he spekithe with uppon hilles where as is grete hepes of erthe namely yn dorset shere and between the howres of xii & one at none[28] or at mydnyghte he usethe they. Wherof the glacke[29] ferrys ys the warst also he saithe that he had a booke of his said mr whiche had greate circles yn hyt where he woolde sett too wax candels a crosse of virgyn wax to raise the famylier sprite[30] of who he wold then aske for a thynge stolen who dyd hit and where the thynge stollen was loste and therby dyd knowe and {as}

---

18. Drayton, in Somerset, 12 miles north of Netherbury.
19. Thirdly.
20. Coughs and fevers.
21. Master.
22. Whom.
23. 'Yt' can mean it, that or yet, as the sentence's sense demands.
24. An especially interesting deletion, as the idea is clearly already being considered in the question before the one where it is recorded in the final draft.
25. Herbs were believed to be hot or cold in accordance with the theory of humours. Walsh's ignorance is clearly seen as suspicious.
26. Fairies.
27. White.
28. Noon.
29. Black.
30. Suddenly Walsh or his recorder slips into an acceptance that he does have a familiar.

farther by the ferrys he know howe psons[31] ar bywitched {by his said mr Rule w[32] the said booke: whiche booke}

Ad viii Inter he beinge demondyd whether ever he had any famylier or no he saithe he had one of his said mr wch famylyer after his booke of circles was taken from hym by one Robert baker of Crekehorne[33] the constable {he cold} beinge then Ao dm[34] 1565 he colde nev do any thyng touchyng his famylier nor the use therof but his famylier dyd then deptt[35] from hym and will nev com to hym agayne as he saithe and farther saithe uppon his othe that his famylier wold somtyme com unto hym like a graye blackysshe culver[36] and somtyme like a brendyd dogg[37] & somtyme like a man yn all proportions savyng that he had cloven fete

Ad ix Articl[38] he beinge demandyd how long he had the use of the famyler he {f} saithe one yere by his said mr life tyme and foure yere after his death and when he wold call hym for a horse stollen or for any other matter wherin he wold use hym he saithe hee must geve hym som lyve thynge a chicken a Catt or a dogge and onse a yere while he had hym he saithe he must geve hym some thynge vidlt[39] ii live thynge once a yere and at the first tyme when he had the sprite, his said m dyd cause hym to delyver one droppe of his bood[40] to the sprite wch bloode the sprite dyde take awaye uppon his pawe

Item x he saithe that when the famylier shuld do any thynge at his comandye yn any arrante[41] he wold not go except firste ii wax candelles of virgyn wax shuld first have ben layed a crosse uppon the circle wt[42] a littel frankinsens {hallowyd} and saynt John his worte {were both} and once lighted and so put owte agayne wch frankensens must be laid then at every ende of the candel a crosse as he saithe and also a litter[43] frankensens wth saynt Johns worte was brente[44] uppon the grownde or ever the famyler wold go and that wold forse hym to go the message[45] and to retorne agayne at the howre appoynted

Item ad xi Articl he being askyd whether thay that do good to suche as ar bewitched whether they kannot also do hurtte yf they liste wherto he answerithe he that dothe hurte kan neaver heale agayne any man nor kan at

---

31. Persons.
32. With.
33. Crewkerne, 6 miles north of Netherbury.
34. Anno Domini (the year of our Lord).
35. Depart.
36. A pigeon or dove.
37. Brindled.
38. Articulum.
39. *Videlicet* (that is).
40. Blood.
41. Errand.
42. With.
43. Little?
44. Burned.
45. Go on the errand.

any tyme do good howbeit he saithe that he whiche hathe the gifte of healinge may do hurte if he liste but his gifte of healyng kan never reterne agayne to any other psons use

Item xii he being demandyd whether that any of the iii kyndes of ferys when they dyd hurt whether they do hit of their owne malygnyte or of the pvocat[46] by any wicked man he answerithe that they do hurte of their owne malignyty not pvoked by anye man & that they have power uppon no man but on suche as onely do wante the faithe wch is the cawse why they have power more of som psons then of any others furthermor he being demandyd to whate ende the famylier dyd serve he answerith that he servithe for no purpose but to fetche owt thynges thefte stollen and for no other purpose at all he being farther demandyd to whate ende the {Tod} Sprites yn the likenes of Todes {and} and the pictures of man or woman made yn wax or claye to whate ende the[47] serve[48] he saithe that theire temperature of pictures made yn wax will cawse the ptie[49] to contynewe sicke ii hole yeres bycawse hit {wilb} wilbe too hole yeres er[50] the wax wilbe consumed and as for the pictures of claye their confection is after this manner ye must take the yerthe of a newe made grave the ribbe bone of a dedde mann or woman bornyd[51] to asshes of a woman for a woman and of a man for a man and a blacke athercobbe[52] wth also the Inner pithe of the ellder tempered all yn water wherin the said Todes must be first wasshed and after all cerymonyes endyd they put a pricke videlt a pynne or a thorne yn any member wherin they wold the ptie shuldbe greved and yf the said pricke be put to the hartte the ptie diethe win[53] ix dayes which Image they burye yn the moste moystie place they kan fynde and as touchynge the usyng of the Todde by the witches he saithe theye have severall names Some greate browning or littell browenyng or Some grate Tom twite, or littell Tom Twite wt other like names wch Todde being callyd the witche strikethe wt too withye sperres[54] on both sides of the hedde and saithe to the sprite their pater noster backeward begynyng at the ende of the pater noster but they wyll neaver saye their crede[55] and when he is stryken he comaundithe the todd to hurtte suche a man or woman as he wold have hurted wherto yf he

---

46. Provocation.
47. *Sic.*
48. An abrupt introduction of a new subject, presumably already partly explored but unrecorded. Walsh distances himself from 'the witches' who use such spirits.
49. Party.
50. Before (ere).
51. Burned.
52. A dialect term for a spider.
53. Within.
54. Willow spurs.
55. Pater noster is the Latin 'Our Father', whilst the Creed lists the beliefs of a church member and must be repeated as a sign of faith.

swelle he will go where he is appoynted either to the deary brewhowse {to the deary} or the drye[56] of malte or to the cattell yn the fild to the Stable to the shepe fold or to any other like places and so returne agen to his place the bodyes of man or woman is hurted by the Images before namyed and mens goodes & cattales[57] ar hurted by the todde and witches yn comandynge and usyng theym as aforesaid as he saithe And if the Todde callyd forthe as aforesaid do not swelle then will the witche that usethe theym call forthe a nother to do the acte wch if he do not then will they spye a nother tyme when they may cause the ptie to be founde {lac} lackyng faithe or elles to be more voide of grace {whe} wherby he may be hurtte farthermore he saithe that who so dothe once yn a daye saye his pater noster & his crede yn pfecte[58] charitie the {devill} witche shalhave no power on his bodye or goodes for that daye

It xiii Interrogatt whither that those wch do heale men or women beinge hurted by Witches kan fynde out those Images under grounde where wth they were tormentyd he affirmythe that they kan

it xiiii Itergat whether he hymself either hathe or had at any tyme any suche Tode or that ever he made any suche Images to hurtte man woman or childe he affirmythe by the othe wch he hathe taken that he never had suche Todes or ever made suche Images.

It xv Interrgat whither that ever he dyd any hurtt to any woman or childe or to their goodes or catteles he saithe by the othe he hathe taken that he never dyd any suche hurtte either yn bodye or goodes.

2. Witches and magistrates: Essex 1582

W.W., A true and just Recorde *(London, 1582)*

In the winter of 1581–2, Brian Darcy, a Justice of the Peace in the English county of Essex, began investigating accusations of witchcraft made against several women in the village of St Osyth. The village was near his family's main home, St Osyth Priory, and according to the published collection of informations and examinations from the case, one of the first accusers was a servant who worked there. Perhaps because of this personal connection, Darcy took his duties very seriously: he examined women, men and children from St Osyth and surrounding villages, and after the case came to court in March, it was publicized by the longest witchcraft pamphlet so far produced.

Darcy's involvement with the publishing project is unclear, but he was the person most likely to benefit from its appearance in print. The booklet was

---

56. Kiln for drying.
57. Probably chattels rather than cattle.
58. Perfect (contraction of 'per').

dedicated to his most powerful relative, Lord Darcy, and it portrayed Brian Darcy as industrious, sharp-witted and motivated by the desire to serve the public good. Therefore, Darcy seems very likely to have been involved both in collecting the papers on which the pamphlet was based and in framing them with suitable sentiments. In particular, Darcy probably wanted the pamphlet to promote the adoption of demonological ideas and questioning techniques from the European continent. In its introduction, by one W.W., the pamphlet enthusiastically quotes the demonologist Jean Bodin, whom Darcy is also shown mentioning to a suspect as part of his encouragement to confess. The pamphlet, citing Bodin, urges that witches ought to be burned (rather than hanged) as enemies of God, and notes that trick questions and false promises of leniency are especially useful in getting confessions from those who are obviously guilty but will not say so. To the modern reader, Darcy appears callous and obsessive, but it is also easy to see that contemporary readers were intended to admire his skill and persistence in a just cause.

As Barbara Rosen suggested, the pamphlet may have been compiled and in part written by William Lowth, who dedicated a devotional text to Brian and his relative in 1581.[59] If he wished to further Darcy's ambitions, he did well: in 1585 Brian Darcy became sheriff of Essex, a high-profile post held for a year, perhaps as a reward for his zealous work for local justice. But it also seems likely that the obvious flaws in Darcy's methods led readers to question the guilt of his victims and both Scot (who directly attacks Darcy) and Gifford use details from *A true and just Recorde* as part of their assertions that witchcraft as Darcy conceived it did not exist and should not be pursued in the ways he advocated.

The pamphlet gives accounts of many different kinds of witchcraft, and different behaviour by accusers and suspects in telling stories of it. It deals with maleficium, cunning magic, witches working alone and in groups sharing familiars. We see suspects accepting blame, striving to throw it on to others, or refusing to admit guilt. There is evidence from both rich and poor people, adults and children. We also know from surviving indictments the outcome of each case, and can begin to speculate about relationships between the nature of the evidence given, the suspect's attitude and the court's verdict. Finally, the pamphlet shows the development of a large number of accusations from one confession, and the spread of accusations over the course of several weeks to other villages.

A true and just Recorde of the Information, Examination and Confession of all the Witches, taken at S. Oses in the countie of Essex: whereof some were executed, and other some entreated according to the determination of lawe. Wherein all men may see what a pestilent people Witches are, and how unworthy to lyve in a Christian Commonwealth. Written orderly, as the cases were tryed by evidence, By W.W.

---

59. Barbara Rosen, *Witchcraft in England 1558–1618* (1969; Amherst: University of Massachusetts Press, 1991), p. 106 n.4.

1. Preface

To the right honourable and his singular good Lorde, the Lord Darcey,[60] W.W. wisheth a prosperous continuaunce in this lyfe to the glory of God, and a dayly preservation in Gods feare to his endlesse joye.

If there hath bin at any time (Right Honorable) any meanes used, to appease the wrath of God, to obtaine his blessing, to terrifie secreete offenders by open transgressors punishments, to withdraw honest natures from the corruption of evil company, to diminishe the great multitude of wicked people, to increase the small number of virtuous persons, and to reforme all the detestable abuses, which the perverse witte and will of man doth dayly devise, this doubtlesse is no lesse necessarye then the best, that Sorcerers, Wizzardes, or rather Dizzardes,[61] Witches, Wisewomen (for so they will be named) are rygorously punished. Rygorously sayd I? Why it is too milde and gentle a tearme for such a mercilesse generation; I should rather have sayd most cruelly executed;[62] for that no punishment can be thought upon, be it never so high a degree of torment, which may be deemed sufficient for such a divelish & damnable practise. And why? Because al the imaginations, al the consultations, al the conference, al the experimentes, finally the attemptes, proceedinges and conclusions of Sorcerers, Witches, and the rest of that hellishe liverie, are meere blasphemers against the person of the most high God; and draw so neere to the nature of idolatrie (for they worshippe Sathan, unto whome they have sworne allegiaunce) that they are by no

---

60. Thomas, Baron Darcy, a cousin of the same generation as Brian's grandchildren. He had become the third Baron in 1581 (for details of Darcy's complex family tree see Walter C. Metcalfe, ed., *The Visitations of Essex*, 2 vols (London: Harleian Society, 1878), vol. 1, pp. 44–6; G. E. Cokayne, *The Complete Peerage*, 13 vols, ed. Vicary Gibbs and H. Arthur Doubleday (London: St Catherine's Press, 1910–59), vol. 4, pp. 78-9).

61. Fools.

62. This passage is translated from Jean Bodin's *De la Demonomanie des Sorciers* (1580; Paris, 1587), pp. 216–17. Bodin says: '*Or s'il y eut oncques moyen d'appaiser l'ire de Dieu, d'obtenir sa benediction, d'estonner les uns par le punition des autres, de conserver les uns de l'infection des autres, de diminuer le nombre des meschans, d'asseurer la vie des bons, & de punir les meschancetez les plus detestables que l'esprit humain peut imaginer, c'est de chastier a toute rigeur les Sorciers: combien que le mot de Rigeur est mal pris, attendu que il n'y a peine si cruelle qui peust suffire à punir les meschancetez des Sorciers, d'autant que toutes leurs meschancetez, blasphemes, & tous leurs desseings se dressent contre la Majesté de Dieu, pour le despiter & offenser par mille moyens.*' In modern English this reads: 'Now if there was ever a way to appease the wrath of God, to obtain his blessing, to frighten some by the punishment of others, to protect some from the contamination of others, to reduce the number of the wicked, to secure the life of the good, and to punish the most dreadful wickednesses that the human spirit can imagine, it is to punish, with utmost rigour, sorcerers: although the word 'rigour' is ill chosen, given that there is no punishment cruel enough to suffice to punish the wickednesses of sorcerers, all the more so since all their wickednesses, blasphemies, and all their designs are set up against the majesty of God, in order to defy and offend him in a thousand ways' (translation by Rebecca Selman and Marion Gibson). It can be seen that the prefacer's translation adds ideas to fit Bodin's theories into an English setting: for example, mentioning wisewomen, and suggesting the burning of witches.

meanes to be exempted from the suspition of that most accursed defection, nay rather they are guiltie of apparaunte apostasie, which is more heynous (considering the circumstances of their ordinarie actions, then any trespasse against the seconde table, which ouglye sinnes of blasphemie, and grosse, or rather divelish idolatrie concurring in no malefactor so roundly, as in sorcerers, witches, Inchaunters &. in whom the meete with a millian of enormities more; as it were in a centre; the magistrates of forren landes, noted so precisely, that weighing the qualitie of the cryme, they kept a due analogie and proportion of punishment, burning them with fire, whome the common lawe of Englande (with more measure of mercie then is to be wished) strangleth with a rope. An ordinary fellon, and a murtherer offending against the morall lawe of justice, is throtled: a Sorcerer, a Witch, (whome a learned Phisitian is not ashamed to avoch innocent, and the Judges, that denounce sentence of death against them no better than hangmen)[63] defying the Lorde God to his face; and trampling the pretious blood of that immaculate lambe Jesus Christ most despitfully under feete is stiffled: the one dyeth on the gallowes, and so doth the other: wherein doubtlesse there is a great inequalitie of justice, considering the inequalitie of the trespasse, which deserveth a death so much the more horrible, by how much the honour of God is eclipsed, and the glorye due to his inviolable name most abhominably defaced, even to the uttermost villanie that they can put in practise.

This I speake (Right Honorable) upon a late viewe of tryall, taken against certaine Witches in the countie of Essex; the orderly processe in whose examinations, together with other accidents, I dilygently observing and considering their trecheries to be notable: undertooke briefly knit up in a fewe leaves of paper, their manifolde abuses: and obtaining the meanes to have them published in print, for that a number of memorable matters are here touched, to present the same unto your Lordship, of whose gentle acceptation though I dooe not doubt, yet will I not be over bolde thereupon to presume: but rather refer the same to your honours judgement and patronage by way of humilyation, that going abrode under coverte of your honourable name, the discourse maye seeme the more credible, your lordship knowing the grounds of this whole booke to be true and justifiable, and therefore the further off from feare of impugning. But supposing I have beene too tedious and sparing to trouble your Lordship with multitude of words, I build upon hope, & so put forth my booke, praying the Lord here to blesse your Honour, and all about you with the

---

63. A marginal note beginning on A3v and continuing on A4 explains that this is Johannes Wier (Weyer, Wierus), who in his *De praestigiis daemonum* of 1563 followed a similar sceptical line to the later English sceptic Scot (see below). Wier's book was attacked by Bodin and his confutation of Wier is given as the source of the prefacer's opinion. *De praestigiis* has been translated as *Witches, Devils and Doctors in the Renaissance*, trans. John Shea, ed. George Mora (Binghampton, NY: Medieval and Renaissance Texts and Studies, 1991).

increase of his grace in this life, and with the presence of his divinitie in the lyfe to come. Amen.

Your Honours to commaund W.W.

2. Beginning – accusation and confession of a cunning woman

Ursley Kempe was the first person to be accused of witchcraft and under pressure she confessed. She was found guilty of committing three murders with Ales Newman (see below) and hanged.

The xix. day of February the xxiiii yeere of the raigne of our Soveraigne Ladie Queene Elizabeth. The information of Grace Thurlowe, the wife of John Thurlowe, taken before mee Brian Darcye the day and yeere above saide, against Ursley Kempe alias Gray, as followeth.

The saide grace sayeth that about xii monethes past, or nere thereabouts, her Sone Davye Thurlowe, beeing strangely taken and greatly tormented, Ursley Kempe alias Grey came unto the said Grace to see how the childe did: At which time the childe lying upon a bed in the chimney corner, shee the said Ursley tooke it by the hande, saying, A good childe howe art thou loden:[64] and so went thrise out of the doore, and every time when shee came in shee tooke the childe by the hande, and saide A good childe howe art thou loden. And so at her departure the said Grace prayed the saide Ursley to come againe unto her at night to helpe her. And thereupon she the saide Ursley replied, and saide, I Warrant thee I thy Childe shall doe well enoughe, and yt night it fell to rest the which it did not of a long time before. And the next day the said Grace going to mille warde[65] meeting the said Ursley, shee asked her howe her childe did, and shee said it tooke good rest this night God be thanked, I I[66] saide the said Ursley, I warrant thee it shall doe well. Note, that the palmes of the childes handes were turned wher the backes shoulde bee, and the backe in the place of the palmes.[67]

The said Grace saith also, that about three quarters of a yeere ago she was delivered of a womanchild, and saith, that shortly after the birth thereof, the said Ursley fell out with her, for that shee woulde not suffer her to have the nursing of that childe, at suche times as she the said Grace continued in woorke at the Lorde Darceys place: And saith, that shee the saide Grace nursing the said childe, within some short time after that falling out, the childe lying in the Cradle, and not above a quarter olde, fell out of the said Cradle, and brake her necke, and died. The which the said Ursley hearing

---

64. Laden, loaded.
65. Going towards the mill.
66. Aye, aye.
67. This disorder was thought to be caused by witchcraft.

to have happened, made answere, it maketh no matter. For shee might have suffered mee to have the keeping and nursing of it.

And the saide Grace saith, that when shee lay in, the saide Ursley came unto her, and seemed to bee very angrie for that shee had not the keeping in of the saide Grace, & for that she answered unto her that shee was provided:[68] And thereupon they entred further into talke, the saide Grace saying, that if shee should continue lame as shee had doone before, shee woulde finde the meanes to knowe howe it came, and yt shee woulde creepe upon her knees to complaine of them to have justice done upon them: And to that shee the saide Ursley saide, it were a good turne: Take heed (said Grace) Ursley, thou hast a naughtie name. And to that Ursley made answere, though shee coulde unwitche shee coulde not witche, and so promised the saide Grace, that if shee did sende for her privily, and send her keeper away, that then shee woulde show the said Grace how shee shoulde unwitch herselfe or any other at any time.

And the said Grace further saith that about halfe a yeere past she began to have a lamenesse in her bones, & specially in her legges, at which time ye said Ursley came unto her unsent for and wtout[69] request, and said she would helpe her of her lamenes, if she the said Grace woulde give her xii. pence, ye which the said Grace speaking her fayre, promised her so to doe, and thereupon for the space of v. weekes after, she was wel & in good case as shee was before. And then the said Ursley came unto the saide Grace, and asked her ye money she promised to her. Wherupon the saide Grace made answere: that shee was a poore and a needie woman, and had no money: & then the said Ursley requested of her cheese for it: but she said she had none. And shee the said Ursley, seeing nothing to be had of the saide Grace, fell out with her, and saide, that she woulde be even with her: and thereupon shee was taken lame, and from that day to this day hath so continued.

And she saith, that when she is any thinge well or beginneth to amend, then her childe is tormented, and so continueth for a time in a very strange case, and when he beginneth to amend: Then shee the saide Grace becometh so lame as without helpe shee is not able to arise, or to turne her in her bed.

The information of Annis Letherdall, wife of Richard Letherdall, taken by mee Brian Darcey Esquire, against Ursley Kempe, alias Grey the xix day of February.

The said Annis saith, that before Michaelmass last, she the said Ursley sent her

---

68. It was usual for a woman lying in at the time of childbirth to be attended to by other women whom she trusted. Grace's failure to choose Ursley as her keeper thus indicates a breakdown in their relationship.

69. Without. Grace, or her recorder, is careful to say that she did not send for Ursley, as her questioner probably disapproves of unwitching activity (see George Gifford below for a discussion of its sinful nature).

sonne to the said Letherdals house, to have scouring sand,[70] and sent word by the said boy, yt his mother would give her the dying of a payre of womens hose for the sand: But the said Annis knowing her to be a naughtie beast sent her none. And after she the said Ursley, seeing her gyrle to carry some to one of her neighbours houses murmured as the said childe said, & presently after her childe[71] was taken as it lay very bigge, with a great swelling in the bottome of the belly, and other privie partes. And the saide Annis saith, yt about the tenth day of Februarie last shee went unto the said Ursley, and tolde her that shee had been foorth with a cunning body,[72] which saide, yt she the said Ursley had bewitched her childe: To yt the said Ursley answered, that shee knewe shee had not so been, and so talking further she said, that she would lay her life that she the said Annis had not been with any: whereupon shee requested a woman being in the house a spinning with the said Ursley, to beare witnesse what shee had said. And the next day the childe was in most piteous case to beholde, whereby shee thought it good to Carry the same unto mother Ratcliffe, for that shee had some experience of her skill. The which when the said mother Ratcliffe did see: shee saide to the saide Annis that shee doubted shee shoulde doe it any good, yet shee ministred unto it &c.

The enformation of Thomas Rabbet, of the age of viii yeres or thereabouts, base[73] son unto the said Ursley Kempe alias Grey, taken before me Brian Darcey esquire, one of her Majesties Justices, the xxv day of February, against his said mother.

The saide Thomas Rabbet saith, that his said mother Ursley Kempe alias Grey hath foure severall spirites, the one called Tyffin, the other Tittey, the third Pygine, & the fourth Jacke: & being asked of what colours they were, saith, that Tyttey is like a little grey Cat, Tyffin is like a white lambe, Pygine is black like a Toad, and Jacke is black like a Cat. And hee saith, hee hath seen his mother at times to give them beere to drinke and of a white Lofe or Cake to eate, and saith that in the night time the said spirites will come to his mother, and sucke blood of her upon her armes, and other places of her body.

This Examinat being asked, whether hee had seene Newmans wife to come unto his mother, saith that one morning he being in the chamber with his mother, his Godmother Newman came unto her, and saith, that then he heard her and his mother to chide, and to fall out. But saith before they parted they were friends: and that then his mother delivered an earthen pot unto her, in the which he thinketh her spirites were, the which she carried away with her under her aperne.

And this examinat saith, that within a fewe daies after the said

---

70. Sand for scouring cooking pots.
71. Another, younger, girl.
72. A wiseman or woman.
73. Illegitimate.

Newmans wife came unto his mother, and yt he heard her to tel his mother that she had sent a spirit to plague Johnson to ye death, and an other to plague his wife . . .

The examination and confession of Ursley Kemp alias Gray, taken at S: Osees, and brought before mee Brian Darsey esquire, one of her Majesties Justices of the peace, the xx. day of Februarie 1582.
Condemned.[74]

The saide Ursley Kempe sayeth, that about tenne or eleven yeeres paste, shee this examinate was troubled with a lamenes in her bones and for ease thereof went to one Cockes wife of Weley,[75] nowe deceased, who telled this examinate that shee was bewitched, and at her entretie taught her to unwitche her selfe. And bad her take hogges dunge and charvell,[76] and put them together and holde them in her left hand, and to take in the other hand a knife, and to pricke the medicine three times, & then to cast the same into the fire, and to take the said knife & to make three pricks under a table, and to let the knife sticke there: & after that to take three leves of sage, and as much of herbe John (alias herbe grace)[77] and put them into ale: and drinke it last at night and first in the morning, & that shee taking the same had ease of her lamenesse.

The sayde examinate sayth, that one Pages wife, and one Grayes wife, beeing eyther of them lame and bewitched, shee beeing requested and sent for to come unto them, went unto them: And saieth, that shee knewe them to bee bewitched and at their desires did minister unto them the foresaid medicine, whereupon they had speedie amendement.

The saide Brian Darcey then promising to the saide Ursley, that if she would deale plainely and confesse the trueth, that shee should have favour & so by giving her faire speeches shee confessed as followeth.[78]

The saide Ursley bursting out with weeping, fel upon her knees, and confessed that shee had foure spirits, wherof two of them were hees and the other two were shees: the two hee spirites were to punishe and kill unto death, and the other two shees were to punishe with lamenes, and other diseases of bodyly harme and also to destroy cattell.

And she this examinate, being asked by what name or names she called the saide spirites, and what maner of thinges, or colour they were of: confesseth and saith: that the one is called Tyttey, being a hee, and is like a

---

74. See note 94.
75. Weeley, a village about 5 miles north of St Osyth.
76. Scot reports a similar spell using the herb chervil. Although the word here has also been read as charnell, suggesting grave-robbing, this seems far less likely, as Barbara Rosen points out (*Witchcraft in England*, p. 114 n.16), although John Walsh (above) asserts that witches do rob graves.
77. St John's wort.
78. At this point, as the pamphlet reveals on 2A8v, the suspect begins confessing to Darcy 'privately'.

gray Cat, the seconde called Jacke, also a hee, and is like a blacke Cat, the thirde is called Pigin, being a she, and is like a blacke Toad, the fourth is called Tyffin, being a shee, and is like a white lambe.[79]

This examinate being further asked, whiche of the saide spirites shee sent to punishe Thorlowes wife, and Letherdalls childe, confessed and sayed, that shee sent Tyttey to punishe Thorlows wife, and Pigin Letherdalls Childe.

And this examinate, without any asking of her owne free will at that present, confessed and saide, yt shee was the death of her brother Kempes wife, and that she sent the spirite Jacke to plague her, for that her sister[80] had called her whore and witche.

And this examinate further confessed, that upon the falling out betweene Thorlowes wife and her, shee sent Tyffin the spirite unto her childe, which lay in the Cradle, and willed the same to rock the Cradle over, so as the childe might fall out thereof, and breake the necke of it.

These foresaide 5. last recited matters, being confessed by the saide Ursley privately to me the saide Brian Darcey, were afterwardes (supper being ended, and shee called agayne before mee, the saide Brian) recited and particularlie named unto her all which shee confessed as before in the presence of us, whose names bee hereunder subscribed.[81]

Also after this examinates aforesaide confession, the saide Thorlows wife, and Letherdalles wife being then in my house,[82] and shee the saide Letherdalls wife having her childe there also, were brought in my presence before this examinate: who, immediatly after some speeches had past betweene them, shee this examinate burst out in teares and fell upon her knees and asked forgivenesse of the saide Letherdalls wife, and likewise of Thorlows wife, and confessed that shee caused Newmans wife to sende a spirite to plague the childe, asking the saide Letherdalls wife, if shee were not afraide that night that the spirite came unto the childe, and telled her about the same hower, and said that shee herselfe by reason thereof was in a great swete. And this examinate confesseth, that shee caused the same Newmans wife, to send a spirite to Thorlowes wife, to plague her where that thought good, &c.

The said Letherdals childe (being a woman childe) at the time of this examination, appeared to bee in most piteous sort consumed, and the privie and hinder partes thereof, to be in a most strange and wonderfull case, as it seemed to verye honest women of good judgement,[83] and not likely to live and continue any long time.

---

79. This statement (20 February) appears to be the origin of 8-year-old Thomas Rabbet's story of his mother's familiars (25 February). Some child evidence appears to have been redated – see note 142.
80. Sister-in-law.
81. The names are missing.
82. Presumably St Osyth Priory, the house of Lord Darcy and his family, rather than Brian's home at Tiptree.
83. Magistrates often asked teams of respectable local women to examine both female victims and suspects for physical evidence.

Note also that it is specially to be considered, that the saide childe beeing an infante and not a yeere olde, the mother thereof carrying it in her armes, to one mother Ratcliffes a neighbour of hers, to have her to minister unto it, was to passe by Ursley this examinates house, and passing bye the wyndowe, the Infante cryed to the mother, wo, wo, and poynted with the finger to the wyndowe wardes: and likewise the chyld used the like as shee passed homewards by the said window, at which she confessed her conscience moved her, so as shee went shortly after and talked with the said Ursley, whereupon shee used suche speeches as mooved her to complaine.

The seconde confession and examination of Ursley Kemp, taken the xxi. day of Februarie.

The said Ursley, being committed to the ward & keeping of the Constable that night, upon some speeches that shee had passed, said, that shee had forgotten to tell M. Darcey one thing, whereupon the next day she was brought before Brian Darcey, & the second time examined, who confessed and said.

That about a quarter of a yeere last past, one Ales Neweman, her nere neighbour came unto this examinates house and fel out with her, and said shee was a witche, and that shee woulde take away her witcherie, and carrie the same unto M. Darcey: But this examinate saieth, shee thought shee did not meane it, but after they had chidden they became friendes, and so shee departed carying away with her, her spirites in a pot, as this examinate sayth.

And shee further sayth, that about Christmas last, shee went to the said Ales Newman, and declared to her that Thorlows wife and shee were fallen out, and prayed the saide Newmans wife, to sende the spirite called Tittey, unto her to plague the sayde Thorlowes wife, where that thought good: The which this examinate saith, shee did, and at the returne of the saide spirite it tolde this examinate, that it had punished Thorlowes wife upon her knee, And then it had a reward by sucking blood of this examinate, and so returned as shee saith to the said Ales Neweman.

This examinate saith, that about three monethes past, shee and one John Stratton fel out, and the saide John called her whore & gave her other evill speeches, whereupon this examinate sayth, that shortly after shee sent her Boy for spices unto the wife of the said John: But shee sayeth, shee sent her none, wherupon this examinate sayeth, shee went unto the saide Newmans wife, and tolde her of the falling out between Stratton and her, and requested the saide Newmans wife, to sende Jacke the spirite unto Strattons wife to plague her, ye which the said Ales Newman promised this examinate to doe the nexte night, as this examinate saith shee did: And the spirite tolde this examinate when it returned, that it had plagued her in the backe even unto death: and the spirite did sucke of this examinate upon the left thigh, the which when she rubbeth (shee saith) it will at all times bleede. And shee sayeth that then the spirite did returne to the sayde Newemans wife agayne, and had the like rewarde of her as shee thynketh.

This examinate sayeth, that about Friday was sevennight[84] beeing about the nienth of Februarie, shee went unto the said Ales Newman, and did shewe her that one Letherdalls wife and shee were fallen out, and sayth, that shee prayed her to sende one of the spirites unto her younge chylde: whereunto shee the sayd Ales answered well she would: and this examinate saith, that at that time shee coulde have no longer talke with her, for that her husband was then present in the house: and this examinat saith that the said Ales sent the spirit Pigin, to plague ye said child where that thought good, and after that it had sucked of this examinate, shee saith it returned to the saide Newmans wife, and more at that time the saide examinate confessed not.

The third examination & confession of Ursley Kempe alias Gray, taken before me Brian Darsey esquire, one of her Majesties Justices of the peace, the xxiiii. day of Februarie.

This examinate, being asked how she knew the said Elizabeth Bennet to have two spirits[85] saith, that about a quarter of a yere past she went unto mother Bennets house for a messe of milke, the which shee had promised her: But at her comming this examinate saith shee knocked at her dore, and no bodie made her any answere, whereupon shee went to her chamber windowe and looked in therat, saying, ho, ho, mother Bennet are you at home? And casting her eyes aside, shee saw a spirit lift up a clothe lying over a pot, looking much like a Ferret. And it beeing asked of this examinate why the spirite did looke upon her, shee said it was hungrie.

This examinate, beeing asked howe shee knewe the names of mother Bennets spirites, sayth that Tyffin her spirite did tell this examinate that shee had two spirites, the one of them like a blacke Dogge, and the other redde like a Lyon, and that their names were Suckin and Lyerd, and sayeth that Suckin did plague Byettes wife unto death, and the other plagued three of his Beastes whereof two of them dyed, and the third leyer fire[86] or drooping, & not likly to live: Byette caused his folkes to make a fire about her: The Cow feeling the heate of the fire, starte up and came her way, and by that occasion was saved.

This examinate saith, that about the foureteene or fifteene day of Januarie last, shee went to the house of William Hunt to see howe his wife did and shee beeing from home, shee called at her chamber window and looked in, and then espied a spirite to looke out of a potcharde[87] from under a clothe,

)

---

84. A week last Friday.

85. The examinate has now become an informant as well as a suspect. There is actually no previous record of Ursley having said that she did know this 'fact'.

86. Rosen suggests plausibly that this should read 'lay sick' and that 'probably the compositor picked up "a fire" from the succeeding sentence as he was setting "lay", since "fire" and "sick" would not be too unlike in Elizabethan handwriting' (*Witchcraft in England*, p. 118 n.22).

87. Potsherd or potshard.

the nose thereof beeing browne like unto a Ferret. And sayeth, that the same night shee asked Tyffin her white spirite, what Huntes wives spirite had done: And then it told this examinate, that it had killed Haywarde of Frowicke sixe beastes which were lately dressed of the gargette.[88] And sayeth, that her sayde spirite tolde her, that Huntes wives spirite had a droppe of her blood for a rewarde: but shee sayeth, that shee asked not her spirite upon what place of her body it was.[89]

This examinate sayeth, that one Michell a shoomaker of Saint Osees did tell her, that he thought that Glascockes wife had bewitched his Chylde, whereof it dyed: Whereupon shee this examinate sayeth, that shee went home, and asked Tyffin her white spirite, whether the same were so: whiche tolde this examinate, that shee had bewitched the sayde chylde, and sent one of her spirites to plague it to the death.

And sayeth also, that the sayde Glascockes wife did bewitche the Base childe that Page and his wife have in keeping, and that her sayde spirite telled her so. And being demaunded, howe many spirits Glascockes wife had, and by what names shee called them, this examinate sayeth, that shee asked not her spirite Tyffin any such questions.[90]

This examinate sayeth, that the sayde Elizabeth Bennette did sende her spirite Suckin to plague one Willingall, whereof hee languished and died: beeyng sicke of an impostume.[91]

This examinate sayeth also, that the sayde Elizabeth sente the sayde spirite to William Willes his wife to plague her, whereof shee languished many yeeres and dyed.

This examinate sayeth, that the sayde Elizabeth (not above three weekes sithence) sent her spirite Lyerd to plague Fortunes wife and his chylde.

This examinate sayeth, that the sayde Elizabeth did sende her spirite Lyerd to Bonners wife to plague her, the whiche her sayde spirite, tolde this examinate to bee done upon the knee.

This examinate saith further, that Ales Newman went unto Johnson beeing Collectour for the poore,[92] and did require him to give her xii. d. for her husbande whiche was sicke. But hee answering her that he had disbursed more money then hee had collected, saying therefore hee coulde not then helpe her with any: The sayde Newemans wife fell out with him very angerly, and the next day after sent one of the spirites that shee had from this examinate to plague the saide Johnson and his wife

---

88. Recently killed, because they had a disease leading to inflamed throats.
89. Ales Hunt was acquitted of bewitching Hayward's cattle and killing Rebecca Durrant. See J. S. Cockburn, *Calendar of Assize Records: Essex: Elizabeth I* (London: HMSO, 1978) for surviving trial records, and J. S. Cockburn, *Introduction* to the calendar series (London: HMSO, 1985) for deaths in prison and pardons.
90. Annis Glascocke was found guilty of killing Martha Stevens, Abraham Hedg and Charity Page. She was reprieved, but died in gaol.
91. Abscess.
92. An official charitable post.

unto the death: And that her spirite called Tyffin did tell the same unto her, and shee beeing asked what woordes the sayde Newemans wife used to Johnson upon the falling out, sayth, that shee asked not her said spirite.

This examinate sayeth, that Newmans wife beeing at Butlers, and asking a peece of meate, was denyed thereof: whereat shee went away mourmuring, And then shortely after sent one of her spirites to punishe him upon the backe: The whiche Tyffin her sayde spirite telleth this examinate was done, whereof hee languisheth and is greatly payned.

This examinate being asked, whether her white spirit called Tyffin did ever at any time tel her any untruths, or whether she had found it at a-[93] time to tell any thing contrary to truth, saith, that the saide spirite did ever tell her true in any matter shee required of it, and saith, that shee never knewe it to tell her otherwise then truth.

This Exam. being asked, whether she sent any of her spirits to plague or punishe John Strattons childe, confesseth and saith, that the spirite which plagued Strattons wife to the death, did also punishe the saide Strattons childe, saying, that the saide childe shoulde not complaine thereof untill the mother were departed.

Note, it is to bee considered, that the saide Ursley Kempe in this her confession hath uttered many thinges well approved and confessed to bee most true: And that shee was brought thereunto by hope of favour.

3. Resistance, trickery and collapse

Ursley Kempe's accusations spread blame to Ales Newman and Elizabeth Bennett. Both were questioned and both initially denied guilt. But the magistrate's manipulation placed both under severe pressure: Ales Newman responded with straightforward denial, Elizabeth Bennett with a slow narrative drift from innocence to an admission of witchcraft which she maintained, pleading guilty at her trial and incurring the death penalty thereby. Newman, charged with Kempe, was found guilty but reprieved and imprisoned, curiously leaving Kempe to bear the brunt of punishment for crimes believed by the court to have been committed jointly. She was released in 1588 under a general pardon.

The Examination and confession of Ales Newman, taken before mee Brian darcie Esquire, the xxi. of February.
Condemned.[94]

---

93. Should read 'any', which is left out in the first line of the next page.
94. One of several errors in reporting sentences. Ales Newman and Ursley Kempe were jointly charged with killing Elizabeth Letherdall, Edena, wife of John Stratton, and Joan Thorlowe: one was hanged, one reprieved.

This examinat saith, that shee went unto the house where the saide Ursley Kempe alias Grey dwelt, and entred into communication with her, and that they fell out greatly and confesseth that shee saide unto the saide Ursley that she knew her to be a witche, but denieth the residue of ye speeches alleadged by the said Ursley against this Examinat.

The said Brian Darcey finding this examinat to bee obstinate, and that shee coulde bee brought to confesse nothing, said to this Examinat, that hee woulde sever and part her and her spirites a sunder, nay sayth shee this examinat, that shal ye not, for I wil carry them with me, and hold being taken of her wordes, after some distance she added (if she have any) . . .

Upon the saide enformation made by Ursley Kempe alias Grey, against Elizabeth Bennet, I Brian Darcey directed my warrant for her apprehension,[95] wherupon she was brought before me the said Brian, whose confession being taken the 22. day of February.
Condemned.[96]

The said Elizabeth Bennet being charged with the foresaid information, denieth the same in generall, & after many and sundrie demands being asked, whether she had not a pot or pitcher of earth standing under a paire of staires in her house & wool in the same, in the which usually the said two spirites did lie, denieth ye same with many othes, saying yt she was wel assured yt she had none such, wherupon it was said to her, if it be proved to your face, what will you say to al the other matters you have bin charged with, are they true? To that she made answere & said yea: Then was the pot brought before her, the which she then confessed to be her pot, but denied yt the wool therin was any of hers, then I calling her unto mee, saide, Elizabeth as thou wilt have favour confesse the truth. For so it is, there is a man of great cunning and knowledge come over lately unto our Queenes Majestie, which hath advertised her what a companie and number of Witches be within Englande: wherupon I and other of her Justices have received Commission for the apprehending of as many as are within these limites, and they which doe confesse the truth of their doeings, they shall have much favour: but the other they shall bee burnt and hanged.[97] At which speeches shee the saide Elizabeth falling upon her knees distilling teares confessed as heereafter followeth.

---

95. Either this is untrue or information is missing. In the records printed in *A true and just Recorde* (all that survives of the case), Ursley Kempe did not mention Elizabeth Bennett until 24 February. However, the opening of Kempe's 24 February examination does suggest missing or unrecorded material (see note 85), as does the opening questioning of Bennett here.
96. Elizabeth Bennett pleaded guilty to killing William and Joan Byett.
97. As Rosen suggests, this man is Jean Bodin, whose visit to the Queen had just ended. Darcy did not have a special commission for his activities, however (*Witchcraft in England*, pp. 121–2 nn.24, 25), and his description of punishments is a lie.

Saying, that one William Byet dwelt in the next house unto her three yeres, saying, yt the first yeere they did agree reasonably well, but ere the second yeare passed they fell out sundry and oftentimes, both with this examinat & her husbande, Byet calling her oftentimes olde trot[98] and olde witche, and did banne and curse this examinat and her Cattell, to which this examinat saith, that shee called him knave saying, winde it up Byet for it wil light upon your selfe:[99] and after this falling out this examinat saith, that Byet had three beastes dyed, whereof hee seeing one of them somewhat to droope, hee did beat the saide Cowe in such sorte (as this Examinat saith, that shee thought the said Cow did die thereof).

This examinat saith further, that Byets wife did beate her swine severall times with great Gybets,[100] and did at an other time thrust a pitchforke through the side of one of this examinats swine, the which Durrant a Butcher did buie, and for that when he had dressed it, it prooved A messell,[101] this Examinat saith, shee had nothing for it but received it againe, &c.

This examinat saith also, that above two yeeres past there came unto her two spirits, one called Suckin, being blacke like a Dogge, the other called Lierd, beeing red like a Lion, Suckin this examinat saith is a hee, and the other a shee. And saith, on a time as this examinat was comming from mill, the spirite called Suckin came unto her and did take her by the coate, and helde her that shee coulde not goe forwarde nor remoove by the space of two houres, at the which (this examinat saith) she was much amased, and shee saith, that the spirite did aske her if she this examinat woulde goe with it: Whereat shee this examinat saide, In the name of God, what art thou? Thou wilt not hurt mee, at the which speeche it said no, & this Examinat saith, that shee then prayed devoutly to Almightie God to deliver her from it: at which time the[102] did depart from her untill shee had gone a good way, and being come within xxx. or xl. rodes[103] of her house, this examinat saith, that the said spirite came againe unto her and tooke her by the coates behind, & held her fast, whereat this examinat saith, that she desired God to deliver her from that evill spirite, and then that did depart to the Wel. And this examinat saith, yt within one houre after, the same[104] spirite came againe unto her she being a sifting of her meale, & saith, the same remained with her untill she had laied her leaven,[105] and then departed.

---

98. Old hag.
99. This probably suggests turning a curse on its speaker: Elizabeth says 'finish the curse with "Byet" for it will fall upon yourself'.
100. Staves, cudgels, pieces of wood.
101. Rosen suggests 'a measled' or with tapeworms (*Witchcraft in England*, p. 122 n.28).
102. Should read 'spirite', which is left out in the first line of the next page.
103. Roods/rods.
104. This word is repeated.
105. Added yeast to her bread mixture.

The saide examinat saith, that the next day shee being a kneading of her bread, the saide spirite came againe unto her, and brought the other spirite with it called Lierd, and that one of them did aske her why she was so snappish yesterday, to that this examinat saith, that shee made answere, I trust I am in the faith of God, and you shall have no power over mee, at which wordes this Examinat saith, the saide spirites departed.

Then shee this examinat saith, that shee beeing a making of a fire in her Oven, the said spirites came againe unto her, and tooke her by the legge, this examinat feeling it to take her by the leg saith she said, God and the holy Ghost deliver me from the evill spirites, at which words this examinat saith, that the said spirites did depart to her thinking.

But this examinat saith, that within halfe an houre after she having a fier fork in her hand, and beeing a stirring of the fire in the Oven, the spirit (called Suckin) came unto her & tooke this examinat by the hippes, and saide, seeing thou wilt not be ruled, thou shalt have a cause, & would have thrust this examinat into ye burning Oven, & so had (as this examinat saith) but for the foresaide forke, but this examinat striving and dooing what shee coulde to her uttermost, the saide spirite burnt her arme, the which burning is apparaunt and evidently too bee seene, and when it had thus doone it did depart.

And this Examinat saith, that about a moneth after or more, shee beeing a walking in a croft[106] neere unto a Barne called Heywoods Barne, the spirite called Suckin came and followed this examinat, she spying the same as she looked backe, at the sight thereof this examinat saith, yt her eies wer like to start out of her heade then she saith yt she did beseech God to governe and guide her from the evill spirites, whereupon shee saith they did depart.

But the same evening she this examinat being set a milking of a red Cowe with a white face, saith that Suckin and Lierd came againe unto her, and saith that Suckin appeared at that time in the likenesse of a blacke dogge, and Lierd in the likenesse of a Hare, the one beeing on the one side of her, the other on the other side of her within lesse then two yardes: And saith, that the Cowe shee was then a milking of, snorted and ranne away, and brake her paile and spilt al her milke, neither coulde she get the said Cow any more that night to stand still, and saith, that for the losse thereof her husband did much chide her, but shee woulde not tell what was the cause: and she praying to the father, the sonne, & the holy ghost, saith thet they did depart, and that shee sawe them not a quarter of a yeere after, not above three times since Midsommer last.[107]

---

106. Field.

107. Despite appearing compliant, the suspect has so far confessed nothing – in fact she has portrayed herself as a victim of devilish tricks, not their instigator. But now she suddenly begins to incriminate herself. Why?

The said exam. saith, that about that time they appeared againe unto her, and saith that a little before there was a falling out betweene her and the saide Byet, whereupon and for that Byet had oftentimes misused her this examinat and her Cattell, shee saith, that shee caused Lyard in ye likenes of a Lion to goe & to plague the saide Byets beastes unto death, and the spirite returning tolde this examinat that it had plagued two of his beastes, the one a red Cow, the other a blacke. And saith that the spirite tolde her, that hee plagued the blacke Cowe in the backe, and the read Cowe in the head.

This Examinate saieth further, that aboute Whitsontyde last past, the spirit called Suckin, did come againe at that tyme unto her, sayeing to this Examinate, that hee had mette Byettes wife two severall tymes, tellyng this Examynate, that it mette her once in this Examinates yarde, and the next day after it sayde, that it met her at the style, going into her grounde: And saieth it tolde this Examinate, it had plagued ye said Byets wife to the death. She this Examinate saying it was done by the spirite, but not by the sending of this Examinate. The sayde spirite sayeing, I knowe that Byet and his wife have wronged thee greatly, and doone thee severall hurtes, and beaten thy swyne, and thrust a pytchforke in one of them, the which the spirite sayde to have doone, to winne credit with this Examinate.[108]

And this Examinate saieth further, that aboute Lammas last past: For that the sayde William Byet had abused her, in calling her olde trot, old whore, and other lewde speaches, shee this Examinate, caused the spirite, called Suckin, to goe and plague the sayde Willyam Byette where that woulde: The which the sayd spyrite did, and at the retourne of it, it tolde this Examinate, that it met Byet in the barne yarde, and that it plagued him in the hippes, even unto death: And saith she gave it a rewarde of mylke: and saith, that many tymes they drinke of her milke bowle. And being asked how shee came by the sayde spirites, she confessed and sayde, that one Mother Turner did sende them unto her to her house (as shee thinketh) for that she had denyed the sayde Mother Turner of mylke:[109] And when, and as often as they did drinke of the mylke: This Examynate saith they went into the sayd earthen pot, and lay in the wooll ...

4. Successful storytelling and escape

Margery Sammon's sister Ales Hunt was named by Ursley Kempe as a suspected witch. With Ales, Margery gave an information implicating her mother's friend Joan Pechey, but she herself was also questioned. Her story was a complex one: it offered the magistrate full cooperation, but limited the suspect's acceptance of blame before transferring it to another. There is no

---

108. Now, despite confessing, the suspect distances herself from the spirit, absolving herself of guilt by claiming it acted autonomously.
109. Elizabeth Bennett clearly sees herself as the victim of witchcraft, but she has also, decisively, confessed to the crime.

record that Margery Sammon was tried in 1582, but she was tried together with another woman for keeping spirits and killing a man in 1583, and acquitted. Where no record remains, it may be that the suspect was never charged, or that an indictment was rejected by the grand jury and destroyed accordingly. Either way, Sammon escaped punishment.[110]

The Examination and confession of Margery Sammon, taken before mee Brian Darcie Esquire, the xxv. of February.

The sayde Margerie Sammon, sister to the sayde Ales Hunt, daughter to one mother Barnes lately deceased, (which mother Barns was accompted to bee a notorious Witche) saith, that shee remayned at home with her mother by the space of halfe a yeare, and saith shee was with her mother several times, when shee laye sicke, and also at the houre of her death: But denyeth the having of any spirites of her sayd Mother, or that her mother had any to her knowledge.

The said Margery yt night being committed to ye ward & keeping of ye cunstable, and the nexte daye brought before mee the saide Bryan in the presence of her sister Ales Hunte, And beeing charged by her sayde Syster to have two spirites like toades, given her by her mother at her death, utterlye denyed the same saying, I defie thee, though thou art my sister, saying she never sawe anye such: At which speaches her sister taking her aside by the arme, whyspred her in the eare: And then presentlye after this Examinate with great submission and many teares, confessed that she had two spirites delyvered her by her mother, the same day shee departed. And that shee this Examinate caryed them awaye with her in the evening, they beeing in a wicker basket, more then half full of white and blacke wooll: And that she asking her mother what shee should doe with them, she bad her keepe them and feede them: This Examinate asking wherewithall: her mother answered, if thou doest not give them mylke, they will sucke of thy blood: And sayeth, she called them by the names of Tom and Robbin. And this Examinate beeing asked how often she had given them meate sithence shee had them, saieth and confesseth, that she fed them twise out of a dyshe with mylke: And beeing asked when shee fed them last, this Examinate sayde, uppon Twesday last past before this examination, and that with mylke.

This Examinate sayeth also, that when shee tooke them of her mother, shee sayde unto her, if thou wilte not keepe the said spirits, then send them to mother Pechey, for I know she is a Witch, and will bee glad of them.[111] And saith further, that shee hearing, that Ursleye Kempe was apprehended, and fearing that shee shoulde bee called in question, saieth thereupon shee tooke

---

110. Margery Sammon appears at the Assizes of March 1583/4 under the name of Margery Barnes of St Osyth (she is referred to as 'Margerie Barnes' on C5v here).

111. Joan Pechey was apparently not tried but died in gaol after she was supposed to have been released.

the saide spirites beeing in a basket, and in the evening wente unto the
grounde of her Master, and so into Reads grounde, and bad them goe to the
sayde mother Pechey: And which wordes they skypped out of the said
basket, and wente before this Examinate, shee this Examinate sayeing, all evill
goe with you, and the Lorde in heaven blesse mee from yee: And sayeth, shee
myghte see the sayde spyrites goeing towarde a barred style, goeing over into
Howe lane: And when they came at the style, shee saieth, they skypped over
the same style and wente the readye waye to mother Pecheyes house: And
saieth shee verilye thinketh the sayde mother Pechey hath them ...

5. Copycat confession

Ales Manfield came from a village 5 miles north-east of St Osyth, and was
accused later in the development of the witchcraft episode, on 13 March. Her
confession eerily echoes Ursley Kempe's. The magistrate clearly questioned
her truthfulness in accusing herself and others, and despite the word
'condemned' here, the only record of her trial is a joint indictment for arson,
of which she was acquitted.

The examination and confession of Ales Manfield, taken at Thorpe,[112] and
brought before me Brian Darcey esquire, one of her Majesties Justices, the
xiii. day of Marche.
Condemned.

The saide Ales Manfielde saieth, that shee is of the age of threescore and
three yeeres or there aboutes, and that about xii. yeeres sithence one
margaret Grevell came unto this examinat and saide, that shee shoulde goe
out of her house yt shee dwelt in unto another house in the towne: And
then telled her that she had foure Impes or spirites the whiche shee woulde
not carrie with her to that house, for feare they shoulde be espied or seene,
and prayed her this examinate that shee woulde keepe them, and also telled
her what they woulde doe for her (saying shee should have them upon
condition that shee the sayde Margaret might have them at her pleasure,
otherwise shee should not have them) and with what, and howe shee
shoulde feede them, and at her desire and request shee sayth that shee was
contented to keepe them: And thereupon shee sayeth it was concluded and
agreed betweene her and this examinate, that shee the sayde Margaret
shoulde have them as often and as many times as shee would at her pleasure,
and that then shee received them.

This examinate being asked, what names they were called by, and of
what likenes, saieth that one of them was called Robin, an other Jack, the
thirde William, the fourth Puppet alias Mamet, & that two of them were
hees and the other two were shees, & were like unto blacke Cats, and

112. Thorpe-le-Soken.

sayth that she kept them in a boxe with woll therein: And yt they did stand upon a shelfe by her bed where she lay. This examinate saith also, yt ye said Margaret Gravel hath commen unto her many & often times sithence ye saide agreement betweene them made, & according to ye said condition hath received of this examinat ye said imps or spirits: shee this examinat being telled of her some times wherfore she would have them, & that some times she knew by asking ye said imps or spirits where they had bin, & what they had done when they returned againe unto her. And being asked how often & when to her remembrance, she this examinat saith, about 7 yeres since ye said mother Gravel came unto this examinate & told her yt Chestons wife & she were fallen out, & had chidden very much: & that she gave her evill speeches, whereupon shee requested to have ye spirit Robin to go to plague his beasts: & then sent it, which said when it returned, yt Cheston being at plow & leaving worke, Yt it had plagued a bullocke of his yt was well liking & lustie, wherof it should pine and die.

This examinate saith, that the saide Margaret Grevell, well neere two yeres after, sent her spirite Jacke to goe plague Cheston, upon the great Toe unto the death.[113] This Examinate saieth, that when it returned it tolde her that it had plagued the saide Cheston upon the Toe even unto death, and that it had sucked blood of the saide Margrettes bodie, and that besides it had of her Beere and Breade for the labour: and saith, that shee this examinate gave it Beare and Breed then also for telling of her.

This examinate saith also, that five yeeres past or there aboutes, her spirit Robin tolde her that Margarette Grevell had sent the saide spirite unto her husband to plague him, where of he pined above halfe a yeere and more, having by that meanes many and severall straunge sores, and thereof died. And this Examinate saith that, that hee woulde eate as much or more then two men woulde doe, and that it sucked blood upon the bodye of the saide Margaret for the labour: she this examinate being asked upon what place, saith the saide spirite did not tell her.

This examinat saith, that on a time she went unto the house of Joan Cheston widow, and desired of her to give her some Curdes: but shee sayeth shee gave her none, whereupon she saith, that shee sent Impe Puppet alias Mamet to plague her Beastes, where that woulde, and so it did: And that when the saide Impe returned, it tolde this examinate that it had plagued foure of her Beastes with lamenesse, and that it did sucke blood upon this Examinates body for a rewarde.

This examinate sayth, that about two yeres past, one John Sayer did fetch doung out of an Orchard, from a pittes banke, neere this examinates house, and did by reason thereof, gulle[114] a greene place before her doore, whereupon shee saieth, shee sent her Impe called Puppet alias Mamet to

---

113. Margaret Grevell was accused of killing Robert Cheston but acquitted.
114. Gulley, erode.

stay the Carte being before the dore, the which it dyd, and shee saieth that shee sawe him and others to lift at the wheeles, and to set his hauser rope, the which did litle good, and that the same hauser rope and other of his horse harnesse burst a sunder, and shee saieth, shee gave her said Impe Beere for the labour.

This examinate saieth, that litle before Michaelmas last, her saide foure Impes saide unto her, saying, I pray you Dame give us leave to goe unto little Clapton to Celles,[115] saying, they woulde burne Barnes, and also kill Cattell, and shee saith, that after their returne they tolde her that they had burnt a barne of Rosses with corne, and also tolde her that Celles his wife knewe of it, and that all they foure were fedde at Cels house by her al ye time they were away from this examinate, wc[116] shee sayeth was about a sevennight: And that Puppet sucked upon this examinates left shoulder at their returne unto her: And the rest had beere.

This examinate saith, that William, one of her Impes not above a sevennight before her apprehension, tolde her that shee shoulde be called in question, and bad her shift for her self: saying, they woulde nowe depart from her and goe unto saint Osees unto mother Gray, mother Torner, or mother Barnes two daughters, but to which of them it was that they would goe shee doth not nowe remember: but they told her yt they to whom they went had hurt men & women to death, & several mens cattel and other thinges.

This examinate saith, yt about a quarter of a yere since, she went unto ye house of mother Ewstace[117] to speake wt her, at wc time she saith, shee saw three imps wc she had standing in a yearthen pot in ye one side of her house nere ye hearth, & saith that one of them was white, ye other gray, & the third blacke, & saith they were like cats. This examinat saith also, that her white spirit told her,[118] yt mother Ewstace their dame, sent her impes to hurt a childe, whereof it shoulde pine and become lame, but whose childe shee remembreth not.

Also this examinate saith, yt upon some conference between mother Ewstace & her, shee this examinate told mother Ewstace, yt mother Grevel did plague her husband, wherof he died, which was done by her spirit Robin: & she saith that she also told mother Ewstace, yt mother Grevel sent her spirite Jacke to plague Cheston to the death: but what answere she the said mother Ewstace then made, shee nowe remembreth not.

This examinate saith, that about a yere since the said mother Gravel

---

115. Little Clacton is 2 miles north-east of St Osyth. The Celles or Selles family consisted of Henry and Cysley (who were both accused of a list of witchcraft and arson attacks (one with Ales Manfield) and both died in gaol) and their children, two of whom gave evidence against them.

116. Which.

117. Elizabeth Ewstace was not tried but discharged.

118. Ales Manfield had said that all her spirits were black but here echoes a phrase of Ursley Kempe's and the shape of Kempe's story about her white spirit confirming sightings of other witches' familiars.

told her, that she had caused her impes to destroy severall brewinges of beere, & batches of bread, being asked where, she saith a brewen at Reades, a brewen at Carters, and a brewen of three or foure bushelles of malte at Brewses.

The said confession being made by the saide Ales in maner and forme aforesaid, I the same Brian in the presence of the cunstables & other the Townesmen of Thorpe, sayde as I had severall tymes before unto the sayde Ales, what a danger it was, and howe highly shee should offende God if shee shoulde charge any person with any thing untrue, and also telled her that her saide confession should bee read agayne unto her, willing her that if shee hearde any thinge read that she knew was not true, that she should speake, and it shoulde be amended, the which being done, shee sayde her confession was true, and the sayde Margaret and Elizabeth beeing then also called before mee, shee affirmed her confession to their faces[119]. . .

6. The end of the case

Almost the last person to be questioned before the Assizes began, Annis Heard was accused of a number of small crimes which were described in great detail to the magistrate. She was also accused by a clergyman of killing his wife. The majority of stories told about her suggest accusers searching their minds for incidents in which they may have angered Heard, and this, together with her profession of innocence, perhaps contributed to her acquittal on charges of bewitching John Wadde's livestock. But it is surprising that there is no record of her alleged murder of Mistress Harrison. As the accusations spread to the north-east and the Assize date arrived, the investigation – for reasons unknown – petered out and ceased.

The enformation of John Wadde, Thomas Cartwrite, Richard Harrison with several others the parishioners of little Okeley,[120] taken by mee Brian Darcey Esquire one of her Majesties justices the 16. day of March.

John Wade saith, that about two moneth sithence Annis Heard, saide unto him, that shee was presented unto the spirituall Courte for a witch,[121] and prayed him to be a meanes to helpe her, that she might answere the same when the dayes were longer: whereunto he said, that hee told her that the Regester dwelt at Colchester,[122] saying, it must be hee that therein may pleasure thee: whereto she saide, that shee woulde goe to John Aldust of

---

119. Perhaps Darcy had spotted her inconsistencies and echoing of Ursley Kempe's confession?
120. Little Oakley is about 10 miles north-east of St Osyth.
121. That she had been accused in the church court of being a witch. From John Wadde's later comment, it appears that he was one of her accusers there.
122. The church court official lives some distance away: Colchester is a major town in Essex, about 13 miles from Little Oakley.

Ramsey[123] to speake unto him, for that he goeth to Colchester that he might speak to the officers for her, and so she departed: this examinat saith, that since that time he drove fortie sheepe and thirtie lambes to a pasture yt he had at Tendring,[124] beeing thereof well neere fourescore Acres, the which hee had spared by some long time, and knew the same to be a good sheepes pasture, and saith, that after they had bin there viii. or ix. dayes, hee went to see them (having neverthelesse appointed one to looke to them): And at his comming he found one to bee dead, another, to bee lame, another to sit drowping, and a lambe in the same case by it, whiche all died, and he founde one other with the necke awry, which is in that case to this day, and one other whiche was so weake that it coulde not arise, & this examinat saith, that sithence he with others that presented her, and sithence shee the saide Annis talked with him, he hath had not so fewe as twentie sheepe and lambes that have died, and be lame and like to die: & hee saith, that hee hath lost of his beasts & other cattell, which have dyed in a strange sort.

Thomas Cartwrite saith, that after a great winde & snowe wel neere three yeeres sithence, there was an arme or boughe of a tree of his that was blowen downe, whereof Annis Herd had removed a peece and laid the same over a wet or durtie place to goe over, which being to this examinat unknowen, hee tooke the same & the rest and carried it home: the which the saide Annis knowing, that hee had carried the same away, she said, that the churle (meaning this examinat) to a neighbour of hers had carried away the peece of the bough that she had laied to go over, saying, that shee woulde bee even with him for it. After which this Examinat saith, within three nights after, there then beeing a snowe two of his beasts went from all the rest, where as they lay as he might well perceive by the snowe, and the head Cowe fell over a great bancke into a ditch on the other side, and there lay with the necke double under her, and the head under the shoulder, but alive, and he saith, he gate it home by good helpe and laied it in his barne, and saith, that it lay fourteene dayes in a groning and piteous sort, but of all that time woulde eate nothing, whereupon hee saith hee tooke an axe & knocked it on the head. And also the other Cowe that was with the said Cow being a calving in a most strange sorte died, the which this examinat saith, yt hee verily thinketh to be done by some witchery by the saide Annis Herd.

Bennet Lane wife of William Lane, saith, yt when she was a widdow,[125] Annis Herd beeing at her house she gave her a pint of milke & also lent her a dish to beare it home, the which dishe she kept a fortnight or 3. weekes, & then ye girle of the said Annis Herds came to her house on a message: & she asked the girle for the dish, & said though I gave thy mother milk to make her a posset I gave her not my dish, she this examinat being then a spinning: & so ye girle went home, & as it seemed told her mother, who by her sent

---

123. A village a mile north-west of Little Oakley.
124. A village 6 miles south-west of Little Oakley.
125. Clearly Lane was not her first husband.

her dish home to her, ye which girle having done her arrand, & being but a while gone: shee this examinat saith, she could no longer spin nor make a thread to hold, whereat she was so greeved yt she could not spin, she saith, she tooke her spindle and went to the grindstone therewith once or twise, & grownd it as smoth as she coulde, thinking it might be by some ruggednesse of ye spindle that did cause her thread to breake, and so when she had grownd it as wel as she could she went againe to worke therewith, thinking that then it would have done, but it would not do no better then it did before: then she saith, yt shee remembred her self and tooke her spindle and put it into ye fire, & made it red hot, & then cooled it gaine[126] and went to worke, and then it wrought as well as ever it did at any time before.

This examinat saith, that an other time the saide Annis Herd owed her two pence, and the time came that shee shoulde pay the Lordes rent,[127] and she beeing a poore woman was constrained to aske her the two pence, and to borow besides (as shee said): whereto she the saide Annis answered, that shee had paied eight or nine shillings that weeke, and shee had it not nowe: saying she should have it the next weeke, whereto shee this Examinat saide, you must needes helpe me with it now, for this day I must paye the Lordes rent, then shee saide shee must goe borrowe it and so went and fetched it, saying, there is your money, whereunto shee this examinat answered, and said, now I owe you a pint of milke, come for it when you will & you shall have it: the which she came for ye next day & had it with ye better,[128] this examinat saith, yt ye next day she would have flete[129] hir milke bowle, but it wold not abide ye fleeting, but would rop & role as it[130] the white of an egg, also the milk being on the fier it did not so soone seath[131] but it woulde quaile, burne by and stincke, the which shee saide shee thought might be long of[132] ye feeding of her beasts, or els that her vessels were not sweete,[133] whereupon she saith, she scalded her vessels, and scoured them with salt, thinking that might helpe, but it was never the better but as before: then she saith, shee was full of care, that shee shoulde loose both milke and creame, then shee saith it came into her minde to approove another way, which was, shee tooke a horse shue and made it redde hote, and put it into the milke in the vessals, and so into her creame: and then she saith, shee coulde seath her milke, fleete her creame, and make her butter in good sort as she had before.

---

126. Again.
127. Tithe.
128. Butter.
129. Skimmed.
130. Should read 'were', which is omitted from the beginning of the page.
131. Boil.
132. 'Along of', because of.
133. Clean.

Andrewe West and Anne saith, that on a time the said Annis Herd came unto his house, saying, she had been at mill, and that she coulde get neither meale nor bread, at which her speeches hee knowing her neede, saith, hee caused his wife to give her a peece of a lofe, and that then he said unto her, Annis, thou art ill thought of for witchcraft, the which she then utterly denyed yt she coulde or did any such thing: whereunto he saith, his wife saide wee have a sort[134] of pigges I wott not what we shall doe with them saying, I woulde some body had one or two of them, to that the said Annis said, that if a poore body should have one of them and bestow cost, & that then if they should die it would halfe undoe them, and said if her Landlord would give her leave to keepe one, she then wished that she would give her one of them, whereunto this examinat said, shee should have one: But for that she came not for it, this examinat saith, that he did thinke that she cared not for it, and after a while one of her neighbours bought two of them, and within ii. or iii. dayes after the said Annis came for one: to whom this examinat said, for yt they had not hard no more of her, that he thought she would have none, and told her that he had sold two of them, and so the said Annis departed and went home.

This examinat saith, yt his wife the next day sent unto the said Annis a pound of wooll to be spun: and that she said to the boy that brought it, saying, can she not have her weeders[135] to spin the same? and that she then said to ye boy, your Aunt might as well give me one of her pigges, as to Penly and this examinat saith, that within two houres after, one of the best pigs that he had set upon a crying as they stood all together before the dore in the yard, and the rest of the pigs went away from yt at the length the pig that cried folowed stackering as though it were lame in the hinder partes, and yt then he called his weeders to see in what strange case the pig was in, and asked them what was best to doe therewith, to which some of them said, burne it, other said, cut of the eares & burn them, and so they did, & then the pig amended by & by. and within two daies after this examinats wife met with the said Annis Herd, and shee then burdened her with that she had said to her boy: To which ye said Annis made answere, yt she did say so: and then this examinats wife told the said Annis in what case her pig was, saying, thou saidest the other day thou hast no skill in witcherie, his saide wife then said, I will say thou hast an unhappie tongue. After which, this examinats wife could not brewe to have any drinke yt was good, so as she was full of care, saying, yt somtimes she put one thing into her brewing fat, sometimes an other thing to see if it could doe it any good, but shee saith, it did none: then she saith one gave her counsell to put a hot yron into her mesh fat,[136] the which she did, and then shee could brewe as well as she did before.

---

134. Large number.
135. Those who she employs to weed.
136. Mash vat. Mash is malt mixed with hot water to form wort.

Edmond Osborne and Godlife his wife, said that a litle before Christmas last past, he bought at Manitree[137] mault, and brought it home, and said to his wife, good wife, let us have good drinke made of it. And the next day shee went in hand to brew the same, and when she had meshed her first worte and did let it goe, that did verye well: Then his said wife having occasion to send her lad to their ground, she bade the lad call at Annis Herds for iii. d. the which shee owed her for a pecke of Aples, and that the lad so did: And she answered him very short, and saide, shee had it not now, saying, she shold have it as soone as ye Wooll man came: and the lad came home, & tolde his dame what she had said. And at yt time, she this examinat was readie to meshe ye seconde time, & when she had done, her mesh fat wrought up as the fat doth when it was set a worke with good beere, and bare up a hand breadth above ye fat, and as they thrust in a sticke or any other thing, it would blow up and then sinked againe, then she saith, yt she did heat an yron redde hot, and put ye same into it, & it rose up no more. And then she let goe, and then shee did seath the wort, and when it was sodden it stancke in suche sorte, as that they were compelled to put ye same in the swill tubbe.

Richard Harrison Clerk, person of Beamond[138] saith, that he and his late wife did dwell at little Okely, in a house of his said wife, & that hee the said Richard Harrison had also the personage of Okely in farme, and about Sommer was twelvemonth,[139] he being at London his wife had a Ducke sitting on certaine egges under a Cherrie tree in a hedge, and when the saide Duck had hatched, his said wife did suspect one Annis Herd a light woman, and a common harlot to have stolen her duckelins, & that his said wife went unto the said Annis Herd & rated her and all too chid her, but she could get no knowledge of her ducklins, and so came home & was very angry against the said Annis. & within a short time after, the said Richard Harrison went into a chamber, and there did reade on his bookes for the space of 2. or 3. houres bidding his said wife to goe to bed wt the children, and yt he would come to her, and she so did: and being a while laid downe in her bed, his wife did crie out: Oh Lord Lorde, helpe me & keepe me, and he running to her, asked her what she ailed? and she said, Oh Lord I am sore afraid, and have bin divers times, but that I would not tell you, and said, I am in doubt husband, that yonder wicked harlot Annis Herd doth bewitch me and ye said Richard, said to his wife, I pray you be content and thinke not so, but trust in God and put your trust in him onely, and he will defend you from her, and from the Divell himselfe also: and said moreover, what will the people say, that I beeing a Preacher shoulde have my wife so weake in faith.

This examinat saith, yt within two moneths after his said wife said unto him, I pray you as ever there was love betweene us, (as I hope there hath been

---

137. Manningtree, 8 miles west of Little Oakley.
138. Parson of Beaumont, a village 4 miles south-west of Little Oakley.
139. A year ago last summer.

for I have v. pretie children by you I thanke God) seeke som remedie for me against yonder wicked beast (meaning the saide Annis Herd). And if you will not I will complaine to my father, and I thinke he wil see som remedie for me, for (said she) if I have no remedie, she will utterly consume me, whereupon this examinat did exhort his said wife as hee had before, & desired her to pray to God, and yt he wold hang her the said Annis Herd if he could prove any such matter and after he went to the personage, and there he saith he gathered plummes: and the said Annis Herd then came to the hedge side and Anwicks wife with her, and said unto him, I pray you give me som plummes sir: and this examinat said unto her, I am glad you are here you vield[140] strumpet, saying, I do think you have bewitched my wife, and as truly as God doth live, if I can perceive she be troubled any more as she hath been, I will not leave a whole bone about thee, & besides I will seeke to have thee hanged: and saith, he saide unto her that his wife would make her father privie unto it, and that then I warrant thee he will have you hanged, for he will make good friends, & is a stout man of himselfe. and saith, yt then he did rehearse divers things to her yt were thought she had bewitched, as Geese & hogges, & as he was comming downe out of the tree, shee the said Annis did sodenly depart from him without having any plummes.

This examinat saith, after which speeches so by him used unto her, and before Christmas, his said wife was taken sore sick, & was at many times afraid both sleeping and waking, & did call this examinat her husbande unto her not above two dayes before her death, and saide unto him, husband, God blesse you and you children, and God send you good friends, for I must depart from you, for I am nowe utterly consumed with yonder wicked Creature, naming the saide Annis Herd, which wordes hee saith were spoken by her in ye presence of John Pollin, & mother Poppe, and within two daies after his said wife departed out of this world in a perfect faith, she divers times in her sicknesse and before, repeating these wordes, Oh Annis Herd, Annis Herd shee hath consumed me.

John Pollin saith he was at master Harrisons when his wife lay sicke, & neere ye departing out of this world, & that her husband gave her good counsell for her salvation, and that she then said, O Annis Herd, Annis Herd.

Brets wife saith, shee heard mistres harrison say, that the said Annis Herd had consumed her even to the death, & that she cryed out upon her to the houre of her death.

The enformation of Annis Dowsing base daughter of Annis Herd, taken before mee Brian Darcey Esquire, one of her Majesties Justices, the xviii. day of March.

The said Annis saith, that shee is of the age of vii. yeeres the Saturday before our Lady day next, and shee being asked whether her mother had any little

---

140. Vile.

things, or any little imps, she saith, that she hath in one boxe sixe Avices or Blackbirds: being asked of what colour, shee saith, they be white speckled, and all blacke, and she saith, that she hath in another boxe, vi. spirits like Cowes (being asked howe big) shee saith, they be as big as Rattes, & that they have little short hornes, & they lie in the boxes upon white and blacke wooll: and she saith, that her mother gave unto her one of the saide Cowes, whiche was called by the name of Crowe, which is of colour black & white. and she saith, yt her mother gave to her brother one of them, which she called Donne, & that is of colour red & white. And she being asked wherewithall she had seene her mother to feed the Avices & blackbirdes, she saith, she hath seene her feed them somtimes wt wheat, barley, somtimes wt otes, & with bread & cheese, & the Cowes yt were like beasts, somtime wt wheat straw, somtime wt barley straw, ote straw, and wt hay, & being asked what she gave them to drinke, she saith, sometimes water & sometimes beere, such drinke as they drunke.

She this examinat saith, yt her brother somtimes seeing them the Avices and blackbirdes, to come about him, saith, that he saith they keepe a tuitling and tetling, and that then hee taketh them and put them into the boxes.

She being asked if she saw them sucke upon her mother, saith, that the Avices & blackbirdes have sucked upon her hands, and upon her brothers legges: being willed to shew the place, she said, here sucked Aves, & here sucked Aves, and heere sucked Blackbird. And being asked how one spot upon the backe of her hands came so somewhat like the other, she saith the same was burnt.

The examination and confession of Annis Herd of little Okeley, taken by me Brian Darcey Esquire, one of her Majesties Justices of the peace, the xvii. day of March.
Continued in prison. [141]

The said Annis Herd saith, that she told one of her neighbors that the churle (meaning Cartwrite) had carried away a bough which she had laid over a flowe in the high way, and saide that she was faine to goe up to the anckle every steppe, and that shee said hee had beene as good hee had not caried it away, for she would fetch as much wood out of his hedges as that doeth come unto. And she saith also that she remembreth she came unto goodman Wad, & telled him that she was presented into the spiritiuall court for a witch, & that then she desired yt she might answere the same when the dayes were longer.

Also she confesseth yt Lannes wife gave her a pinte of milk & lent her a dish to carie it home in, & that she kept the dishe a fortnight or longer, & then sent it home by her girle, & also that Lannes wife came to her for ii. d. which shee ought her.

Also she confesseth that she came to the house of her neighbour West, &

---

141. There is no record that this was the case.

telled him that she had bin at mille, but she could get no meale, nor yet no bread, & that he gave her a piece of a loafe: and she confesseth the speeches that then were of the pigs: And that she saide to ye boy that brought woll, yt his Aunt might aswell have let her have one as Penley. She saith also, yt shee remembreth yt she came to goodwife Osborne, & bought of her 3. peckes of aples, & confesseth yt shee ought unto her iii.d. but denieth that the boye or ladde came to her for any money.

Also she remembreth that mistres Harison charged her to have stollen her ducklings, & that she called her harlot & witch, & confesseth yt she came unto M. Harison, he being at ye parsonage a gathering of plumms, & that shee prayed him to give her some plumms: But denieth that she hath any imps Aveses or blackebirds, or any kine called Crowe or Donne:[142] And all and every other thing in generall, or that shee is a witch or have any skill therein.[143]

3. Witchcraft at the Assizes: Northamptonshire, 1612

A Brief abstract of the Arraignment of nine Witches at Northampton, 1612

In 1612 at the Lent Assizes held at Northampton Castle a number of women and a man were tried for witchcraft of various kinds, ranging from murder to the bewitching of pigs. There are two accounts of witches tried at the Assizes, which cross-reference in a number of ways but which also differ importantly over how many witches were tried, who they were and precisely what they were said to have done.

One account is a manuscript of unknown authorship, now known as B.L. (British Library) Sloane 972 (f. 7). The writer seems likely to have been an educated observer of the Assizes, who was particularly interested in two of the witches' victims, Mistress Elizabeth Belcher and her brother Master William Avery. He recorded in some detail their pious response to bewitchment, especially that of Mr Avery, and had little interest in the witches themselves or in the verdicts of their trials, which he does not report. The author of the pamphlet of the same year (*The Witches of North-amptonshire* (London, 1612)) is also unknown, but he had a different focus. For him, the meaning of witchcraft could be found in the (allegedly) debased

---

142. The examinations of mother and daughter have presumably been 'helpfully' dated: Annis Heard is asked on 17 March to respond to Annis Dowsing's accusation of keeping familiars, which is dated 18 March here. The same thing happens with the evidence of the Celles children. This dating suggests that children's (potentially less reliable) evidence only supports adult confessions rather than being used to extract them.

143. For readers who want to know more, the complete text of this pamphlet, with full annotation, is available in Gibson, ed., *Early Modern Witches.*

and immoral lives of the witches as well as in the godliness of their victims, and he was interested in guilt and its rightful punishment. He seems less well informed on some aspects of the Belcher/Avery story than the author of the manuscript, and his descriptions of his sources for this account point to a random collection of gossip rather than personal acquaintance with events. He was not apparently aware of three of the cases tried at the Assizes, which the manuscript describes in some detail. Nevertheless, he possessed information (or at least, anecdote) which the manuscript's writer lacked or did not report, such as the cause of the dissension between witches and victims in the Belcher/Avery case. He probably attended some of the witch trials of 1612, and he describes the cases of three other witches apparently unknown to the writer of the manuscript.

Each account thus gives a different list of witches tried at the Summer Assizes in 1612. The pamphleteer takes as his main focus Agnes Browne and her daughter Joan Browne or Vaughan, Arthur Bill, Hellen Jenkenson and Mary Barber. Bill, Jenkenson and Barber were unconnected with the Belcher/Avery case and came from different areas of Northamptonshire. The pamphlet also includes in passing some material about Catherine Gardiner and Jane Lucas. The manuscript's author, however, names Browne and Vaughan, Jane Lucas, Alce Harrys, Catherine Gardiner, and Alce Abbott, and says that these were jointly indicted for harming Belcher and Avery. He does not mention Bill, Jenkenson or Barber, but instead describes the case of three women of the Wilson family, the context of which he does not seem to know.

It is puzzling that each writer could remain in ignorance of the cases well known to the other. It is possible that the witches were arraigned on different days, by different juries, and that each writer was present at only some of the trials, missing others. The sensational Belcher/Avery case, with its well-born and strangely afflicted victims, was clearly one of the highlights of the Assizes, with other witches probably playing secondary roles either because their cases were fairly everyday or because they were seen as less directly involved in the main events. Some of the witches may even have been acquitted, and thus were potentially of less interest to reporters and readers, although in other published works and manuscripts, it can be seen that acquittal does not guarantee that accusations against once-suspected witches will be kept out of print, or that the acquitted will be treated as innocent.

The manuscript account is reproduced in full here, together with extracts from the printed pamphlet, *The Witches of Northamptonshire* (London, 1612). The full pamphlet text is available in Gibson, ed., *Early Modern Witches*.

A Brief abstract of the Arraignment of nine Witches at Northampton: July 21th[144] 1612.

Inditements: The witches names: 1 Jane Lucas. 2 Alce Harrys. 3 Catherine Gardiner. 4 Agnes Brown. 5 Jone Brown. 6 Alce Abbott.

There were two bills on Inditement: the one for torturing Eliz. Belcher wife to Dabriscourt Belcher Esquier,[145] and Wil. Avery her own Brother, for wch inchantments were six accused. 1 Jane Lucas. 2 Alce Harrys. 3 Katherine Gardiner. 4 Agnes Brown. 5 Jone Brown. 6 Alce Abbot. The other for killing two porkets, & one Cow & for bewitching a Mare for wch facts there stood three arraigned. 1 Agnes Wilson widow. 2 Alce Wilson her daughter. 3 Jane Wilson her sonns wife or daughter in law. The evidences are these.

The Evidences: Mrs Belcher.

1 That Mrs Belcher had bene strangely afflicted and tormented in al her body for the space of a yeare and quarter, & using all lawful meanes of phisick could find no ease, neither did any purgation were it never so forcible work upon her or doo her any good. So it was generally suspected to bee witchcraft, but shee would never bee so perswaded by any of her friends for almost a yeares space, till March[146] 15th last past, when being in her fit, some spectators by nominated sundry suspected parties, wch shee still disclaimed, & at last naming Jone Brown daughter to Agnes Brown, shee replied, hath shee done it, then they named her again, & Mrs Belcher answered again, did shee & so from that time forth persisted to accuse Jone Brown, & being in her fits seemed still to see her tormenting her, and would presently recover out of her fits, if shee could touch her or draw blood of her.[147]

---

144. *Sic.*
145. Dabriscourt Belcher (variously spelt Dabrisecourt, Daubridgcourt Belchier (in his *DNB* entry) and Dawbridge-court) was a country gentleman, traveller and a dabbler in literature. He is completely absent from both accounts of his wife's illness, and the fact that he settled in Utrecht around 1600, and that his wife's brother is the one who assists her in 1612, suggests that he lived apart from Elizabeth Belcher for at least part of the time.
146. This word has clearly been overwritten and is unclear.
147. *The Witches of Northamptonshire* gives a history of the accusation on B2v–B3: 'This Joane Vaughan, whether of purpose to give occasion of anger to the said Mistris Belcher, or but to continue her vilde, and ordinary custome of behaviour, committed something either in speech, or gesture, so unfitting, and unseeming the nature of woman-hood, that it displeased the most that were there present: But especially it touched the modesty of this Gentlewoman, who was so much mooved with her bold, and impudent demeanor, that shee could not containe her selfe, but sodainely rose up and strooke her, howbeit hurt her not, but forced her to avoide the company: which this Chicken of her Dammes hatching, taking disdainefully and beeing also enraged (as they that in this kind having power to harme, have never patience to beare) at her going out told the Gentlewoman that shee would remember this injury, and revenge it: To whom Mistris Belcher answered, that shee neither feared her nor her mother: but bad her doe her worst ... being alone in her

Mr Avery.

Mr Avery her Brother moved to revenge went toward Agnes Browns house to beate her & her daughter, but by the way was so confounded that he could not goe forward, but went back very well, then hee assaied again, and coming to the same place had no power to goe forth, but returned & so wthin 2 daies after April 6th fell into strange fits and convulsions having sundry visions and apparitions of divers, witches & such like.[148]

1 hee saw Agnes Brown bring a molewarp,[149] and perswaded him to let it suck his toe, but hee defied them both & would not suffer it, wth many godly prayers & meditations in his fit.

2 Agnes Brown appeared to him naked above the middle wth a knife in ech hand, inciting him to deliver the one to his Sister Belcher to kill herself, & to murther himself wth the other in wch fit hee so diligently observed her, that hee detected a black wart as big as a fetch under left arm,[150] wch upon search was found & seen by many: yea, though hee never saw nor knew the woman by face, yet by the apparitions hee being brought where shee was amongst other women, instantly said this is shee who hath wrongd my sister & mee.

3 Sundry other witches appeared to him in his fits, whome hee exhorted to repent in time, for the divel their master would bring them to a shameful end: some hee called novices in the trade, & wisht them to desist from those abhominable practises, & to ask god forgivenes &c.

4 hee heard many of them railing at Jane Lucas, laying the fault on her that they were thus accused: and hee saw Alce Abbot, Cath: Gardiner & Alce Harrys riding on one walkers sow: and there appeared to him a bloody man desiring him to have mercy on his Mistris Agnes Brown and to cease from impeaching of her.[151]

---

cont.

    house, she was sodainely taken with such a griping, and gnawing in her body, that shee cried out, and could scarce bee held by such as came unto her, And being carried to her bed her face was many times so disfigured by beeing drawn awrie that it bred both feare, and astonishment to all the beholders, and ever as shee had breath, she cried, Heere comes Joane Vaughan, away with Joane Vaughan ...'

148. The pamphlet confirms this story and Avery's subsequent decline into illness.

149. A mole.

150. *Sic.*

151. The pamphlet treats the sow story as fact, not a vision on signature C: 'It was credibly reported that some fortnight before their apprehension, this Agnes Browne, one Ratherine [Katherine] Gardiner, and one Joane Lucas, all birds of a winge, and all abyding in the Towne of Gilsborough did ride one night to a place (not above a mile off) called Ravenstrop [Ravensthorpe, 2 miles from Guilsborough] all upon a Sowes backe, to see one mother Rhoades, an old Witch that dwelt there, but before they came to her house the old Witch died, and in her last cast cried out, that there were three of her old friends comming to see her, but they came too late. Howbeit shee would meete with them in another place within a month after.'

5 Being at Northampton in his fit he said that the witches in prison were at variance & that if any one would goe down hee should heare their voices, but would not understand a word distinctly whereupon Mr Brown a Mr[152] of Arts of Trinity College Oxford went to the prison being about two a clock in the morning, & heard a confused noise of much chattering & chiding but could not discern a ready word.

6 when he was caried from Northampton in a Coch, hee said if they did not take him out of the coch, hee should break his neck at such a place in the high way, and that such a mans mare fell dead in the said place at that very instant wch was two miles of and as they rode on, the man met them wth saddle & bridle on his back, and affirmd so much of the strange & soudain death of his mare: whereat Mr Avery being come out of his fit, stept forth and on his knees gave god thanks for his delivery wch the mans wife seeing thought to join wth him in prayer, but was soudainly taken in the same maner as Mr Avery had bene, & so after being in a house & put into a chaire, the very chaire danced exceedingly to the admiration of all the beholders: so the woman continueth still bewitched.[153]

7 Hee saw a black ugly villain in his fit daring him to come down to the yard, but hee would not, yet still defied him & Agnes Brown wch sent him, wth such like words:, thou divell! thou filthy black rogue! thou damned whore! thou hast done thy worst to my sister, & brought knives to mee to kill my sister & my child that I might be damned as thou art, but I care not for thee, & thou ugly fiend wouldst have mee come down to thee, but I care not for thee. thou filthy whore thou hast committed 14 murthers sparing nor young nor old women nor children: and thou hast gotten a swift page that will run 24 miles in a moment, & will follow thee to the gallows. then hee said, look how the black rogue comes stealing up the staires & peeps into the dore, & now hee comes creeping in by the walls to my bedside: but let him doo his worst, hee cannot doo mee harm: my saviour doth still defend mee &c.

All these visions and speaches delivered in his fits wth many others of like nature were ratified and confirmed by sundry persons there present of good credite, and reputation.

---

152. Master.
153. The pamphlet tells a different version of the story on B4–B4v: 'Not long after Maister Avery and his Sister having beene both in Northampton and having drawne blood of the Witches, Ryding both homewards in one Coach, there appeared to their view a man and a woman ryding both upon a blacke horse, M. Avery having spyed them a farre off, and noting many strange gestures from them, sodainely spake to them that were by, and (as it were Prophetically) cryed out in these words, That either they or their Horses should presently miscarry, And imediately the horses fell downe dead. Whereupon Maister Avery rose up praysing ye grace and mercies of God, that he had so powerfully delivered them ...'

8 There appeared to him Agnes Browns spirit, & hee said what art thou? art thou Arouta, or Cramega, or Arachne? no thou art Cramega with a pox I know thee too well.

9 being in a fit at Northampton hee desired to goe to the prison, & there amongst others pickt out Agnes Brown, threw her down on the ground, & so the blood sprung out of her eye wth the fall, whereat hee presently recovered.

10 Hee was once stricken on the eyes & his heeles tript up & so cast into his fit: & another time hee was thrown from his horse twenty paces of wthout any harme at all.

There were others who accused some of those witches, as one Hugh Lucas a youth of 12 yeares who looking stark[154] on Jane Lucas at the Church, shee askt him whether hee would outface her, but the boy being afraid replied not but went home, & being on a wall fell into a trance, & so continued 12 hours, & in his fit said hee saw J: Lucas come to his bed side 4 times: but the next day hee met wth her, tript up her heeles, beate her, and so had never any more fits. also John Walker being stricken very lame in all his limbs & suspecting Alce Harrys desired to scratch her, but being brought to her could not a long time draw any blood from her hands or face, yet at length wth much adoo got a little & so recovered instantly & cast away his crutches. All these women were searcht by women sworn,[155] who found marks or teates on some of them but on some none: and Alce Abbot being for trial cast into the water wth her hands & feete bound could not sink to bottome by any meanes.

Mrs Belcher being in the castle yard amongst the people before the arraignment began fell into a strange fit, & desired to have Jone Brown brought to her, wch the Judg granted, & so touching her did partly recover, yet was not able to deliver her mind fully at barr, but made signs for pen and inck & wrote these words (Jone Brown.) & so being brought before her shee started back shrikt wept & presently came to her perfect senses & shee then spake very modestly & would accuse none but Jone Brown, whome in her conscience shee thought had bene the instrument to afflict her in that strange fashion.

Mr Avery having bene all night grievously tormented & very sore in his body was sent for to the bench: but when hee alighted out of the coch at castle gate, hee fell into his fit & so was brought in that case to the bench, where all the witches were brought to touch him, yet hee recovered not but was carried forth & at last came to his perfect understanding, & so

---

154. Boldly.
155. The team of women employed to search suspects for suspicious marks and deliver their opinion on oath.

being brought to barr spake very discreetly, christianly & charitably to every point.

The witches: 1 Agnes Wilson. 2 Alce Wilson. 3 Jane Wilson.

The second inditement touched 3 others for killing cattle: who had bene long suspected of witchcraft, so about Easter last Mr Harrison minister of their parish[156] examined and catechised them 3 or 4 times before witnessed, who answered most blasphemously.

1 Agnes Wilson the mother saying her Creed would leave out I beleeve in Jesus Christ & could not bee induced to say it after the Minister: then hee askt her, how many gods shee did acknowledg, who answered two, god the father and the divell.[157]

2 Alce Wilson being demanded what her godfathers promised for her in baptism, shee said 3 things. 1 to forsake the world. 2 the pomp & vanity thereof. 3 the lusts of the flesh: but shee would by no meanes say, I forsake the divell & all his works, being askt the reason, because (said shee) the divell never did mee harme. Then being urged to say after the minister, shee would still say, I forsake god and all his works. When shee was brought before the Justices & threatned wth death except shee would say I forsake the divell &c shee would strive to say it, but a thing did rise & swell up in her throat ready to choke her. but since shee will say it and saith shee could not then for want of grace.[158]

The minister caused them to bee sercht, especially in their mouths, where in ech of them were found teats, wch being toucht presently yeelded blood: but wthin two daies after dried up & could not bee seen.

The facts laid to their charge were only 3: 1 that March 10. 1612 two porkets fell into strange fits, ran mad & died. 2 that March 20th 1612, a Cow of the same parties[159] fell into like passions & so languished,

---

156. This nonspecificity suggests that the writer is uncertain about where the Wilson family lived, suggesting that he only encountered them at the Assize stage of their prosecution.

157. This ranking of the devil alongside God corresponds with the heresy of Manichaeanism, justifying the writer's opinion that the women answered questions 'most blasphemously'. Manichaean beliefs, which stated that the devil ruled over the world in parity with God who ruled the heavens, were held by some of the early Medieval European sects accused of witchcraft. However, the emphasis on the devil in English Catholic and Protestant teaching could easily lead an innocently conformist parishioner to the conclusion that the devil rivalled God in his omnipotence. The interest in the Wilson women displayed by their minister suggests that he perceived in them either great ignorance or equally unwelcome free thinking (see John Cotta, below, for further comment).

158. Clearly this woman was not executed, as her crimes were not serious enough even if she was convicted. After her trial, the writer shows her producing a properly godly response. The verdicts of the Wilsons' trials are not known.

159. The victim is not named, suggesting little familiarity with pre-trial documents from the case.

consumed & died. 3 that a Mare of the same mans was in like case, & being mad brake down a wall, came into the house & being caried away, ran in again bounct at dore, & so being let into the hall ran to the chimney, put her head into the chimney where a wad of straw was put into the fire, & so held her head in the smoke til the fire kindled, singed her haire in the flame, & afterward being burnt rubd his[160] head in the ashes, & so perfectly recovered & went away very sound.

160. *Sic.*

THREE

ENGLISH DEMONOLOGIES

1. Warnings from a witchcraft believer

George Gifford, A Dialogue concerning Witches and Witchcraftes *(London, 1593)*

George Gifford (d. 1600) was an Essex minister of non-conformist views, for which he lost his position as incumbent of All Saints with St Peter's church in Maldon in 1584. The title page of his book thus describes him simply as 'minister of Gods word in Maldon', adding that his book is one 'in which is laide open how craftely the Divell deceiveth not onely the Witches but many other and so leadeth them awrie into many great errours'. Stoutly controversial, he argued a position which would now be labelled 'puritan' and was then described as 'godly': his work on witches suggests a deeply Protestant concern with reforming the (implicitly popish) superstitions and ignorance of 'the people' by evangelizing with the word of God.

Gifford felt that far too much power was attributed to witches and to the devil and stated repeatedly that nothing could happen in the world without God's providence: he having permitted, indeed instigated, it. If his purposes in this were inscrutable, it was not for Man to question them. In particular, Gifford condemned recourse to counter-magic against witches as ungodly. To go to magical healers or soothsayers for treatment or to find out if one was bewitched, was playing into the devil's welcoming hands, he argued. The correct response was to pray for God's help and submit to his trials and/or punishments, often inflicted using the devil as 'God's executioner'.

This essentially simple philosophy led Gifford, among other godly writers, to construct a frighteningly complex devil as the omnipresent enemy of humankind: if God was the universal answer, then the devil was the universal problem. Satan was potentially behind everything, and his master-stroke was to be not only pulling the strings of the witches, whom he kept as deluded and powerless puppets, but also to be the force behind the 'cunning people' and thus frequently behind those who accused witches. The devil carried out the magical harm on witches' victims, but he also set up accusations by cunning people and deluded victims to condemn innocent and guilty alike, increasing human misery and sinfulness.

Gifford's argument that some condemned witches were innocent, and the evidence against them unreliable, made him in a sense a sceptical writer on the subject, because he could conceive of witchcraft as an unreal crime, perpetrated by the devil and not by human agents. In this he approvingly and openly echoed Johannes Wier, the physician whose *De praestigiis daemonum* was sceptical about many aspects of supposed witchcraft (Gifford G4v; see also *A true and just Recorde* above). King James, writing his *Daemonologie* as King of Scotland two years before George Gifford's *Dialogue*, said that Wier had produced 'a publick apologie' (defence) of witches and so must himself be one (*Daemonologie*, p. xii).[1] Yet like Wier and Reginald Scot (below), Gifford mocked accusers for their crude understanding of witchcraft, and he left open severe doubts about any given accused witch – he or she might be the victim of satanic deceit and illusion, and thus guiltless. But he also argued that real witches, when identified, should be executed for their desire to cause harm, and especially for entering into a league with the devil. This latter definition of witches included – indeed, deliberately focused attention on – cunning people, whom Gifford said used magical means, often to accuse innocent people.

Gifford certainly believed in real witches, and had his own unsound methodology for distinguishing them from the innocent. His insistence that they, the cunning people and the devil, were let loose in the dark pre-apocalypse world aligned him firmly with less complex theorists of witchcraft. In the year of Gifford's first work on witches, 1579, a pamphleteer stated that

among the punishementes whiche the Lorde GOD hath laied uppon us, for the manifest unpietie and carelesse contempt of his woorde, aboundyng in these desperate daies, the swarmes of Witches, and Inchaunters, are not the laste nor the leaste. For that old Serpent Sathan, suffred to be the scourge for our sinns, hath of late yeares greatly multiplyed the broude of them, and muche encreased their malice.[2]

Many readers must have taken from Gifford's far more subtle and problematic text a similarly simple message: that the devil and witches were everywhere. But others must have questioned the very basis of their belief in witches, for in Gifford's text the most active witch-hunters are the thoughtless and the ignorant. Gifford's argument stands here as a statement of godly belief in the power the devil exercised through witches, a sample of the reservations about delusion and magical testing which came to dominate even the most assured demonology, and a brilliantly articulated example of the careful discriminations involved in any statement on witchcraft.

---

1. King James VI and I, *Daemonologie* (1591; London: The Bodley Head, 1924), p. xii.
2. *A Rehearsall straung and true* (London, 1579), A2. For the pamphlet's account, see Marion Gibson, ed., *Early Modern Witches*, pp. 33–40.

The Epistle

To the Right Worshipfull Maister Robert Clarke, one of her Majesties Barons of her Highnes Court of Exchequer.[3]

Certaine yeares now past, right Worshipfull, I published a small Treatise concerning Witches, to lay open some of Sathans sleightes, and subtile practices, least the ignoranter sort should be carried awry and seduced more and more by them.[4] The errors be farre more grosse, and the sinnes much greater, into which by the meanes of Witches he seduceth multitudes, then in common opinion they be esteemed. It falleth out in many places even of a suddaine, as it seemeth to me, and no doubt by the heavy judgement of God, that the Divels as it were let loose, doe more prevail, then ever I have heard of. For when men have set so light by the hearing of Gods voice to be instructed by him, they are justly given over to be taught by the Divels, and to learne their waies. Sathan is now hearde speake, and beleeved. He speaketh by conjurors, by sorcerers, and by witches, and his word is taken. He deviseth a number of thinges to be done, and they are put in practise and followed. The high providence of God Almighty and soveraigne rule over all, is set forth so unto us in the Scriptures, as that without him a Sparrow can not fall upon the ground. All the haires of our head are numbred. The Devils would hurt and destroy with bodily harmes, both men and beastes and other creatures: but all the Divels in Hell are so chained up and bridled by this high providence that they can not plucke the wing from one poore little Wrenne, without speciall leave given them from the ruler of the whole earth. And yet the Witches are made beleeve that at their request, and to pleasure them by fulfilling their wrath, their spirites doe lame and kill both men and beastes. And then to spread this opinion among the people, these subtill spirites bewray[5] them, and will have them openly confesse that they have done such great things, which all the Divels at any mans request cold never doe. For if they could, they would not stay to be intreated.[6] God giveth him[7] power sometimes to afflict both men and beastes with bodile harmes: If he can, he will doe it, as intreated and sent by Witches, but for us to imagin either that their sending doth give him power, or that he would not doe that which God hath given him leave to doe, unlesse they should

---

3. Robert Clarke was an eminent lawyer and judge who was a natural choice as Gifford's patron and dedicatee. He took many tours of duty on the Assize circuits, as Gifford suggests later in his epistle, and judged the cases of witches as part of this work. In addition he owned several estates in Gifford's home county, Essex, and had sympathies with Gifford's religious views. Knighted in 1603, he died in 1607.
4. George Gifford, *A Discourse of the Subtill Practises of Devilles by Witches and Sorcerers* (London, 1587).
5. Betray.
6. They would not wait to be asked.
7. The devil.

request and send him, is most absurd. There be many diseases in the bodies of men and beastes which he seeth will breake forth unto lamenes or unto death, he beareth the witches in hand he doth them:[8] He worketh by his other sort of Witches, whome the people call cunning men and wise women to confirme all his matters, and by them teacheth many remedies, that so he may be sought unto and honored as God. These things taking root in the hearts of the people, and so making them afraide of Witches, and raising up suspitions and rumors of sundry innocent persons, many giltles are uppon mens othes condemned to death, and much innocent bloud is shed. How subtilly he continueth these matters, I have to my smal skill laide open in this slender Treatise. I have done it in waye of a Dialogue, to make the fitter for the capacity of the simpler sort. I am bolde to offer it unto your Worship, not unto one as needeth to be taught in these thinges, being zealously affected to the Gospell, and so grounded in the faith of the high providence, that I have been delighted to heare and see the wise and godly course used uppon the seat of Justice by your Worship, when such have beene arraigned. I offer it therefore as a testimony of a thankeful mind for favours and kindnesse shewed towardes me: and so intreat your Worshippe to accept of it. If it doe good unto any of the weaker sort in knowledge I shall be glad. If I erre in any thing being shewed it, I will be ready to correct it.

Your Worships in all dueties to commaund.

George Giffard.

THE SPEAKERS.

Samuell. Daniell. The wife of Samuell. M.B. Schoolemaister. The good wife R.

Sam. You are well mette olde acquaintance, I am glad to see you looke so well, howe doe all our good friendes in your Countrey.[9]

Dan. I trust they be all in good health, they were when I came from home, I am sorry to see you looke so pale, what have you beene sicke lately?

Sam. Truely no, I thanke God I have had my health pretily well, but yet me thinke my meate[10] doth me no good of late.

Dan. What is the matter man, doe you take thought and care for the world? take heede of that, for the Scripture saith, worldly sorrow worketh

---

8. He deludes the witches into belief that he is the cause of the diseases.
9. County, 'part of the world'.
10. Food.

death. 2 Cor. 7.10. It is a great sinne rising from unbeleefe, and distrust in Gods providence, when men be over pensive for the world.[11]

Sam. Indeede my minde is troubled, but not for that which you say, for I hope in God I shall not want[12] so long as I live.

Dan. Is it any trouble of conscience for sinne? If it be, that may turne to good.

Sam. O, no, no. I know no cause why.

Dan. Why, what is it then, if I may be so bold, I pray you tell me. I think you take me for your friend.

Sam. Indeede I have alwaies found you my very good friend, and I am sure you will give me the best counsell you can, truely we dwell here in a bad countrey, I think even one of the worst in England.

Dan. Is it so? I thinke you dwell in a fine countrey, in a sweete wholesome aire and fruitfull grounds.

Sam. Aire man? I finde no fault with the aire, there be naughty people.

Dan. Naughty people? Where shall a man dwell, and not finde them? swearers, liars, raylers, slaunderers, drunckards, adulterers, riotous, un-thriftes, dicers, and proude high minded persons, are every where to be founde in great plenty.[13]

Sam. Nay, I doe not meane them, I care not for them. These witches, these evill favoured[14] old witches doe trouble me.

Dan. What doe you take your selfe to be bewitched?

Sam. No, no, I trust no evill spirite can hurt me, but I heare of much harme done by them: they lame men and kill their cattle, yea they destroy both men and children. They say there is scarce any towne or village in all this shire, but there is one or two witches at the least in it. In good sooth, I may tell it to you as my friend, when I goe but into my closes,[15] I am afraide, for I see nowe and then a Hare; which my conscience giveth me is a witch, or some witches spirite, shee stareth so uppon me. And sometime I see an ugly weasell runne through my yard, and there is a foule great catte sometimes in my Barne, which I have no liking unto.[16]

---

11. This apparently inconsequential opening, with Daniel's scriptural citation, actually serves two purposes: it engages Gifford's target readership with its homely accessibility and it establishes Daniel as a godly sage with God's word on any given matter at his fingertips.

12. Samuel, though a 'simple' character with mistaken ideas on witchcraft, echoes the 23rd Psalm to establish his fundamental goodness: if God is with him, he will never be in need. But to differentiate him from the omniscient and righteous Daniel, he does not attribute this wisdom properly to the Bible.

13. Daniel's concern with sin is also Gifford's: these sins are favourite godly targets.

14. Ugly – but also probably evil-natured.

15. Fields.

16. These details suggest that Gifford had been reading pamphlet accounts of witches as sources for his treatise. The witch as hare and the foul cat occur in tandem in a work of the previous year, G.B.'s *A Most Wicked worke of a wretched Witch* (London, 1592), where, interestingly, they are victimizing a farm worker like Samuel. For the pamphlet's account, see Gibson, ed., *Early Modern Witches*, pp. 138–45.

Dan. You never had no hurt done yet, had you by any witch?

Sam. Trust me I cannot tell, but I feare me I have[17] for there be two or three in our towne which I like not, but especially an old woman, I have beene as carefull to please her as ever I was to please mine own mother, and to give her ever anon one thing or another, and yet me thinkes shee frownes at me now and then. And I had a hogge which eate his meate with his fellowes and was very well to our thinking over night, and in the morning he was starke dead. My wife hath had five or six hennes even of late dead. Some of my neighbours wishe me to burne some thing alive, as[18] a henne or a hogge. Others will me in time to seeke helpe at the handes of some cunning man, before I have any further harme. I wold be glad to do for the best.

Samuel tells several stories of friends of his who have allegedly received help from cunning people. Then Daniel tells him 'it is most certaine you are bewitched'. Samuel is horrified, but Daniel explains . . .

Dan. Nay I doe not thinke that the olde woman hath bewitched you, or that your body is bewitched, but the divell hath bewitched your minde, with blindnes and unbeleefe, to draw you from God, even to worship himselfe, by seeking help at the hands of devils . . . It is not in these matters to be taken as we imagine, but as the word of God teacheth. What though a man think he worshippeth not devils, nor seeketh not help at their handes, as he is persuaded, nor hath any such intent, is he ever the neere,[19] when as yet it shall be found by Gods word, that he doth worship them, and seek unto them for help?

Sam. Doe you thinke then that there be no witches? Doth not God suffer wicked people to doe harme? Or doe you thinke that the cunning men doe helpe by the devill? I would be glad to reason with you, but I have smal knowledge in the scripturs. We have a Schoolemaister that is a good pretie scholler, they say, in the Latine tongue, one M.B. he is gone to my house even now, I pray you let me intreat you to go thither, you two may reason the matter . . .

Daniel and Master B. establish parameters for their discussion, following orthodox demonology derived, ironically, from European Catholic writers. Daniel stresses that 'I go not about to defend witches. I denie not but that the devill worketh by them. And that they ought to be put to death. We ought also to seeke remedie against them . . .' and Master B. assents: 'If you have this

---

17. Samuel changes his view – or expresses his true unease – as Gifford shows us an accusation developing.
18. For example.
19. Perhaps a word is missing here?

meaning, that witches and sorcerers ar bewitched by the devil, that they forsake God, and follow him, that they worship and obey him, and doe sacrifice to him, and commit manie hainous sinnes, I agree with you . . .'. But they diverge when Daniel asserts that he also means 'that multitudes are seduced and led from God, to follow the devil, by meanes of witches and conjurors: yea, I speak it of those, not which are caried of a godlie zeale, but of a blinde rage and mad furie against them [witches]'. Daniel then begins to define the nature of the relationship between witch, devil and victims: devils use witches as a distraction from the real harm they do in the world, so that the devil is not the witches' tool, but quite the opposite.

Dan. . . . mark this, the devils continuallie compasse the soule of man about, to shoot it full of their fierie dartes. Ephes. 6. even to wound it to death with all wicked sinnes. The devill goeth about like a roring lion, seeking whome hee may devoure. 1. Pet. 5. And they by this craft which they use by meanes of the witches, make the blind[20] people imagin that they never come nigh them, but when the witches are angrie and doe send them, and that they are easilie driven away when they do come, as by burning some quick[21] thing, as henne or hogge, or by beating and drawing bloud upon the witch. Such people as can thus drive him away, or by thrusting a spitte red hot into their creame,[22] are farre from knowing the spirituall battel, in which we are to warre under the banner of Christ against the devill, much lesse doe they know how to put on (as S. Paule willeth) the whole armour of God, to resist and overcome him. Ephes. 6. He may deale with their soules even as he listeth, when they take him not present but upon such sending, and where such hurt doth follow in their bodies or goods.

M.B. I doe not denie, but that the devils seeke chiefly for to destroy the soules of men . . . But I thought we had fullie agreed in this, that the witches do send their spirits, and doe manie harmes both unto men and beasts: because we have it confirmed by daylie experience: and unlesse you will denie that which is manifest, I doubt not but we shall accorde in these.

Dan. I say the witches do send their spirits.

M.B. What shal we need then to stand upon that point in which we are agreed?

Dan. Yes – though we agree that they send them, yet we may dissent in divers thinges about this sending. As first, tell me, whether doe you thinke that the witch or the Devill is the servaunt, which of them commaundeth, and which obeyeth?

M.B. How can I tell that? It is thought hee becommeth her servaunt, and

---

20. Ignorant, deluded.
21. Living.
22. A detail from *A true and just Recorde* (above), which also contains the counter-magical burning of live creatures and drawing blood from the suspected witch.

where she is displeased, and would be revenged, she hyreth him for to doe it. The witches themselves have confessed thus much: and for my part, I think no man can disproove it.

Dan. They that doe the will of God are the children and servants of God. And they which fulfill the lustes of the devill, and obey him, are his children and his servantes, Joh. 8. vers. 44. Act. 13. vers. 10. Are they not?

M.B. I graunt all this?

Dan. The devilles are the rulers of the darknesse of this world. Ephes. 6. ver. 12.

M.B. The text is plaine.[23]

Dan. The darknesse of this world, is not meant of the darknesse of the night, which is but the shadow of the earth, but it is the spiritual darknes, which consisteth in the ignorance of God, in infidelitie, and in sinne.

M.B. I am of your mind in this also.

Dan. And doe you not thinke then that the devill hath his throne, his dominion and kingdom in the hearts of ignorant blind infidels?

M.B. I must needs thinke he hath, the word of God doth force me thereunto: seeing he is the Prince of darkenesse.

Dan. And is there anie greater infidelitie and darknesse in anie, than in witches, conjurors, and such as have familiaritie with devils?

M.B. I tak it they be the depest overwhelmed in darknesse and infidelitie of all other.

Dan. Lay all these thinges together which you confesse, and see whether it doth not follow upon the same, that the witch is the vassal of the devill, and not he her servant; he is Lord and commaundeth, and she is his drudge and obeyeth.

M.B. Yea, although he be Lord, yet he is content to serve her turne, and the witches confesse, they call them forth and send them: and that they hire them to hurt such in their bodies, and in the cattell, as they bee displeased withall.[24]

Dan. I am sorie you are so farre awrie, it is pitie any man should be in such errour, especiallie a man that hath learning, and should teach others knowledge.

---

23. Gifford affirms the vital importance of God's word in the method of his argument as well as its content: Daniel attempts to crush Master B. with the unquestionable authority of the Bible before embarking on any merely human reasoning – the approved method for demonologies.

24. Master B.'s stubborn restatement gives Gifford the opportunity to enlarge on his argument with further anecdote and biblical citation. In this way the text's appeal and authority are both increased with the realism of Gifford's characters. Unlike most dialogues of this kind, Master B. is rather more than a mere straw man to be set up and knocked down.

M.B. Nay, I may returne this upon you, for if you will denie this, it is but a follie to reason any further: I will never be driven from that which I knowe: There was one olde mother W. of great T. which had a spirite like a Weasill: she was offended highlie with one H.M. home she went, and called forth her spirite, which lay in a pot of woll under her bed, she willed him to goe plague the man: he required what she would give him, and he would kill H.M. She said she would give him a cocke, which shee did, and he went, and the man fell sicke with a great paine in his bellie, languished and died: the witch was arraigned, condemned, and hanged, and did confesse all this.[25]

Dan. I told you before that I do not deny these things, but you are deceived about the doing: you marke not the cunning sleightes of the devill: Tel me, is not this the truth which S. Peter speaketh, that the devil goeth about like a roaring lion, seeking whom he may devoure. 1. Pet. 5.

M.B. What then?

Dan. What then? can you be so simple as to imagine that the devill lieth in a pot of wooll, soft and warme, and stirreth not, but when he is hired and sent? The devils conspire together in their worke, they bestirre them, and never take rest night nor day: they are never wearie, they be not a colde, they care not for lying soft: These be fooleries by which hee deceiveth the witches, and bewitcheth the mindes of many ignorant people: And whereas you say he is hired, it is but deceit ... You say the witch commeth home angrie, who hath kindled this wrath in her heart but the devill? Who inflameth her mind with malice, to be revenged, and to doe mischiefe but the devill? doth he not rule in her heart?

M.B. I muste needes confesse hee stirreth her up to wrath and malice.

Dan. Then he lieth not at home in his pot of wool: nor he is not hyred to this: hitherto[26] she is his drudge, and obeyeth him, and not he her, being led by his suggestion ... I pray you let me aske you this question, doth the witch or the devill the harme unto men and cattell?

M.B. Why, the devill doth it at their sending though I confesse it must needs be as you said, that the devil worketh al in the mind of the witch, & mooveth her to send him.

Dan. The devill hath a kingdome, but it is in darkenesse and corruption of sinne. He hath no right nor power over Gods creatures, no not so much as to kill one flye, or to take one eare of corne out of anie mans barne, unlesse power be given him. You know when Christ cast the devils out of the man possessed, they aske leave for to goe into the heard of swine. Then tell me, who giveth the devill this power then, when the witch sendeth him, to kill

---

25. This seems to be lifted directly from *The Examination and Confession of certaine Wytches* (London, 1566), B2, B3v–B4, where the pot of wool, the location under the bed and the cockerel all occur. For the pamphlet's account, see Gibson, ed., *Early Modern Witches*, pp. 10–24.

26. Therefore.

or to lame man or beast? doth the witch give it him? Do you think he had power to doe harme, but no mind[27] till she mooved him? Or doe you take it that her sending giveth him power, which he had not?

M.B. It is a question indeed worth the asking: For doubtlesse, the devill hath not power untill it be given him, to touch any creature, to hurt, or to destroy the body, but onely to tempt and to lead into sin: I am also sure that the witch cannot give him power, but onlie God above.

Dan. Lay these together then, that the devill only hurteth,[28] and that none can give him power, neither man nor woman, but only God, and tell me whether the people be not wonderfully carried away in a rage. For, when as they should consider, that the devill is the Lordes executioner:[29] And then finding that he hath any power given him to molest, to hurt and vexe them in theyr bodies or goods, to know certainly it commeth from the Lord, and then gather from thence (as the trueth is) that the Lord is displeased with them for their offences. And to seeke unto him, humbly craving pardon and deliverance from this enemy, seeking to be armed with the mighty power of faith, to cast him foorth, and to resist him, as the Lord willeth, 1. Pet. 5. Here is no such matter, no looking so high among the people, but running deeper into errour, and into sinne, as if the witches did it, and that it commeth from their anger and not from their owne sinnes and infidelity,[30] here is no repentance, no humbling themselves by fasting and prayer, but running for helpe unto devilles, using meanes which those devils by the cunning men & women appoint, scratching and clawing, thirsting after guiltles blood as raging against those whome they imagine to be witches, which many times are not, because they imagine, that if there were no witches, ther should be no such plagues ...

M.B. ... doe you cleare the witches, because God, and not they, giveth the devil power ...?

Dan. That I say God alone, and not the witches, giveth power unto the devils to plague and torment: it is so evident as that I suppose a man shall hardlie meete with anie man so grosse but will confesse it. But this doeth not cleare the witches at all; for their sinne is in dealing with devils, and that they imagine that their Spirits do those harmes, requested and hyred by them ... As I said before, here is the deepe craft of Satan, that he will covet to bee sent by witches, whereas indeed God hath sent him, seeing none can sende him but God. Againe, wee must consider that there bee naturall causes in the bodies of men and beastes of grievous tormentes and diseases, yea even causes of death. Nowe, they cannot be so secrete, but the devill knoweth them, and even when they are like to take effect. Then doth he

---

27. No desire to do so.
28. Only the devil does harm.
29. The one who executes God's commands.
30. The accusers' own sin and faithlessness.

plie it with the witch, setteth her in a furie, she sendeth him, even upon this sending the man or the beast suddainlie and strangely are tormented, fall lame, or die. Then the witch is suspected, examined, and confesseth that she killed such a man, or such a mans cattell, or made them lame. Here the people are set in a wonderfull maze and astonishment, as if witches could plague men in their wrath, by sending their spirits, because they confesse they did it, when their spirits doe lie and had no power, but the tormentes came by naturall causes. And to drive the people into a deeper madnes in this, & to mak them beleeve, that strange and suddaine torments and languishing diseases come by witches, he hath his other sort of witches, the cunning men and women, which tell even upon his worde, which you know is to be trusted,[31] that they be bewitched, that they bee haunted with fayries, and that ther be thus many witches therabout, in everie town some.

M.B. That is most true no doubt, which you speake. I doe not for my part knowe how to gainsay any one point thereof. Only I wonder at the craftinesse of the devils in these things ... If it be thus, then how should a Jurie condemne by their verdict any witch? For she hath not killed, nor the devill at her request, but maketh her beleeve he did it at her request.

Dan. A witch by the word of God ought to die the death[32] not because she killeth men, for that she cannot (unlesse it be those witches which kill by poyson, which eyther they receive from the devill, or he teacheth them to make) but because she dealeth with devils. And so, if a Jurie doe finde proofe that she hath dealt with devils, they may and ought to find them guiltie of witchcraft.

M.B. If they find them guilty to have dealt with devils, and cannot say they have murdered men, the law doth not put them to death.[33]

Dan. It wer to be wished, that the law were more perfect in that respect, even to cut off all such abhominations.[34] These cunning men and women which deale with spirites and charmes seeming to doe good, and draw the people into manifest impieties, with all other which have familiaritie with devils, or use conjurations, ought to bee rooted out, that others might see and feare ...

Having made this draconian pronouncement, Daniel is asked to comment on several specific cases in which M.B. and Samuel have been involved. Yet instead

---

31. Assured sarcasm creeps into Daniel's voice as he sums up his theory.
32. Gifford several times has Daniel quote from Exodus, 'Thou shalt not suffer a witch to live' (22.18).
33. See the Witchcraft Act of 1563 (above).
34. The law actually contained provisions that, if so interpreted and enforced, would have dealt with cunning people as well as malefic witches. But Gifford's zeal for further reform marks him out as a troublemaker in the eyes of the establishment and aligns him with 'puritans' who wished to see secular society remake its laws and customs to conform with (their interpretation of) biblical commands and inferences.

of endorsing wholeheartedly the punishment of individuals, he examines carefully the quality of accepted evidence against them. He says that in a court case no evidence which might be traced back to the devil's lies should be accepted, and adds that Satan sometimes 'pursueth the innocent with suspicion upon suspicion, that men may be guilty of innocent blood'. M.B. is perplexed and makes an excellent point against Daniel which, perhaps revealingly, he does not answer satisfactorily – how can real proof of witchcraft be distinguished from false? But Gifford's work draws towards its close with a devastating dismissal of the amiable Samuel's concrete instances of evidence given at a witch trial – the more compelling because of its typically detailed nature and the uncompromising brevity of Daniel's judgement of Samuel's mistake.

M.B. You say the testimony of the devill is not to bee taken, although it be manifest that he doth many times tell the trueth, because when he speaketh the trueth, hee doeth it of a bad purpose. And you hold it the testimony of the devill, not only which he speaketh when anie charge him,[35] but also which the cunning men & women give, in as much as they can say nothing but upon his word. Moreover, unles I mistake you, the testimony of a witch in many things at her death, is not as you say any other than the testimonie of the devill, because the devill hath deceived her, and made her beleeve things which were nothing so. Besides al this, you wil have likelihoods and suspitions to be of no waight, nor common fame and opinion to moove the conscience of a Jurie, because Satan is exceeding subtill in all these. Then how shall a Jurie finde a witch? What proofes will you have?

Dan. Men are upon their oath to deale, & it doth touch life, if they doe finde any guiltie of witchcraft. This is a most waightie matter: whereupon it followeth, that there must be eyther due proofe by sufficient witnesses, or els the confession of the witch.[36] For if the testimony be such as may be false, as al that commeth from devils is to be suspected: or if it be but upon rumors, and likelihoods, in which there may be exceeding sleights of Satan, as for the most parte there be: how can that Jury answere before God, which upon their oath are not sure, but that so proceeding they may condemne the innocent, as often it commeth to passe ... If the party be a witch which is suspected, & yet no proofe, the Jury doeth more rightly in acquitting, than in condemning, for what warrant have they upon their oath to goe by gesse, or to find that which they knowe not? ...

Sam. I pray you give me leave a litle ... I have my selfe sundry times bene of the Jurie when witches have bene arraigned, we have found them guiltie upon common fame, upon likelihoods, and upon such testimonie as you

---

35. Daniel has been discussing possession cases, where the devil, being 'charged' to answer truly in the name of God, speaks using his supposed victim's voice.

36. Yet Daniel has shown how, in his terms, both of these sources of proof may be contaminated by delusion caused by the devil.

disalow. They have indeed taken it upon their deaths that they were innocent, but that never made me to doubt but that they were witches: for it is saide, the devill hath such power over them, that he will not suffer them to confesse ... I was of a Jurie not many yeares past, when there was an old woman arraigned for a witch. There came in eight or ten which gave evidence against her. I doe not remember every particular: but the chiefe for some thinges were of small value. One woman came in and testified uppon her oath that her husband upon his death bed, tooke it upon his death, that he was bewitched, for he pined a long time. And he sayde further, he was sure that woman had bewitched him. He tooke her to be naught,[37] and thought she was angry with him, because she would have borrowed five shillinges of him, and he denyed to lend it her. The woman tooke her oath also, that she thought in her conscience that the old woman was a witch, and that she killed her husband. There came in a man that halted, he told a shrewde[38] tale. I once, sayd he, had both my legges sound. This old woman and I fell out and did chide.[39] She sayd she would be even with me. Within three daies after I had such a paine in my knee that I could not stand. And ever since I go haulting[40] of it, and now and then feele some paine. There came in an other, a little fellowe that was very earnest, me thinkes I see him yet. He tooke his oath directly that she was a witch: I did once anger her saide he, but I did repent me: for I looked somewhat would follow.[41] And the next night, I saw the ugliest sight that ever I saw: I awaked suddainely out of my sleepe, and there was me thought a great face, as bigge as they use to set up in the signe of the Saracens-head, looked full in my face. I was scarce mine owne man two dayes after. An other came in, a woman and her child dyed with greevous paine,[42] & she tooke her oath, that in her conscience she[43] killed her child. Then followed a man, and he sayde he could not tell, but he thought she was once angry with him because she came to begge a few pot-hearbes, and he denied her: and presently after he heard a thing as he thought to whisper in his eare, thou shalt be bewitched. The next day he had such a paine in his back, that he could not sit upright: he sayd he sent to a cunning woman, shee tolde he was bewitched, and by a woman that came for pot-hearbes. But she sayd he should recover of it, and so he sayd he did within some tenne dayes. Then came in two or three grave honest men, which testified that she was by common fame accounted a witch. We found her giltie, for what could we doe lesse, she was condemned and executed: and upon the ladder she made her prayer, and

37. Naughty, malign.
38. Bitter.
39. Argue.
40. Limping.
41. I thought something would result.
42. A woman whose child died ...
43. The witch.

tooke it upon her death shee was innocent and free from all such dealings. Do you thinke we did not well? . . .

Dan. . . . let us see in all these which one could proove that she must needes be a witch. One saith her husband tooke it upon his death that she killed him, because he would not lend her five shillinges: doth this proove she bewitched him? Can the devill kill a man at his pleasure, to gratifie the witch? Is it not rather to be judged he dyed of some pining sicknesse growing from an evill constitution of body, which the devill did know, and would set him at some variance with one old woman or other, that so it might breede suspition of witchcraft.

Sam. You see there were some things which could not be done but by the devill.

Dan. Indeede the great face which the man thought he saw, was an illusion of the devill. But is this a good proofe, the devill appeareth to a man after he hath displeased a woman, therefore she sent him? . . . What reason did the woman shew which tooke it upon her conscience that the olde woman killed her child, to proove it was so? If shee thought so in her conscience, and tenne thousand more with her upon bare imagination, was that a warrant for you to sweare solemnly that it was so? As for the testimony of the cunning woman that he was bewitched which had the paine in his backe, upon the deniall of pot-hearbes, it was the testimony but of the devill, as I shewed before. And what is common fame grounded upon imaginations?

Sam. Then you thinke we did amisse do you?

Dan. I would not upon mine oath doe such a thing for to gaine a kingdome . . .

2. Sweeping sceptic

Reginald Scot, **The Discoverie of Witchcraft** *(London, 1584)*

As the very long title of Reginald Scot's monumental work implies, the *Discoverie of Witchcraft* covers a vast range of topics and it does not shrink from vigorous controversy in exposing anything that its author sees as fraud, stupidity or wickedness. The full title indicates that it is a book: 'wherein the lewde[44] dealing of witches and witchmongers is notablie detected, the knaverie of conjurors,[45] the impietie of inchanters, the follie of soothsaiers, the impudent falshood of cousenors,[46] the infidelitie of atheists, the pestilent practises of

---

44. Ignorant, base, sinful.
45. Those who raise, or pretend to raise, spirits.
46. Tricksters.

Pythonists,[47] the curiositie of figurecasters,[48] the vanitie of dreamers, the beggerlie art of Alcumystrie,[49] the abhomination of idolatrie, the horrible art of poisoning, the vertue and power of naturall magike, and all the conveiances of Legierdemaine[50] and juggling are deciphered: and many other things opened, which have long lien hidden, howbeit verie necessarie to be knowne'. It discusses everything from the torture of witchcraft suspects deployed in some European countries to the party-tricks of illusionists: and all its arguments contribute to the central thesis that witchcraft and magic, as conventionally defined, do not exist.

Scot believed that almost all experiences of witchcraft and magic could be explained away as psychological delusion, trickery, ignorant misbelief in God (especially, he thought, Catholic belief) or naturally occurring phenomena. Steering a very careful line, he examined biblical definitions of witchcraft – sometimes rather sophistically – as well as what he saw as the ridiculous lies of European demonologists. He concluded that when the Bible spoke of witchcraft, it meant something entirely unlike the post-medieval witch conceived by demonologists, which is certainly true. But he added for good measure a specifically Protestant version of the Deist assertion that the Bible spoke of times when God was closer to his people, establishing their faith by miracles and by Christ's incarnation as man. These miracles, Scot said, were now ceased (despite the claims of the Catholic church), and thus the relationships that the Bible described, of the divine and satanic to the material world, were changed too. Therefore even if the Bible did speak of witches with any recognizably modern elements, they no longer existed, and belief that they did was a misunderstanding both of religion and the nature of the physical world.

By the end of the book, Scot's examination of witchcraft belief – one small element of the political and religious orthodoxy of his time – had questioned many of the beliefs in which his culture had invested its deepest significances. If the Bible could be read as history or metaphor rather than the prescription for modern living which many of Scot's godly contemporaries believed it to be, and if such fundamentals as its apparently straightforward endorsement of the killing of witches in Exodus (22.18) could be questioned, then dangerous lines of enquiry into religion and authority were opened up.

Although they were not unique, as his careful attributions often show, Scot's views and his bluntness of expression would have been profoundly shocking to most Elizabethans. On St Augustine, he remarks '. . . he verifieth the starkest lie that ever was invented, of the two alewives that used to transforme all their

---

47. Those who conjured the dead and often projected their voices – also known as ventriloquists.
48. The (by implication deceitful) arcane complexities of astrologers.
49. Alchemy. Alchemists who failed to find the philosopher's stone and turn base materials to gold (in other words, all of them) were seen as likely to be reduced to beggary by their experiments, but this phrase also implies that the art itself is a poor one.
50. Sleight of hand.

ghests in horsses ... And therefore I saie with Cardanus,[51] that how much Augustin saith he hath seen with his eies, so much I am content to beleeve.' With classical authorities he is even brusquer: when the Roman writer Plutarch extols the power of augury, Scot retorts that 'Plutarch doteth by his leave, for all his learning'. All Scot's explanations of his iconoclasm (Catholic corruption of ancient texts, authors' paganism) cannot alter the reader's perception that Scot has no reverence for any opinion simply because it is old, well-established or pious. His views on witchcraft were roundly condemned by writers on the subject. King James, writing in 1591, said that Scot 'is not ashamed in publike print to deny, that ther can be such a thing as Witch-craft: and so mainteines the old error of the Sadducees, in denying of spirits'.[52] While Scot repeatedly stated that he did believe in witchcraft and spirits, his arguments, and especially the sweepingly condemnatory tone of his rhetoric, leave the slimmest possible space for their existence.

Relatively little is known of Scot: born about 1538 and also known as Raynolde Scot, he was a Kentish gentleman farmer, whose only other known work was a treatise promoting the successful cultivation of hops in England. Educated at Hart Hall, Oxford, he was encouraged in his studies by his kinsman Sir Thomas Scot, to whom the *Discoverie* is in part dedicated. Living at Smeeth, he certainly attended at least one Kentish witch trial, and may, because of his position in society and relationship to Sir Thomas, have played a role in the administration of local justice. He was certainly an MP for New Romney, 1588–9. He married Jane Cobbe in 1568, and they had a daughter, Elizabeth. When Jane died, Reginald remarried, for in his will he mentions his wife Alice and a stepdaughter Marie. He died in 1599, leaving land in several Kentish parishes and some money, and protesting in his will that but for his wife he would have died penniless.

Scot's arguments juxtapose interestingly with those of George Gifford. Although Gifford wrote after Scot, Scot was responding to other statements (by writers from the early church onwards) of similar positions, and he would very likely have defined Gifford as, on the whole, a 'witchmonger'. Yet the two men share a scepticism about evidence against witches, about the proper definition of their activities and about those who see witches at the root of all evils. Instead, Gifford privileges the role of the devil, whilst Scot is more 'modern' in seeing only human factors at work. Near neighbours in the adjoining counties of Essex and Kent, both men grappled with the same problems in the same revisionist English Protestant context. Were there really witches, in the way the Bible and European demonologists suggested? Was English law just? How might communities avoid condemning innocents? Both at odds with mainland Europe's Catholic tradition of demonology, with its sabbats and flying devil-worshippers, their very different responses set the parameters of English thinking on witchcraft for the centuries to follow.

---

51. Girolamo Cardano or Jerome Cardan, the Italian physician whose books, published in the 1550s and 1560s, speculated on the nature of magic and natural science.
52. King James VI and I, *Daemonologie* (1591; London: The Bodley Head, 1924), pp. xi–xii.

Dedications, *The Discoverie of Witchcraft*

To the Honorable, mine especiall good Lord, Sir Roger Manwood Knight, Lord cheefe Baron of hir Majesties Court of the Eschequer.[53]

... In somuch as your Lordship knoweth, or rather exerciseth the office of a judge, whose part it is to heare with courtesie, and to determine with equitie; it cannot but be apparent unto you, that when punishment exceedeth the fault, it is rather to be thought vengeance than correction ... Howbeit, it is naturall to unnaturall people, and peculiar unto witch-mongers, to pursue the poore, to accuse the simple, and to kill the innocent; supplieng in rigor and malice towards others, that which they themselves want in proofe and discretion, or the other in offense or occasion ... I will bring before you, as it were to the barre, two sorts of most arrogant and wicked people, the first challenging to themselves, the second attributing unto others, that power which onelie apperteineth to God, who onelie is the Creator of all things, who onelie searcheth the heart and reines,[54] who onelie knoweth our imaginations and thoughts, who onelie openeth all secrets, who onelie worketh great wonders, who onelie hath power to raise up & cast downe; who onelie maketh thunder, lightning, raine, tempests, and restraineth them at his pleasure; who onelie sendeth life and death, sicknesse & health, wealth and wo; who neither giveth nor lendeth his glorie to anie creature.[55]

And therefore, that which greeveth me to the bottome of my heart, is, that these witchmongers cannot be content, to wrest out of Gods hand his almightie power, and keepe it themselves, or leave it with a witch: but that, when by drift of argument they are made to laie downe the bucklers,[56] they yeeld them up to the divell, or at the least praie aid of him, as though the raines of all mens lives and actions were committed into his hand; and that he sat at the sterne, to guide and direct the course of the whole world, imputing unto him power and abilitie inough to doo as great things, and as strange miracles as ever Christ did.

But the doctors of this supernaturall doctrine saie somtimes, that the witch doth all these things by vertue of hir charmes; sometimes that a spirituall, sometimes that a corporall divell doth accomplish it; sometimes

---

53. Roger Manwood (1525–92) was a judge with substantial interests in Kent, and thus a particularly suitable dedicatee for Scot. He had powerful friends and had made himself useful to the government in a number of state trials. Knighted in 1578, he was Chief Baron of the Exchequer from 1578–92, the year of his death, although by this time he was in disfavour at court.
54. Literally, the loins but also the supposed seat of the emotions.
55. This passage is heavily annotated by Scot with biblical references. It establishes his godliness, just as a passage above it (omitted here) praises the Queen, establishing him as a good subject.
56. When they are forced to surrender, lay down their shields.

they saie that the divell doth make the witch beleeve she doth that which he himselfe hath wrought; sometimes that the divell seemeth to doo that by compulsion, which he doth most willinglie. Finallie, the writers hereupon are so eloquent, and full of varietie; that sometimes they write that the divell dooth all this by Gods permission onelie; sometimes by his licence, somtimes by his appointment: so as (in effect and truth) not the divell, but the high and mightie king of kings, and Lord of hosts, even God himselfe, should this waie be made obedient and servile to obeie and performe the will & commandement of a malicious old witch … as the revenger of a doting old womans imagined wrongs, to the destruction of manie innocent children, and as a supporter of hir passions, to the undoing of manie a poore soule. And I see not, but a witch may as well inchant, when she will; as a lier may lie when he list: and so should we possesse nothing, but by a witches licence and permission …

And although some saie that the divell is the witches instrument, to bring hir purposes and practises to passe: yet others saie that she is his instrument, to execute his pleasure in anie thing, and therefore to be executed. But then (me thinks) she should be injuriouslie dealt withall, and put to death for anothers offense: for actions are not judged by instrumentall causes; neither dooth the end and purpose of what is done, depend upon the meane instrument. Finallie, if the witch doo it not, why should the witch die for it? But they saie that witches are persuaded, and thinke, that they doo indeed those mischeefs; and have a will to performe that which the divell committeth: and that therefore they are worthie to die. By which reason everie one should be executed, that wisheth evill to his neighbor …

But (my Lord) it shalbe proved in my booke, and your Lordship shall trie it to be true, as well here at home in your native countrie, as also abrode in your severall circuits,[57] that (besides them that be *Veneficae*, which are plaine poisoners) there will be found among our witches onelie two sorts; the one sort being such by imputation, as so thought of by others (and these are abused, and not abusors) the other by acceptation, as willing so to be accompted (and these be meere cousenors) …

To the right worshipfull Sir Thomas Scot Knight, &c.

Sir, I see among other malefactors manie poore old women convented[58] before you for working of miracles, other wise called witchcraft, and therefore I thought you also a meet person to whom I might commend my booke … See first whether the evidence be not frivolous, & whether the proofes brought against them be not incredible, consisting of ghesses, presumptions, & impossibilities contrarie to reason, scripture, and nature.

---

57. In Manwood's home county of Kent as well as on the official tours he undertook to judge Assizes in other counties.
58. Summoned.

See also what persons complaine upon them, whether they be not of the basest, the unwisest, & most faithles kind of people. Also may it please you to waie what accusations and crimes they laie to their charge, namelie: She was at my house of late, she would have had a pot of milke, she departed in a chafe[59] bicause she had it not, she railed, she curssed, she mumbled and whispered, and finallie she said she would be even with me: and soone after my child, my cow, my sow, or my pullet died, or was strangelie taken.[60] Naie (if it please your Worship) I have further proofe: I was with a wise woman, and she told me I had an ill[61] neighbour, & that she would come to my house yer it were long, and so did she; and that she had a marke above hir waste, & so had she: and God forgive me, my stomach hath gone against hir[62] a great while. Hie mother before hir was counted a witch, she hath beene beaten and scratched by the face till bloud was drawne upon hir, bicause she hath beene suspected, & afterwards some of those persons were said to amend. These are the certeinties that I heare in their evidences.

Note also how easilie they[63] may be brought to confesse that which they never did, nor lieth in the power of man to doo:[64] and then see whether I have cause to write as I doo ...

To the right worshipfull his loving friends, Maister Doctor Coldwell Deane of Rochester, and Maister Doctor Readman Archdeacon of Canterburie, &c.

... My question is not (as manie fondlie[65] suppose) whether there be witches or naie: but whether they can doo such miraculous works as are imputed unto them ... O Maister Archdeacon, is it not pitie, that that which is said to be doone with the almightie power of the most high God, and by our saviour his onelie sonne Jesus Christ our Lord, shouldbe referred to a baggage old womans nod or wish, &c? Good sir, is it not one manifest kind of Idolatrie, for them that labor and are laden, to come unto witches to be refreshed? If witches could helpe whom they are said to have made sicke,

---

59. Temper.
60. Scot's caricature of accusers' stories and vocabulary is intended to establish them as ignorant and foolish (see *A true and just Recorde*, which he later states that he used as a source for this kind of material) and he uses diminishing gravity of result here to sharpen his humorous point, going on to emphasize the vagueness of evidence, its origin as hearsay and the role of cunning people in accusation. Gifford later used exactly the same rhetorical techniques.
61. Wicked.
62. I have disliked her.
63. Suspected witches.
64. Here, Scot implicitly brushes aside the existence of any agent other than man. Taken with his earlier dismissal of the common idea that the devil, with God's permission, carries out magical harm (see Gifford, above), it is easy to see how contemporaries could believe that he found the supernatural and superhuman incredible concepts.
65. Foolishly.

I see no reason, but remedie might as well be required at their hands, as a pursse demanded of him that hath stolne it. But trulie it is manifold idolatrie, to aske that of a creature, which none can give but the Creator. The papist hath some colour of scripture to mainteine his idoll of bread,[66] but no Jesuiticall distinction can cover the witchmongers idolatrie in this behalfe. Alas, I am sorie and ashamed to see how manie die, that being said to be bewitched, onelie seeke for magicall cures, whom wholsome diet and good medicines would have recovered. I dare assure you both, that there would be none of these cousening kind of witches, did not witchmongers mainteine them, followe them, and beleeve in them and their oracles: whereby indeed all good learning and honest arts are overthrowne ...

To the Readers.

... My request unto all you that read my booke shall be no more, but that it would please you to conferre my words with your owne sense and experience, and also with the word of God ...[67] And till you have perused my booke, ponder this in your mind, to wit, that *Sagae, Thessalae, Striges, Lamiae* (which words and none other being in use do properlie signifie our witches)[68] are not once found written in the old or new testament; and that Christ himselfe in his gospell never mentioned the name of a witch. And that neither he, nor Moses ever spake anie one word of the witches bargaine with the divell, their hagging, their riding in the aire, their transferring of corne or grasse from one feeld to another, their hurting of children or cattell with words or charmes, their bewitching of butter, cheese, ale, &c: nor yet their transubstantiation;[69] insomuch as the writers hereupon[70] are not ashamed to say, that it is not absurd to affirme that there were no witches in Jobs time. The reason is, that if there had beene such witches then in beeing, Job would have said he had beene bewitched. But indeed men tooke no heed in those daies to this doctrine of divels; to wit, to these fables

---

66. Scot mocks the Catholic belief in transubstantiation; namely, that the communion bread literally becomes the body of Christ.

67. Scot's insistence on empirical experience *before* the word of God is interesting.

68. One of the battles between 'witchmongers' and sceptics was over the Latin, Greek and Hebrew words for persons with prodigious powers. Sceptics argued that most of them did not mean 'witch' in its modern sense ('our witches') but signified poisoners or soothsayers.

69. Transformation (into animals, for example), with an anti-Catholic thrust again.

70. Scot's marginal note refers the reader to Heinrich Kramer and Jacob Sprenger, *Malleus Maleficarum* (1486). The *Malleus* or *Hammer of Witches* is one of Scot's main targets: written by Catholic inquisitors, it is a concise statement of the most extreme European beliefs, regarded by Scot as lurid fantasies.

of witchcraft, which Peter saith shall be much regarded and hearkened unto in the latter days ...[71]

God that knoweth my heart is witnes, and you that read my booke shall see, that my drift and purpose in this enterprise tendeth onelie to these respects. First, that the glorie and power of God be not so abridged and abased, as to be thrust into the hand or lip of a lewd old woman: whereby the worke of the Creator should be attributed to the power of a creature. Secondlie, that the religion of the gospell may be seene to stand without such peevish trumperie. Thirdlie, that lawfull favour and christian compassion be rather used towards these poore soules, than rigor and extremetie. Bicause they, which are commonlie accused of witchcraft, are the least sufficient of all other persons to speake for themselves; as having the most base and simple education of all others; the extremetie of their age giving them leave to dote, their povertie to beg, their wrongs to chide and threaten (as being void of anie other waie of revenge) their humor melancholicall to be full of imaginations,[72] from whence cheeflie proceedeth the vanitie of their confessions; as that they can transforme themselves and others into apes, owles, asses, dogs, cats, &c: that they can flie in the aire, kill children with charmes, hinder the comming of butter, &c ... Now bicause I mislike the extreame crueltie used against some of these sillie[73] soules (whom a simple advocate having audience and justice might deliver out of the hands of the inquisitors themselves) it will be said, that I denie anie punishment at all to be due to anie witch whatsoever. Naie, bicause I bewraie[74] the follie and impietie of them, which attribute unto witches the power of God: these witch-moongers will report, that I denie there are anie witches at all: and yet behold (saie they) how often is this word [Witch] mentioned in the scriptures? Even as if an idolator should saie in the behalfe of images and idols, to them which denie their power and godhead, and inveigh against the reverence doone unto them; How dare you denie the power of images, seeing their names are so often repeated in the scriptures? But truelie I denie not that there are witches or images: but I detest the idolatrous opinions conceived of them; referring that to Gods work and ordinance, which they impute to the power and malice of witches; and

---

71. Job's continual misfortunes and his patient reaction to them are the biblical precedent for accepting God's will no matter how seemingly harsh. Peter warned of false prophets in the world's last days (2 Peter 2.1). While most demonologists saw the increasing numbers of witches and cunning people in this light, Scot sees witchmongers as the harbingers of the world's end.

72. An idea Scot has borrowed from Wier's *De praestigiis daemonum*. The physician believed that witches, as (he said) predominantly post-menopausal women, were susceptible to the melancholy humour and its delusions, and thus their evidence against themselves was untrustworthy. See below for an example.

73. Innocent, foolish.

74. Expose.

attributing that honour to God, which they ascribe to idols. But as for those that in verie deed are either witches or conjurors, let them hardlie suffer such punishment as to their fault is agreeable,[75] and as by the grave judgement of lawe is provided.

The dedications finished, Scot lists well over 200 authors and/or individual texts which he used in preparing his book and then proceeds to the main text. It is a rich source of anecdotes which illustrate his claims. In book 1, chapter 2, is the following:

At the assises holden at Rochester, Anno 1581, one Margaret Simons, the wife of John Simons, of Brenchlie in Kent, was araigned for witchcraft, at the instigation and complaint of divers fond and malicious persons; and speciallie by the meanes of one John Ferrall vicar of that parish: with whom I talked about that matter and found him both fondly assotted[76] in the cause, and enviouslie bent towards hir: and (which is worse) as unable to make a good account of his faith, as shee whom he accused. That which he, for his part, laid to the poore womans charge, was this.

His sonne (being an ungratious boie, and prentise to one Robert Scotchford clothier, dwelling in that parish of Brenchlie) passed on a daie by hir house; at whome by chance hir little dog barked. Which thing the boie taking in evill part, drewe his knife, & pursued him therewith even to hir doore: whom she rebuked with some such words as the boie disdained, & yet neverthelesse would not be persuaded to depart in a long time. At last he returned to his maisters house, and within five or sixe daies fell sicke. Then was called to mind the fraie betwixt the dog and the boie: insomuch as the vicar (who thought himselfe so privileged, as he little mistrusted that God would visit his children with sicknes) did so calculate; as he found, partlie through his owne judgement, and partlie (as he himselfe told me) by the relation of other witches, that his said sonne was by hir bewitched. Yea, he also told me, that this his sonne (being as it were past all cure) received perfect health at the hands of another witch.

He proceeded yet further against hir, affirming, that alwaies in his parish church, when he desired to read most plainelie, his voice so failed him, as he could scant be heard at all. Which hee could impute, he said, to nothing else, but to hir inchantment. When I advertised the poore woman hereof, as being desirous to heare what she could saie for hir selfe; she told me, that in verie deed his voice did much faile him, speciallie when he strained himselfe to speake lowdest. How beit, she said that at all times his voice was hoarse and lowe: which thing I perceived to be true. But sir, said she, you shall understand, that this our vicar is diseased with such a kind of hoarsenesse, as divers of our neighbors in this parish, not long since, doubted that he had

75. Appropriate.
76. Besotted, infatuated.

the French pox; & in that respect utterly refused to communicate with him:[77] untill such time as (being thereunto injoined by M.D. Lewen the Ordinarie)[78] he had brought from London a certificat, under the hands of two physicians, that his hoarsenes proceeded from a disease in the lungs. Which certificat he published in the church, in the presence of the whole congregation: and by this meanes hee was cured, or rather excused of the shame of his disease. And this I knowe to be true by the relation of divers honest men of that parish. And truelie, if one of the Jurie had not beene wiser than the other, she had been condemned thereupon, and upon other as ridiculous matters as this. For the name of a witch is so odious, and hir power so feared among the common people, that if the honestest bodie living chance to be arraigned thereupon, she shall hardlie escape condemnation.

In book 1, chapter 3, Scot lays out concisely his understanding of how an accusation and confession originate:

One sort of such as are said to bee witches are women which be commonly old, lame, bleare-eied, pale, fowle, and full of wrinkles; poore, sullen, superstitious, and papists;[79] or such as knowe no religion: in whose drousie minds the divell hath goten a fine seat; so as, what mischeefe, mischance, calamitie, or slaughter is brought to passe, they are easilie persuaded the same is doone by themselves; imprinting in their minds an earnest and constant imagination hereof. They are leane and deformed, shewing melancholie in their faces, to the horror of all that see them. They are doting, scolds, mad, divelish; and not much differing from them that are thought to be possessed with spirits; so firme and stedfast in their opinions, as whosoever shall onelie have respect to the constancie of their words uttered, would easilie beleeve they were true indeed.

These miserable wretches are so odious unto all their neighbors, and so feared, as few dare offend them, or denie them anie thing they aske: whereby they take upon them; yea, and sometimes thinke, that they can doo such things as are beyond the abilitie of humane nature. These go from house to house, and from doore to doore for a pot full of milke, yest, drinke, pottage, or some such releefe; without the which they could hardlie live: neither obtaining for their service and paines, nor by their art, nor at the divels hands (with whome they are said to make a perfect and visible

---

77. To take communion with him.
78. Being requested to do so by the diocesan official.
79. The idea that witches were often poor and elderly women is very familiar, but Scot's suggestion that witches were frequently Catholic is perhaps less so. Evidence does suggest that older, poorer people tended to retain Catholic habits well after 1558, when Elizabeth I's accession re-established Protestantism as the state faith (see John Walsh, above). If accused of witchcraft, this could help to condemn them. Scot's defence of Catholic witches interestingly mingles pity and contempt.

bargaine) either beautie, monie, promotion, welth, worship, pleasure, honor, knowledge, learning, or anie other benefit whatsoever.

It falleth out many times, that neither their necessities, nor their expectation is answered or served, in those places where they beg or borrowe; but rather their lewdnesse is by their neighbors reprooved. And further, in tract of time the witch waxeth odious and tedious to hir neighbors; and they againe are despised and despited of hir: so as sometimes she cursseth one, and sometimes another; and that from the maister of the house, his wife, children, cattell, &c. to the little pig that lieth in the stie. Thus in processe of time they have all displeased hir, and she hath wished evill lucke unto them all; perhaps with cursses and imprecations made in forme.[80] Doubtlesse (at length) some of hir neighbors die, or fall sicke; or some of their children are visited with diseases that vex them strangelie: as apoplexies, epilepsies, convulsions, hot fevers, wormes, &c. Which by ignorant parents are supposed to be the vengeance of witches. Yea and their opinions and conceits are confirmed and maintained by unskilfull physicians: according to the common saieng; *Inscitiae pallium malificium & incantatio*, Witchcraft and inchantment is the cloke of ignorance: whereas indeed evill humors, & not strange words, witches, or spirits are the causes of such diseases. Also some of their cattell perish, either by disease or mischance. Then they, upon whom such adversities fall, weighing the fame that goeth upon this woman (hir words, displeasure, and cursses meeting so justlie with their misfortune) doo not onelie conceive, but also are resolved, that all their mishaps are brought to passe by hir onelie meanes.

The witch on the other side exspecting hir neighbours mischances, and seeing things sometimes come to passe according to hir wishes, cursses and incantations (for Bodin himselfe confesseth, that not above two in a hundred of their witchings or wishings take effect)[81] being called before a Justice, by due examination of the circumstances is driven to see hir imprecations and desires, and hir neighbors harmes and losses to concurre, and as it were to take effect: and so confesseth that she (as a goddes) hath brought such things to passe. Wherein, not onelie she, but the accuser, and also the Justice are fowlie deceived and abused; as being thorough hir confession and other circumstances persuaded (to the injurie of Gods glorie) that she hath doone, or can doo that which is proper onelie to God himselfe.

Scot summarizes for his readers the methods of interrogation and torture which he has found in his reading of European demonologists, with specific attack reserved for Bodin and the *Malleus Maleficarum*. He comments that:

---

80. Formally, Scot admits that some suspects actually do believe themselves to be witches, and try to use cursing spells.
81. Jean Bodin, one of Scot's chief targets, the French jurist and demonologist and author of *De la Demonomanie des Sorciers* (1580; Paris, 1587) cited in *A true and just Recorde* (above). Scot cites book 2, chapter 8, here.

I neede not staie to confute such parciall and horrible dealings, being so apparentlie impious, and full of tyrannie ... supposing that the citing of such absurdities may stand for a sufficient confutation thereof.

But sometimes he cannot help retorting to what he sees as evident absurdities or cruelties, becoming deeply engaged in several key debates: whether a devil has or can assume a corporeal body, how melancholic delusions affect the mind, and whether devils can have sex with human beings. Quoting from the works he criticizes, Scot provides answers to their assertions about witches:

They use incestuous adulterie with spirits.
Ans. This is a stale ridiculous lie, as prooved apparentlie hereafter.
They boile infants (after they have murthered them unbaptised) untill their flesh be made potable.[82]
Ans. This is untrue, incredible, and impossible ...
That the joining of hands with the divell, the kissing of his bare buttocks, and his scratching and biting of them, are absurd lies; everie one having the gift of reason may plainlie perceive: in so much as it is manifest unto us by the word of God, that a spirit hath no flesh, bones, nor sinewes, whereof hands, buttocks, claws, teeth, and lips doo consist. For admit that the constitution of a divels bodie (as Tatian[83] and other affirme) consisteth in spirituall congelations, as of fier and aire; yet it cannot be perceived of mortal creatures. What credible witnesse is there brought at anie time, of this their corporall, visible, and incredible bargaine; saving the confession of some person diseased both in bodie and mind, wilfullie made, or injuriouslie constrained? ...

He also offers further evidence from his own experience:

... that it may appeere, that even voluntarie confession (in this case) may be untrulie made, though it tend to the destruction of the confessor; and that melancholie may moove imaginations to that effect: I will cite a notable instance concerning this matter, the parties themselves being yet alive, and dwelling in the parish of Sellenge in Kent, and the matter not long sithence in this sort performed.

One Ada Davie, the wife of Simon Davie, husbandman, being reputed a right honest bodie, and being of good parentage, grew suddenlie (as hir husband informed mee, and as it is well knowne in these parts) to be somewhat pensive and more sad than in times past. Which thing though it greeved him, yet he was loth to make it so appeere, as either his wife might be troubled or discontented therewith, or his neighbours informed thereof;

---

82. Drinkable.
83. Tatianus, 110–80 AD, an early Christian writer, later accused of heresy.

lest ill husbandrie should be laid to his charge (which in these quarters is much abhorred). But when she grew from pensivenes, to some perturbation of mind; so as hir accustomed rest began in the night season to be withdrawne from hir, through sighing and secret lamentation; and that, not without teares, hee could not but demand the cause of hir conceipt[84] and extraordinarie moorning. But although at that time she covered the same, acknowledging nothing to be amisse with hir: soone after notwithstanding she fell downe before him on hir knees, desiring him to forgive hir, for she had greevouslie offended (as she said) both God & him. Hir poore husband being abashed at this hir behaviour, comforted hir, as he could; asking hir the cause of hir trouble & greefe: who told him, that she had, (contrarie to Gods lawe) & to the offense of all good christians, to the injurie of him, & speciallie to the losse of hir owne soule, bargained and given hir soule to the divell, to be delivered unto him within short space. Whereunto hir husband answered, saieng; Wife, be of good cheere, this thy bargaine is void and of none effect: for thou hast sold that which is none of thine to sell; sith[85] it belongeth to Christ, who hath bought it, and deerlie paid for it, even with his bloud, which he shed upon the crosse; so as the divell hath no interest[86] in thee. After this, with like submission, teares, and penitence, she said unto him; Oh husband, I have yet committed another fault, and doone you more injurie: for I have bewitched you and your children. Be content (quoth he) by the grace of God, Jesus Christ shall unwitch us: for none evill can happen to them that feare God.

And (as trulie as the Lord liveth) this was the tenor of his words unto me, which I knowe is true, as proceeding from unfeigned lips, and from one that feareth God. Now when the time approched that the divell should come, and take possession of the woman, according to his bargaine, he watched and praied earnestlie, and caused his wife to read psalmes and praiers for mercie at Gods hands: and suddenlie about midnight, there was a great rumbling beelowe under his chamber windowe, which amazed them exceedinglie. For they conceived, that the divell was beelowe, though he had no power to come up, bicause of their fervent praiers.

He that noteth this womans first and second confession, freelie and voluntarilie made, how everie thing concurred that might serve to adde credit thereunto, and yeeld matter for hir condemnation, would not thinke, but that if Bodin were foreman of hir inquest,[87] he would crie; Guiltie: & would hasten execution upon hir; who would have said as much before any judge in the world, if she had beene examined; and have confessed no lesse, if she had beene arraigned thereupon. But God knoweth, she was innocent of anie these crimes: howbeit she was brought lowe and pressed downe

---

84. State of mind.
85. Since.
86. Investment, ownership.
87. Foreman of the jury at her trial.

with the weight of this humor, so as both hir rest and sleepe were taken awaie from hir; & hir fansies troubled and disquieted with despaire, and such other cogitations as grew by occasion thereof. And yet I beleeve, if any mishap had insued to hir husband, or his children; few witchmongers would have judged otherwise, but that she had bewitched them. And she (for hir part) so constantlie persuaded hir selfe to be a witch, that she judged hir selfe worthie of death; insomuch as being reteined in hir chamber, she sawe not anie one carrieng a faggot to the fier, but she would saie it was to make a fier to burne hir for witcherie.[88] But God knoweth she had bewitched none, neither insued there anie hurt unto anie, by hir imagination, but unto hir selfe.[89]

And as for the rumbling, it was by occasion of a sheepe, which was flawed, and hoong by the wals,[90] so as a dog came and devoured it; whereby grew the noise which I before mentioned: and she being now recovered, remaineth a right honest woman, far from such impietie, and shamed of hir imaginations, which she perceiveth to have growne through melancholie ...

Before moving on to deal with magic, prophecy and trickery, Scot must deal with the thorny issue of witchcraft and sex. Wishing to present himself as a serious and godly inquirer, he prefaces his remarks with a statement of reluctance, and proceeds to refute logically all that he can, but there is an enjoyment in his writing suggesting a bawdy sense of humour at odds with his assertions.

A request to such readers as loath to heare or read filthie or bawdie matters (which of necessitie are heere to be inserted) to passe over eight chapters.

But in so much as I am driven (for the more manifest bewraieng and displaieng of this most filthie and horrible error) to staine my paper with writing thereon certeine of their beastlie and bawdie assertions and examples, whereby they confirme this their doctrine (being my selfe both ashamed, and loth once to thinke upon such filthinesse, although it be to the condemnation thereof) I must intreat you that are the readers hereof, whose chaste eares cannot well endure to heare of such abhominable lecheries, as are gathered out of the bookes of those witchmongers (although doctors of divinitie, and otherwise of great authoritie and estimation) to turne over a few leaves, wherein (I saie) I have like a groome thrust their bawdie stuffe (even that which I my selfe loath) as into a

---

88. Witches were not burned in England, but people at the time routinely said that they were. This seems to be a conflation of the English punishment for heretics with the practice in some European states of burning witches as heretical devil-worshippers.

89. Scot says that he does not believe Ada Davie had bewitched anyone: but does he mean that she had not even tried to do so by making a bargain (however imaginary) with the devil? Elsewhere, his argument hangs on the inefficacy of such bargains and spells, not on the suspect's utter innocence of such activities.

90. Flayed (skinned) and hung.

stinking corner: howbeit, none otherwise, I hope, but that the other parts of my writing shall remaine sweet, and this also covered as close as may be . . .

Howbeit, *M. Mal.*[91] proceedeth, affirming that All witches take their beginning from such filthie actions, wherein the divell, in likenes of a prettie wench, lieth prostitute as Succubus to the man, and reteining his nature and seede, conveieth it unto the witch, to whome he delivereth it as Incubus.[92] Wherein also is refuted the opinion of them that hold a spirit to be unpalpable. *M. Mal.* saith, There can be rendred no infallible rule, though a probable distinction may be set downe, whether Incubus in the act of venerie doo alwaies powre seed out of his assumed bodie. And this is the distinction; Either she is old and barren or young and pregnant. If she be barren, then dooth Incubus use hir without decision of seed; bicause such seed should serve for no purpose. And the divell avoideth superfluitie as much as he may; and yet for hir pleasure and condemnation togither, he goeth to worke with hir. But by the waie, if the divell were so compendious,[93] what should he need to use such circumstances, even in these verie actions, as to make these assemblies, conventicles, ceremonies, &c: when he hath alreadie bought their bodies, and bargained for their soules? Or what reason had he, to make them kill so manie infants, by whom he rather loseth than gaineth any thing; bicause they are, so farre as either he or we knowe, in better case than we of riper yeares by reason of their innocencie?[94] Well, if she be not past children, then stealeth he seed awaie (as hath beene said) from some wicked man being about that lecherous busines, and therewith getteth yoong witches upon the old.

And note, that they affirme that this businesse is better accomplished with seed thus gathered, then that which is shed in dremes, through superfluitie of humors: bicause that is gathered from the vertue of the seed generative. And if it be said that the seed will wax cold by the waie, and so lose his naturall heate, and consequentlie the vertue: *M. Mal.*, Danaeus,[95] and the rest doo answere, that the divell can so carrie it, as no heate shall go from it, &c.

Furthermore, old witches are sworne to procure as manie yoong virgins for Incubus as they can, whereby in time they growe to be excellent bawds: but in this case the preest plaieth Incubus . . .

Scot's problematic strategy of refusing to refute in detail what he saw as obvious idiocy made his work liable to becoming a straightforward conduit for the ideas of Continental demonologists to reach an English audience. But his continual need to mock usually resurfaces, as in the last line above, so that

---

91. *Malleus Maleficarum.* Scot cites question 1, part 1.
92. Succubus: a devil in the shape of a woman. Incubus: a devil in the shape of a man.
93. Efficient.
94. Therefore more likely to go to heaven, presumably.
95. Lambert Daneau, whose *A Dialogue of Witches* (1575) was a Protestant demonology.

readers are forced to imbibe his scepticism along with the lurid material he reproduces. The results can be seen in plays like Thomas Middleton's *The Witch*, below. For example, Scot said that incubus was a natural disease, a nightmare causing paralysis and a feeling of being oppressed by a heavy body, and went on to deal with the belief that witches stole men's penises by retelling from the *Malleus* the stories of young men so afflicted. His conclusion soberly brings the reader back to the heart of Scot's book, which for all its gleeful insults, anti-Catholic jokes and devastating ripostes, is a work intended to save lives.

Item, a reverend father, for his life, holinesse, and knowledge notorious, being a frier of the order and company of Spire, reported, that a yoong man at shrift made lamentable moane unto him for the like losse: but his gravitie suffered not to beleeve lightlie any such reports, and therefore made the yoong man untrusse his codpiece point, and sawe the complaint to be true and just. Whereupon he advised or rather injoined the youth to go to the witch whome he suspected, and with flattering words to intreat hir, to be so good unto him, as to restore him his instrument: which by that meanes he obtained, and soone after returned to shew himselfe thankfull; and told the holie father of his good successe in that behalfe: but he so beleeved him, as he would needs be *Oculatus testis*, and made him pull downe his breeches, and so was satisfied of the troth and certaintie thereof.[96]

Another yoong man being in that verie taking, went to a witch for the restitution thereof, who brought him to a tree, where she shewed him a nest, and bad him climb up and take it. And being in the top of the tree, he tooke out a mightie great one, and shewed the same to hir, asking hir if he might not have the same. Naie (quoth she) that is our parish preests toole, but take anie other which thou wilt. And it is there affirmed, that some have found 20. and some 30. of them in one nest, being there preserved without provender, as it were at the racke and manger, with this note, wherein there is no contradiction (for all must be true that is written against witches) that If a witch deprive one of his privities, it is done onlie by prestigious[97] meanes, so as the senses are but illuded. Marie by the divell it is reallie taken awaie, and in like sort restored.[98] These are no jestes, for they be written by them that were and are judges upon the lives and deaths of those persons.

---

96. Scot puns on the Latin phrase meaning eyewitness, for *testis* also means testicle. There is a hint of accusation of priestly homosexuality to sweeten this joke for the unsympathetic reader presupposed in Scot's preface to this section.
97. Illusory.
98. If the witch removes it, it is only an illusion, but the devil can really remove it.

3. Expert observer

John Cotta, The Triall of Witch-craft shewing the true and right methode of the Discovery: with a Confutation of erroneous wayes *(London, 1616)*

John Cotta was a Northamptonshire physician whose interest in witchcraft was stimulated by contact, as part of his medical practice, with those who claimed to be bewitched. As a good doctor, he prided himself on his ability often to identify their complaints as being of natural origin, but the limited medical knowledge of the time and his own strong belief that witchcraft did indeed exist left him frankly confusing in attempting an explanation of his beliefs in *The Triall of Witch-craft*. Cotta's book shows him fighting on several fronts: attempting to convince patients that their complaints are natural, and thus can be naturally treated; fending off the claims of magical healers; trying to decide whether such healers are mere imposters or are themselves actually witches, who may harm. The book focuses attention on (often male) witches attempting devilish cures, rather than malignant old women causing illness. In doing this, it emphasizes the diversity of beliefs about what lay at the heart of the 'witchcraft problem', echoing the concerns of George Gifford. But, secondly, like the work of Scot, it illustrates the attempts of an ordinary professional man to comprehend, adapt to his own experience and apply demonological theory. Other examples from the period include Edward Jorden's 1603 *A Brief Discourse of a Disease called the Suffocation of the Mother*, an hysterical affliction thought by many to be the cause of those symptoms often (Jorden polemically stated) misdiagnosed by lesser physicians as demonic possession, and Robert Burton's discussions of witchcraft (and delusion) in his 1621 *Anatomy of Melancholy*.[99]

Describing himself as 'a meane wit', Cotta humbly offers to 'adventure ammidest so many doubts and ambiguities' because he passionately believes that a combination of reasoning and experience (a word which carries some of the modern sense of 'experiment') can help solve the old puzzles. In the past, men have not sufficiently carefully searched the scriptures, he argues, and – more importantly, it transpires – they have not 'seriously consulted with that wisedome and prudence, which by the light of nature and reason Almightie God hath left discoverable . . .'. Cotta is thus an early natural scientist, working on the boundaries of the Galenic medicine of the past, in the difficult new territory of inductive reasoning – a method of reaching conclusions about phenomena that was promoted by, among others, Francis Bacon. Reversing the traditional deductive method, inductive reasoning began not with assumptions about the world which might be tested by thought and (sometimes) experiment, but with a particular experiment from which conclusions are then drawn, no matter how

---

99. For Jorden, see Michael MacDonald, ed., *Witchcraft and Hysteria in Elizabethan London* (London and New York: Routledge, 1991).

little they may appear to fit in with assumptions about the world. The world of Galen, with its humours and hot and cold remedies (see John Walsh, above) would eventually be destroyed by experiment and induction, because medical phenomena did not in fact fit Galen's assumptions at all well. By dissecting deceased patients he had been unable to cure, Cotta learned more about disease, and as he did so he became more convinced that magic neither caused nor cured it. From this practical experimental base, Cotta moved outwards to discuss demonology. But here, traditional assumptions took over. Cotta's book is an excellent illustration of the epistemological confusion surrounding witchcraft, and the way that belief in it was ingrained so that despite possessing a methodology that would eventually undermine belief in witches, early English Renaissance people were largely unable to use it.

Cotta began his book with a dedication to the Lord Chief Justice, Sir Edward Coke, and boldly took issue with the state of English law.

... What Lawe or Nation in the detection of Witches and Witch-craft, hath as yet ever appeared competent, or from just exception[100] exempt? How uncertaine are among all people differing judgements? Some judge no witches at all, others more then too many, others too few by many, in so opposite extremes, so extremely opposite: I doe not presume to prescribe how a lawe may become more absolute or perfect, I onely labour and enquire to learne ...

To The Reader.

Ingenious Reader, in this subject of Witch-craft which I here present unto thee, thou art not ignorant, what obscuritie, difficultie, difference, contrarietie and contradiction hath among Authors and learned men in all ages arisen. From the effusion of generall ignorance, or supersitious blindnesse herein, willing to withdraw the vulgar illusion; I have indeavoured demonstratively to declare what portion of certainety in such uncertainties, God and Nature hath destined & allowed ... The envious haply may cavill, that a Physician out of his own supposed precincts, should rush into sacred lists, or enter upon so high points of Divinitie, as by an unavoidable intercurrence, do necessarily insert themselves in this proposed subject. Divinitie it selfe doth herein answere them. In the theory of Theologie, it is the duety and praise of every man, to bee without curiositie[101] fruitfully exercised.

Cotta concludes his preface by restating the central role of the clergy in demonology: he does not want to usurp their place but says that he will 'submit unto the grave censure and dictature of the learned and reverend Divine'.

---

100. Censure, as in 'to take exception'.
101. Peculiarity, self-indulgence.

Finally, he warns the reader that if they do not wish to investigate and know the truth about witchcraft, 'truth shall judge thee'. Cotta's concern with serving the truth is immediately made clear in his first section, a discussion of knowledge and how it is acquired; namely, by inward processes (innate knowledge, and subsequent reasoning) and outward senses. His starting point, his professional interest in curing disease, is also evident.

... all the Philosophers have determined the two onely instruments of all true Arts, to bee Reason and Experience, which Galen[102] doth call the two legges whereupon the Art of Physike doth consist ... hee who doth all things in his subject of Physike, according to right rule of reason, is the most excellent Physicion ... All diseases that happen unto the body of man are either outward or inward, and therefore either seene by the eye, and deprehended[103] by the outward sense, or conceived only by Reason and the inward Understanding. Inward diseases, and subject onely to reason and understanding doe sometimes appeare clearely and certainly to reason and understanding; sometimes they do not appeare certaine, or by certaine notes or signes, but by likely markes onely, which are the grounds of artificiall[104] conjecture. And as some diseases are apparent to outward sense, some evident to inward reason, some by artificiall conjecture only in learned, exact search and perquisition[105] pursued unto their discovery: so also are many diseases hidden from all these wayes of investigation, and therefore remaine as remembrances of mans manifold ignorance in this life, and of the secret reservation of Gods decree and prohibition ...

That it may the better appeare, that beyond these waies and lights, the Physicion cannot finde any knowledge or discovery of Diseases: let us view some particular examples ... There happened unto my selfe this yeere last past, a Patient, a very worthy Gentleman, who being extremely vexed with the Strangury, Disurie, and Ischurie together with pissing of blood in great abundance, and the stone,[106] who by the use and accommodation of remedies, found much ease ... Notwithstanding, for that there were certaine indications of an Ulcer in the body or capacitie of the Bladder, his recoverie was not expected, but after his decease, in the dissection of his body, his Bladder was found rotten, broken and black, without any manifest matter therein as cause thereof, or so much as one stone ... This I produce, being fresh in memory, as an instance of impossibilitie of knowledge unto a Physicion in many and frequent cases.

... Thus hath been at large manifested, that nothing can bee unto the

---

102. Roman physician of Greek origin, c. 130–c. 200 AD. His discoveries on circulation were revolutionary but by 1616 his orthodoxies were very outdated.
103. Detected.
104. Artful.
105. Inquiry.
106. Urine retention, painful urination and a concretion in the bladder or kidneys.

Physicion in his Art and Science knowne, which either by outward sense
or inward is not apparent, or by likely and artificiall conjecture from both,
is not detected or discerned. The like might be urged concerning the trials
of lawe and justice, and inquisitions of offences and errors against the law,
which are the diseases of a Common-weale, as the former of the body of
man. Many offences against the law are apparent unto the outward sense, as
sight or hearing: and therefore being witnessed by hearers or beholders, are
without doubt or difficulty immediately dispatched, sentenced, and
adjudged. Many also are evident to reason, which therefore are held and
reputed invincibly and infallibly to convince.[107] Many offences also there
are, neither manifest to sense, nor evident to reason, against which only
likelihood and presumption doe arise in judgement; whereby, notwithstanding, through narrow search and sifting, strict examination, circum-
spect and curious view of every circumstance, together with every materiall
moment[108] and oddes thorowly, and unto the depth and bottome by subtil
disquisition fadomed,[109] the learned, prudent, and discerning Judge doth
oft detect and bring unto light many hidden, intestine,[110] and secret
mischiefes, which unsensibly and unobservedly would otherwise oppresse
and subvert the Common-weale. When by none of these wayes of
extrication, the truth can possibly be gained, the wise and upright Judge
unto necessity in want of due warrant unto just proceeding, doth with
patience and sobriety submit . . .

It remaineth now to enquire concerning one particular subject of Witchcraft, whether in the common way of all other detection of truths, it ought
likewise consist; or whether by it selfe it have other priviledges beyond all
other trials. If reason be the sole eye and light of naturall understanding
which God hath given unto reasonable man (as is before proved). If without
it can be no naturall knowledge, no Art, no Science no discovery. If lawe
among all people and nations be so just in all things, as to do or allow
nothing against true reason (in which consisteth right). If God himselfe, and
all flourishing Comon-weales have tryed men and lawes, and the decision
by them of all doubts, questions and controversies, either unto right proofe,
evidence and allegation, according unto reason, or at least, faire likelihood,
presumption, and probabilitie, and beyond these there never was, is, or can
be any just judgement or triall: How is it possible than man can attaine any
knowledge of Witch-craft, if not by those meanes, by which only his nature
is capable of whatsoever is allotted to be known thereto? . . . It may bee and
is objected, that it is a hard and difficult matter to detect Witch-craft, by the
former and ordinary courses, as is oft seene and found apparent. So is it
likewise equally difficult, and as hard by the same meanes oft-times, for

---

107. Convict.
108. Small detail, cause or consideration.
109. Fathomed.
110. Internal.

many a just man to prove and cleere his opposed innocency, and for many
an injuriously wronged wretch to prove his right, to defend his goods, yea,
life it selfe from violence; notwithstanding, this is no allowance unto
another way . . . out of the way of Reason, Justice, and Lawe . . .

The modern reader probably concludes at this point in Cotta's book that he is
another Scot, and is going in effect to return a verdict of 'not proven' on
witchcraft cases. However, Cotta's reasoning, and the assumptions on which it
is based, leads him into a much more convoluted statement of belief, far more
typical of his era. He first discusses the differences between the work of devils
acting alone and the work of devils acting within a contract with a witch, both of
which he believes are possible. He moves through the usual demonological
territory: devils counterfeit bodies and transport witches; charmers (of whom
the literary characters Medea and Circe are cited as reliable examples) can
cause tempests, transport corn from fields, and so on. Finally, Cotta shows his
true target – not the female maleficial witch, but a much more personal enemy –
and in doing so betrays the flaws in his definition of rationality.

He that doth undertake voluntarily, doth present himselfe and doth
promise, and according to promise, cause to be performed that which is in
anothers power, and impossible unto himselfe, doth thereby necessarily and
unanswerably proove himselfe to have an interest, a power, a contract with
that other, which for any man to have with the Divell, is society with
Divels, which is Witch-craft and Sorcerie . . . An objection here may be
made, that many of the former workes may seeme manifest to the sense,
which indeed and truth are deceits of the imagination and illusion . . . It is
truly[111] answered, He that wanteth so much true judgement, as to
distinguish when he doth see a certain true object offered unto his sight
from without, and when he is incountred only with a resemblance thereof
from within his fancie and imagination, is diseased in body, or mind, or
both, and therfore is no competent Judge or witnesse in these or other
weighty affaires . . . If men could not certainely discerne betweene that
which they do really see, and that they falsely imagine in visions, dreames
and fancie, then were the life of man most miserable . . .[112]

Cotta's inability to imagine the possibility of convincing Satanic illusion goes
against the grain of almost all writings by demonologists, both sceptics and
believers. It shows a vigorous modern assertion of the rational over the power
of the supernatural, but Cotta never explains how judgement may be tested, or
those of unfit mind kept from witnessing against or judging witches. In his

111. In the sentence following this point, the word 'not' (or similar) has been omitted,
      inverting Cotta's point; however, a note here makes it very clear: 'Things imagined and
      fancied, easily discerned from those things which are reall & true objects of the sense.'
112. See Cotton Mather (below) for a similar argument.

relentless pursuit of the cunning man, whose invitation to others to consult him on supernatural matters is held to condemn him instantly as a witch, Cotta may be referring to the case of Mistress Belcher (see 'Witchcraft at the Assizes: Northamptonshire 1612', above). Certainly his description resembles her illness, although the dates do not quite match, and Cotta very probably attended the 1612 trials of witches (see below).

There is a very rare, but true, description of a Gentlewoman, about sixe yeares past, cured of divers kinds of convulsions, and other apoplecktike, epileptike, cataleptike, and paralytike fits, and other kinds of accidents of affinitie therwith.[113] After she was almost cured of those diseases, but the cure not fully accomplished, it was by a reputed Wisard whispered, and thereupon beleeved, that the Gentlewoman was merely bewitched, supposed Witches were accused, and after executed. The Gentlewoman hath been free from all those accidents there mentioned, the space of sixe yeares now past. In this last past seventh yeare, since the writing of that history, some of the former fits are critically again returned: the same Wisard or Deceiver resorted unto and enquired at, doth now againe avouch her to be bewitched; upon opinion whereof and trust in his illusion, the timely use and benefit of due counsell hath beene much omitted and neglected . . . For in true reason and judicious discerning, it is as cleere as the brightest day, that no accident befalling the Gentlewoman mentioned, can be other than naturall, or farther super-naturall, then either the Divels credit with a Witch, or an Impostours credit with deceived and seduced men is able to inchaunt perswasion unto vain affiance[114] in them . . .

Cotta's certainty that most diseases he himself had witnessed were unquestionably natural had no impact on his belief that there were diseases caused by witchcraft, and that witches could be found and judged relatively easily. The character of the suspect was as important as the fact that they should be seen as having incriminated themselves by offering to perform magic.

. . . let us suppose a person of a curious[115] and inquisitive disposition in things hidden or inhibited, a man voide of the feare and knowledge of God, a searcher after Sorcerers, and their divelish Arts, educate among them, by Kindred, affinity, or neighbour-hood, with them having generall opportunitie unto inchoation[116] in to that Diabolicall mysterie, a man

---

113. Apoplexy, epilepsy, catalepsy (inanimate fits) and paralysis are very different: the case sounds increasingly like possession.
114. Alliance.
115. Cotta footnotes William Perkins, *A Discourse of the Damned Art of Witchcraft* (Cambridge, 1608), chapter 1, p. 11.
116. Induction.

likely and prone to become a receptacle of Divels, expressed by his long observed, or knowne flying from or hating all occasions or places, where the name, mention, worship, or adoration of Almighty God is in any kinde used; a man out of whose cursed lips hath at any time beene heard, the[117] renouncing of God, or voluntary profession of love & friendship unto the Divell (all which with horror sometimes my owne eares did hear, in a[118] woman at an open assise, being there indited upon suspicion of Witch-craft . . .

When therefore men that are prudent, judicious, and able to discerne, do first advisedly upon good ground and reason, adjudge a supernaturall act evidently done, or at least worthy to be suspected: secondly, shall by just and reasonable proofe, or at least, likely and faire presumption, detect the contract, affection, or consent of any man in that act, then and not before, is the accusation, inquisition, and inditement of Witch-craft, against any man equall and just.

---

117. Cotta footnotes Perkins, chapter 2, p. 48.
118. Cotta's note here says, 'She was easie and ready to professe, that she renounced God and all his workes, but being required to say that shee renounced the Divell and all his workes, she did refuse it with this addition of the reason, (*videlicet*) for that the Divell had never done her any hurt.' This is almost certainly a reference to the trial of Alce Wilson (see 'Witchcraft at the Assizes: Northamptonshire 1612', above).

FOUR

STAGE AND PAGE – WITCHES IN
LITERATURE

1. Comedy

Thomas Middleton, **The Witch** *(1613–15?)*

Middleton's 120-year-old witch Hecate, with her lusty band of followers, was probably created between 1613 and 1615 and has obvious origins both in European demonologies such as the *Malleus Maleficarum* and in Scot's English scepticism about such claims as the *Malleus* makes. Hecate's witches are lecherous, murderous and perverse in the traditional demonological way, but they are also funny, vulnerable and uncomfortably necessary to the maintenance of state power and social position by those who resort to them.

In writing the play, Middleton was probably influenced by recent events at the English court – the murder by poison of Sir Thomas Overbury and the plot between the Countess of Essex and several cunning people to make her husband impotent, so that she might gain a divorce and marry her lover. Middleton therefore shows quite clearly that whilst what the witches do is ugly, sinful and self-serving, it is no worse than what is done by outwardly respectable figures at court. Even the 'good' characters are implicated in plotting with the witches, and the witches sabbath can be read as an arena for the displacement on to others of all the desires and fears of respectable society, suggesting (together with the blackly comic tone) that Middleton is less than wholehearted in his belief in the reality of such sabbaths. Nevertheless, he is very willing to use magic for the purposes of stage spectacle and it is an important dramatic assumption in the play that spells work – literally, like a charm.

The play is set in Italy – perhaps to distance it from English affairs – but Middleton welds together witchcraft practices from several different cultures, many of them borrowed conspicuously from Scot, so that the witches carry out both perverse high magic rituals and everyday maleficium, both boiling babies and spoiling butter-making in an all-encompassing attempt to do mischief. There is a hint that witches are an organized Satanic cult, with references to the witches' 'master' and to their taking of oaths, but despite a hodge-podge of grotesque detail, they seem really rather harmless. *The Witch* was clearly designed to entertain, and perhaps – following Scot – to satirize Catholic European beliefs in witches. But with a demonologist king on the English throne and scandal enveloping his court it would also have targets nearer to home, which might explain why Middleton later implied (in a dedication of a manuscript of the play to Thomas Holmes) that it had been unsuccessful and fallen into obscurity as being 'ignorantly ill-fated'.

Middleton (1580–1627) was certainly more famous for other works – his city comedies such as *A Chaste Maid in Cheapside* (1613?), tragi-comedies like *The Changeling* (written with William Rowley, 1622) and his political satire *A Game at Chess* (1624). But *The Witch* is still entertaining, displaying its creator's careful research into demonology using Scot, as well as his obsession with laughing at and reproving human wickedness. And it offers a surprising perspective on witchcraft: even in a time when hundreds of people were being executed for the crime, there were those who recognized its potential for humour and celebration. Middleton prefers here to see witchcraft as a subject for satire, rather than as a terrifying spectre stalking the world.

The story is as follows: Sebastian, a young gentleman, returns to Ravenna from the wars to find that his fiancée, Isabella, believes him to be dead, and is about to be married to the powerful and lecherous Antonio. Although he cannot stop the wedding, he resolves to win Isabella back and visits the witches …

Act 1, Scene 2[1]
[Enter Hecate]

Hecate: Titty and Tiffin,
          Suckin and Pidgen,
          Liard and Robin,[2]
          White spirits, black spirits;
          Grey spirits, red spirits;
          Devil-toad, devil ram;
          Devil-cat, and devil-dam.
          Why Hoppo and Stadlin, Hellwain and Puckle!

Stadlin [within]:   Here, sweating at the vessel.

Hecate: Boil it well.

Hoppo [within]:   It gallops now.[3]

---

1. The text used here is based on Peter Corbin and Douglas Sedge, eds, *Three Jacobean Witchcraft Plays* (Manchester: Manchester University Press, 1986), and is quoted with their kind permission. Their excellent notes have been very helpful in preparing this abridged text. Throughout this volume, notes on plays are by the present editor, but sometimes draw on other editors, with attribution. *All* editors' additions to the text and *all* stage directions (whether original or added) are in square brackets: readers who need detailed bibliographical information are therefore usually referred to the editions specified. *The Witch* existed only in manuscript form during its author's lifetime.
2. These names, for familiar spirits, are taken from *A true and just Recorde* (London, 1582) above.
3. It's boiling now.

Hecate: Are the flames blue enough?
            Or shall I use a little seeton more?[4]
Stadlin [within]:   The nips of fairies upon maids' white hips
            Are not more perfect azure.[5]
Hecate: Tend it carefully.
            Send Stadlin to me with a brazen dish
            That I may fall to work upon these serpents,
            And squeeze 'em ready for the second hour.
            Why, when!

[Enter Stadlin with a brazen dish]

Stadlin: Here's Stadlin and the dish.
Hecate: Here, take this unbaptised brat; [giving the dead body of a baby]
            Boil it well, preserve the fat.
            You know 'tis precious to transfer
            Our 'nointed flesh into the air,
            In moonlight nights o'er steeple-tops,
            Mountains and pine-trees, that like pricks or stops[6]
            Seem to our height; high towers and roofs of princes
            Like wrinkles in the earth. Whole provinces
            Appear to our sight then even leek[7]
            A russet mole upon some lady's cheek,
            When hundred leagues in air we feast and sing,
            Dance, kiss and coll,[8] use everything.
            What young man can we wish to pleasure us
            But we enjoy him in an incubus?
            Thou knowst it, Stadlin?
Stadlin: Usually that's done.
Hecate: Last night thou got'st the Mayor of Whelplie's son.
            I knew him by his black cloak lined with yellow;
            I think thou'st spoiled the youth – he's but seventeen.
            I'll have him the next mounting. Away, in!
            Go feed the vessel for the second hour.
Stadlin: Where be the magical herbs?
Hecate: They're down his throat;
            His mouth crammed full; his ears and nostrils stuffed.
            I thrust in *eleoselinum* lately,

---

4. 'Seeton' is not in *OED*, but Corbin and Sedge suggest it is a chemical which, like salt, makes flames burn blue (Corbin and Sedge, eds, *Three Jacobean Witchcraft Plays*, p. 222, note to line 11).
5. Fairies were believed to pinch lazy servants.
6. Dots, full stops/periods.
7. Like.
8. Embrace.

        Aconitum, frondes populeus, and soot –
        You may see that, he looks so black i'th'mouth –
        Then *sium, acarum vulgaro* too,
        Pentaphyllon, the blood of a flittermouse,
        Solanum somnificum et oleum.[9]

Stadlin: Then there's all, Hecate?

Hecate: Is the heart of wax
        Stuck full of magic needles?

Stadlin: 'Tis done, Hecate.

Hecate: And is the farmer's picture and his wife's
        Laid down to th'fire yet?

Stadlin: They're a-roasting both, too.[10]

Hecate: Good.
        Then their marrows are a-melting subtly
        And three months' sickness sucks up life in 'em.
        They denied me often flour, barm[11] and milk,
        Goose-grease and tar, when I ne'er hurt their charmings,[12]
        Their brew-locks, nor their batches,[13] nor forespoke[14]
        Any of their breedings. Now I'll be meet with 'em.
        Seven of their young pigs I have bewitched already
        Of the last litter, nine ducklings, thirteen goslings,
        And a hog fell lame last Sunday, after evensong too;[15]
        And mark how their sheep prosper, or what sop
        Each milch-kine gives to th'pail. I'll send
        Those snakes shall milk 'em all beforehand.
        The dewed-skirted dairy wenches shall stroke
        Dry dugs for this and go home cursing.
        I'll mar their syllabubs and frothy feastings
        Under cows' bellies with the parish youths.

---

9. The ingredients are: mountain parsley, poisonous aconite or wolf's bane, poplar leaves, yellow watercress, myrtle, cinquefoil, bat's blood, deadly nightshade (containing belladonna and with hallucinogenic properties often thought by sceptics to be responsible for the flying fantasies of witches) and oil. Much of this is taken from Scot, book 10, chapter 8, where he lists ingredients and discusses some of the flying and sexual activities of witches (Corbin and Sedge, eds, *Three Jacobean Witchcraft Plays*, p. 222, notes to lines 38–45).

10. Picture: an image, usually of wax like the waxen heart above. See John Walsh, above. The images could be melted or buried, with or without pins or thorns stuck in them, to cause illness and death in those they represented.

11. Yeast.

12. Churnings.

13. Brewing vessels and batches of baking.

14. Bewitched.

15. Although the victims are devout, churchgoing has (interestingly) offered them no protection. Middleton takes Gifford's view that the godly may be afflicted by witches just like anyone else.

       Where's Firestone? Our son, Firestone?

[Enter Firestone]

Hecate: Here, take this brazen dish full of dear ware ...
          Go, and take heed you shed not by the way.
          The hour must have her portion, 'tis dear syrup;
          Each charmed drop is able to confound
          A family consisting of nineteen
          Or one-and-twenty feeders ...

Firestone: Mother, I pray you give me leave to ramble abroad tonight with the Nightmare, for I have a great mind to overlay a fat parson's daughter.[16]

Hecate: Who shall lie with me then?

Firestone: The great cat
          For one night, mother. 'Tis but a night –
          Make shift with him for once.[17]

Hecate: You're a kind son!
          But 'tis the nature of you all, I see that.
          You had rather hunt after strange women still
          Than lie with your own mothers. Get thee gone;
          Sweat thy six ounces out about the vessel
          And thou shalt play at midnight. The Nightmare
          Shall call thee when it walks.

Firestone: Thanks, most sweet mother. [Exit]

Hecate: Urchins, Elves, Hags, Satyrs, Pans, Fawns,
          Silens, Kit-with-the-candlestick, Tritons, Centaurs,
          Dwarfs, Imps, the Spoorn, the Mare, the Man-i'-th'-oak,
          The Hellwain, the Fire-drake, the Puckle, *A ab hur hus!*[18]

---

16. As the modern term 'nightmare' suggests, this incubus-demon could be explained by sceptics, including Scot, as a bad (and possibly sexual) dream in which the sleeper became paralysed as if by a heavy body lying on them. It's not clear how Firestone intends to cooperate with the creature, but he clearly wants sex with the nightmare's victim.

17. Middleton's witches have sex with their animal familiars – when the more mundane incest is not on offer – instead of the usual English suckling of spirits. There are a few English accusations of sex with man-shaped spirits (for example, *The most strange and admirable discoverie of the three Witches of Warboys* (London, 1593)) or incest (*A true and just Recorde* (London, 1582)) but the blending of demon-lover and animal is from the European sabbath. The cat appears later played by an actor, so it is intended to be an unnaturally large animal.

18. From Scot, book 7, chapter 15, where they appear similarly herded together as a list of childish and outmoded superstitious creations. Scot conflates English, European and Classical spirits, mythic creatures and deities: urchins were fairies, and elves, dwarfs and imps are also fairy-related creatures, although the European term 'dwarfs' also applied to people of restricted growth, and imps could be witches' familiars; hags are female evil spirits; satyrs, pans, fawns, sylens or silvans (a kind of satyr or a wood-spirit), tritons and centaurs are all human-animal creatures from classical mythology; Kit-with-the-candlestick and the fire-drake are both will-o'-the-wisp, the glowing marsh-gas often

[Enter Sebastian]

Sebastian [aside]:   Heaven knows with what unwillingness and hate
I enter this damned place; but such extremes
Of wrongs in love fight 'gainst religious knowledge,
That were I led by this disease to deaths
As numberless as creatures that must die,
I could not shun the way ...
[To Hecate] Whate'er thou art, I have no spare time to fear thee,
My horrors are so strong and great already
That thou seem'st nothing. Up and laze not ...
I'm in great need of help; wilt give me any?

Hecate: Thy boldness takes me bravely ...
I rise and bid thee welcome. What's thy wish now?

Sebastian: O my heart swells with't? I must take breath first.

Hecate: Is't to confound some enemy on the seas?
It may be done tonight. Stadlin's within;
She raises all your sudden ruinous storms
That shipwreck barks[19] and tears up growing oaks,
Flies over houses and takes *Anno Domini*
Out of a rich man's chimney[20] – a sweet place for't!
He would be hanged ere he would set his own years there;
They must be chambered in a five-pound picture,
A green silk curtain drawn before the eyes on't –
His rotten diseased years![21] Or dost thou envy
The fat prosperity of any neighbour?
I'll call forth Hoppo, and her incantation
Can straight destroy the young of all his cattle,
Blast vineyards, orchards, meadows, or in one night

---

cont.

thought to be a spirit; the spoorn is a now-forgotten type of spectre; the mare is the nightmare; the man-i'-the-oak is a tree-spirit; the hellwain and puckle refer to Hecate's colleagues but also to the cart thought to drag sinners to hell and to Puck-like fairy creatures. Scot's list is intended to obscure the boundaries between different types of 'bugs' as he calls them, and some of the things he mentions do not survive in printed sources to be identified: but his inclusion of witches and incubus in his catalogue shows that he meant to ridicule all such beliefs. Middleton's use of selected 'bugs' in his set-piece witches' invocation suggests either a satirical intent or a complete disregard for what witches were actually thought to do in favour of impressive-sounding names. *A ab hur hus* is quoted by Scot (book 12, chapter 14) as part of a charm against toothache but certainly seems intended as a grand peroration here (Corbin and Sedge, eds, *Three Jacobean Witchcraft Plays*, pp. 223–4, notes to lines 105–8).

19. Boats.
20. The date of building the house was often recorded on the chimney.
21. The rich man will not admit his age and mortality, although he is vain enough to have an expensive portrait painted: Middleton makes his satirical focus on the sins of the world clear as the witch criticizes the supposedly respectable citizen.

Transport his dung, hay, corn, by ricks, whole stacks
Into thine own ground.

Sebastian: This would come most richly now
To many a country grazier; but my envy
Lies not so low as cattle, corn or vines.
'Twill trouble your best powers to give me ease.

Hecate: Is it to starve up generation?
To strike a barrenness in man or woman?[22]

Sebastian: Ha!

Hecate: Ha? Did you feel me there? I knew your grief.

Sebastian: Can there be such things done?

Hecate: Are these the skins
Of serpents? These of snakes?

Sebastian: I see they are.

Hecate: So sure into what house these are conveyed, [giving skins to
Sebastian]
Knit with these charmed and retentive knots,
Neither the man begets nor woman breeds;
No, nor performs the least desires of wedlock,
Being then a mutual duty. I could give thee
Chiroconita, adincantida,
Archimadon, marmaritin, calicia,[23]
Which I could sort to villainous barren ends;
But this leads the same way. More I could instance:
As the same needles thrust into their pillows
That sews and socks up dead men in their sheets;
A privy gristle of a man that hangs
After sunset – good, excellent! Yet all's there, sir.

Sebastian: You could not do a man that special kindness
To part 'em utterly now? Could you do that?

Hecate: No, time must do't. We cannot disjoin wedlock.
'Tis of heaven's fastening. Well may we raise jars,[24]
Jealousies, strifes and heart-burning disagreements,
Like a thick scurf o'er life, as did our master
Upon that patient miracle,[25] but the work itself
Our power cannot disjoint.

---

22. Some European witches were said to be able to remove male genitalia, as well as simply impeding conception by attacking male or female partners (see Scot, above, quoting the *Malleus Maleficarum*). Probably closer to Middleton's own experience, although a less common English notion, witchcraft was said to have made the Earl of Essex impotent.
23. See Scot, book 6, chapter 3.
24. Marital disharmony.
25. As the devil afflicted Job in the Bible.

Sebastian: I depart happy
    In what I have then, being constrained to this.
    [Aside] And grant, you greater powers that dispose men,
    That I may never need this hag again.

Hecate: I know he loves me not, nor there's no hope on't;
    'Tis for the love of mischief I do this,
    And that we're sworn to – the first oath we take . . .[26]

A dissolute, comic courtier also visits Hecate's witches.

[Enter Almachildes] . . .

Hecate [aside]:   'Tis Almachildes – fresh blood stirs in me! –
    The man that I have lusted to enjoy.
    I have had him thrice in incubus already.[27]

Almachildes: Is your name Goody Hag?

Hecate: 'Tis anything.
    Call me the horrid'st and unhallowed'st things
    That life and nature trembles at; for thee
    I'll be the same.[28] Thou com'st for a love-charm now?

Almachildes: Why, thou'rt a witch I think.[29]

Hecate: Thou shalt have choice
    Of twenty, wet or dry.

Almachildes: Nay, let's have dry ones!

Hecate: If thou wilt use't by way of cup and potion,
    I'll give thee a remora shall bewitch her straight.

Almachildes: A remora? What's that?

Hecate: A little suck-stone;[30]
    Some call it a sea-lamprey, a small fish.

Almachildes: And must't be buttered?

Hecate: The bones of a green frog too, wondrous precious,
    The flesh consumed by pismires.[31]

Almachildes: Pismires? Give me a chamber-pot!

---

26. Middleton's witches have clearly entered into a contract with Satan as detailed in almost all contemporary demonologies, and as questioned by Scot.
27. The devil in Almachildes' shape has had sex with Hecate already.
28. Hecate is unexpectedly passionate and vulnerable as the young man she desires insults her.
29. Irony. In the seventeenth century a lucky guess provoked joking accusation: 'You must be a witch!'
30. The remora fish was thought to suck the hulls of ships and stop them moving. Presumably in a spell to cause impotence it might be thought to impede other processes.
31. Ants.

Firestone [aside]:   You shall see him go nigh to be so unmannerly he'll
          make water before my mother anon.

Almachildes: And now you talk of frogs, I have somewhat here;
          I come not empty-pocketed from a banquet –
          I learned that of my haberdasher's wife.
          Look, goody witch, there's a toad in marchpane for you.
          [Gives][32]

Hecate: O, sir, you've fitted me.

Almachildes: And here's a spawn or two
          Of the same paddock-brood too, for your son. [Gives]

Firestone: I thank your worship, sir. How comes your handkercher so
          sweetly thus berayed? Sure, 'tis wet sucket, sir.[33]

Almachildes: 'Tis nothing but the syrup the toad spit.
          Take all, I prithee.

Hecate: This was kindly done, sir.
          And you shall sup with me tonight for this.

Almachildes: How? With thee? Dost think I'll eat fried rats
          And pickled spiders?

Hecate: No; I can command, sir,
          The best meat i'th'whole province for my friends,
          And reverently served in too.

Almachildes: How?

Hecate: In good fashion.

Almachildes: Let me see but that, and I'll sup with you.

[She conjures, and enter Malkin, a Spirit like a Cat, playing on a fiddle, and
Spirits with meat]

· ·

Act 2, Scene 2

Almachildes: What a mad toy took me to sup with witches?
          Fie of all drunken humours! By this hand
          I could beat myself when I think on't; and the rascals
          Made me good cheer too; and to my understanding then
          Ate some of every dish, and spoiled the rest.
          But coming to my lodging, I remember,
          I was as hungry as a tired foot-post.[34]
          What's this? [Takes from his pocket a ribbon] O, 'tis the charm

---

32. A piece of marzipan shaped like a toad or 'paddock'.
33. The handkerchief must be dirty with the remains of preserved fruits (suckets).
34. The food offered by witches was usually illusory. Almachildes is still hungry, like a tired
     carrier of messages.

her hagship gave me
For my duchess' obstinate woman; wound about
A threepenny silk ribbon of three colours,
Necte Tribus nodis ternos Amoretta colores,
Amoretta! – why there's her name indeed.
Necte – Amoretta – again, two boughts;[35]
Nodo et Veneris dic vincula necte …[36]
The whoreson old hellcat would have given me the brain of a
cat once, in my handkercher – I bad her make sauce with't with
a vengeance! – and a little bone in the nethermost part of a
wolf's tail – I bad her pick her teeth with't, with a pestilence!
Nay this is somewhat cleanly yet and handsome – a coloured
ribbon? A fine, gentle charm; a man may give't his sister, his
brother's wife, ordinarily.[37] See, here she comes luckily.

[Enter Amoretta]

Amoretta: Blest powers, what secret sin have I committed
That still you send this punishment upon me?

Almachildes: 'Tis but a gentle punishment; so take it.

Amoretta: Why, sir, what mean you? Will you ravish me?

Almachildes: What, in the gallery? And the sun peep in?
There's fitter time and place.

[As he embraces her, he thrusts the ribbon into her bosom]
                                      [Aside] 'Tis in her bosom now.

Amoretta: Go, you're the rudest thing e'er came at court.

Almachildes: Well, well. I hope you'll tell me another tale
Ere you be two hours older – a rude thing!
I'll make you eat your word; I'll make all split else. [Exit]

Amoretta: Nay, now I think on't better, I'm to blame too.
There's not a sweeter gentleman at court;
Nobly descended too, and dances well.
Beshrew my heart, I'll take him when there's time;
He will be catched up quickly. The duchess says
She's some employment from him and has sworn me
To use my best art in't. Life of my joys,
There were good stuff! I will not trust her with him.
I'll call him back again. He must not keep
Out of my sight so long; I shall go mad then …

---

35. Knots.
36. 'I take three colours, Amoretta, in three knots, and say "These are the chains of Venus
   that I twine"' (trans. E.V. Rieu). As Corbin and Sedge point out (*Three Jacobean Witchcraft
   Plays*, p. 226, note to lines 11–14), this is adapted from Virgil, Eclogue VIII.
37. Almachildes speculates how he might seduce his sister-in-law.

Amoretta runs after the man she has been bewitched into loving, and meanwhile, at the centre of the play in Act Three, Scene Three, the witches celebrate their powers and prepare for their own sexual adventures in a sabbath.

Act 3, Scene 3
[Enter Hecate, Stadlin, Hoppo, three other Witches and Firestone carrying eggs, herbs and so forth]

Hecate: The moon's a gallant; see how brisk she rides!

Stadlin: Here's a rich evening, Hecate.

Hecate: Ay, is't not, wenches,
            To take a journey of five thousand mile?

Hoppo: Ours will be more tonight.

Hecate: O, 'twill be precious!
            Heard you the owl yet?

Stadlin: Briefly in the copse
            As we came through now.

Hecate: 'Tis high time for us, then.

Stadlin: There was a bat hung at my lips three times
            As we came through the woods and drank her fill.
            Old Puckle saw her.

Hecate: You are fortunate still;
            The very screech-owl lights upon your shoulder
            And woos you like a pigeon. Are you furnished?
            Have you your ointments?

Stadlin: All.

Hecate: Prepare to flight, then.
            I'll overtake you swiftly.

Stadlin: Hie thee, Hecate:
            We shall be up betimes.

Hecate: I'll reach you quickly.

[Exeunt all the Witches except Hecate]

. . . .

Hecate [to Firestone]:   ... Look well to the house tonight; I am for aloft.

Firestone [aside]:   Aloft, quoth you? I would you would break your neck
            once, that I might have all quickly![38] [Music in the air. To
            Hecate] Hark, hark, mother! They are above the steeple already,
            flying over your head with a noise of musicians.

---

38. Firestone is desperate to inherit his mother's goods: his repeated disrespect and lack of
     love, shown in comic asides to the audience, emphasize again Hecate's unexpectedly
     warm nature, and her friendly relations with her 'sisters'.

Hecate: They are there indeed. Help, help me! I'm too late else.

Song [sung by voices in the air]:

> Come away, come away,
> Hecate, Hecate, come away!
> Hecate: I come, I come, I come, I come,
> With all the speed I may,
> With all the speed I may.
> Where's Stadlin?

[Voice] in the air: Here.

Hecate: Where's Puckle?

[Voices] in the air: Here.

> And Hoppo too and Hellwain too;
> We lack but you, we lack but you;
> Come away, make up the count.

Hecate: I will but 'noint and then I mount.

[Hecate anoints herself]

[Malkin] above: There's one comes down to fetch his dues;

> A kiss, a coll, a sip of blood;

[Malkin a Spirit like a Cat descends]

> And why thou stay'st so long
> I muse, I muse.
> Since the air's so sweet and good.

Hecate: O, art thou come?

> What news, what news?

[Malkin]:   All goes still to our delight,

> Either come or else
> Refuse, refuse.

Hecate: Now I am furnished for the flight.

[Malkin sings]

Firestone: Hark, hark? The cat sings a brave treble in her own language!

Hecate, going up [with Malkin]:   Now I go, now I fly,

> Malkin, my sweet spirit, and I.
> O, what a dainty pleasure 'tis
> To ride in the air
> When the moon shines fair
> And sing and dance and toy[39] and kiss;
> Over woods, high rocks and mountains,
> Over seas, our mistress' fountains,[40]

---

39. Flirt.

40. The text is disputed here, but the 'mistress' may mean the moon, which draws up the seas.

>Over steeples, towers and turrets
>We fly by night, 'mongst troops of spirits;
>No ring of bells to our ears sounds,
>No howls of wolves, no yelps of hounds.
>No, not the noise of water's breach
>Or canon's throat our height can reach

[**Voices**] **above**:   No ring of bells, etc.... .

Several plot-twists later, the Duchess, having used Almachildes in her schemes as Amoretta mentioned, wants to get rid of him and comes to Hecate for help.

Act 5, Scene 2
[Enter Duchess, Hecate, Firestone; a cauldron in the centre]

Hecate: What death is't you desire for Almachildes?

Duchess: A sudden and a subtle.

Hecate: Then I have fitted you.
Here lie the gifts of both sudden and subtle.
His picture made in wax and gently molten
By a blue fire kindled with dead men's eyes
Will waste him by degrees.

Duchess: In what time, 'prithee?

Hecate: Perhaps in a moon's progress.

Duchess: What? A month?
Out upon pictures if they be so tedious!
Give me things with some life.

Hecate: Then seek no farther.

Duchess: This must be done with speed. Dispatched this night
If it may be possible.

Hecate: I have it for you;
Here's that will do't. Stay but perfection's time
And that's not five hours hence.

Duchess: Can'st thou do this?

Hecate: Can I?

Duchess: I mean so closely?

Hecate: So closely do you mean too?

Duchess: So artfully, so cunningly?

Hecate: Worse and worse: doubts and incredulities!
They make me mad. Let scrupulous greatness[41] know:

---

41. Hecate refers to the Duchess herself: distrustful and high-and-mighty.

Cam volui ripis ipsis mirantibus amnes
In fontes rediere suos, concussaque sisto,
Stantia concutio, cantu freta nubila pello,
Nubilaque induco, ventos, abigoque vocoque
Viperias rumpo verbis et carmine fauces,
Et siluas moueo, iubeoque tremiscere montes
Et mugire solum, manesque exire sepulchris.
Teque, luna, traho.[42] Can you doubt me then, daughter?
That can make mountains tremble, miles of woods walk,
Whole earth's foundation bellow and the spirits
Of the entombed to burst out of their marbles,
Nay, draw yond moon to my involved[43] designs?

Firestone [aside]:   I know as well as can be when my mother's mad and
our great cat angry: for one spits French then and th'other spits
Latin.

Duchess: I did not doubt you, mother.

Hecate: No? What did you?
My power's so firm, it is not to be questioned.

Duchess: Forgive what's past; and now I know th'offensiveness
That vexes art, I'll shun th'occasion ever.

Hecate: Leave all to me and my five sisters, daughter.
It shall be conveyed in at howlet-time.[44]
Take you no care, my spirits know their moments.
Raven or screech-owl never fly by th'door
But they call in – I thank 'em – and they lose not by't.
I give 'em barley soaked in infant's blood.
They shall have *semina cum sanguine*,[45]
Their gorge crammed full, if they come once to our house.
We are no niggard ...

Hecate: Give me some lizard's brain. Quickly, Firestone!

[Firestone brings the different ingredients for the charm as Hecate calls for
them]

---

42. This passage from Ovid (*Metamorphoses*, 7.199) appears in Scot but, as Corbin and Sedge
show (*Three Jacobean Witchcraft Plays*, p. 230, note to lines 18–25), because Middleton
omits a line in the same way as Bodin does in his *Daemonomania*, it has been suggested
that he took it from Bodin directly. Scot's translation is: The rivers I can make retire, Into
the fountains whence they flo, (Whereat the banks themselves admire), I can make the
standing waters go, With charmes I drive both sea and clowd, I make it calme and blowe
alowd. The vipers jawes, the rockie stone, With words and charmes I breake in twaine,
The force of earth congeald in one, I moove and shake both woods and plaine; I make the
soules of men arise. I pull the moon out of the skies (Scot, book 12, chapter 7).
43. Underhand.
44. At night, when the owls are active.
45. Seed with blood.

Where's Grannam Stadlin and all the rest o'th'sisters?

Firestone: All at hand, forsooth.

[Enter Stadlin, Hoppo, and the three other Witches]

Hecate: Give me marmaritin; some bear-breech.[46] When!

Firestone: Here's bear-breech and lizard's brain, forsooth.

Hecate: Into the vessel;
And fetch three ounces of the red-haired girl
I killed last midnight.

Firestone: Whereabouts, sweet mother?

Hecate: Hip; hip or flank. Where is the *acopus*?[47]

Firestone: You shall have *acopus*, forsooth.

Hecate: Stir, stir about, whilst I begin the charm.

[They sing a charm-song about a vessel]

Black spirits and white; red spirits and grey,
Mingle, mingle, mingle, you that mingle may.
Titty, Tiffin,
Keep it stiff in;
Firedrake, Puckey,
Make it lucky;
Liard, Robin,
You must bob in.[48]
Round, around, around, about, about!
All ill come running in, all good keep out!

First Witch: Here's the blood of a bat.

Hecate: Put in that, O put in that!

Second Witch: Here's libbard's bane.[49]

Hecate: Put in a grain.

First Witch: The juice of toad, the oil of adder.

Second Witch: Those will make the younker[50] madder.

Hecate: Put in – there's all; and rid the stench.

Firestone: Nay, here's three ounces of the red-haired wench.

All [Witches]:   Round, around, around, etc.

Hecate: So, so, enough. Into the vessel with it.
There, 't hath the true perfection. I am so light
At any mischief; there's no villainy
But is a tune methinks.

---

46. Acanthus.
47. A soothing salve.
48. The spirits' names are again from *A true and just Recorde*.
49. Leopard's bane, doronicum.
50. Youngster.

Firestone [aside]:   A tune? 'Tis to the tune of damnation, then, I warrant
you, and that song hath a villainous burden.

Hecate: Come, my sweet sisters. Let the air strike our tune
Whilst we show reverence to yond peeping moon.

[Here they dance The Witches Dance and exeunt][51]

As court events come to a bloody conclusion of conflicting intrigues, it is interesting that those who consulted the witches (Sebastian, Almachildes and the Duchess) escape relatively lightly. Contrastingly, the witches' main victim Antonio and his corrupt followers are those who suffer most – he is made impotent and later dies in an accident just as Sebastian had hoped. The witches seem to be on the side of good, despite the problematic nature of their clients' requests and their own repulsive and exploitative practices.

2. Tragedy

William Shakespeare, Macbeth *(1606?)*

William Shakespeare's *Macbeth* is perhaps the most famous depiction of witches on the stage. The 'weird sisters', with their economical, rhythmic and riddling speeches, create in a few short scenes an oppressive atmosphere of evil and mystery which blights the whole play. The drama of Macbeth and Lady Macbeth, who murder King Duncan to seize the throne of Scotland after the witches prophesy Macbeth's succession, is played out amid constant unresolved questioning. Did the witches cause the murder and those that come after it? Did they simply bring out Macbeth's own evil? Is Lady Macbeth a witch? What are the witches themselves – Nordic goddesses (Norns), Fates, sibyls, fairies, sorceresses?[52] Attention is directed towards the source of evil, but nothing is revealed and the audience and readers, like the characters, are left unsatisfied.

Shakespeare's witches are ambiguous creatures, partly because of the play's context and partly because they are drawn from a variety of sources. Firstly, the play is Jacobean, and is framed to accommodate the new Scottish king's well-known interest in demonology, without committing itself to many specific details. Shakespeare probably drew on James' own encounter with witches in 1591, when a group of them were accused of trying to sink his ship

---

51. This seems also to be used in *Macbeth* (below) and is possibly the dance that Ben Jonson conceived for his witches in *The Masque of Queenes* (below), consisting of dancing back-to-back, with strange gestures contrary to all usual human motion.

52. John Dover Wilson best sums up the sisters' nature: 'too witch-like to be Norns, too Norn-like to be witches' (*The Works of Shakespeare edited for the Syndics of the Cambridge University Press: Macbeth* (Cambridge: Cambridge University Press, 1947), p. xxi).

and do him other harms,[53] as well as Raphael Holinshed's *Chronicles*, with its 'Historie of Scotland' mentioning witches at Forres, and other Scottish histories.[54] Witches and Scots were both of particular interest to early Jacobean Londoners, and it is hard to read Shakespeare's blending of the two without seeing a compliment to the king and also a certain advantage in leaving demonological conclusions elusive. It is even possible that the play was performed before James, but no evidence of a specific occasion exists.

Secondly, Shakespeare returned repeatedly to the creation of witches, spirits, fairies, semi-divine characters and soothsayers as drivers and resolvers of plot in his plays, often synthesizing imagery from different literary and oral sources so that he combined Greek myth with English folklore, Classical and European high magic with New World travellers' tales, implying everything from complete scepticism about magic (*The Comedy of Errors, Henry IV Part 1*) to willing immersion in the otherworldly (*A Midsummer Night's Dream, The Tempest* – the two examples above). We do not know how his Scottish witches were portrayed in the first productions (comic or sinister?), and Shakespeare's sources and previous writings give us only limited clues.

From a series of much-debated topical references, the play has been dated most convincingly to late 1606, but there is further textual confusion in that it appears to survive as a revised, rather than an original text. Certainly, as printed in the First Folio of Shakespeare's plays in 1623, it shares some text with Thomas Middleton's *The Witch* (see above and below). Victorian and early-twentieth-century critics delighted in condemning different parts of the play, including the first witch-scene and the anecdote of the sailor's wife, as 'turgid bombast ... ludicrous and impertinent', and (therefore) clearly not by Shakespeare.[55] Most of the play is, however, now thought to be his, and it has been argued (for example, by Nicholas Brooke in the Oxford edition)[56] that it was not wantonly vandalized but sparingly revised for performance, perhaps at the Blackfriars theatre. The Blackfriars had machinery enabling the witches to fly, and it was an indoor space, unlike the Globe, charging higher ticket prices and providing a more courtly form of entertainment, with more song and dance. Thus, Middleton or another dramatist probably added material (it is unclear precisely when, just as *The Witch*'s date is unclear), notably the parts of the text featuring Hecate, the songs in 4.1, and The Witches' Dance. Certainly, astrologer Simon Forman saw the play at the Globe in 1611 and did not

53. See *Newes from Scotland* (London, 1591), which is reprinted together with James' *Daemonologie* and documents from the North Berwick trials in Lawrence Normand and Gareth Roberts, eds, *Witchcraft in Early Modern Scotland* (Exeter: University of Exeter Press, 2000).
54. For Holinshed's version, see Kenneth Muir, ed., *The Arden Shakespeare: Macbeth*, rev. edn. (1951; London: Methuen, 1984), Appendix A.
55. Henry Cunningham, ed., *The Works of Shakespeare: Macbeth* (London: Methuen, 1912), pp. xxiii–xxviii.
56. Nicholas Brooke, ed., *The Oxford Shakespeare: Macbeth* (Oxford: Oxford University Press, 1999). This edition includes the maximum amount of text taken from *The Witch*.

mention these elements, although Forman is not the most reliable of critics.[57] Recent scholarship agrees that the text we have is probably a revision interwoven with a script from the playhouse itself, rather than a fully integrated text intended for publication.

As some of the probable additions – the songs – are indicated only by a few words, and an expansion from those words is found in *The Witch,* scholars are unsure how much text the two plays share, and modern editions choose differently how much of *The Witch* to incorporate. The text used here is edited from the First Folio in the Folger Shakespeare Library, and also indebted to the New Cambridge edition, edited by A. R. Braunmuller, which does not add the full text of the songs, or additional dialogue, to the Folio text. Readers can find the song texts and dialogue that may have been added to *Macbeth* in *The Witch* itself (above).[58]

Act 1, Scene 1
[Thunder and lightning. Enter three Witches][59]

First Witch: When shall we three meet again?
                      In thunder, lightning, or in rain?
Second Witch: When the hurly-burly's[60] done,
                      When the battle's lost, and won.[61]
Third Witch: That will be ere the set of sun.
First Witch: Where the place?
Second Witch: Upon the heath.
Third Witch: There to meet with Macbeth.
First Witch: I come, Gray-malkin.
Second Witch: Paddock calls.
Third Witch: Anon.[62]
All: Fair is foul and foul is fair,
              Hover through the fog and filthy air. [Exeunt]

---

57. For Forman's account, see Muir, ed., *The Arden Shakespeare: Macbeth*, pp. xv–xvi.
58. Professor Braunmuller's excellent notes have been very helpful in preparing this abridged, re-edited text, with his kind permission.
59. The word 'witch' occurs only once in the play's speeches (1.3.5) but original stage directions repeatedly use the word.
60. Commotion.
61. The play begins as King Duncan emerges victorious from a bloody battle with Nordic invaders and Scottish rebels, in which Macbeth had fought fiercely for the King.
62. The three women are responding to the calls of familiars – a cat (malkin), toad (paddock) and another, later named Harpier. The Folio has all three witches speak the last four lines, but this appears to be an error.

Act 1, Scene 3
[Thunder. Enter the three Witches]

First Witch: Where hast thou been, sister?

Second Witch: Killing swine.

Third Witch: Sister, where thou?

First Witch: A sailor's wife had chestnuts in her lap
                    And munched, and munched, and munched. 'Give me', quoth I.
                    'Aroint thee, witch', the rump-fed runnion cries.[63]
                    Her husband's to Aleppo gone, master o'th'Tiger:[64]
                    But in a sieve I'll thither sail,[65]
                    And like a rat without a tail,
                    I'll do, [and] I'll do, and I'll do.

Second Witch: I'll give thee a wind.

First Witch: Th'art kind.

Third Witch: And I another.

First Witch: I myself have all the other,
                    And the very ports they blow,
                    All the quarters that they know
                    I'th'shipman's card.[66]
                    I'll drain him dry as hay:[67]
                    Sleep shall neither night nor day
                    Hang upon his penthouse lid;[68]
                    He shall live a man forbid.[69]
                    Weary sennights, nine times nine,[70]
                    Shall he dwindle, peak, and pine.
                    Though his bark[71] cannot be lost,
                    Yet it shall be tempest-tossed.
                    Look what I have.

---

63. 'Aroint' is similar to the better-known 'avaunt!', whilst the 'rump-fed runnion' suggests a well-fed, fat-rumped woman – a term of abuse.

64. Aleppo is in modern Syria; *Tiger* is the name of the man's ship.

65. The North Berwick witches, in whose trial King James took part, said they sailed in sieves (see Normand and Roberts, *Newes from Scotland*, p. 314 etc.). They also attempted to divert or sink his ship with stormy weather.

66. The four directions from which winds might come, on the 'card' or chart the compass.

67. This sounds sexual. See *The Witch* for succubic witches who 'spoil' their victims.

68. Eyelid.

69. Cursed, forespoken.

70. Eighty-one weeks. In 1956 E. A. Loomis identified an actual stormy voyage of this length made by a ship named *Tiger*, from Cowes, Isle of Wight, to Japan, via the Middle East. This ship, returning in June 1606, probably helps date the play to late summer 1606 (see Brooke, ed., *The Oxford Shakespeare: Macbeth*, pp. 61–2, for discussion).

71. Ship, barque.

Second Witch: Show me, show me.

First Witch: Here I have a pilot's thumb,
        Wrecked, as homeward he did come.

[Drum within]

Third Witch: A drum, a drum;
        Macbeth doth come.

All: The weird[72] sisters, hand in hand,
        Posters[73] of the sea and land,
        Thus do go, about, about,
        Thrice to thine, and thrice to mine,
        And thrice again, to make up nine.
        Peace, the charm's wound up.[74]

[Enter Macbeth and Banquo]

Macbeth: So foul and fair a day I have not seen.

Banquo: How far is't called to Forres?[75] What are these,
        So withered, and so wild in their attire,
        That look not like th'inhabitants o'th'earth,
        And yet are on't? Live you, or are you aught
        That man may question? You seem to understand me,
        By each at once her choppy[76] finger laying
        Upon her skinny lips; you should be women,
        And yet your beards forbid me to interpret
        That you are so.

Macbeth: Speak if you can: what are you?

First Witch: All hail Macbeth, hail to thee, Thane of Glamis.[77]

---

72. The Folio spelling means that this word wavers awkwardly throughout the play between 'wayward' and 'weird' (weyward, weyard), and the famous spelling here has been used since Lewis Theobald's 1733 edition, based on Holinshed's use of 'weird'. Holinshed was following an early Scottish chronicle describing 'werd' sisters (Andrew of Wyntoun, *The Orygnale Cronykil of Scotland, c.* 1424), and John Bellenden's translation of Hector Boece's *Scotorum Historiae* using 'weird' (*The Hystory and Croniklis of Scotland, c.* 1540). The word 'weird' was used for the three Fates, and implied a power over destiny. For the fullest recent discussion, see Braunmuller, ed., *Macbeth*, pp. 239–40. Onions suggests 'perverted' as an appropriate gloss of 'weyward' here (C. T. Onions, *A Shakespeare Glossary* (ed. Robert D. Eagleson), rev. edn (Oxford: Clarendon Press, 1986), p. 313).
73. Travellers.
74. Elizabeth Bennett (see *A true and just Recorde* above) also suggests charms are 'wound up' – ended and bound into efficacy. Witches sometimes made corresponding knot charms, such as Hecate's love charm in *The Witch* (above).
75. In north-west Scotland near Inverness. It is not clear where Macbeth and Banquo are coming from, but Banquo is asking how far away Forres is.
76. Chapped.
77. Macbeth is head of his clan (thane) and his castle is in Glamis, near Dundee (usually pronounced 'Glarms').

Second Witch: All hail Macbeth, hail to thee, Thane of Cawdor.[78]

Third Witch: All hail Macbeth, that shalt be king hereafter.

Banquo: Good sir, why do you start and seem to fear
       Things that do sound so fair? I'th'name of truth
       Are ye fantastical,[79] or that indeed
       Which outwardly ye show? My noble partner
       You greet with present grace, and great prediction
       Of noble having, and of royal hope
       That he seems rapt withal: to me you speak not.
       If you can look into the seeds of time,
       And say, which grain will grow, and which will not,
       Speak then to me, who neither beg nor fear
       Your favours, nor your hate.

First Witch: Hail.

Second Witch: Hail.

Third Witch: Hail.

First Witch: Lesser than Macbeth, and greater.

Second Witch: Not so happy, yet much happier

Third Witch: Thou shalt get[80] kings, though thou be none.
       So all hail Macbeth and Banquo.

First Witch: Banquo and Macbeth, all hail.

Macbeth: Stay, you imperfect speakers, tell me more.
       By Finel's death, I know I am Thane of Glamis;[81]
       But how of Cawdor? The Thane of Cawdor lives
       A prosperous gentleman; and to be king
       Stands not within the prospect of belief,
       No more than to be Cawdor. Say from whence
       You owe this strange intelligence, or why
       Upon this blasted heath you stop our way
       With such prophetic greeting? Speak, I charge you.

[Witches vanish]

Banquo: The earth hath bubbles, as the water has,
       And these are of them: whither are they vanished?

---

78. In 1.2 the audience heard of the Thane of Cawdor's recently discovered treachery and death, and saw King Duncan promising to confer his title on Macbeth, who has not yet heard the news.

79. Imaginary.

80. Beget.

81. As Braunmuller explains, he has substituted 'Finel' for the traditional reading 'Sinel' because that is based on a confusion in Holinshed between 'f' and a long 's'. Finel was the historical Macbeth's father (Braunmuller, ed., *Macbeth*, p. 113 n.69).

Macbeth: Into the air, and what seemed corporal,
              Melted, as breath into the wind. Would they had stayed …

Macbeth returns home to his wife, and she urges him to murder King Duncan, taking on witch-like attributes herself as she (metaphorically?) summons spirits to unsex her, and fill her with cruelty. Macbeth kills the king, and blames the murder on his attendants, who are executed for it. Duncan's sons flee, fearing for their own safety, and Macbeth becomes king. However, he becomes increasingly suspicious of other lords and has Banquo murdered because he is afraid of the witches' prophecy that Banquo's children will succeed to the throne. Banquo's son escapes, and Banquo's ghost returns to haunt the increasingly haggard and sleepless Macbeth. At this moment, the witches reappear.

Act 3, Scene 5
[Thunder. Enter the three Witches, meeting Hecate]

First Witch: Why how now, Hecate,[82] you look angerly?[83]
Hecate: Have I not reason (beldams)[84] as you are?
              Saucy and over-bold, how did you dare
              To trade, and traffic with Macbeth
              In riddles, and affairs of death;
              And I the mistress of your charms,
              The close contriver of all harms,
              Was never called to bear my part
              Or show the glory of our art?
              And which is worse, all you have done
              Hath been but for a wayward son,
              Spiteful, and wrathful, who (as others do)
              Loves for his own ends, not for you.
              But make amends now. Get you gone,
              And at the pit of Acheron[85]
              Meet me i'th'morning: thither he
              Will come to know his destiny.
              Your vessels, and your spells provide,

---

82. The Folio reads 'Hecat', showing the pronunciation demanded by the rhythm.
83. This is the first appearance of Hecate and has led many critics to suspect Middleton's or another's hand. Hecate's verse has different patterns to that previously used by the witches (iambic rhythm as against trochaic; see G. K. Hunter, ed., *The New Penguin Shakespeare: Macbeth* (London: Penguin, 1967), pp. 42–3, for discussion) and her anger seems out of place: actually, the three witches have precipitated spectacular chaos in Scotland with a few well-chosen words.
84. Hags.
85. A river in Hades. Suddenly the witches are shifted into a classical landscape and specifically to the classical hell.

Your charms; and everything beside.
I am for th'air. This night I'll spend
Unto a dismal and a fatal end.
Great business must be wrought ere noon.
Upon the corner of the moon
There hangs a vap'rous drop, profound;[86]
I'll catch it ere it come to ground;
And that distilled by magic sleights,
Shall raise such artificial sprites
As by the strength of their illusion
Shall draw him on to his confusion.[87]
He shall spurn fate, scorn death, and bear
His hopes 'bove wisdom, grace, and fear.
And you all know, security
Is mortals' chiefest enemy.

[Music, and a song. Sing within. 'Come away, come away', etc.][88]

Hark, I am called: my little spirit, see,
Sits in a foggy cloud, and stays for me. [Exit]

First Witch: Come, let's make haste; she'll soon be back again. [Exeunt]

Act 4, Scene 1
[Thunder. Enter the three Witches with a cauldron]

First Witch: Thrice the brindled cat hath mewed.
Second Witch: Thrice, and once the hedge-pig[89] whined.
Third Witch: Harpier cries, ''Tis time, 'tis time.'[90]
First Witch: Round about the cauldron go;
In the poisoned entrails throw
Toad, that under cold stone,
Days and nights has thirty-one:
Sweltered venom sleeping got,
Boil thou first i'th'charmed pot.
All: Double, double, toil and trouble;
Fire burn, and cauldron bubble.
Second Witch: Fillet of a fenny[91] snake,

---

86. The moon was believed to drip a magical substance.
87. The references to artifice and illusion may suggest deceit: without this passage, the spirits the witches later raise become more truthful and independent.
88. Compare with *The Witch* (above). The two stage directions fused here were originally separated (after 'song') by Hecate's last two lines, but must refer to the same music, as Hecate's 'I am called' indicates.
89. Hedgehog.
90. See note 62.
91. Fenland, marshland.

> In the cauldron boil and bake:
> Eye of newt, and toe of frog,
> Wool of bat, and tongue of dog.
> Adder's fork, and blind-worm's[92] sting,
> Lizard's leg, and howlet's[93] wing:
> For a charm of powerful trouble,
> Like a hell-broth, boil and bubble.

All: Double, double, toil and trouble;
> Fire burn, and cauldron bubble.

Third Witch: Scale of dragon, tooth of wolf,
> Witches' mummy,[94] maw and gulf[95]
> Of the ravined[96] salt-sea shark;
> Root of hemlock,[97] digged i'th'dark;
> Liver of blaspheming Jew,[98]
> Gall of goat, and slips of yew,[99]
> Slivered in the moon's eclipse;
> Nose of Turk, and Tartar's lips;
> Finger of birth-strangled babe,
> Ditch-delivered by a drab,[100]
> Make the gruel thick, and slab.[101]
> Add thereto a tiger's chawdron,[102]
> For th'ingredience of our cauldron.

All: Double, double, toil and trouble;
> Fire burn, and cauldron bubble.

Second Witch: Cool it with a baboon's blood,
> Then the charm is firm and good.

[Enter Hecate, and the other three Witches]

Hecate: O well done! I commend your pains,
> And every one shall share i'th'gains;
> And now about the cauldron sing

---

92. Slow-worm, actually a harmless snake-like creature neither blind nor slow.
93. Owlet's.
94. Dead flesh, which witches were thought to use in charms. See Middleton's Hecate's use of body-parts and ointment made from children's boiled fat (above).
95. Mouth, voracious belly or appetite.
96. Greedily gorged.
97. A plant used to make poison.
98. Jews were held to blaspheme by being 'misbelievers'. See also the Muslim Turks and Tartars below.
99. A poisonous tree.
100. A victim of infanticide, the child is born in a ditch to a whore.
101. Viscous. Gruel was usually thin.
102. Entrails.

Like elves and fairies in a ring,
Enchanting all that you put in.

[Music, and a song, 'Black spirits, etc.' Exeunt Hecate and the other three Witches][103]

Second Witch: By the pricking of my thumbs,
Something wicked this way comes;
Open locks, whoever knocks.

[Enter Macbeth]

Macbeth: How now, you secret, black, and midnight hags?
What is't you do?

All the Witches: A deed without a name.

Macbeth: I conjure you by that which you profess
(Howe'er you come to know it) answer me:
Though you untie the winds, and let them fight
Against the churches; though the yeasty[104] waves
Confound and swallow navigation up;
Though bladed corn be lodged,[105] and trees blown down,
Though castles topple on their warders'[106] heads;
Though palaces and pyramids do slope
Their heads to their foundations; though the treasure
Of nature's germen[107] tumble altogether
Even till destruction sicken: answer me
To what I ask you.

First Witch: Speak.

Second Witch: Demand.

Third Witch: We'll answer.

First Witch: Say, if thou'dst rather hear it from our mouths,
Or from our masters'?[108]

Macbeth: Call 'em: let me see 'em.

First Witch: Pour in sow's blood, that hath eaten
Her nine farrow;[109] grease that's sweaten
From the murderer's gibbet, throw
Into the flame.

---

103. See *The Witch* (above). It is assumed that Hecate and the 'other three' witches exit here.
104. Frothing.
105. Flattened.
106. Wardens'.
107. Usually 'germens' but Braunmuller follows the Folio's singular here. The essence or material 'germ' of Nature's creativeness.
108. The masters are clearly plural, not (for example) simply Satan.
109. Piglets.

All the Witches: Come high or low:
        Thyself and office deftly show.

[Thunder. Enter First Apparition, an armed Head]

Macbeth: Tell me, thou unknown power --
First Witch: He knows thy thought;
        Hear his speech, but say thou nought.
First apparition: Macbeth, Macbeth, Macbeth: beware Macduff,
        Beware the Thane of Fife.[110] Dismiss me. Enough. [He descends]
Macbeth: Whate'er thou art, for thy good caution, thanks;
        Thou hast harped my fear aright. But one word more –
First Witch: He will not be commanded. Here's another,
        More potent than the first.

[Thunder. Enter Second Apparition, a bloody Child]

Second apparition: Macbeth, Macbeth, Macbeth.
Macbeth: Had I three ears, I'd hear thee.
Second apparition: Be bloody, bold, and resolute: laugh to scorn
        The power of man; for none of woman born
        Shall harm Macbeth. [Descends]
Macbeth: Then live, Macduff: what need I fear of thee?[111]
        But yet I'll make assurance double sure,
        And take a bond of fate: thou shalt not live,
        That I may tell pale-hearted fear, it lies,
        And sleep in spite of thunder.

[Thunder. Enter Third Apparition, a Child crowned, with a tree in his hand]

                         What is this,
        That rises like the issue[112] of a king,
        And wears upon his baby-brow, the round
        And top of sovereignty?
All the Witches: Listen, but speak not to't.
Third apparition: Be lion-mettled, proud, and take no care
        Who chafes, who frets, or where conspirers are:

---

110. A peninsula south of Glamis. Macbeth will later have Macduff's family murdered at their
    castle there.
111. The vision leads Macbeth into a trap – Macduff was not, technically, born but delivered
    by Caesarean operation. He will kill Macbeth, thus fulfilling the letter of the prophecy.
112. Child.

Macbeth shall never vanquished be, until
Great Birnam Wood, to high Dunsinane hill
Shall come against him.[113] [Descends]

Macbeth: That will never be:
Who can impress the forest, bid the tree
Unfix his earthbound root? Sweet bodements,[114] good.
Rebellious dead,[115] rise never till the wood
Of Birnam rise, and our high-placed Macbeth
Shall live the lease of nature, pay his breath
To time, and mortal custom.[116] Yet my heart
Throbs to know one thing: tell me, if your art
Can tell so much; shall Banquo's issue ever
Reign in this kingdom?

All the Witches: Seek to know no more.

Macbeth: I will be satisfied. Deny me this,
And an eternal curse fall on you: let me know! [Cauldron
descends. Hautboys]
Why sinks that cauldron? And what noise is this?

First Witch: Show!

Second Witch: Show!

Third Witch: Show!

All the Witches: Show his eyes, and grieve his heart,
Come like shadows, so depart.

[Enter a show of eight kings, and the last with a glass in his hand; Banquo's
Ghost following][117]

---

113. Once again, a deceiving truth. The forces of Duncan's sons cut tree branches from the
wood to shield them in their advance on Macbeth's castle – hence the wood does appear
to move, and Macbeth is defeated by 'it'.
114. Predictions.
115. Banquo.
116. Macbeth thinks he will live out his natural term of life.
117. In general terms, these are the eight Stuart kings, the last being James I, omitting the Stuart
Queen Mary (of Scots, 1542–87). James spent much of his younger life in political conflict
with Mary, his mother, who was eventually executed by the English, and her omission is
probably tactful. However, the detail is very confused. The Folio stage direction and text
suggest difficulty over who is carrying the glass (mirror, but more likely scrying glass or
'crystal ball' to see future kings). The stage direction suggests it is Banquo (this is emended
by Braunmuller, like other modern editors), but Banquo appears to be separated from the
lineal show at the end of Macbeth's description of it. The double and triple signs of
kingship presumably refer to James as king of both England and Scotland (to say nothing of
Wales, Ireland and notionally France). In 1951, Richard Flatter wrote to the *Times Literary
Supplement* to suggest that if *Macbeth* had been performed at court, an ordinary mirror could
have been held by the eighth king to show James his own face and his descendants'
(23.3.51, p. 181). Although the argument on which the more fanciful ideas of royal
involvement were based has been rebutted, this element remains a seductive idea.

Macbeth: Thou art too like the spirit of Banquo. Down!
Thy crown does sear mine eyeballs. And thy hair
Thou other gold-bound brow, is like the first;
A third, is like the former. Filthy hags,
Why do you show me this? – A fourth? Start, eyes!
What, will the line stretch out to th'crack of doom?
Another yet? A seventh? I'll see no more:
And yet the eighth appears, who bears a glass,
Which shows me many more: and some I see,
That two-fold balls and treble sceptres carry.
Horrible sight! Now I see 'tis true,
For the blood-boltered[118] Banquo smiles upon me,
And points at them for his. [Exeunt show of kings and Banquo's Ghost]
What? Is this so?

First Witch: Ay, sir, all this is so. But why
Stands Macbeth thus amazedly?
Come sisters, cheer we up his sprites,[119]
And show the best of our delights.
I'll charm the air to give a sound,
While you perform your antic round:
That this great king may kindly say,
Our duties did his welcome pay.

[Music. The Witches dance, and vanish]

3. Tragi-comic documentary

John Ford, Thomas Dekker and William Rowley, The Witch of Edmonton *(1621)*[120]

In 1621 a London minister, Henry Goodcole, wrote a pamphlet entitled *The wonderfull discoverie of Elizabeth Sawyer a Witch, late of Edmonton, her conviction and condemnation and Death.* Published shortly after the witch's execution in April, it detailed Goodcole's conversation with her after her

---

118. Blood-clotted.
119. The sudden breaking of the mood again suggests revision, introducing the witches' dance. The final lines hardly apply to Macbeth, and it is tempting to wonder if they were addressed to James, either in a possible court performance or in the abstract.
120. The play also appears in Peter Corbin and Douglas Sedge, eds, *Three Jacobean Witchcraft Plays*, and their excellent notes have been very helpful in preparing this text.

conviction, in his capacity as a prison chaplain. This was a role that Goodcole had used before to gather material for publications of a moralistic kind, and like his earlier pamphlets *The wonderfull discoverie* was intended to teach its readers to beware of sin. As part of that lesson it gave the convicted felon a voice within its text, setting up a dialogue between the questioning Goodcole and the answering, penitent Sawyer, and it was perhaps partly this vivid representation of the condemned woman that interested the playwrights in her story. Goodcole's portrait of Elizabeth Sawyer is not a sympathetic one, showing her as old, ugly, ignorant and guilty of great wickedness, but it does show her also as a victim of the devil's bullying and lust for creating human misery. Both these viewpoints found their way into the play based on Goodcole's pamphlet, which was performed in 1621.

However, the playwrights added material of their own. The creation of the play's main plot, in which the devil induces a young man to commit murder, was the most substantial change. The playwrights also demonstrated their demonological reading by inserting discussions of the devil's abilities and methods, and added a titillating succubus. But, most interestingly, the character of the witch herself was given depth and background, building on details from Goodcole and adding a social context for witchcraft which is the target of both moral censure and satire in the play. By emphasizing her poverty (which Goodcole mentions only in passing), her consequent vulnerability to abuse and violence from her neighbours (especially the playwrights' invention, the vicious Old Banks), and her isolation, they gave her clear and understandable motives for turning to the devil. In this they were almost certainly influenced by Scot and Gifford (above). The Elizabeth Sawyer of the play is memorable as a combined incarnation of Scot's stereotypical victim of witchcraft accusation, a desperate, miserable old woman seeking charity and acceptance, and Gifford's stereo-typical sinner, who was first led astray and then betrayed by the wily devil. Where Goodcole flattens Sawyer's character, evidently tailoring his account of her to promote the moral of his story, the playwrights expand it and set up a moving and suspenseful relationship between the woman, her fellow-villagers and her devil-dog which is unlike any other representation of witchcraft in the theatre.

Frustratingly little is known about the writing of the play. The relationship between the three named dramatists is uncertain, and likely to remain so. It was not uncommon for teams of writers to work together on a script, each being assigned to different areas of the plot, and there may even have been other collaborators on the project. *The Witch of Edmonton* is the first known play of John Ford (1586–*c.* 1640) and perhaps marks his first engagement with writing about the victims of social convention and prejudice. Two of his later plays dealt with the misery of an unwanted arranged marriage and the theme of incestuous love (*The Broken Heart* (1629) and *'Tis Pity She's a Whore* (first performed 1632)). Thomas Dekker (*c.* 1570–1632) was already an experienced dramatist, collaborating with John Marston, Thomas Middleton and Philip Massinger in a long and prolific career, concentrating on comedy and pamphlet satires. William Rowley (*c.* 1585–1626), another of Middleton's collaborators, was also an actor and may have played the role of Cuddy Banks.[121] Despite early success, the play was not published until 1658. The text used here is in the Huntington Library.

Like Middleton's *The Witch* (above), the play begins with characters from respectable society – instead of Italian courtiers, they are English farmers and country gentlemen – whose sins and difficulties are leading them towards a collision with the magical, devilish world of the witches. Sir Arthur Clarington has made his servant Winnifride pregnant, and plans to marry her to her other, unsuspecting, lover Frank Thorney so that her child will seem to be Frank's. However, Frank's landowner father wants his son to marry the virtuous Susan Carter and has agreed the mutually beneficial match with her father, a rich yeoman. The ironically named Frank, already married to Winnifride, weakly agrees to the bigamous second wedding because it will make him and his family rich, and is therefore trapped by his former lust and present shame and greed. The play chooses this moment to introduce the witch. Like Winnifride, she is a victim of her own desires and the callousness of others, and like Frank she will soon fall victim to the temptations of power and love.

Act 2, Scene 1
[Enter Elizabeth Sawyer gathering sticks]

Elizabeth Sawyer: And why on me? Why should the envious world
Throw all their scandalous malice upon me?
'Cause I am poor, deformed and ignorant,
And like a bow buckled and bent together,
By some more strong in mischiefs than myself?
Must I for that be made a common sink,
For all the filth and rubbish of men's tongues
To fall and run into? Some call me witch;
And being ignorant of myself, they go
About to teach me how to be one; urging,
That my bad tongue (by their bad usage made so)
Forespeaks their cattle, doth bewitch their corn,
Themselves, their servants, and their babes at nurse.

[Enter Old Banks]

This they enforce upon me: and in part
Make me to credit it.[122] And here comes one
Of my chief adversaries.

121. See Simon Trussler's introduction to Dekker, Ford and Rowley, *The Witch of Edmonton* (London: Methuen, 1983), p. ix.
122. It is hard to imagine a clearer statement of Scot's ideas. Although unconvincingly placed in the mouth of an old, poor, uneducated woman, this speech sets the tone of the play.

Old Banks: Out, out upon thee, witch!

Elizabeth Sawyer: Dost call me witch?

Old Banks: I do, witch, I do: and worse I would, knew I a name more hateful. What makest thou upon my ground?

Elizabeth Sawyer: Gather a few rotten sticks to warm me.

Old Banks: Down with them when I bid thee, quickly; I'll make thy bones rattle in thy skin else.

Elizabeth Sawyer: You won't, churl, cut-throat, miser! [Throws down sticks] There they be. Would they stuck 'cross thy throat, thy bowels, thy maw, thy midriff.

Old Banks: Sayest thou me so? Hag, out of my ground! [Beats her]

Elizabeth Sawyer: Dost strike me, slave? Curmudgeon, now thy bones ache, thy joints cramp, and convulsions stretch and crack thy sinews!

Old Banks: Cursing, thou hag! Take that and that. [Beats her and exit]

Elizabeth Sawyer: Strike, do, and withered may that hand and arm
Whose blows have lamed me, drop from that rotten trunk.
Abuse me! Beat me! Call me hag and witch!
What is the name? Where and by what art learned?
What spells, what charms or invocations?
May the thing called Familiar be purchased? . . .

Then arrive a group of morris-dancers and Cuddy Banks, son of Old Banks. They flee from her, mocking her missing eye, a detail taken from Goodcole's account.

All: Away with the Witch of Edmonton!

[Exeunt in strange postures]

Elizabeth Sawyer: Still vexed? Still tortured? That curmudgeon Banks
Is ground of all my scandal. I am shunned
And hated like a sickness: made a scorn
To all degrees[123] and sexes. I have heard old beldames
Talk of familiars in the shape of mice,
Rats, ferrets, weasels and I wot not what,
That have appeared, and sucked, some say, their blood.
But by what means they came acquainted with them
I'm now ignorant: would some power good or bad
Instruct me which way I might be revenged
Upon this churl, I'd go out of myself
And give this fury leave to dwell within

---

123. Classes.

This ruined cottage, ready to fall with age;[124]
Abjure all goodness, be at hate with prayer,
And study curses, imprecations,
Blasphemous speeches, oaths, detested oaths,
Or anything that's ill; so I might work
Revenge upon this miser, this black cur,
That barks, and bites, and sucks the very blood
Of me, and of my credit.[125] 'Tis all one,
To be a witch, as to be counted one.[126]
Vengeance, shame, ruin, light upon that canker!

[Enter Dog]

Dog: Ho! Have I found thee cursing? Now thou art mine own.[127]

Elizabeth Sawyer: Thine? What art thou?

Dog: He thou hast so often
Importuned to appear to thee, the devil.

Elizabeth Sawyer: Bless me! The devil?

Dog: Come, do not fear, I love thee much too well
To hurt or fright thee. If I seem terrible,
It is to such as hate me. I have found
Thy love unfeigned; have seen and pitied
Thy open wrongs, and come out of my love,
To give thee just revenge against thy foes.

Elizabeth Sawyer: May I believe thee?

Dog: To confirm't, command me
Do any mischief unto man or beast,
And I'll effect it, on condition
That uncompelled thou make a deed of gift
Of soul and body to me.

Elizabeth Sawyer: Out, alas!
My soul and body?

Dog: And that instantly,

---

124. Sawyer's old, damaged body.
125. Old Banks, the uncharitable witchmonger, here appears as the devilish familiar. This both suggests to the devil a shape to take when he appears, and highlights the play's Scot/Gifford-inspired equation of the devil with those who accuse witches.
126. Being a witch is just the same as being thought to be one.
127. This introduction paraphrases Goodcole's account, C–Cv. Goodcole's godly concern with regulating Sawyer's blasphemous, cursing tongue hangs on the devil's opening words to the witch, and his account shapes this passage, with the devil alternately wooing and threatening his victim. His *The wonderfull discoverie* is available in Gibson, ed., *Early Modern Witches*, pp. 299–315.

And seal it with thy blood: if thou deniest,
I'll tear thy body in a thousand pieces.

Elizabeth Sawyer: I know not where to seek relief: but shall I
After such covenants sealed, see full revenge
On all that wrong me?

Dog: Ha, ha! Silly woman!
The devil is no liar to such as he loves.
Didst ever know or hear the devil a liar
To such as he affects?

Elizabeth Sawyer: Then I am thine, at least so much of me,
As I can call my own.

Dog: Equivocations?
Art mine or no? Speak or I'll tear –

Elizabeth Sawyer: All thine.

Dog: Seal't with thy blood.

[Sucks her arm, thunder and lightning][128]

                         See, now I dare call thee mine;
For proof, command me, instantly I'll run,
To any mischief; goodness can I none.

Elizabeth Sawyer: And I desire as little. There's an old churl,
One Banks –

Dog: That wronged thee: he lamed thee, called thee witch.[129]

Elizabeth Sawyer: The same: first upon him I'd be revenged.

Dog: Thou shalt. Do but name how.

Elizabeth Sawyer: Go, touch his life.

Dog: I cannot.

Elizabeth Sawyer: Hast thou not vowed? Go, kill the slave.

Dog: I wonnot.[130]

Elizabeth Sawyer: I'll cancel then my gift.

Dog: Ha, ha!

Elizabeth Sawyer: Dost laugh?
Why wilt not kill him?

---

128. Unlike the learned, male 'witches' Dr Faustus or Peter Fabel (see *Dr Faustus* and *The Merry Devil of Edmonton* below) the ignorant, female Elizabeth Sawyer need not write a deed to confirm her contract with the devil. It was believed to be sealed by her words and by the sucking of blood – a practice not unique to female witches but very suggestive of suckling a child (see *A true and just Recorde* above).

129. The dog's completion of Sawyer's train of thought emphasizes their growing closeness. The implication is that they are now bound together (whether repentance and escape is possible is hotly debated in *Dr Faustus*, below), and from this bond evil grows quickly.

130. Will not, won't.

Dog: Fool, because I cannot.
Though we have power, know, it is circumscribed,
And tied in limits: though he be curst to thee,
Yet of himself he is loving to the world,
And charitable to the poor. Now men
That, as he, love goodness, though in smallest measure,
Live without compass of our reach. His cattle
And corn, I'll kill and mildew: but his life
(Until I take him, as I late found thee,
Cursing and swearing) I have no power to touch.

Elizabeth Sawyer: Work on his corn and cattle then.

Dog: I shall.
The Witch of Edmonton shall see his fall,
If she at least put credit in my power,
And in mine only; make orisons[131] to me,
And none but me.

Elizabeth Sawyer: Say how, and in what manner?

Dog: I'll tell thee. When thou wishest ill,
Corn, man or beast would spoil or kill,
Turn thy back against the sun
And mumble this short orison:
If thou to death or shame pursue 'em,
Sanctibicetur nomen tuum.[132]

Elizabeth Sawyer: If thou to death or shame pursue 'em,
Santibecetur nomen tuum.

Dog: Perfect. Farewell. Our first-made promises
We'll put in execution against Banks. [Exit]

Elizabeth Sawyer: *Contaminetur nomen tuum.*[133] I'm an expert scholar;
Speak Latin, or I know not well what language,
As well as the best of 'em. But who comes here?

[Enter Young Banks]

The son of my worst foe. To death pursue 'em
Et sanctabecetur nomen tuum.

---

131. Prayers.
132. Another direct borrowing from Goodcole, C4v. The phrase is in fact a misspelled part of the Latin Lord's Prayer: 'Hallowed be thy name'. Elizabeth Sawyer's inability below to get even this mangled phrase right is, Corbin and Sedge suggest, an important suggestion by the dramatists of her ignorance and vulnerability (*Three Jacobean Witchcraft Plays*, p. 237, note for lines 176–90) and not simply a compositor or printer error.
133. 'Contaminated be thy name'.

Young Banks: What's that she mumbles? The devil's *pater noster?*[134] Would it were else. Mother Sawyer, good morrow ...

    ... witch or no witch, you are a motherly woman: and though my father be a kind of God-bless-us, as they say, I have an earnest suit to you ... If he has hurt the head of thy credit, there's money to buy thee a plaster [gives her money]: and a small courtesy I would require at thy hands.

Elizabeth Sawyer: You seem a good young man, [aside] and I must dissemble, the better to accomplish my revenge. [To him] But for this silver, what would'st thou have me do? Bewitch thee?

Young Banks: No, by no means; I am bewitched already.[135] I would have thee so good as to unwitch me, or witch another with me for company.

Elizabeth Sawyer: I understand thee not. Be plain, my son.

Young Banks: As a pike-staff, mother: you know Kate Carter?

Elizabeth Sawyer: The wealthy yeoman's daughter. What of her?

Young Banks: That same party hath bewitched me.

Elizabeth Sawyer: Bewitched thee?

Young Banks: Bewitched me, *hisce auribus.*[136] I saw a little devil fly out of her eye like a burbolt,[137] which sticks at this hour up to the feathers in my heart. Now my request is, to send one of thy what d'ye call 'ems, either to pluck that out, or stick another as fast in hers ...

Elizabeth Sawyer: It's enough. What art can do, be sure of: turn to the west, and whatsoe'er thou hearest or seest, stand silent, and be not afraid.

[She stamps. Enter the Dog; he fawns and leaps upon her] ...

Elizabeth Sawyer: To scandal and disgrace pursue 'em,
    Et santabicetur nomen tuum ... A ball well bandied:[138] now the set's half won.
    The father's wrong I'll wreak upon the son.

Elizabeth Sawyer has told Young Cuddy Banks to follow the first living thing he meets that night at his father's pea-field. It will lead him to Kate (Katherine) Carter, who will flee coyly from him – but he must pursue her ...

---

134. Cuddy Banks accurately identifies the quotation from the Latin Lord's Prayer.
135. The first of the play's equations of women's beauty, or lust for it, as bewitching. Both beldams and *belles dames* are dangerous witches.
136. By these ears.
137. Bird-bolt, an arrow-like bird-killer.
138. Rallied, a ball-game metaphor.

Act 3, Scene 1
[Enter Dog]

Young Banks: Ha! My guide is come. A water-dog ... That way? Nay,
which way thou wilt, thou knowst the way better than I.
[Aside] Fine gentle cur it is, and well brought up, I warrant him.
[To Dog] We go a-ducking, spaniel; thou shalt fetch me the
ducks, pretty kind rascal.

[Enter a Spirit in the shape of Katherine, vizarded, and takes the mask
off][139]

Spirit [aside]:   Thus throw I off mine own essential horror,
And take the shape of a sweet lovely maid
Whom this fool dotes on. We can meet his folly,
But from his virtues must be runaways.
We'll sport with him: but when we reckoning call,
We know where to receive: th'witch pays for all.
[Dog barks]

Young Banks: Aye? Is that the watchword? She's come. Well, if ever we
be married, it shall be at Barking church[140] in memory of thee.
Now come behind, kind cur.
And have I met thee, sweet Kate?
I will teach thee to walk so late.
O, see, we meet in metre. What? Dost thou trip[141] from me? O
that I were upon my hobby horse,[142] I would mount after thee
so nimble.
'Stay, nymph, stay, nymph' singed Apollo:
Tarry and kiss me; sweet nymph, stay;
Tarry and kiss me, sweet.
We will to Chessum Street,
And then to the house stands in the highway.[143]

---

139. The boy actor playing Katherine would presumably enter wearing a devil's head mask,
and take it off to reveal himself/herself. The actor's sex would add a further uneasy
tension to the sexual ambiguity of the devil-woman.

140. A pun, but maybe also an allusion to the Witch of Barking (Barking, at the time, being a
small town east of London) described in a pamphlet of 1574, *The Examination and
Confession of a notorious Witch named Mother Arnold* (London, 1574). There are other
allusions to this woman in contemporary pamphlets and the story was reprinted in 1595
in *A World of Wonders* (see Gibson, ed., *Early Modern Witches*, pp. 146–50).

141. Run away.

142. The hobby horse is part of the equipment of Banks' team of morris men.

143. As Corbin and Sedge point out (*Three Jacobean Witchcraft Plays*, p. 239, notes to lines 89–
93), Cuddy Banks is adapting a ballad, 'When Daphne did from Phoebus fly', adding an
obscure allusion to Cheshunt Street. Perhaps the house is an inn or brothel?

Nay, by your leave, I must embrace you. [Exeunt Spirit and Young Banks]

[Within] O, help, help! I am drowned, I am drowned![144]

Dog: Ha, ha, ha, ha!

[Enter Young Banks wet]

Young Banks: This was an ill night to go a-wooing in; I find it now in Pond's almanac.[145] Thinking to land at Katherine's Dock, I was almost at Gravesend.[146] I'll never go to a wench in the dog-days again; yet 'tis cool enough.[147] Had you never a paw in this dog-trick? A mangie[148] take that black hide of yours: I'll throw you in at Limehouse in some tanner's pit or other.[149]

Dog: Ha, ha, ha ha!

Young Banks: How now? Who's that laughs at me? Hist to him.

[Dog barks]

Peace, peace; thou didst but thy kind neither. 'Twas my own fault.

Dog: Take heed how thou trustest the devil another time.

Young Banks: How now? Who's that speaks? I hope you have not your reading tongue about you?

Dog: Yes, I can speak.

Young Banks: The devil you can. You have read Aesop's fables, then: I have played one of your parts then; the dog that catched at the shadow in the water.[150] Pray you, let me catechise[151] you a little: what might one call your name, dog?

---

144. Cuddy Banks' offstage fall into the pond was obviously a highlight of the comedy, as it is shown in the woodcut decorating the title-page of the play's first edition.

145. Cuddy suggests that the almanac, published by Edward Pond, would have shown him it was an inauspicious time for wooing.

146. The euphemism 'Katherine's dock' is a bawdy joke; Gravesend is a funereal word-play; the geographical references and Cuddy's wet state suggest that he has been metaphorically swept downriver from London's St Katherine's Dock to Gravesend in Kent.

147. The dog-days are in the months when the dog-star, Sirius, is dominant – proverbially, the hottest days of the summer.

148. Mange.

149. Limehouse was a London district famous for its smelly tanneries.

150. Aesop's dog lost the meat he was carrying because he attacked his own reflection in the water, believing he was dropping his own food to steal some more from another dog (Corbin and Sedge, *Three Jacobean Witchcraft Plays*, p. 239, note to lines 111–13). Even this small allusion adds to the themes of greed, desire, aggression and delusion in the play.

151. Question.

Dog: My dame calls me Tom.

Young Banks: 'Tis well; and she may call me Ass: so there's an whole
one betwixt us, Tom-Ass. She said, I should follow you,
indeed. Well, Tom, give me thy fist; we are friends. You shall
be mine ingle.[152] I love you; but pray let's have no more need of
these ducking devices.

Dog: Not, if you love me. Dogs love where they are beloved. Cherish
me, and I'll do anything for you.

Young Banks: Well, you shall have jowls and livers: I have butchers to
my friends that shall bestow 'em, and I will keep crusts and
bones for you, if you'll be a kind dog, Tom.

Dog: Anything: I'll help thee to thy love.

Young Banks: Wilt thou? That promise shall cost me a brown loaf,
though I steal it out of my father's cupboard. You'll eat stolen
goods, Tom, will you not?

Dog: O, best of all. The sweetest bits, those.

Young Banks: You shall not starve, Ningle Tom; believe that; if you
love fish, I'll help you to maids and soles. I'm acquainted with a
fishmonger.[153]

Dog: Maids and soles? O, sweet bits! Banqueting stuff, those …

Meanwhile, the devil-dog has more serious business, foreshadowed by Cuddy
Banks' pursuit of Katherine, but made more terrible by the contrast between
Cuddy's fate and that of the devil's next victim. By Act Three, Frank Thorney has
bigamously married Susan Carter, Katherine's sister. In Act Three, Scene Three,
the devil, unprompted by the witch, spots an opportunity to lead him deeper into
sin as he leaves Susan early one morning to run away with Winnifride …

Act 3, Scene 3
[Enter Dog][154]

Dog: Now for an early mischief and a sudden:
The mind's about it now. One touch from me
Soon sets the body forward.

---

152. Literally, lover. Although Cuddy Banks seems to mean 'friend', his choice of word
interestingly suggests sexual sin. The suggestion of over-intimacy with the seductive
Satan hangs over both Cuddy and Elizabeth Sawyer.
153. Cuddy Banks is talking about fish and their suppliers, but again language betrays its user
and he seems to be talking about a pimp (fishmonger, a slang term), girls (maids) and
souls – 'Freudian' slips which delight the devil.
154. No one in this scene mentions the presence of the dog, and Corbin and Sedge conclude
that he is 'invisible' to everyone except the audience (*Three Jacobean Witchcraft Plays*,
p. 240, note to stage direction). However, Frank seems to address the dog indirectly later
in the scene, leaving his status mysterious and disturbing.

[Enter Young Frank Thorney and Susan]

Frank Thorney: Your request is out:[155] yet will you leave me?
Susan: What?
        So churlishly? You'll make me stay forever,
        Rather than part with such a sound from you.
Frank Thorney: Why, you almost anger me. Pray you be gone.
        You have no company, and 'tis very early;
        Some hurt may betide you homewards.
Susan: Tush, I fear none.
        To leave you, is the greatest hurt I can suffer:
        Besides, I expect your father and mine own,
        To meet me back, or overtake me with you.
        They began to stir when I came after you:
        I know they'll not be long.
Frank [aside]:   So, I shall have more trouble.

[Dog rubs him]

        Thank you for that.[156] Then I'll ease all at once.
        'Tis done now: what I ne'er thought on.
        [To her] You shall not go back.
Susan: Why? Shall I go along with thee? Sweet music!
Frank Thorney: No, to a better place.
Susan: Any place, I:
        I'm there at home, where thou pleasest to have me.
Frank Thorney: At home? I'll leave you in your last lodging.
        I must kill you.
Susan: O fine! You'd fright me from you.
Frank Thorney: You see I had no purpose: I'm unarmed.
        'Tis this minute's decree, and it must be.
        Look, this will serve your turn. [Draws a knife]
Susan: I'll not turn from it,
        If you be earnest, sir. Yet you may tell me
        Wherefore you'll kill me.
Frank Thorney: Because you are a whore.
Susan: There's one deep wound already: a whore?
Frank: Yes, I'll prove it,

---

155. Susan had innocently asked to accompany Frank over one final field before parting.
156. It seems at this moment that Frank may be able to see the dog, at least on a subconscious
     level.

> And you shall confess it. You are my whore.
> No wife of mine. The word admits no second.
> I was before wedded to another, have her still.
> I do not lay the sin unto your charge,
> 'Tis all mine own. Your marriage was my theft.
> For I espoused your dowry, and I have it:
> I did not purpose to have added murder;
> The devil did not prompt me: till this minute[157]
> You might have safe returned; now you cannot:
> You have dogged your own death.

[Stabs her]

Susan dies with speeches forgiving Frank, and welcoming death as better than her unwitting adultery. Frank wounds himself to make it seem that they have both been attacked by a third party, and the devil-dog helps tie him to a tree. Frank comments:

> So, so, I'm fast. I did not think I could
> Have done so well behind me. How prosperous
> And effectual mischief sometimes is . . .

And as he cries murder, the dog leaves him to the consequences of his crime, which include accusing two other men of killing Susan. One is Cuddy Banks' rival for Katherine's affections, leading Cuddy to suspect that the dog has been working mischief to promote his cause. Meanwhile, action is being taken against Elizabeth Sawyer, perceived as a far greater public danger than the devious Frank or the devil himself.

Act 4, Scene 1
[Enter Old Banks and two or three Countrymen]

Old Banks: My horse this morning runs most piteously of the glanders, whose nose yesternight was as clean as any man's here now coming from the barber's; and this, I'll take my death upon't, is long of this jadish witch, Mother Sawyer.

First Countryman: I took my wife and a servingman in our town of

---

157. This line sums up the devil's involvement as a 'prompt', since it reads as a unit of sense in its own right despite its overt punctuation. It is clear that the playwrights endorse Gifford's and Scot's assertions that the devil can and does do harm without the instruction of a witch, but the physical nature of his suggestion to Frank has more to do with dramatic device than theological debate. The pun in Frank's last words to Susan here (meaning that she has stubbornly pursued her own death) leaves that reality open to debate: how much is the dog a metaphor?

Edmonton, thrashing in my barn together, such corn as country wenches carry to market; and examining my polecat why she did so, she swore in her conscience she was bewitched: and what witch have we about us, but Mother Sawyer?

Second Countryman: Rid the town of her, else all our wives will do nothing else but dance about other country maypoles.

Third Countryman: Our cattle fall, our wives fall, our daughters fall and maidservants fall; and we ourselves shall not be able to stand, if this beast be suffered to graze amongst us.[158]

[Enter W. Hamluc, with thatch and link][159]

Hamluc: Burn the witch, the witch, the witch, the witch!

All: What hast got there?

Hamluc: A handful of thatch plucked off a hovel of hers; and they say, when 'tis burning, if she be a witch, she'll come running in.[160]

Old Banks: Fire it, fire it: I'll stand between thee and home for any danger.

[As that burns, enter the Witch Elizabeth Sawyer]

Elizabeth Sawyer: Diseases, plagues; the curse of an old woman follow and fall upon you!

All: Are you come, you old trot?

Old Banks: You hot whore, must we fetch you with fire in your tail?

First Countryman: This thatch is as good as a jury to prove she is a witch.

All: Out, witch! Beat her, kick her, set fire on her!

Elizabeth Sawyer: Shall I be murdered by a bed of serpents? Help, help!

[Enter Sir Arthur Clarington and a Justice][161]

---

158. This exchange is full of bawdy puns. A polecat is a whorish woman, and there are jokes about thrashing, maypoles, falling and standing.

159. Lantern.

160. A detail from Goodcole (A4). Like the Justice, Goodcole condemns this practice as 'ridiculous'.

161. The playwrights have separated from the symbolically named 'Justice' the character of Sir Arthur, who seems to be named after Arthur Robinson, the magistrate who in Goodcole's account committed Elizabeth Sawyer for trial. Whilst the Justice offers, by the standards of his time, a fair hearing, we have already seen Sir Arthur prejudging cases, such as that of the two men arrested for Susan's murder, as well as seducing and marrying off his servant Winnifride. Are the playwrights commenting on the real events portrayed by Goodcole?

All: Hang her, beat her, kill her!

Justice: How now? Forbear this violence!

Elizabeth Sawyer: A crew of villains, a knot of bloody hangmen set to torment me I know not why.

Justice: Alas, neighbour Banks, are you a ringleader in mischief? Fie, to abuse an aged woman!

Old Banks: Woman? A she hell-cat, a witch: to prove her one, we no sooner set fire on the thatch of her house, but in she came running, as if the devil had sent her in a barrel of gunpowder; which trick as surely proves her a witch, as the pox in a snuffling nose is a sign a man is a whore-master.[162]

Justice: Come, come; firing her thatch? Ridiculous. Take heed, sirs, what you do: unless your proofs come better armed, instead of turning her into a witch, you'll prove yourselves stark fools.

All: Fools?

Justice: Arrant fools.

Old Banks: Pray, Master Justice What do you call 'em, hear me but in one thing. This grumbling devil owes me, I know, no good will ever since I fell out with her.

Elizabeth Sawyer: And breakest my back with beating me.

Old Banks: I'll break it worse.

Elizabeth Sawyer: Wilt thou?

Justice: You must not threaten her: 'tis against law. Go on.

Old Banks: So, sir, ever since, having a dun cow tied up in my backside,[163] let me go thither, or but cast my eye at her, and if I should be hanged, I cannot choose, though it be ten times in an hour, but run to the cow, and taking up her tail, kiss (saving your worship's reverence) my cow behind; that the whole town of Edmonton has been ready to bepiss themselves with laughing me to scorn.[164]

Justice: And this is long of her?

Old Banks: Who the devil else? For is any man such an ass, to be such a baby, if he were not bewitched?

Sir Arthur: Nay, if she be a witch, and the harms she does end in such sports, she may 'scape burning.

---

162. This may recall Scot's story (above) of Margaret Simons and the hoarse vicar.
163. Backyard or lot.
164. This story is from Gifford's *Dialogue* (above, although this particular section, L4v and M2v, has not been included). When told this story, and asked what he thinks of it, Gifford's character Daniel brushes it off as 'fantasies' and 'foolish imaginations', with the unexpectedly flippant remark: 'I say he was farre in love with his cow'.

Justice: Go, go; pray vex her not. She is a subject, and you must not be judges of the law to strike her as you please.

All: No, no, we'll find cudgel enough to strike her.

Old Banks: Aye, no lips to kiss but my cow's – ?

[Exeunt Old Banks and Countrymen]

Elizabeth Sawyer: Rots and foul maladies eat up thee and thine!

Justice: Here's none now, Mother Sawyer, but this gentleman, myself and you; let us to some mild questions, have you mild answers? Tell us honestly and with a free confession (we'll do our best to wean you from it) are you a witch or no?

Elizabeth Sawyer: I am none!

Justice: Be not so furious.

Elizabeth Sawyer: I am none. None but base curs so bark at me. I am none. Or would I were: if every poor old woman be trod on thus by slaves, reviled, kicked, beaten, as I am daily, she to be revenged had need to turn witch.

Sir Arthur: And you to be revenged have sold your soul to th'devil.

Elizabeth Sawyer: Keep thine own from him.

Justice: You are too saucy, and too bitter.

Elizabeth Sawyer: Saucy? By what commission can he send my soul on the devil's errand, more than I can his? Is he a landlord of my soul, to thrust it when he list out of door?

Justice: Know whom you speak to.

Elizabeth Sawyer: A man: perhaps no man. Men in gay clothes, whose backs are laden with titles and honours, are within far more crooked than I am; and if I be a witch, more witch-like.

Sir Arthur: You're a base hell-hound. And now, sir, let me tell you, far and near she's bruited for[165] a woman that maintains a spirit that sucks her.

Elizabeth Sawyer: I defy thee.

Sir Arthur: Go, go, I can, if need be, bring an hundred voices, e'en here in Edmonton, that shall loud proclaim thee for a secret and pernicious witch.

Elizabeth Sawyer: Ha, ha!

Justice: Do you laugh? Why laugh you?

Elizabeth Sawyer: At my name: the brave name this knight gives me, witch.

---

165. Named as, gossiped about.

Justice: Is the name of witch so pleasing to thine ear?

Sir Arthur: Pray, sir, give way, and let her tongue gallop on.

Elizabeth Sawyer: A witch? Who is not?
> Hold not that universal name in scorn then.
> What are your painted things in princes' courts,
> Upon whose eyelids lust sits, blowing fires
> To burn men's souls in sensual hot desires:
> Upon whose naked paps,[166] a lecher's thought
> Acts sin in fouler shapes than can be wrought?

Justice: But these work not as you do.

Elizabeth Sawyer: No, but far worse:
> These by enchantments, can whole lordships change
> To trunks of rich attire; turn ploughs and teams
> To Flanders mares[167] and coaches; and huge trains
> Of servitors, to a French butterfly.[168]
> Have you not city-witches who can turn
> Their husband's wares, whole standing shops of wares,
> To sumptuous tables, gardens of stol'n sin?
> In one year wasting, what scarce twenty win?
> Are not these witches?

Justice: Yes, yes;[169] but the law
> Casts not an eye on these.

Elizabeth Sawyer: Why then on me,
> Or any lean old beldame? Reverence once
> Had wont to wait on age. Now an old woman
> Ill-favoured grown with years, if she be poor,
> Must be called bawd or witch. Such so abused
> Are the coarse witches: t'other are the fine,
> Spun for the devil's own wearing.

Sir Arthur: And so is thine.

Elizabeth Sawyer: She on whose tongue a whirlwind sits to blow
> A man out of himself, from his soft pillow,
> To lean his head on rocks and fighting waves,
> Is not that scold a witch? The man of law
> Whose honeyed hopes the credulous client draws,

---

166. Breasts.
167. Carriage horses, but also with the connotation of 'loose women'. Flanders was proverbially noted for its prostitutes. Honest necessities are replaced with sinful luxuries.
168. A fancy courtier with French affectations.
169. An important admission. Technically, of course, the courtesans and adulteresses are not witches, but the playwrights clearly wish to compare different sins to suggest that some 'witches' are worse than others.
170. Rattling basins and pans was said to be a way of attracting swarms.

(As bees by tinkling basins)[170] to swarm to him,
From his own hive to work the wax in his;
He is no witch, not he.

Sir Arthur: But these men-witches
Are not in trading with hell's merchandise
Like such as you are, that for a word, a look,
Denial of a coal of fire, kill men,
Children and cattle.

Elizabeth Sawyer: Tell them, sir, that do so:
Am I accused for such a one?

Sir Arthur: Yes, 'twill be sworn.

Elizabeth Sawyer: Dare any swear I ever tempted maiden
With golden hooks flung at her chastity,
To come and lose her honour? And being lost,
To pay not a denier[171] for't? Some slaves have done it.
Men-witches can, without the fangs of law
Drawing once one drop of blood, put counterfeit pieces
Away for true gold.

Sir Arthur: By one thing she speaks,
I know now she's a witch, and dare no longer
Hold conference with the fury.[172]

Justice: Let's then away:
Old woman, mend thy life, get home and pray.

[Exeunt Sir Arthur Clarington and Justice][173]

Elizabeth Sawyer: For his confusion.

[Enter Dog]

                              My dear Tom-boy, welcome!
I am torn in pieces by a pack of curs.
Clapped all upon me, and for want of thee:
Comfort me; thou shalt have the teat anon.[174]

Dog: Bow, wow: I'll have it now.

Elizabeth Sawyer: I am dried up
With cursing and with madness; and have yet
No blood to moisten these sweet lips of thine.

---

171. A coin of small value.
172. Sir Arthur recognizes his own crime in Sawyer's words.
173. The Justice does not have Elizabeth Sawyer sent for trial. The dramatists choose to
     postpone her arrest, making it appear that the Justice does not believe her accusers and, as
     they are not shown giving formal informations, he would not in reality be obliged to act.
174. In Goodcole, Sawyer was searched and a supposed teat found (B3v).

Stand on thy hind-legs up. Kiss me, my Tommy,
And rub away some wrinkles on my brow,
By making my old ribs to shrug for joy
Of thy fine tricks. What hast thou done? Let's tickle. [They embrace]
Hast thou struck the horse lame as I bid thee?

Dog: Yes, and nipped the sucking child.[175]

Elizabeth Sawyer: Ho, ho, my dainty,
My little pearl! No lady loves her hound,
Monkey, or parakeet, as I do thee.

Dog: The maid has been churning butter nine hours; but it shall not come.

Elizabeth Sawyer: Let 'em eat cheese and choke.

Dog: I had rare sport
Among the clowns i'th'morris.

Elizabeth Sawyer: I could dance
Out of my skin to hear thee. But, my curl-pate,
That jade, that foul-tongued whore, Nan Ratcliffe,
Who, for a little soap licked by my sow,
Struck, and almost had lamed it; did not I charge thee,
To pinch that quean to th'heart?[176]

Dog: Bow, wow, wow: look here else.

[Enter Anne Ratcliffe mad]

Anne Ratcliffe: See, see, see; the Man i'th' Moon has built a new windmill, and what running there's from all quarters of the city to learn the art of grinding!

Elizabeth Sawyer: Ho, ho, ho! I thank thee, my sweet mongrel.

Anne Ratcliffe: Hoyda! A pox of the devil's false hopper! All the golden meal runs into the rich knaves' purses, and the poor have nothing but bran. Hey derry down! Are you not Mother Sawyer?

Elizabeth Sawyer: No, I am a lawyer.

---

175. Sawyer was acquitted of killing two nurse-children, but confessed to Goodcole that she was guilty of the crimes (C2).
176. Goodcole reports Sawyer's conviction for killing Agnes Ratcliefe after the incident with the sow, some of Ratcliefe's husband's testimony in court, and Sawyer's continued denial that she was responsible (Bv–B2, B3v, C2v, C4). The playwrights have added Anne Ratcliffe's madness and suicide, turning her into the Ophelia-like female version of the 'wise fool' character, present in many Renaissance plays, whose lunacy allows her to express the true corruption of the world.

Anne Ratcliffe: Art thou? I prithee let me scratch thy face; for thy pen has flayed off a great many men's skins. You'll have brave doings in the vacation; for knaves and fools are at variance in every village. I'll sue Mother Sawyer, and her own sow shall give in evidence against her.

Elizabeth Sawyer [to Dog]:   Touch her. [Dog rubs against Anne Ratcliffe]

Anne Ratcliffe: O, my ribs are made of a paned hose,[177] and they break. There's a Lancashire hornpipe in my throat: hark how it tickles it, with doodle, doodle, doodle, doodle. Welcome, serjeants: welcome, devil. Hands, hands; hold hands and dance around, around, around.

[Enter Old Banks, his son Young Banks the Clown, Old Ratcliffe and Country fellows]

Old Ratcliffe: She's here; alas, my poor wife is here.

Old Banks: Catch her fast, and have her into some close chamber: do, for she's as many wives are, stark mad.

Young Banks: The witch, Mother Sawyer, the witch, the devil!

Old Ratcliffe: O, my dear wife! Help, sirs!

[Old Ratcliffe and the Country fellows carry her off]

Old Banks: You see your work, Mother Bumby.[178]

Elizabeth Sawyer: My work? Should she and all you here run mad, is the work mine?

Young Banks: No, on my conscience, she would not hurt a devil of two years old.

[Enter Old Ratcliffe and the rest]

How now? What's become of her?

Old Ratcliffe: Nothing: she's become nothing, but the miserable trunk of a wretched woman. We were in her hands as reeds in a mighty tempest: spite of our strengths, away she brake; and nothing in her mouth being heard but 'the devil, the witch, the witch, the devil', she beat out her own brains and so died.

Young Banks: It's any man's case, be he never so wise, to die when his brains go a-wool-gathering.

177. Striped or pleated hose liable to split at the seams.
178. Mother Bumby or Bombie is mentioned by Scot, and John Lyly wrote a comedy about her supposed activities (*Mother Bombie*, 1594). The name became associated with malign witches, although Lyly's character is a well-intentioned seer, who, like Peter Fabel in *The Merry Devil of Edmonton* (below), assists in matchmaking.

Old Banks: Masters, be ruled by me; let's all to a justice. Hag, thou hast done this, and thou shalt answer it.

Elizabeth Sawyer: Banks, I defy thee.

Old Banks: Get a warrant first to examine her, then ship her to Newgate:[179] here's enough, if all her other villainies were pardoned, to burn her for a witch. You have a spirit, they say, comes to you in the likeness of a dog; we shall see your cur at one time or other. If we do, unless it be the devil himself, he shall go howling to the gaol in one chain, and thou in another.

Elizabeth Sawyer: Be hanged thou in a third, and do thy worst!

Young Banks: How, father? You send the poor dumb thing howling to th'gaol? He that makes him howl, makes me roar ...

Dog: Bow, wow, wow, wow!

All: O, the dog's here, the dog's here![180]

Old Banks: It was the voice of a dog.

Young Banks: The voice of a dog? If that were a dog's, what voice had my mother? So am I a dog: bow, wow, wow! It was I that barked so, father, to make coxcombs of these clowns ...

[Exeunt Old Banks, Old Ratcliffe, and Countrymen]

Young Banks: Ningle, you had like to have spoiled all with your bowings. I was glad to put 'em off with one of my dog-tricks on a sudden ... [Exit]

Dog: Bow, wow, wow, wow.

Elizabeth Sawyer: Mind him not, he's not worth thy worrying: run at a fairer game, that foul-mouthed knight, scurvy Sir Arthur, fly at him, my Tommy, and pluck out's throat.

Dog: No, there's a dog already biting's conscience.

Elizabeth Sawyer: That's a sure bloodhound. Come, let's home and play. Our black work ended, we'll make holiday. [Exeunt]

Frank Thorney's murder of Susan is discovered and he is arrested, partly on the accusation of his first wife Winnifride. Another betrayal is also taking place ...

Act 5, Scene 1
[Enter Mother Elizabeth Sawyer alone]

Elizabeth Sawyer: Still wronged by every slave? And not a dog
                      Bark in his dame's defence? I am called witch,
                      Yet am myself bewitched from doing harm.

---

179. Suspected felons from Middlesex were sent to Newgate prison in London to await trial.
180. The dog is invisible again.

Have I given up myself to thy black lust
Thus to be scorned? Not see me in three days?
I'm lost without my Tomalin: prithee come,
Revenge to me is sweeter far than life;
Thou art my raven on whose coal-black wings
Revenge comes flying to me. O my best love!
I am on fire (even in the midst of ice)
Raking my blood up, till my shrunk knees feel
Thy curled head leaning on them. Come then, my darling.
If in the air thou hover'st, fall upon me
In some dark cloud; and as I oft have seen
Dragons and serpents in the elements,
Appear thou now so to me. Art thou i'th' sea?
Muster up all the monsters from the deep,
And be the ugliest of them: so that my bulch[181]
Show but his swart cheek to me, let earth cleave
And break from hell, I care not! Could I run
Like a swift powder-mine[182] beneath the world,
Up would I blow it, all to find out thee,
Though I lay ruined in it.[183] Not yet come!
I must then fall to my old prayer,
Sanctibiceter nomen tuum.
Not yet come! Worrying of wolves, biting of mad dogs, the
manges and the –

[Enter Dog, now white][184]

Dog: How now! Whom art thou cursing?

Elizabeth Sawyer: Thee! Ha! No, 'tis my black cur I am cursing, for not
attending on me.

Dog: I am that cur.

Elizabeth Sawyer: Thou liest: hence, come not nigh me.

Dog: Bow, wow!

Elizabeth Sawyer: Why dost thou thus appear to me in white,
As if thou wert the ghost of my dear love?

Dog: I am dogged, list not[185] to tell thee, yet, to torment thee: my
whiteness puts thee in mind of thy winding sheet.

---

181. Bull-calf, a term of endearment.
182. A gunpowder explosive.
183. This declaration of love is full of imagery used in sonnets of the period. Fire and ice is the
most obvious and begins the sequence.
184. Goodcole reports that Sawyer's familiar came as either black or white, white when she
was praying (C2v, Dv), but the playwrights give his colour further significance here.
185. Don't want to.

Elizabeth Sawyer: Am I near death?

Dog: Yes, if the dog of hell be near thee. When the devil comes to thee as a lamb, have at thy throat!

Elizabeth Sawyer: Off, cur!

Dog: He has the back of a sheep, but the belly of an otter: devours by sea and land. Why am I in white? Didst thou not pray to me?

Elizabeth Sawyer: Yes, thou dissembling hell-hound:
Why now in white more than at other times?

Dog: Be blasted with the news; whiteness is day's foot-boy, a forerunner to light, which shows thy old rivelled[186] face. Villains are stripped naked, the witch must be beaten out of her cockpit.

Elizabeth Sawyer: Must she? She shall not; thou art a lying spirit.
Why to mine eyes art thou a flag of truce?
I am at peace with none; 'tis the black colour,
Or none, which I fight under. I do not like
Thy puritan paleness: glowing furnaces
Are far more hot than they which flame outright.
If thou my old dog art, go and bite such
As I shall set thee on.

Dog: I will not.

Elizabeth Sawyer: I'll sell my self to twenty thousand fiends,
To have thee torn in pieces then.

Dog: Thou canst not: thou art so ripe to fall into hell, that no more of my kennel will so much as bark at him that hangs thee.

Elizabeth Sawyer: I shall run mad.

Dog: Do so, thy time is come to curse, and rave, and die. The glass of thy sins is full, and it must run out at gallows.

Elizabeth Sawyer: It cannot, ugly cur, I'll confess nothing;
And not confessing, who dare come and swear
I have bewitched them? I'll not confess one mouthful.

Dog: Choose, and be hanged or burned.[187]

Elizabeth Sawyer: Spite of the devil and thee, I'll muzzle up my tongue from telling tales.

Dog: Spite of thee and the devil, thou'lt be condemned.

Elizabeth Sawyer: Yes, when?

Dog: And ere the executioner catch thee full in's claws, thou'lt confess all.

Elizabeth Sawyer: Out, dog!

---

186. Wrinkled, shrivelled.
187. Of course, in reality there was no such choice.

Dog: Out, witch! Thy trial is at hand:
            Our prey being had, the devil does laughing stand.

[The Dog stands aloof. Enter Old Banks, Ratcliffe and Countrymen]

Old Banks: She's here; attach her. Witch, you must go with us.

Elizabeth Sawyer: Whither? To hell?

Old Banks: No, no, no, old crone; your mittimus[188] shall be made
            thither, but your own jailors shall receive you. Away with her!
            [They seize her]

Elizabeth Sawyer: My Tommy! My sweet Tom-boy! O thou dog!
            Dost thou now fly to thy kennel and forsake me?
            Plagues and consumptions –

[Exeunt all but Dog]

Dog: Ha, ha, ha, ha!
            Let not the world, witches or devils condemn;
            They follow us, and then we follow them.

The dog meets Cuddy Banks and confesses his trick with the false Katherine,
whilst Cuddy reproaches him for betraying the witch. He reminds Tom that their
relationship is that of man and dog, not man and devil, but, intrigued by devils'
ability to assume female shape, questions the dog about the forms devils can
take.

Dog: Any shape to blind such silly eyes as thine, but chiefly those coarse
            creatures, dog or cat, hare, ferret, frog, toad.

Young Banks: Louse or flea?

Dog: Any poor vermin.

Young Banks: It seems you devils have poor thin souls, that you can
            bestow yourselves in such small bodies: but pray you, Tom, one
            question at parting – I think I shall never see you more – where
            do you borrow those bodies that are none of your own? The
            garment-shape you may hire at broker's.[189]

Dog: Why wouldst thou know that? Fool, it avails thee not.

Young Banks: Only for my mind's sake, Tom, and to tell some of my
            friends.

Dog: I'll thus much tell thee: thou art never so distant
            From an evil spirit, but that thy oaths,

---

188. Warrant. The implication is that the witch is bound to be committed to Hell eventually,
     but in the meantime will merely be jailed.
189. Cuddy Banks means that clothes may be hired, but not bodies.

> Curses and blasphemies pull him to thine elbow.
> Thou never tellst a lie, but that a devil
> Is within hearing it; thy evil purposes
> Are ever haunted. But when they come to act,
> As thy tongue slandering, bearing false witness,
> Thy hand stabbing, stealing, cosening, cheating,
> He's then within thee. Thou playst, he bets upon thy part;
> Although thou lose, yet he will gain by thee.[190]

Young Banks: Aye? Then he comes in the shape of a rook.[191]

Dog: The old cadaver of some self-strangled wretch
> We sometimes borrow, and appear human.
> The carcass of some disease-slain strumpet
> We varnish fresh, and wear as her first beauty.
> Didst never hear? If not, it has been done.
> An hot luxurious lecher in his twines,
> When he has thought to clip his dalliance,
> There has provided been for his embrace
> A fine hot flaming devil in her place.

Rejecting Tom's offer of service, Cuddy Banks saves himself from the devil but for Elizabeth Sawyer it is too late.

[**Voices within**]:   Away with her! Hang her, witch!

[Enter Elizabeth Sawyer to execution, Officers with halberds, and Country-people]

Old Carter: The witch, that instrument of mischief! Did not she witch the devil into my son-in-law, when he killed my poor daughter? Do you hear, Mother Sawyer?

Elizabeth Sawyer: What would you have? Cannot a poor old woman Have your leave to die without vexation?

Old Carter: Did you not bewitch Frank to kill his wife? He could never have done't without the devil.

Elizabeth Sawyer: Who doubts it? But is every devil mine?
> Would I had one now whom I might command
> To tear you all in pieces: Tom would have done't
> Before he left me.

Old Carter: Thou didst bewitch Anne Ratcliffe to kill herself.

---

190. This is very like Goodcole's conclusion that the devil is eternally vigilant, and that sin such as swearing 'brings the devil to you' (D3).
191. A cheat.

Elizabeth Sawyer: Churl, thou liest; I never did her hurt.[192]
Would you were all as near your ends as I am,
That gave evidence against me for it.

First Countryman: I'll be sworn, Master Carter, she bewitched
Gammer Washbowl's sow, to cast her pigs a day before she
would have farrowed; yet they were sent up to London, and
sold as good Westminster dog-pigs, at Bartholomew Fair, as
ever great-bellied ale-wife longed for.[193]

Elizabeth Sawyer: These dogs will mad me: I was well resolved
To die in my repentance; though 'tis true
I would live longer if I might.[194] Yet since
I cannot, pray torment me not; my conscience
Is settled as it shall be. All take heed
How they believe the devil; at last he'll cheat you.

Old Carter: Thou'dst best confess all truly.

Elizabeth Sawyer: Yet again?
Have I scarce breath enough to say my prayers?
And would you force me to spend that in bawling?
Bear witness, I repent all former evil;
There is no damned conjuror like the devil.

All: Away with her, away! ...

4. Poetry

Edmund Spenser, The Faerie Queene (Books 1–3, 1590)[195]

Edmund Spenser (*c.* 1552–99) a poet and courtier-administrator, wrote the epic
The Faerie Queene as a celebration of Protestant England and a compliment to
Queen Elizabeth, whose carefully cultivated attributes appear in several of its
heroines. As antitheses to these, witches and magicians figure prominently
among its villains, with allusions to Mary Queen of Scots and the Roman

---

192. Are we to see this as a lie or not? We saw Sawyer urging the dog to attack Anne Ratcliffe, but in both pamphlet and play Sawyer denies causing her harm. Unlike Goodcole's version, the play's mad woman ended her own life. Like Gifford (above) the playwrights seem to be suggesting a complex relationship between the agency of the witch and the devil, and emphasizing the slippery nature of truth.

193. Although the pigs were stillborn, they were sold as good meat at London's Bartholomew Fair. Once again, everyday lies and con-tricks are laid alongside witchcraft for comparison. The point is sharpened by the probable reference to Ben Jonson's play *Bartholomew Fair* (1614), which is all about such tricks, and the peculiar lusts of human beings as exemplified by the pregnant ale-wife's longing for pork.

194. A direct borrowing from Goodcole, Dv.

195. The text used here is the 1590 edition of *The Faerie Queene* (three books) in the British Library. The best modern edition is Thomas P. Roche, ed., *The Faerie Queene* (London: Penguin, 1978).

Catholic Church attached to them. In Book One is Spenser's most notorious witch Duessa (Doubleness), a false and seductive scarlet-clad woman who wears a popish mitre, and preys on honest men. Duessa is a powerful female magician who has elements of the characters of Classical witches such as Circe and Medea, and she is the Whore of Babylon, representing religious misbelief in Revelation. But she is also a folkloric figure who waits for the (especially male) unwary or erring and leads them to their doom. Spenser's deliberately archaic language and Arthurian setting recall Morgan le Fay and the temptresses of medieval myth. Duessa is very unlike English witches of Spenser's time, but shares some of the terrors associated with them: a horror of women's sexual power and arcane skills is very evident in this extract.

Spenser's poem muses on witchcraft, and especially the seductive dangers of magic, on several occasions. Duessa, the villainess of Book One, is amplified in Acrasia, the Circe-like temptress of Book Two, whose feminine magic turns men into swine and enfeebles her lovers to the point of near emasculation. That she and her world, the Bower of Bliss, are so attractive is an essential teaching tool of this didactic poem: like the knight of Book Two, and as with Duessa in Book One, the reader must reject magic's artificiality and allow the Bower to be destroyed and the witch captured. But Spenser also introduces less attractive witch-figures, male and female. Archimago, the arch image-maker of Book One, is a deceitful, malicious wizard, as is Book Three's cruel Busyrane, who keeps the pining lover Amoret under a spell inflicting continual torture as an allegory of the pains of excessive love. Book Three also contains a conventional witch-figure, an old woman living in a small cottage with her oafish son. This ugly witch too has the power of seductive femininity, however: as Archimago does in Book One, she makes a fake body for a wicked spirit, and allows it to impersonate a beautiful woman. Throughout his explorations of witchcraft, Spenser (like many other writers of his time) repeatedly associates magic with deceit, cruelty, love and effeminacy, often figuring it as a trap that women set for men.

In Book One, the Redcrosse Knight (Holiness) encounters two people who have been turned into trees by Duessa. The unfortunate male tree, Fradubio (Brother Doubt), explains how, unaware of Duessa's true identity, he had to choose between her and his erstwhile love Froelissa (Frailty). Duessa decided to force his hand:

The wicked witch now seeing all this while
The doubtful balance equally to sway,
What not by right, she cast to win by guile,
And by her hellish science raised straightway
A foggy mist, that overcast the day,
And a dull blast, that breathing on her[196] face,
Dimmed her former beauty's shining ray,
And with foul ugly form did her disgrace:

---

196. Froelissa's.

Then was she fair alone, when none was fair in place.
Then cried she out, fie, fie, deformed wight,[197]
Whose borrowed beauty now appeareth plain
To have before bewitched all men's sight;
O leave her soon, or let her soon be slain ...

Fradubio almost kills Froelissa, but Duessa pretends to pity her and she is turned into a tree. Meanwhile, Fradubio receives a shock:

Thenceforth I tooke Duessa for my Dame,
And in the witch unweeting[198] joyed long time,
Ne ever wist,[199] but that she was the same,
'Till on a day (that day is every Prime,[200]
When Witches wont do penance for their crime)
I chaunst to see her in her proper hew,[201]
Bathing her selfe in origane and thyme:[202]
A filthy foul old woman I did view,
That ever to have touched her, I did deadly rue.[203]

Her nether partes misshapen, monstruous,
Were hid in water, that I could not see,
But they did seeme more foul and hideous,
Then woman's shape man would believe to be.
Thenceforth from her most beastly company
I gan[204] refrain, in mind to slip away,
Soon as appeared safe opportunity:
For danger great, if not assured decay
I saw before mine eyes, if I were known to stray.

The divelish hag, by chaunges of my cheer[205]
Perceived my thought, and drowned in sleepy night,
With wicked herbs and ointments did besmear
My body all, through charms and magic might,
That all my senses were bereaved quite:

---

197. Person.
198. Unknowing.
199. Knew.
200. Springtime.
201. True colours.
202. Used to heal scabs. Later we hear that Duessa has a fox-tail, an eagle's claw and a bear's paw and that she is a toothless, wrinkled hag.
203. I regretted deeply.
204. Began to.
205. Mood.

Then brought she me unto this desert waste,
And by my wretched lover's side me pight,[206]
Where now enclosed in wooden walls full fast,
Banished from living wights, our weary days we waste ...

The reader learns of Fradubio's fate with horror, for the disguised witch Duessa is now the companion of the unsuspecting Redcrosse Knight ...

Ben Jonson, The Masque of Queenes (1609)[207]

Ben Jonson (1572–1637) was one of the premier playwrights and poets of his time. His greatest strengths lay in comedy, and a selection from his play *The Alchemist* appears in Chapter 7. But his masques, despite their tendency to be overburdened by a desire to demonstrate Jonson's classical learning, are also outstanding examples of their genre, as entertainments designed to entertain the court and display some of its supposed virtues. Jonson, who came from a relatively poor background, and was at one time an apprentice bricklayer, became in effect Poet Laureate, and in his ardent efforts to please his royal patron, James I, he naturally focused on some of the king's interests. Witchcraft was one of these, and in 1608–9 Jonson created *The Masque of Queenes* to set off the virtues of the court (and especially the queen and her ladies in waiting) against the noxious vices of female witches. Jonson trawled classical and modern works, both of fiction and demonology, for details to incorporate into his masque: Delrio, Ovid, Bodin, Apuleius, della Porta, Remy, Martial, the *Malleus Maleficarum*, Lucan, Homer, Agrippa, Seneca, Nider, the king's own book, and (silently) Scot, whose work the king despised, are all assembled in his lengthy notes to the masque, to flatter his patron's expertise.

In the masque, performed on 2 February, the witches are discovered at a hellish 'convent' or sabbath, and begin to summon their 'Dame', the leading witch, with charms. She is a figure straight from Graeco-Roman nightmare: 'naked-armed, bare-footed, her frock tucked, her hair knotted, and folded with vipers; in her hand a torch made of a dead man's arm, lighted, girded with a snake'. Opposites to Fame and Glory, the witches have allegorical signifi-cances, and are named Ignorance, Suspicion, Credulity, Malice and so on: but also, like the witches in the recent *Macbeth*, they describe various practical tasks they have been performing: stealing skulls from charnel-houses, killing children, gathering the horrid ingredients for spells. They plan a spell to cast the world into dark chaos. The Dame witch begins an invocation full of inversions, based on those by Ovid's and Seneca's Medea:

---

206. Placed.
207. The text used is from Jonson's *Workes* (London, 1616) in the British Library.

You fiends and furies (if yet any be
Worse than ourselves) you, that have quaked to see
These knots untied; and shrunk, when we have charmed.
You, that (to arm us) have yourselves disarmed,
And to our powers resigned your whips and brands,
When we went forth, the scourge of men and lands.[208]
You, that have seen me ride, when Hecate
Durst not take chariot; when the boisterous sea,
Without a breath of wind, hath knocked the sky;
And that hath thundered, Jove not knowing why:
When we have set the elements at wars,
Made midnight see the sun, and day the stars;
When the winged lightning, in the course hath stayed,
And swiftest rivers have run back, afraid,
To see the corn remove, the groves to range,[209]
Whole places alter, and the seasons change;
When the pale moon, at the first voice down fell
Poisoned, and durst not stay the second spell.
You, that have oft been conscious of these sights;
And thou three-formed star,[210] that, on these nights
Art only powerful, to whose triple name
Thus we incline, once, twice, and thrice the same;
If now with rites profane, and foul enough,
We do invoke thee: darken all this roof,
With present fogs. Exhale earth's rottenest vapours,
And strike a blindness through these blazing tapers . . .[211]

However, the charms are doomed to fail. Despite an inverted 'magical dance' in which witches, Jonson notes, 'do all things contrary to the custom of men, dancing back to back, and hip to hip, their hands joined, and making their circles backward, to the left hand, with strange fantastic motions of their heads and bodies', Heroic Virtue and his twelve famous queens (played by Queen Anne and her ladies) sweep the 'anti-masque' of witches from the stage simply by appearing with a blast of harmonious music. Order is restored, and the court can proceed with self-congratulation. The spectacle has resonances of King James and Queen Anne's encounter with witches at North Berwick during their honeymoon (immortalized in a pamphlet, *Newes from Scotland*, in 1591, see note 53 in this chapter), as well as offering a commentary on the wider anarchic significance of witchcraft in the supposedly decorous and controlled Jacobean world. Ironically, one of the twelve virtuous queens was played by Frances

208. The furies carried these whips and brands.
209. Move about.
210. Hecate, the three-formed goddess.
211. The lights in the King's court.

Howard, Countess of Essex, upon whose scandalous resort to witches during her attempts to obtain a divorce, Middleton would base his play *The Witch*.

Miles Gale (?), 'Witchcraft ye practice of deluded minds'

This poem appears in a British Library collection of manuscripts on witchcraft, and the history of the Gale family (Add. MS 32496). Miles Gale (1647–1721), whose epitaph appears on the first page of the collection, seems likely to have been the collector and transcriber, and probably wrote the poem, which is used to preface Edward Fairfax's 'Discourse' (see below). Its date is not known. Gale, a graduate of Cambridge University, was the rector of Keighley, Yorkshire for 41 years (1680–1721) and the poem probably dates from this time. He was interested in local antiquities, compiling memoirs of his family and local histories, but the poem and the many imaginative illustrations of witches and familiars accompanying the texts suggest that he also had an eye for the artistic. The poem's sentiments are entirely appropriate to a rector and it constitutes a kind of sermon on witchcraft.

Witchcraft ye practice of deluded minds,
Where grace is wanting soon admission finds.
With golden promises of life and wealth,
The tempter takes unwary souls by stealth.
In this his seeming clemency appears,
That he will give them back a lease for years.
But that expired, how dismal is their end!
And case, when he a fiend shall for them send.
'Tis death to think of mending when too late,
And glories[212] given for so vile a rate,
As power to hurt another, and to sin
With greater freedom, from control within.
That laws divine, and human, should not be
The least restraint to their impiety.
That reason should be set aside, and death
Become their choice, when they resign their breath.
That piety should be of no esteem,
Nor faith in him, that only can redeem.
All their conceived pleasures come to this,
When yelling they descend ye grand abyss.

---

212. Glory is.

FIVE

POSSESSION – THE DEVIL AND THE WITCH

1. The Boy of Burton

Jesse Bee and others, **The Most Wonderfull and True Storie, of a certaine Witch named Alse Gooderige ...** *(London, 1597)*

As the rest of the pamphlet's title explains, Alse was a woman 'of Stapenhill, who was arraigned and convicted at Darbie at the Assises there'. The pamphlet not only promises to tell her story but adds in a subtitle a description of what will actually become the pamphlet's main theme 'a true report of the strange torments of Thomas Darling, a boy of thirteene yeres of age, that was possessed by the Devill, with his horrible fittes and terrible Apparitions by him uttered at Burton upon Trent in the Countie of Stafford, and of his marvelous deliverance'.[1] The pamphlet describes many of the typically bizarre symptoms of possession and the response of some ministers to these.

The main body of the established Church of England was extremely sceptical about exorcism as a remedy for possession, arguing that it was an ancient Catholic practice and that it implied dialogue with the devil, thus granting him at least a sense of importance and at worst a hold over those who engaged with him. But a small body of ministers on the 'puritan' wing of the Church wished to reclaim Protestantism's right to exorcize, and in the 1580s, 1590s and early 1600s a group of these from the English Midlands carried out spectacular exorcisms by prayer and fasting (rather than the traditional Catholic rites) which they and others documented in pamphlets. Naturally, this drew the fire of the Church's authorities, and the group's *de facto* leader, Nottinghamshire preacher John Darrell (b. 1562), was investigated by commissioners of the Archbishop of York, tried in London by an ecclesiastical court, and judged to be not merely exorcizing without permission but also to be a fraud. Without formalizing a verdict, the court stripped him of his ministry and imprisoned him and his colleague George More. As no more was heard from him after 1602, it is possible that Darrell died in prison. Whether this is so or not, Darrell was heavily punished for exorcizing Darling and others, and for publishing accounts of his work.

---

1. Alse's alleged victim came from Staffordshire, but the suspect herself lived just over the border in Derbyshire: hence, she was sent to the county town of Derby to be tried.

In 1597, however, Darrell and his fellow-ministers, such as Arthur Hildersham who attended Darling, were in the exciting midst of the possession controversy, and the notorious case of the 'Boy of Burton' as he became known, provided another test-case for their theories. Unfortunately, however, it also provided ammunition for their opponents, as Darling later confessed to the court that he had faked his symptoms. This was, of course, precisely what the court wished to hear (and pro-exorcism accounts claim that the confession was tricked and beaten out of him), although it suggested Darrell had been Darling's dupe rather than a charlatan. What Darling actually experienced in 1597, as with all possessions, is in doubt: possession symptoms have been ascribed to the devil, psychological disorders related to hysteria and possibly to abuse, fevers, poisoning by ergot fungus, attention-seeking pretence or a combination of several different factors in each case. In common with many possession victims, Darling was young, lived among pious people, apparently began his possession after becoming demonstrably ill, performed feats that, as reported here, could not easily be explained by fraud, and subsequently gained great celebrity both locally and nationally. The reader may choose how to interpret the information we have about him, and extracts from the main account, later attributed to Jesse Bee, a saddler from Burton-on-Trent, follow below.

The attribution to Bee, a relative by marriage of Darling, was made by Samuel Harsnet, who helped investigate and prosecute Darrell and wrote several vitriolic attacks on Protestant and Catholic exorcists and alleged demoniacs, most notably *A Discovery of the Fraudulent Practises of John Darrell* (London, 1599) and *A Declaration of Egregious Popish Impostures* (London, 1603). But other contributors were also named: Thomas Saunders and Edward Wightman or Weightman, who took over the note-taking of events while Bee was away, and John Denison, minister, who abridged these notes for publication. Bee and Denison abjectly confessed to the court that they had striven to make the possession appear as plausible as possible, and Harsnet also alleged that Darrell and Hildersham had further edited the account.[2] John Denison, who probably wrote the account's preface (signed J.D.) confirmed that the work was 'compiled by a private Christian & man of trade' and that Jesse Bee 'tooke the notes' without mentioning any further input. Whatever the truth, what emerged was an entirely typical possession narrative, which helped fuel the controversy and later contributed significantly to the public humiliation of its main protagonists.

To the Reader ... In a worde, I thinke there can scarcely be any instance shewed (the holy Scriptures excepted) whereby both the peevish opinion, that there are no witches, and the Popish assertion that only their priests can dispossesse, may be better controlled than by this ...

---

2. Samuel Harsnet, *A Discovery of the Fraudulent Practises of John Darrell* (London, 1599), Mmv–Mm2v.

A report of the torments and deliverance of Thomas Darling, (a Boy of thirteene yeares of age) that was possessed by Sathan, at Burton upon Trent.

Upon Saterday (being the xxvii. of Februarie) Robert Toone (dwelling in Burton upon Trent in the Countie of Stafford, Uncle to this Thomas Darling) going to Winsell Wood (which is distant from Burton about half a myle) to hunt the hare, took the Boy with him; and being earnest in following his game, lost him: who (after he had a while wandred up & downe, and could not finde his Uncle) returned home to his uncles house, where he sojourned. Being come home, he wexed[3] heavie, and afterward grew to be verie sicke, vomiting & casting up what he had eaten at dinner: and so was got to bed. The next morning hee had sore fits, with extreame vomitings, that all which sawe him, judged it to bee some strange ague. In the time of this extremitie in these hys fits, he would manie times poynt with his hand, saying; Looke where greene Angels stand in the window, and not long after would often complaine, that a green Cat troubled him: which thing was judged by his friends to proceede of lightnes in his head; manie other things fell out also in these times worthie the noting, whereof (in respect of the unexpected event) there was no note kept. His sicknes wexing more vehement, his Aunt went to a Phisition with his urine:[4] who said he saw no signes of anie natural disease in the Child, unles it were the wormes. His sicknes still increasing (notwithstanding anie thing prescribed or ministered[5]) she went againe with his urine to the Physition; who judged as before, saying further, he doubted that the Childe was bewitched: which shee (holding incredible) imparted it to no bodie; rather imagining it to bee (though some strange, yet) a naturall disease: as divers also judged it to bee the Falling sicknes,[6] by reason that it was no continuall distemperature, but came by fits, with sodaine staring, striving and strugling verie fiercely, and falling downe with sore vomits; also it tooke awaye the use of his legs, so that he was faine to bee carried up and downe, save in his fits, For then hee was nimble inough. How hee spent the time betweene his fits, it is woorth the observing; his exercises were such as might well have beseemed[7] one of riper yeares; wherein he shewed the frutes of his education, which was religious and godly. With those that were good Christians he took great pleasure to conferre; to whom he would signifie his daily expectation of death, and his resolute readinesse to leave the World, and to be with Christ: and all his love to the world, he said extended thus farre (if God had so been

---

3. Became, began to feel.
4. The family were well-off and respectable and did what such people usually did when faced with strange illness. Much is made of their refusal to consult cunning people or accept a diagnosis of supernatural affliction. Many possession accounts start in this way, establishing the credibility of victim/s and witnesses.
5. Administered. See physician John Cotta (above) for this, a sign of bewitchment.
6. Epilepsy.
7. Become, graced.

pleased) he might have lived to be a preacher to thunder out the threatenings of Gods word, against sinne and all abhominations, wherewith these dayes doe abound.[8] In these fits and such like speeches, he continued till Mid-lent Sunday, being the xxi. of March. That day (besides that his wonted fit tooke him) he began in other and more strange manner to bee vexed: for hee sweyed downe as one in a swound. Foorthwith they tooke him up, and layd him upon a bed: where (having layne some smal space) he arose up sodainly, striving and strugling in such sort, that it was enough for two or three to hold him. Then fell hee sodainly upon his backe, and (lying in such manner) raysed up his leggs one after the other so stifly, that the standers by[9] could not beow them in hamme:[10] and thus continuing a whyle with greevous roaring, at last he raysed himselfe up on his feete and his head, his belly standing much above hys head or feete, continuing so a little space he fell downe upon his backe groning verie pittifully. Then rising up, he ran round on his hands and his feete, keeping a certaine compasse: after that striving and strugling with groning, he fel a vomiting, and then comming to himselfe, saide, the Lordes name bee praised. This was the first fit that hee had; and after this manner was hee ordinarily handled during the time of his possession (save that hee did seldome turne round in that manner that is aforesaid:) which being thus ended, he fell upon his knees sodainly in prayer, and that so pithily that the standers by wondered thereat, as much as they did at his strange visitation, beeing no lesse comforted by the one, than they were before greeved at the other . . .

Thomas Darling entreated his friends to pray for him, but when they became distraught at his agonies and could not go on, he asked that Jesse Bee be sent for and asked him to read from the Bible at any point in the text that Bee chose. It seems likely that demonic activity was already suspected by some for Bee read from John, chapter 11, and at verse 4 Thomas Darling had a fit. The fourth verse was regarded by many of the godly as diagnostic in possession cases: it reads 'When Jesus heard that, he said, This sickness is not unto death, but for the glory of God, that the Son of God might be glorified thereby'. It was clear to those watching Darling that this was a direct message about his own illness. Bee remained to read to the patient . . .

---

8. Darling's godly sentiments persisted when he went to university at Oxford. After publicly denouncing the Vice-Chancellor and the Bishop of London (the latter of whom had been one of the chief antagonists of Darrell) as papists, he was sentenced to be whipped and have his ears cropped. The punishment was at least partly carried out, as a contemporary letter reveals (Sarah Williams, ed., *Letters Written by John Chamberlain* (London: Camden Society, 1861), pp. 178–9).

9. Note that Darling's 'friends' (his immediate family and acquaintance) have been replaced by 'standers by': the possession is becoming an audience event, as was often the case.

10. Bend the knees.

When Jesse either ceased to speake of anie comfortable[11] matter, or to read the scriptures, the Boy was quiet from his fits: but when he was so religiously occupied, they came thick upon him; which Jesse Bee considering and observing, told the Boyes Aunt he suspected that the Boy was bewitched. Upon which occasion, (though she doubted of the matter) she told him as before, both her going to the Physition and the Physitions judgement concerning the Boyes sicknesse, which he[12] over-hearing, yet said nothing. The next morning, he said unto the maide that made him readie, I heard my Aunt tell Jesse Bee, that I was bewitched: the same Saterday that my sicknes tooke me, I lost my Uncle in the Wood, and in the Coppice I met a little old woman; she had a gray gown with a black fringe about the cape, a broad thrumd hat,[13] and three warts on her face: I have seene her begging at our doore, as for her name I know it not, but by sight I can know her againe. As I passed by her in the Coppice, I chanced (against my will) to let a scape;[14] which she taking in anger sayd, Gyp with a mischiefe, and fart with a bell: I wil goe to heaven, and thou shalt goe to hell; and forthwith she stooped to the ground. I stood still and looked at her, viewing everie part of her, mervailing what she stooped for; so I came home, and she went to Winsell. Hereupon a more vehement suspition arising, some judged it to be the Witch of Stapenhill:[15] others, because she was olde and went little abroad, rather thought it to be Alice Gooderidge her daughter, who was had in great suspition of manie to bee a dooer in those divellish practises ...

On 8 April the boy's grandmother Mistress Walkeden and another aunt came to visit, and sent for the suspected witch.

When (with much adoo) she was come, they brought her into the chamber where the Boy was; at which time, the Boy fell sodainly into a marvellous sore fit: which being ended, Mistres Walkeden asked her if she knew that boy? She answered she knew him not. Manie other questions were asked; but in vaine, for she would not confesse anye thing. Some of the standers by, perswaded the Boye to scratch her: which he did upon the face, and back of the hands, so that ye blood came out apace: she stroked the back of her hand upon the child, saying; take blood enough child, God helpe thee.

The narrator discourses briefly on the practice of scratching the witch to obtain a cure for bewitchment, concluding that it is itself a witchcraft, but clearly approves of the next tests set for the suspect.

---

11. Spiritually comforting.
12. Darling.
13. A hat covered in tufts, shaggy.
14. A fart.
15. From later information given about Alse's mother, 'the Witch of Stapenhill', Elizabeth Wright, it appears that she certainly attempted a spell to cure a cow, and thus she may have been a cunning woman (B3v).

When Robert Toone the Boyes Uncle and his Schoolemaster saw that mistres Walkeden could nothing prevaile with this bad woman, they tooke her aside: to whom (after many questions) she granted, that she was in the Wood that Saterday which the Boy spake of, and that she saw no boy but Sherrats boye. Further they demanded of her when she received the Communion? She sayd, a twelve month agoe ... They caused her to say the Lords Praier and the Creed, which she huddled up wyth much adoo: but when she came to these words in ye Lords Praier, And lead us not into temptation; and in the Creed either to Jesus Christ, The Holy Ghost, or The Catholicke Church, she would not say anie of those words.

The suspect is established as being present at the scene of the crime, as being a person of bad character who fails to attend church, and as unable to utter holy words. Witches commonly missed out one or more lines of the Lord's Prayer, it was believed, because the Devil would not allow them to say such words. More prosaically, their failure to recite them presumably stemmed from anxiety or occurred because they had originally learned it in Latin in the time before the re-establishment of Protestantism in 1558. Alse's age in 1597 is given as 'almost 60'. Witches also stumbled over the Creed, in listing the beliefs of a true Christian. Perhaps Alse Gooderige believed the men were trying to trap her into a heretical statement on the Trinity or a profession of Roman Catholicism? These tests were enough evidence for Jesse Bee, who took her to a magistrate on 10 April, where both she and her mother were examined about Darling's illness. The magistrate set up more tests, asking the suspects to look at and pray for the boy. Both women were searched for unusual teats, and evidence of warts, and warts that had been cut off, were found. Alse Gooderige was jailed to await trial, but her mother was freed.

The next day the boy had a very greevous fit, in which lying still a while, hee beganne to throw up both his feete sodainely, beating them against the ground with great vehemencie, and at length being in a traunce, he spake saying, Doost thou say thou art my god, and that I am thy sonne? Avoyde Sathan, there is no God save the Lord of hosts. Pawzing a while, at last he said againe, And wouldest thou have me worship a moulten calf?[16] I will worship nothing but the Lord God, and him only wil I serve. Againe being silent awhile, he saide; Wilt thou give mee three townes if I will worship thee? Avoyde Sathan, it is written, I shall worship the Lord God onely. And dost thou say, that if I wil not worship thee, thou wilt torment me three times more; if thou torment me three hundred times, yet canst thou not touch my soule. After this hee was tormented three severall times over every part of his body, which being ended, he desired to goe to the windowe, to refresh himselfe, being hote and faint: there he praysed God for his mercies, telling them that stoode by, If Sathan

---

16. Like that made by the erring Aaron in Exodus 32.4.

came againe, hee woulde aske him many questions, and charge him with many things ... he was throwne into two severall fittes, matchable with the former in crueltie, and at the last spake saying, I charge thee by the living God to tell me who sent thee? Doost thou tel me thy mistris sent thee? What is thy mistris name? ...

'Satan' replied that he would tell Darling tomorrow, but he did not do so. Fits continued, with dialogue revealing a devil named Wrythe inside the boy, and local gentry came to observe the spectacle. One nameless visitor was not so welcome to Thomas Darling. He, said Darling, 'bade me I should not dissemble, saying that there was no witches'. Cunning people called to offer help, and were rebuffed. Finally, Alse Gooderige was brought on a visit from prison and confessed she had hurt Darling, mistaking him for Sherrat's boy who, she said, had broken a basket of her eggs. 'If they would forgive her', she said 'it should cease'. Under duress she confessed she had asked a devil-dog to hurt the boy, and had bent over vomiting herself to show him how it should be done. But, of course, no confession could help free her and she was returned to jail in Derby. Finally, an acceptable healer arrived ...

... at 3 came M. Hildersham of Ashby de la Zouch, with divers other godly ministers.[17] M. Hildersham after that by certaine questions, hee had made triall of the boys faith, said openly, that howsoever the Papists boasted much of the power their priests had to cast out divells, and the simple everie where noted it as a great discredit to the Ministers of the Gospel, that they do want this power, yet he did professe there was no such gift in them, that thogh the Lord oft in these daies, by the praiers of the faithful casts out divels, yet could he not assure them to cure him. To holde this faith of myracles to remaine still in the church, is an opinion dangerous ... al which notwithstanding, that there is a good use of praier in such a case, and of fasting also ... In which perswasion, hee being the mouth of the rest, they all prayed, during which time the childe was not interrupted.

Hildersham and a crowd of others prayed and fasted, and were rewarded when Darling began to have visions of Job, Christ and heaven, crying out 'See Maister Hildersham, preach and teach, Oh fast and pray night and day.' On 27 May John Darrell arrived to offer advice.

there came one John Dorell (a faithful Preacher of the Word) to him; who

---

17. Arthur Hildersham (1563–1632) had been a lecturer at Ashby since 1587, and vicar since 1593. John Darrell had preached at Ashby also, and the men shared a religious viewpoint. After Darrell's downfall, Hildersham was active in promoting Church reform from within (the 'Millenary Petition', 1604, asked the king to drive out vestiges of Catholicism from Church of England practice). Increasingly in conflict with his bishop, he too was imprisoned for his beliefs (1615, 1616) and published tracts on his theological views.

seeing him in divers of his fits, assured his Frends and him he was possessed with an unclean spirit: telling him (out of S. James 4 chapt. vers. 7)[18] that the onely way for his deliverance was to resist sathan; in which if he failed, he shuld sin against God: because it was a breach of a Commandement, Resist the divell. &c. That for his further incouragement, he had a promise of victorie, in that it is said, he will or shall flee; That by the divell is not to be understood onely the temptations of the divel, but even sathans verie person. And proceeding to confirme the Childes faith in this Resistance, he afterwards exhorted his Parents and whole Familie to prepare themselves against the next day to that holy exercise of Prayer and Fasting; alledging (to put by all doubts) the words of Christ, This kinde goeth not out but by Praier & Fasting.[19]

Darrell himself was not present at the event, but, even so, Thomas Darling began to be cured. He spoke in the voices of several devils: as one, Brother Radulphus, he said 'Brother Glassap, we cannot prevaile, his faith is so strong, and they fast and pray, and a Preacher prayeth as fast as they.' The devil-voices plotted to stop the prayers but eventually Darling was again sick and pointed to a corner of the room, saying 'Looke, looke, see you not the Mouse that is gone out of my mouth.' The devil was gone and although he apparently tried subsequently to obsess Darling, from without, the new trances soon ended. Darrell's critics were to represent this final demonic assault as a repossession showing the inefficacy of prayer and fasting, but this pamphlet ends triumphantly by noting that Alse Gooderige died in jail, and promising further stories of Darrell's dispossessions to come.

2. Frustrations of a failed witch-hunter

Edward Fairfax, 'A Discourse of witchcraft' (1621–2)

From British Library Additional Manuscript 32496.

Edward Fairfax (d. 1635) was a Yorkshire gentleman, a poet, famous translator of Tasso and an uncle of the Parliamentarian general Thomas Fairfax, and his attempts to prosecute and bring to conviction those he believed responsible for an outbreak of possession in his family in 1621–2 are the topic of his unpublished manuscript 'A Discourse of witchcraft as it was acted in the family of Mr. Edward Fairfax'. Fairfax's daughters, 21-year-old Helen and 7-year-old Elizabeth, together with a neighbour's daughter, Maud Jeffray, began to exhibit the symptoms of possession or obsession in October 1621. After the traditional

18. Darrell offers an exegesis of James 4.7 'Resist the devil, and he will flee from you'.
19. Matthew 17.21; Mark 9.29. Christ is referring to a possessing spirit.

resistance to belief that witches were the cause, Fairfax accused six women of bewitching his children. But other members of his community, including the vicar of Fuystone or Fewston where the family lived, defended the women, and told Fairfax he must be mistaken. He managed to have the accused brought to trial, but although he took the case to two separate Assizes, the magistrates, Judge and jury were convinced that the affair was a hoax. The six were acquitted and Fairfax, fuming and blaming his neighbours for intriguing against him, had to drop the matter.

Fairfax's account is notable for the freshness of the appeal it makes to the reader. The combative author anticipates and deals directly with possible criticisms, is precise and unapologetic about the circumstances of his life and beliefs, and justifies his activities vigorously. His expressions of hurt and anger are undimmed by time. However, the reader is also constantly tantalized by the possibility that there are unacknowledged factors at work in the circumstances of the case: why was Fairfax so spectacularly unsuccessful? Did specific suspicions about his family and the Jeffrays or a more general scepticism – perhaps based on reports of other faked possessions – influence decision makers locally and at York? What local tensions lie behind the antagonism between Fairfax and other families? Fairfax does not provide answers, but his narrative suggests both that there are hidden stories within the account of his experience, and that it was certainly not always easy to accuse and prosecute witches. How many stories of failure like Fairfax's were not recorded?

There are a number of versions of Fairfax's 'Discourse', including the incomplete BL Add. MS 32495. Each version differs slightly, but the version chosen is BL Add. MS 32496. The published text recommended in the Bibliography is the first complete printed edition, William Grainge's *Daemonologia* (Harrogate, 1882), differing quite substantially from 32496 in a variety of phrasing, spelling and punctuation, and based on a transcription by Ebenezer Sibley. Those differences are not noted here, as they are very many and mostly minor, but readers are referred to Grainge's edition for comparison. The text below was probably transcribed by Miles Gale, rector of Keighley, Yorkshire (see above, Chapter 4 under Gale(?), 'Witchcraft ye practice of deluded minds').[20]

I present yee, Xian[21] reader, a narration of Witchcraft, of wch I am a wofull wittness, and soe can best report it, read ys[22] wthout vindicating passion, & in reading, let thy discretion proeceed thy judgement: I set down ye actions

---

20. William Grainge quotes R. M. Milnes as confirming the MS is in Gale's handwriting (Grainge, *Daemonologia*, p. 22).
21. Christian.
22. This. The writer routinely abbreviates that (yt), than and then (yn), them (ym), thus (yus), when (wn) and so forth.
23. *Sic.*

& ye accidents truly, observe ym seriously wth learning, if yu[23] be furnished yt way: if not, yet with wisedome & religion, ye enquiry will afford yee matter enough, to assure ye wise phisitian, yt here is more[24] yn naturall desease. To answer ye superstitious ignorant: yt ye Actors in ys be noe walking Ghosts, nor danceing Fairies, and to stop ye mouths of ye incredulous (who deny Witches), for in ys appeareth ye work of Sathan, nor merely his own, but assisted with some wicked coadjutors, by whose cooperation, these Innocents be yus cruelly afflicted ... I intreat yee to be assured, yt for my selfe I am in religion nether a fantastick Puritan, nor superstitious Papist, but soe settled in conscience, yt I have ye sure ground of God's word, to warrant all I beleeve, & ye commendable ordinances of our English Church, to approve all I practice in wch course I live a faithful Xian, & an obedient subject, & soe teach my family. Of ye Patients 2 are my Daughters: of whome ys was ye estate wn ye Witches began wth ym. ye Elder Hellen Fairfax a maid of 21 years, of person healthfull, of complexion sanguine: free from melancholy, of capacitie not apprehensive of much, but rather hard to learn things fit, slow of speech, patient of reproofe, of behaviour wthout offence, educated only in my own house, and therefore not knowing much. Elizabeth my younger Daughter an Infant of scarce 7 years, of a pleasant aspect, quick witt, active spirit able to receive any instruction, and willing to undergoe pains ...[25]

Fairfax mentions Maud Jeffray, the other original possession victim and a daughter of John Jeffray, gentleman, but says he knows little of her or her family. He also describes the suspects.

The 1st is called Margaret Waite a Widdow yt some yeares agoe came to dwell in these parts, wth a Husband who brought wth ym an evill report for Witchcraft & theft, ye man dyed by ye hand of ye Executioner, for stealing, and his relickt hath increased ye report shee brought wth her, for Witcherie. her familiar spirit is a deformed thing, wth many feet, black of collure, rough wth hair, ye bigness of a Cat, ye name of it unknown. ye next is her Daughter, a young Woman, aggreeing wth her Mother in name & conditions (as is thought) to wch shee added impudency, & lewd behaviour, for shee is young & not deformed, & their house is holden for a receptacle for some of ye worst sort practiceing night picooies[26] & small larcenies: her spirit, a white Cat, spotted wth black & named Inges.

---

24. The writer abbreviates 'more' to +.
25. To work hard. Fairfax's detailed, and notably different, assessment of his daughters' characters is unexpected and demonstrates his willingness to allow the reader access to private matters so that they may make a correct judgement. The family dynamics are interesting: after their father's 1635 death, Helen married Christopher Yates (1636), while the much younger Elizabeth married Philip Richardson (1635), but died sometime before 1648.
26. Not in the *Oxford English Dictionary*, this word is perhaps related to 'picaro' or 'picaroon', a knave or brigand?

Ye 3 is Jennit Dible, a very old widdow reputed a Witch for many yeares, and a constant report affirmeth yt her Mother, two Ants, 2 sisters, her Husband, & some of her children, have all been long esteemed Witches, for yt it seemeth hereditary to her family her spirit is in ye shape of a great black Catt, called Gibbe, wch hath attended her now above 40 years.

These are made up a Mass by Margaret Thorpe, Daughter of Jennit Dibble lately a Widdow for wch shee beareth some blame. This Woman if you read ye sequell, will perhaps seeme unto you, not wthout great reason to be an obedient childe and docible[27] scholler of soe skillfull a parent: her Familiar is in ye shape of a bird, yellow of colour, about ye bigness of a Crow, ye name of it, is Tewhit.

The 5th is Elizabeth Fletcher, Wife of Tho. Fletcher, Daughter to one Grace Foster, dead not long since, a woman notoriously famed for a Witch, who had soe powerful a hand over ye wealthiest neighbours about her, yt none of ym refused to doe any thing shee required, yea unbesought they provided her of fire, & meat from their own tables, & did wht else they thought would please her. ne illis noceat[28]

ye halfe dozen is made up by Elizabeth Diconson, wife of Wm Diconson, of whome I cannot say much of certain knowledge nether is her spirit known unto us ... There is a 7th who much afflicteth ye Children, very frequent in apparitions,[29] & talkings unto ym, but they know her not, & therefore call her ye strange woman, ys individuum vagum,[30] hath a spirit in likeness of a white Cat, wch she calleth Fillie she hath kept yt 20 years ...

So far, the matter seems straightforward: three victims, six identifiable suspects. But problems began almost at once.

Wn 1st quaestioned by way of justice some of these women, they wanted not both Counsellers & supporters of ye best, able & most understanding about ym. these men (at feasts & meetings) spread reports, and moved doubts, inferring a supposall of counterfeiting, & practice in ye Children, and yt it was not serious, but a combination proceeding of malice:[31] these things they suggested to our next[32] Justices where it found a wellcome, ether for ye person's sake, who presented yt, or for yt those Magistrates are incredulous of things of ys kind, or perhaps for both those reasons ...

---

27. Docile.
28. To prevent her harm(ing them).
29. The witches often appeared to their victims as ghostly apparitions. See the section in Chapter 8 on American witchcraft in the 1690s for the most heated discussion of this phenomenon.
30. Vague or unsettled inseparable creature. The phrase makes more sense as 'vague individual', but this is not its literal meaning.
31. A plot growing from malice.
32. Nearest.

Fairfax goes on to say that 'some divines and physicians', among others, attributed the victims' symptoms to natural disease. These included 'trances and fits ... convulsions and distortions of divers members' and 'strange wringings in their bellies'. Fairfax was even lent medical books in an attempt to convince him that his children were not possessed. With this groundwork laid, he begins the story of the afflictions of his daughters. On Sunday 28 October 1621, Helen was found in a trance on the floor. She seemed dead, but several hours later began to breathe and speak. Her words suggested that she thought she was in Leeds, at a sermon preached by Alexander Cooke (vicar of Leeds 1614–32 and a noted anti-Catholic writer). The next day she seemed recovered but then began to hold conversations with brothers and sisters of hers who had died – the Fairfax family had lost yet another baby, Ann, in October 1621. It was decided that she was suffering from 'the mother', an hysterical disease thought especially likely to afflict young women. But throughout November she had visions: a cat which breathed poison into her mouth, a handsome and fashionable young man who came as a suitor to her but turned out to be the devil, and Mr Cooke, who drove Satan away. Fairfax still had no suspicion of witchcraft but on 23 November ...

I was in ye Kitchin, wth many of my family, & there some speeches were moved of Charmers, & Lookers (as our rude people call ym) & ye names of many were reckoned up, who were thought to be skillfull therein, & it was said yt such as goe to these Charmers, carry & give ym a single penny. these words gave occasion to my Wife[33] to remember & tell it, yt she had a single pennie given her, amongst other money, by Margaret Wait, sen. wch she paid for Corn ye woman desired her to keep ye penny, for she would come for it again, wch she did accordingly, a few dayes after, & demanded it, affirmeing yt she would not lack it for any thing, for it kept her from dreaming: she said, yt it had a hole in it, by wch she did use to hang it about her neck, in a thred: at wch words, such as were present laughed heartily, especially Wm. Fish, yn my servant, wth whome ye woman was very angry for laughing, & departed in anger, wthout her penny ...

Fairfax was troubled by this evidence of cunning magic and determined to destroy the penny. But it was missing from the locked desk where it had been kept. Helen saw a vision of a man who said he had taken it, and it later returned, at which time Fairfax burned and pounded it to pieces. William Fish, meanwhile, had fallen terribly sick and his foot had rotted from his leg. Fairfax was now suspicious that witchcraft was in operation, and this was confirmed for him when on 5 December Helen saw a vision of Margaret Wait, who threatened her that she would suck out her heart's blood and gave her a baby which sucked on Helen's breast. Helen was then sick, and was only comforted when she was told the witch was lying to her. On 6 December, one of those who was to be a

---

33. Dorothy Fairfax, née Laycock.

chief opponent of the prosecution, neighbour Henry Graver, came to see Helen, but Fairfax had by now determined to confront Margaret Wait. When she denied any wrongdoing ...

I sent for Henry Graver & for Mr. Smithson ye Vicar of Fuystone,[34] to whome, (as my good neighbours) I reported ye strangeness of ye case, and of ym expected advice & comfort, as soe great a perturbation needfully required. but I found my selfe deceived in yt expectation, for these men were great friends to yt woman, & turned all their speeches to entreaties yt I would suffer ye woman to depart, & to make further tryall before I brought her in quaestion; to wch I condescended ...

Wait was released but touched Fairfax as she left, leading him and his fearful wife to suspect that she wished to gain power to bewitch him. Another woman was now accused by Helen, whose visions continued. A young man appeared to her praising Graver and Smithson for not bearing with, or believing, Helen. She retorted that anyone who bore with witches was not a fit vicar, and that Graver was afraid of the demonic apparition. In January 1622 Elizabeth also began to go into trances and Helen's accusations took a new direction. A vision told her that the witches 'were hired to bewitch her' by 'the best man in Fuystone parish'. Helen identified this man as Henry Graver.

It was at this point that Fairfax moved against the six female suspects. They appeared at Assizes in early April, and again in August, although the precise course of events and charges are not recorded. Fairfax first complains about the court's verdict, then gives details of the August trial, so for the sake of clarity these extracts are presented in reverse order.

Upon ye 8 of August, I preferred sundry Inditements, against ye women quaestioned, & my selfe, & all other ye wittnesses, delivered our evidence upon our oathes before ye grand Jury, who were all of ym Gentlemen of such wisedome & discretion, yt they can hardly be parraleld by any Jury, for divers years past, if ye comparison be made for all things. six of ym were Justices of peace & they received alsoe a good caveat[35] by a message from ye Judge, to be very carefull in ye matter of ye Witches, wch message was delivered to ym in my hearing, soe they proceeded wth much advisedness & diligence in quaestioning me, & all ye other wittnesses. Soe as I thinck nothing was left undone, or said, wch ye witt of man could esteeme needfull for ye searching out of ye truth, & in gieveing satisfaction of ye certainty of soe strange a case in ye end they were all soe fully persuaded in their consciences, and so abundantly satisfyed in all their doubts and curious demands,[36] yt wthout difficulty, they found every Inditement to be Billa Vera ...

34. Nicholas Smithson, Vicar of Fewston 1591–1632.
35. Caution.
36. Detailed questions.

On 9 August, therefore, Fairfax again gave evidence, whilst all three girls fell into deathlike trances in court. But when they were carried out, several justices decided to carry out further trial of their stories. Fairfax is unclear about the details, but argues that the justices had an 'intention, as it seemed, to find out some imposture'. The accusers were forcibly cut off from all the people who had come to court with them but, speaking of Elizabeth first, Fairfax protests as if certain that she and Helen confessed nothing.

how they proceeded wth her, I know not: but they found nothing in her wch could cause ym thinck[37] yt her innocency should dissemble those things of her sister alsoe they made some experiments more violent, whereof ye marks remained for a time after, yet in her alsoe their curiosity found nothing but sincerity. How they dealt wth Jeffray's daughter I will not examine, but they returning to ye bench, reported yt ys was a practice confessed ...

Subsequently Maud Jeffray denied confessing, and none of the three was asked to repeat a confession in court.

but ye Judge, upon wht occasion moved, I know not, after some good plausible hearing of ye evidence for a time, at last told ye Jury yt ye evidence reached not to ye point of ye statute, and soe wthdrew ye offenders from their tryall, by the Jurie of Life and Death, & dismissed ym at liberty: at wch manner of proceeding many wiser men yn I am greatly wonder. It hath since been told me yt one John Dibb, son to Dib's wife & brother to Thorp's wife, procured a certificate to ye Judge yt these women were of good fame, & never before yt time ill reported of for witchcraft, & yt Henry Graver solicited & induced many persons to set there hands to ye same: upon advantage of wch certificate such Magistrates as are incredulous in these things, worke their deliverance ...

Fairfax had said previously that he thought the judge was motivated by the fact 'that the children were presented in court alive and well-liking' or in good health, which suggests that the judge felt they were not, as the statute decreed, 'killed, destroyed, wasted, consumed, pined or lamed in his or her bodie, or any parte thereof', although had he wished to find ways around this objection, he could certainly have done so. Fairfax added that he was not sorry the witches had escaped death, since so many lives ought to be precious to a charitable Christian, but concluded 'the proceedings which made the way easy for their escape, I fear, was not fair'.

The Fairfax family returned home disconsolate, whilst John Jeffray was imprisoned. Fairfax bitterly explains the effects of the judgment on his own reputation, providing an interpretation of events which sums up many of the unanswered questions about his family.

---

37. *Sic.*

... upon my selfe was put an aspersion not of dishonesty, but of simplicity & it was given out yt Jeffray & his family devised ye practice, to wch they drew my eldest daughter & she ye younger, and yt I (like a good Innocent)[38] beleeved all wch I heard or saw to be true & not feigned; they add an end my children should aim at in ys, Vid[39] to be ye more cherished.

38. Like a fool.
39. *Videlicit*: which was.

SIX

LEARNED MEN AND MAGIC

1. Tragedy

Christopher Marlowe, **The Tragical History of Dr Faustus** *(A text; London, 1604)*

Christopher Marlowe (1564–93) probably wrote *Dr Faustus* in the late 1580s, basing his play on the existing story of a German magician, an amalgam of several real and fictional characters. Translated into English, this story gave Marlowe several images and episodes. But he added a great deal of depth to the character of the magician, creating an archetypal image of a Renaissance man driven by questions and desires to transgress the most fundamental laws of a restrictive culture and religion. He explored the possibilities of devil worship and magic in succulent verse, itself innovatory, circling obsessively around the moment of damnation until audience and reader are no longer sure exactly when God withdraws his mercy, and the magician is finally doomed to hell. The original story of Faust is a clear-cut moral tale of an interestingly bad man justly punished for his iniquity: Marlowe's play leaves us wondering why the magician chooses (and keeps choosing) as he does and whether his punishment is just. The play's tensions are not only between God and the devil, but between human aspiration and human limitations, and between two forms of writing: the medieval morality play and the Renaissance revival of classical tragedy. Marlowe's boldness in *Dr Faustus* was to take the protagonist of a morality tale and rework him to demand that we have some imaginative sympathy with a man variously defined as a witch, a conjuror and a devil-worshipper.

Marlowe and his magician share a reputation for scandalous unorthodoxy and doomed dissent. At the time of his death in a brawl in 1593, Marlowe was suspected of atheism, which in Elizabethan times most commonly took the form of questioning and deriding received truths about God and biblical figures, rather than denying God's existence. Certainly Marlowe must have been aware, through a network of acquaintances, of these 'atheist' views, although his background was soundly orthodox. Born in Canterbury, he attended Cambridge University where militant Protestantism was at its height, and was at one time suspected of wishing to convert to Catholicism. In the light of this polarized biography, critics have read *Dr Faustus* both as an endorsement of contemporary atheism and a condemnation of it, suggesting that Marlowe left a genuine ambivalence in the text despite the resoundingly repressive Epilogue, included below. Ambivalence is appropriate to the demonological subject: the secret, forbidden world Marlowe created for the scholar Faustus is that of the Renaissance magus, a learned man who treads a dangerous line between satanic and divine, and who may or may not remain on the side of the angels.

'Real' magi, such as English court astrologer John Dee, and lesser oracles like Simon Forman and Francis Coxe, argued that they harnessed the power of natural energies, good spirits, or God's name to command demons, but demonologists thought otherwise, and stories persisted of learned men who, like common witches, had trafficked with Satan to learn secrets and gain power (see John Walsh above and The Merry Devil of Edmonton below). Marlowe thus drew on contemporary anxieties about witches and magicians to create the classic English depiction of contracting with the devil. In doing so, his play perfectly sums up human fascination with magic: on the one hand it is an abomination, gratifying worldly ambition and vanity, but on the other it offers unlimited imaginative power and a reckless defiance of the prudent and the proper. Theatre, through illusion and pretence, gave an opportunity to engage with this attraction/repulsion for it could flirt with danger and withdraw untainted. The devils were only actors and the spells just cues.

There are two early texts of Dr Faustus, both of which can claim some relationship to the play as conjecturally first written and performed (the first known performance was in 1594). The extracts below are edited from the 1604 'A' text, but the notes include reference to any significant differences in the revised 'B' text of 1616. For a full discussion of the play and its texts, readers are referred to David Bevington and Eric Rasmussen's introduction to both texts in The Revels Plays edition of Doctor Faustus (Manchester: Manchester University Press, 1993).[1]

The play begins with a Prologue introducing its protagonist's story and his first appearance on the stage.

Prologue: Now is he born, his parents base of stock,
            In Germany, within a town called Rhodes:[2]
            Of riper years to Wittenberg[3] he went,
            Whereas[4] his kinsmen chiefly brought him up.
            So soon he profits in divinity,
            The fruitful plot of scholarism graced,[5]
            That shortly he was graced with doctor's name,

---

1. The editors' excellent notes have been very helpful in preparing this text, which is taken from the 2nd edition of the 'A' text in the Bodleian Library.
2. Roda.
3. University town, famous for its strident Protestantism.
4. Where.
5. Divinity is seen as the most fruitful and 'graced' subject of study.

Excelling all whose sweet delight disputes[6]
In heavenly matters of theology;
Till, swoll'n with cunning of a self-conceit,[7]
His waxen wings did mount above his reach,
And melting heavens conspired his overthrow.[8]
For, falling to a devilish exercise,
And glutted more with learning's golden gifts,
He surfeits upon cursed necromancy;[9]
Nothing so sweet as magic is to him,
Which he prefers before his chiefest bliss.
And this the man that in his study sits.

When we see Dr Faustus in his study, we soon learn that he has become frustrated with the limitations of conventional subjects. He dismisses Logic, Medicine, Law and Divinity before choosing a new study which promises to give him power to do whatever he can imagine.

Act 1, Scene 1

Faustus: These metaphysics of magicians
              And necromantic books are heavenly.
              Lines, circles, signs,[10] letters, and characters:
              Aye, these are those that Faustus most desires.
              O, what a world of profit and delight,
              Of power, of honour, of omnipotence,
              Is promised to the studious artisan?[11]
              All things that move between the quiet poles
              Shall be at my command. Emperors and kings
              Are but obeyed in their several provinces;
              Nor can they raise the wind or rend the clouds:
              But his dominion that exceeds in this
              Stretcheth as far as doth the mind of man.

---

6. Whose delight is dispute, i.e., formal argument on theological topics.
7. A richly suggestive phrase. Cunning meant knowing but also deceit, and here also suggests artfulness and skill. Conceit meant idea or concept, so that Faustus is at once self-obsessed, skilful and 'conceited' in the modern sense.
8. In Greek myth, Icarus flew using a pair of wings made of feathers glued with wax. When he soared too high, the wax was melted by the sun (heavens) and Icarus fell to his death. The idea of heavens 'conspiring' is interesting: do Christian heavens conspire Faustus' fall in a pejorative sense?
9. Original reads 'negromancy'; black magic as opposed to divination by conjuring the dead?
10. Original reads 'sceanes'.
11. Worker, but also the practiser of an art.

A sound magician is a mighty god.[12]
Here, Faustus, try thy brains to gain a deity.

Angels – good and bad spirits – appear to give him advice on the choice of this
course.

Good Angel: O Faustus, lay that damned book aside
And gaze not on it, lest it tempt thy soul,
And heap God's heavy wrath upon thy head,
Read, read the Scriptures. That[13] is blasphemy.

Evil Angel: Go forward, Faustus, in that famous art
Wherein all nature's treasury is contained:
Be thou on earth as Jove[14] is in the sky,
Lord and commander of these elements. [Exeunt Angels]

Faustus: How am I glutted with conceit of this?
Shall I make spirits fetch me what I please,
Resolve me of all ambiguities,
Perform what desperate[15] enterprise I will?
I'll have them fly to India for gold,
Ransack the ocean for orient pearl,
And search all corners of the new-found world[16]
For pleasant fruits and princely delicates:[17]
I'll have them read me strange philosophy
And tell the secrets of all foreign kings.
I'll have them wall all Germany with brass
And make swift Rhine circle fair Wittenberg.[18]
I'll have them fill the public schools with silk,[19]
Wherewith the students shall be bravely clad.
I'll levy soldiers with the coin they bring
And chase the Prince of Parma from our land,[20]

---

12. 'B' text reads 'demigod'.
13. The necromantic book.
14. God.
15. Reckless, extravagant.
16. America.
17. Delicacies.
18. These defensive measures, and plans to support the rights of his pupils (below), also
suggest Faustus' capacity for self-display, excess and superficiality: are they good or bad?
Will moving the river Rhine, clothing students in silk, or fighting a war with new
technologies to drive out invaders count as 'good works'? As it transpires, we hear no
more of these ideas.
19. Original reads 'skill'.
20. The Prince led the Spanish forces occupying the Protestant Netherlands. As Bevington
and Rasmussen point out, English audiences would have approved of his removal (*Doctor
Faustus*, p. 117, note to line 95).

> And reign sole king of all our provinces:
> Yea, stranger engines for the brunt of war
> Than was the fiery keel at Antwerp's bridge,[21]
> I'll make my servile spirits to invent.

After Faustus has chosen his aims, he must summon a devil.

Act 1, Scene 3[22]

Faustus: Now that the gloomy shadow of the earth,
               Longing to view Orion's drizzling look,
               Leaps from th'Antarctic world unto the sky
               And dims the welkin with her pitchy breath,[23]
               Faustus, begin thy incantations,
               And try if devils will obey thy hest,
               Seeing thou hast prayed and sacrificed to them.[24]

[He draws a circle]

> Within this circle is Jehovah's[25] name,
> Forward and backward anagrammatised,
> The breviated[26] names of holy saints,
> Figures of every adjunct to the heavens,
> And characters of signs and erring stars,[27]
> By which the spirits are enforced to rise,
> Then fear not, Faustus, but be resolute,
> And try the uttermost magic can perform.
> *Sint mihi dei Acherontis propitii! Valeat numen triplex Jehovae! Ignei,*
> *aerii, aquatici, terreni, spiritus, salvete! Orientis princeps Lucifer,*
> *Beelzebub, inferni ardentis monarcha, et Demogorgon, propitiamus vos,*
> *ut appareat et surgat Mephistopheles! Quid tu moraris? Per Jehovam,*

---

21. An innovatory and frightening device, this was a fireship used in 1585 to burn the bridge.
22. In the 'B' text, five devils are already on the stage, invisible to Faustus, but overseeing his conjuration. The 'B' text records revisions, and implies a bigger, more spectacular production with more actors and expensive costumes, so the demonological import of the devils waiting invisibly for Faustus to transgress might be secondary to the desire to feast the audience's eyes.
23. *Dr Faustus* is full of imagery taken from cosmological debates where science and magical lore meet – whether the sun is the centre of the universe, how the planets orbit in their 'spheres'. Here, a partly personified night (the earth's shadow) moves *north*wards from Antarctica to see the (supposedly rainy) constellation Orion, dimming the sky as 'she' does so.
24. Marlowe does not show these rites.
25. God's.
26. Abbreviated.
27. Charts of the skies, including zodiac signs and planets.

> *Gehennam, et consecratam aquam quam nunc spargo, signumque crucis*
> *quod nunc facio, et per vota nostra, ipse nunc surgat nobis dicatus*
> *Mephistopheles!* [28]

[Faustus sprinkles holy water and makes a sign of the cross]

[Enter a Devil, Mephistopheles][29]

> I charge thee to return and change thy shape,
> Thou art too ugly to attend on me.
> Go, and return an old Franciscan friar,
> That holy shape becomes a devil best.[30] [Exit Devil
> Mephistopheles]
> I see there's virtue in my heavenly words.
> Who would not be proficient in this art?
> How pliant is this Mephistopheles,
> Full of obedience and humility,
> Such is the force of magic and my spells.
> Now,[31] Faustus, thou art conjurer laureate,[32]
> That canst command great Mephistopheles.
> *Quin redis, Mephistopheles, fratris imagine!*[33]

---

28. May the gods of Acheron (the hellish river) be propitious to me! Let the threefold power of Jehovah be strong! Spirits of fire, air, water, and earth, all hail! Lucifer, Prince of the East, Beelzebub, monarch of burning hell, and Demogorgon, we ask your favour that Mephistopheles may appear and rise. Why do you delay? By Jehovah, Gehenna, and the holy water I now sprinkle, and by the sign of the cross I now make, and by our prayers, may Mephistopheles himself rise at our command! (translated by Bevington and Rasmussen, eds, *Doctor Faustus*, p. 126, note to lines 16-23). Some of the words are supplied from the 'B' text as they are omitted from 'A'.

29. In the 'B' text, the word 'dragon' appears here. Was the character of Mephistopheles to enter as an actor costumed as a dragon, or perhaps represented by an inanimate 'creature effect'? By 1598 the Admiral's Men theatre company possessed among their costumes and props a 'dragon in fostes', as theatre manager Philip Henslowe's surviving diary shows (W. W. Greg, ed., *Henslowe's Diary* (London, 1904)). Thus this may well have been part of the original conception of the play rather than a spectacular extra. Faustus' reaction to such an appearance is entirely appropriate. The devil was often represented by a dragon, as in Revelation.

30. As with many episodes in the play, there is an awkward relationship here between anti-Catholicism and anti-Christianity. If the joke is that friars are like devils, then this is anti-Catholic and Faustus is adopting an awkwardly pro-Protestant (and thus pro-Christian) position. If Faustus' aim is to mock friars by having their evil inverse, a devil, inhabit their robes, then it cannot help suggesting Catholicism is a force for good, since in devilishly attacking it, Faustus is pointing to its holiness.

31. Original reads 'No'.

32. Crowned with laurel, celebrated.

33. Why don't you return, Mephistopheles, in the guise of a friar! (translation by Bevington and Rasmussen, eds, *Doctor Faustus*, p. 128, note to line 35).

[Enter Mephistopheles disguised as a friar]

Mephistopheles: Now, Faustus, what wouldst thou have me do?

Faustus: I charge thee wait upon me whilst I live,
To do whatever Faustus shall command,
Be it to make the moon drop from her sphere
Or the ocean to overwhelm the world.

Mephistopheles: I am a servant to great Lucifer
And may not follow thee without his leave;
No more than he commands must we perform.

Faustus: Did not he charge thee to appear to me?

Mephistopheles: No, I came now hither of mine own accord.

Faustus: Did not my conjuring speeches raise thee? Speak.

Mephistopheles: That was the cause, but yet *per accidens*.[34]
For when we hear one rack the name of God,
Abjure the Scriptures and his Saviour Christ,
We fly, in hope to get his glorious soul,
Nor will we come, unless he use such means
Whereby he is in danger to be damned:
Therefore, the shortest cut for conjuring
Is stoutly to abjure the Trinity
And pray devoutly to the prince of hell.

Faustus: So Faustus hath
Already done, and holds this principle:
There is no chief but only Beelzebub,
To whom Faustus doth dedicate himself.
This word 'damnation' terrifies not him,
For he confounds hell in Elysium.
His ghost be with the old philosophers.[35]
But leaving these vain trifles of men's souls,
Tell me what is that Lucifer thy lord?

Mephistopheles: Arch-regent and commander of all spirits.

Faustus: Was not that Lucifer an angel once?

Mephistopheles: Yes, Faustus, and most dearly loved of God.

Faustus: How comes it then that he is prince of devils?

---

34. Not as a matter of cause and effect, but simply as giving occasion to the devil to come.
35. Faustus equates the Christian hell with the classical underworld. There was much debate about where moral pre-Christians might spend eternity after God's revelation of himself. To suppose them damned as heathens suggested unfair retrospective judgement, and whilst the Catholic Limbo provided one answer, this fudging of definitions was another.

Mephistopheles: O, by aspiring pride and insolence,
For which God threw him from the face of heaven.

Faustus: And what are you that live with Lucifer?

Mephistopheles: Unhappy spirits that fell with Lucifer,
Conspired against our God with Lucifer,
And are forever damned with Lucifer.

Faustus: Where are you damned?

Mephistopheles: In hell.

Faustus: How comes it then that thou art out of hell?

Mephistopheles: Why, this is hell, nor am I out of it:
Think'st thou that I, who saw the face of God,
And tasted the eternal joys of heaven,
Am not tormented with ten thousand hells
In being deprived of everlasting bliss?
O, Faustus, leave these frivolous demands,
Which strike a terror to my fainting soul!

Faustus: What, is great Mephistopheles so passionate,
For being deprived of the joys of heaven?
Learn thou of Faustus manly fortitude,
And scorn those joys thou never shalt possess.
Go bear these tidings to great Lucifer:
Seeing Faustus hath incurred eternal death
By desp'rate thoughts against Jove's deity,
Say he surrenders up to him his soul,
So he will spare him four-and-twenty years,
Letting him live in all voluptuousness,
Having thee ever to attend on me,
To give me whatsoever I shall ask,
To tell me whatsoever I shall demand,
To slay mine enemies and aid my friends,
And always be obedient to my will.
Go and return to mighty Lucifer,
And meet me in my study at midnight,
And then resolve me of thy master's mind.

Mephistopheles: I will, Faustus. [Exit]

Faustus: Had I as many souls as there be stars,
I'd give them all for Mephistopheles:
By him I'll be great emperor of the world
And make a bridge through the moving air
To pass the ocean with a band of men;
I'll join the hills that bind the Afric shore,
And make that land continent to Spain,
And both contributory to my crown.

> The Emp'ror shall not live but by my leave,
> Nor any potentate of Germany:[36]
> Now that I have obtained what I desire,
> I'll live in speculation[37] of this art
> Till Mephistopheles return again. [Exit]

However, Faustus contemplates not just his art, but the price he must pay –
and, he implies, that he has already paid – for it.

Act 2, Scene 1

[Enter Faustus in his study]

Faustus: Now, Faustus, must thou needs be damned,
　　　　　And canst thou not be saved?[38]
　　　　　What boots it[39] then to think of God or heaven?
　　　　　Away with such vain fancies and despair,
　　　　　Despair in God and trust in Beelzebub:
　　　　　Now go not backward. No, Faustus, be resolute,
　　　　　Why waverest thou? O, something soundeth in mine ears:
　　　　　'Abjure this magic, turn to God again'.
　　　　　Ay, and Faustus will turn to God again.
　　　　　To God? He loves thee not.
　　　　　The god thou servest is thine own appetite,
　　　　　Wherein is fixed the love of Beelzebub.
　　　　　To him I'll build an altar and a church,
　　　　　And offer lukewarm blood of new-born babes.

[Enter Good Angel and Evil Angel]

Good Angel: Sweet Faustus, leave that execrable art.
Faustus: Contrition, prayer, repentance: what of them?
Good Angel: O, they are means to bring thee unto heaven.
Evil Angel: Rather illusions, fruits of lunacy,
　　　　　That makes men foolish that do trust them most.
Good Angel: Sweet Faustus, think on heaven and heavenly things.
Evil Angel: No, Faustus, think of honour and wealth. [Exeunt Angels]

---

36. In the Renaissance period, Germany was a confederation of over 300 states, under the rule of the 'Holy Roman' Emperor.
37. Contemplation.
38. In the 'B' text these are questions.
39. What use is it?

Faustus: Of wealth,
Why, the seignory of Emden[40] shall be mine.
When Mephistopheles shall stand by me,
What god[41] can hurt thee, Faustus? Thou art safe;
Cast no more doubts. Come, Mephistopheles,
And bring glad tidings from great Lucifer:
Is't not midnight? Come, Mephistopheles!
Veni, veni, Mephistophile![42]

[Enter Mephistopheles]

Now tell, what says Lucifer thy lord?
Mephistopheles: That I shall wait on Faustus whilst he lives,[43]
So he will buy my service with his soul.
Faustus: Already Faustus hath hazarded[44] that for thee.
Mephistopheles: But, Faustus, thou must bequeath it solemnly
And write a deed of gift with thine own blood,
For that security craves great Lucifer:[45]
If thou deny it, I will back to hell.
Faustus: Stay, Mephistopheles, and tell me, what good will my soul do
thy lord?
Mephistopheles: Enlarge his kingdom.
Faustus: Is that the reason he tempts us thus?
Mephistopheles: *Solamen miseris socios habuisse doloris.*[46]
Faustus: Have you any pain, that tortures others?[47]
Mephistopheles: As great as have the human souls of men:
But tell me, Faustus, shall I have thy soul?
And I will be thy slave, and wait on thee,
And give thee more than thou hast wit to ask.
Faustus: Ay, Mephistopheles, I give it thee.
Mephistopheles: Then stab thine arm courageously,

---

40. Governance of a rich north-German port city.
41. 'B' text reads 'power'.
42. Come, come, Mephistopheles!
43. Original reads 'I live'.
44. Endangered, gambled away.
45. Many demonologists discussed the 'security' of a contract with the devil, either written or verbal (see Scot on the case of Ada Davie, above): Mephistopheles implies that it is binding and damning, but another reading suggests that the prospect of God's forgiveness is held out up to and including Act Five.
46. It is a comfort to the wretched to have had companions in misery (translation by Bevington and Rasmussen, eds, *Doctor Faustus*, p. 140, note to line 42).
47. Have you, who torture others, any pain?

And bind thy soul that at some certain day
Great Lucifer may claim it as his own,
And then be thou as great as Lucifer.

Faustus [cutting his arm]:   Lo, Mephistopheles, for love of thee
I cut mine arm, and with my proper blood
Assure my soul to be great Lucifer's,
Chief lord and regent of perpetual night.
View here the blood that trickles from mine arm,
And let it be propitious for my wish.

Mephistopheles: But Faustus, thou must write it in manner of a deed of gift.

Faustus: Ay, so I will. [He writes] But Mephistopheles,
My blood congeals, and I can write no more.

Mephistopheles: I'll fetch thee fire to dissolve it straight. [Exit]

Faustus: What might the staying of my blood portend?
Is it unwilling I should write this bill?
Why streams it not, that I may write afresh?
'Faustus gives to thee his soul': ah, there it stayed!
Why shouldst thou not? Is not thy soul thine own?
Then write again: 'Faustus gives to thee his soul'.

[Enter Mephistopheles with a chafer of coals][48]

Mephistopheles: Here's fire. Come Faustus, set it on.

Faustus: So now the blood begins to clear again,
Now will I make an end immediately. [He writes]

Mephistopheles [aside]:   O, what will not I do to obtain his soul?

Faustus: *Consummatum est.*[49] This bill is ended,
And Faustus hath bequeathed his soul to Lucifer.
But what is this inscription on mine arm?
'*Homo, fuge!*'[50] Whither should I fly?
If unto God, he'll throw thee down to hell.[51]
My senses are deceived, here's nothing writ.
I see it plain, here in this place is writ
'*Home, fuge!*' Yet shall not Faustus fly.

Mephistopheles [aside]:   I'll fetch him somewhat to delight his mind.

---

48. Metal grate filled with hot coals.
49. It is finished. These were Christ's last words (John 19.30).
50. Man, fly! Another biblical echo (1 Timothy 6.11, where man is urged to flee from pride, questionings and the love of money, and to fight for faith).
51. 'B' text reads 'If unto heaven, he'll throw me down ...', leaving the thrower's identity unclear. Later, devils are said to pull Faustus away from heaven, but the 'A' text implies a vengeful God will repel him.

[Enter Mephistopheles with Devils, giving crowns and rich apparel to Faustus, and they dance and then depart]

Faustus: Speak, Mephistopheles, what means this show?

Mephistopheles: Nothing, Faustus, but to delight thy mind withal
And to show thee what magic can perform.

Faustus: But may I raise up spirits when I please?

Mephistopheles: Ay, Faustus, and do greater things than these.

Faustus: Then there's enough for a thousand souls.[52]
Here, Mephistopheles, receive this scroll,
A deed of gift of body and of soul:
But yet conditionally, that thou perform
All articles prescribed between us both.

Mephistopheles: Faustus, I swear by hell and Lucifer
To effect all promises between us made.

Faustus: Then hear me read them.
'On these conditions following:
First, that Faustus may be a spirit in form and substance.[53]
Secondly, that Mephistopheles shall be his servant, and at his command.
Thirdly, that Mephistopheles shall do for him and bring him whatsoever.
Fourthly, that he shall be in his chamber or house invisible.
Lastly, that he shall appear to the said John Faustus at all times in what form or shape soever he please.
I, John Faustus of Wittenberg, Doctor, by these presents,[54] do give both body and soul to Lucifer, Prince of the East, and his minister Mephistopheles; and furthermore grant unto them that four-and-twenty years being expired, the articles above written inviolate,[55] full power to fetch or carry the said John Faustus, body and soul, flesh, blood, or goods, into their habitation wheresoever. By me, John Faustus.'

Mephistopheles: Speak, Faustus. Do you deliver this as your deed?

Faustus [giving the deed]:   Aye, take it, and the devil give thee good on't.[56]

Mephistopheles: Now, Faustus, ask what thou wilt.

---

52. This remark, quantifying the magician's loss and gain, is missing from 'B'.

53. This is a much-debated line. Later in the play it is implied that because Faustus is a spirit (a devil?) he cannot be saved (see Bevington and Rasmussen's introduction, *Doctor Faustus*, p. 19, for further debate) but what precisely is meant by 'spirit' is unclear.

54. A legal phrase: in these present papers.

55. A potential get-out clause: if these agreements have not been broken.

56. Ironic commonplace: the devil give you joy of it.

Faustus: First will I question thee about hell.
Tell me, where is the place that men call hell?

Mephistopheles: Under the heavens.

Faustus: Aye, but whereabout?[57]

Mephistopheles: Within the bowels of these elements,
Where we are tortured and remain for ever.
Hell hath no limits, nor is circumscribed
In one self place, for where we are is hell,
And where hell is, must we ever be:
And, to conclude, when all the world dissolves,
And every creature shall be purified,
All places shall be hell that is not heaven.

Faustus: Come, I think hell's a fable.

Mephistopheles: Aye, think so still, till experience change thy mind.

Faustus: Why? Think'st thou then that Faustus shall be damned?

Mephistopheles: Aye, of necessity, for here's the scroll
Wherein thou hast given thy soul to Lucifer.

Faustus: Aye, and body too. But what of that?
Think'st thou that Faustus is so fond
To imagine that after this life there is any pain?
Tush, these are trifles and mere old wives' tales.

Mephistopheles: But, Faustus, I am an instance to prove the contrary,
For I am damned and am now in hell.

Faustus: How? Now in hell? Nay, an this be hell,
I'll willingly be damned here: what, walking, disputing, etc.?[58]
But leaving off this, let me have a wife, the fairest maid in
Germany, for I am wanton and lascivious and cannot live
without a wife.

Mephistopheles: How, a wife? I prithee, Faustus, talk not of a wife.

Faustus: Nay, sweet Mephistopheles, fetch me one, for I will have one.

Mephistopheles: Well, thou wilt have one. Sit there till I come. I'll fetch
thee a wife, in the devil's name. [Exit]

[Enter Mephistopheles with a Devil dressed like a woman, with fire-works][59]

Mephistopheles: Tell, Faustus, how dost thou like thy wife?

---

57. 'B' text has Faustus cannily point out 'Ay, so are all things else', increasing our sense of
Mephistopheles' evasion.
58. 'B' text adds sleeping and eating, sensual as opposed to intellectual delights.
59. 'B' text describes 'a woman Devil', a succubus, which Faustus rejects, as opposed to the
devil in woman's clothes here.

Faustus: A plague on her for a hot whore!

Mephistopheles: Tut, Faustus, marriage is but a ceremonial toy. If thou
                lovest me, think no more of it ...

Faustus' other demands are treated in a similar way. The scene ends with
Mephistopheles presenting Faustus with a series of books which he says will
tell Faustus all he wants to know of spells, astrology, and herbs, but Faustus
still doubts the worth of what he has received in the contract, and
Mephistopheles' assurances remain unproven. In subsequent scenes, Faustus
questions Mephistopheles on heaven and the planets but is disappointed by the
'slender trifles' he is given as answers. Mephistopheles offers nothing new, and
will not discuss God, taunting Faustus with his damnation. Throughout the play
the Good and Evil Angels appear when Faustus reaches a crisis of decision
between following the devil or returning to God, and each time he is distracted
from the Good Angel's advice by a devilish show, or by outright threats of
violence from devils.

   He is, however, given an aerial tour of the world, encouraged to play magic
tricks on the Pope and others, and his conjuring skills are celebrated at various
courts. He raises spirits representing Homer and Helen of Troy, prompting
Marlowe's best-known, and some of his most beautiful, lines, such as, 'Was this
the face that launched a thousand ships, And burnt the topless towers of Ilium?'
But we never see Faustus make any attempt to gain the power he had
promised himself in early speeches, nor does Mephistopheles volunteer to give
it to him. The play reaches its climax when, after twenty-four years, Faustus'
contracted lifespan nears its end. The unremitting final scene is a horrifying
warning of the fate of those who bargain with the devil.

Act 5, Scene 2

Faustus: Ah, Faustus,
                Now hast thou but one bare hour to live,
                And then thou must be damned perpetually:
                Stand still, you ever-moving spheres of heaven,[60]
                That time may cease and midnight never come!
                Fair nature's eye,[61] rise, rise again, and make
                Perpetual day, or let this hour be but
                A year, a month, a week, a natural day,
                That Faustus may repent and save his soul!

---

60. Before Copernicus' ideas, the universe was thought to be made of spheres centred around
    the earth, which moved along with the stars and planets, marking the passing of time.
61. The sun.

O lente, lente currite noctis equi![62]
The stars move still; time runs; the clock will strike,
The devil will come, and Faustus must be damned.
O, I'll leap up to my God! Who pulls me down?
See, see where Christ's blood streams in the firmament![63]
One drop would save my soul, half a drop. Ah, my Christ!
Ah, rend not my heart for naming of my Christ!
Yet will I call on him. O, spare me, Lucifer!
Where is it now? 'Tis gone; and see where God
Stretcheth out his arm, and bends his ireful brows![64]
Mountains and hills, come, come and fall on me,
And hide me from the heavy wrath of God!
No, no!
Then will I run headlong into the earth:
Earth, gape! O, no, it will not harbour me.
You stars that reigned at my nativity,
Whose influence hath allotted death and hell,[65]
Now draw up Faustus like a foggy mist
Into the entrails of yon labouring cloud,
That when you vomit forth into the air,
My limbs may issue from your smoky mouths,
So that my soul may but ascend to heaven.[66]

[The watch strikes]

Ah, half the hour is past:
'Twill all be past anon.
O God,
If thou wilt not have mercy on my soul,[67]
Yet for Christ's sake, whose blood hath ransomed me,[68]
Impose some end on my incessant pain.
Let Faustus live in hell a thousand years,

---

62. O run slowly, slowly, ye horses of the night! From Ovid's *Amores* (1.13.40), translated by
    Bevington and Rasmussen, eds, *Doctor Faustus*, p. 195, note to line 74. As they point out,
    in Ovid the line refers to a lover's desire for the night to last, suggesting that even in his
    holy terror Faustus cannot detach his mind from pleasure.
63. This last sign of God's mercy is missing from 'B'.
64. God is not named directly in 'B', either here or two lines later, giving him less personal
    involvement in damning the magician, a pattern repeated below.
65. Faustus suggests that his damnation was predetermined by his horoscope.
66. If Faustus is raised up, even by evaporation, and killed by a thunderbolt, he vainly hopes
    he may be able to get to heaven.
67. 'B' reads 'O, if my soul must suffer for my sin'.
68. Christ's sacrifice redeemed humans, who otherwise would have been damned. But
    Faustus is damned because of his own personal, not original, sin.

A hundred thousand, and at last be saved.
O, no end is limited to damned souls.
Why wert thou not a creature wanting soul?
Or why is this immortal that thou hast?
Ah, Pythagoras' *metempsychosis*, were that true,
This soul should fly from me and I be changed
Unto some brutish beast:[69]
All beasts are happy, for, when they die,
Their souls are soon dissolved in elements;
But mine must live still to be plagued in hell.
Curst be the parents that engendered me!
No, Faustus, curse thyself, curse Lucifer,
That hath deprived thee of the joys of heaven.

[The clock striketh twelve]

O, it strikes, it strikes! Now, body, turn to air,
Or Lucifer will bear thee quick to hell.

[Thunder and lightning]

O soul, be changed into little waterdrops,
And fall into the ocean, ne'er be found!
My God, my God, look not so fierce on me![70]

[Enter Lucifer, Mephistopheles, and other Devils]

Adders and serpents, let me breathe a while!
Ugly hell, gape not. Come not, Lucifer!
I'll burn my books. Ah, Mephistopheles!

[The Devils exeunt with him]

[Epilogue]

[Enter Chorus]

Chorus: Cut is the branch that might have grown full straight,
And burned is Apollo's laurel bough[71]

---

69. Pythagoras, a Greek philosopher, held that souls could 'transmigrate' between creatures in a kind of reincarnation.
70. 'B' reads 'O, mercy, heaven, look not so fierce on me!'
71. Apollo, with his symbol the laurel, was associated with poetry and thus tangentially with study: but the epitaph suits Marlowe better than Faustus.

That sometime grew within this learned man:
Faustus is gone. Regard his hellish fall,
Whose fiendful fortune may exhort the wise
Only to wonder at unlawful things,
Whose deepness doth entice such forward wits
To practise more than heavenly power permits. [Exit]

2. Comedy

Anon., The Merry Devil of Edmonton *(1604?)*

The Merry Devil of Edmonton was first published in 1608 but was being
performed as early as 1604, when it was mentioned by T.M. in his *Blacke Book*.
There is, however, no record of its authorship and despite attempts to attribute
it to such diverse writers as William Shakespeare, Michael Drayton and
Thomas Heywood its creator remains anonymous. The play was, however,
very successful, and Ben Jonson mentioned it in his 1616 *The Devil Is an Ass*
as the 'dear delight' of audiences.

   The Merry Devil is one of those many bland, pleasant plays in which a
young man and his friends must plot and plan, with the involvement of a witch
or magician, in order to work out a complicated tangle of love and marriage.
Examples include Thomas Heywood's *The Wise Woman of Hogsdon* (see
below), Robert Greene's comedy *Friar Bacon and Friar Bungay*, and John
Lyly's comic *Mother Bombie*. The tragi-comic *The Witch* and the tragedy *The
Witch of Edmonton* (see above) are more sophisticated variations on the
theme. As do several of these plays, *The Merry Devil* combines the love-plot
with a mythologized piece of English history, for Peter Fabel, the scholarly
magician who is 'the merry devil' of the play, did indeed practise alchemy and
magic in fifteenth-century Edmonton.

   The opening scene of the play retells the story of how Fabel cheated the
devil, whilst the final scene emphasizes the role that such magical mentors
often play in drama – that of the fixer, the *deus ex machina*, bringing about a
happy ending. Witches and magicians on the Renaissance stage are often
relatively benign and communitarian – an illuminating contrast with their
malignant and outcast counterparts in the courts, which suggests a continuing
desire to believe in the potential of good magic, and a determination to tell a
story no matter how ill its subject matter fitted with contemporary beliefs about
reality. In this play, it is stressed that Fabel did not actually use his magic in
resolving the play's affairs, but only ordinary human cunning, so the playwright
is able to flirt with the idea of the good magician whilst being protected from the
uneasiness surrounding magical coercion which haunts such plays as *The
Witch*, Shakespeare's *The Tempest* and *A Midsummer Night's Dream*.

   Briefly, when the play begins, the young gentleman Raymond Mounchensey is about to lose the love of his life, Millicent Clare, to his friend Frank Jerningham. This is because Old Mounchensey (Raymond's father) and Sir Arthur Clare (Millicent's father) have fallen out and Clare has arranged a new match for his daughter. The young people work together with Fabel, Raymond Mounchensey's former university tutor, to thwart their parents. But first Fabel has a problem of his own ...

The Prologue[72]

Prologue: Your silence and attention, worthy friends,
That your free spirits may with more pleasing sense
Relish the life of this our active scene:
To which intent, to calm this murmuring breath,
We ring this round[73] with our invoking spells;
If that your listening ears be yet prepared
To entertain the subject of our play,
Lend us your patience.
'Tis Peter Fabel, a renowned scholar,
Whose fame hath still been hitherto forgot
By all the writers of this latter age.
In Middlesex his birth and his abode,
Not full seven mile from this great famous city,[74]
That, for his fame in sleights and magic won,
Was called the Merry Fiend of Edmonton.
If any here make doubt of such a name,
In Edmonton yet fresh unto this day,
Fixed in the wall of that old ancient church,
His monument remaineth to be seen;
His memory yet in the mouths of men,
That whilst he lived he could deceive the devil.
Imagine now that whilst he is retired
From Cambridge[75] back unto his native home,
Suppose the silent, sable-visaged night
Casts her black curtain over all the world;
And whilst he sleeps within his silent bed,
Toiled with the studies of the passed day,
The very time and hour wherein that spirit
That many years attended his command

72. The text is that of 1655 in the Huntington Library, with some minor emendations from C. F. Tucker-Brooke, ed., *The Shakespeare Apocrypha* (Oxford: Clarendon, 1918).
73. The theatre itself, with its Elizabethan circular shape.
74. London.
75. Fabel is a university lecturer.

And often times twixt Cambridge and that town
Had in a minute borne him through the air,
By composition[76] twixt the fiend and him,
Comes now to claim the scholar for his due.

[Draw the curtains][77]

Behold him here, laid on his restless couch,
His fatal chime prepared at his head,[78]
His chamber guarded with these sable sleights,
And by him stands the necromantic chair,
In which he makes his direful invocations,
And binds the fiends that shall obey his will.
Sit with a pleased eye, until you know
The comic end of our sad tragic show. [Exit]

[Induction]

[The Chime goes, in which time Fabel is oft seen to stare about him, and hold up his hands]

Fabel: What means the tolling of this fatal chime?
           O, what a trembling horror strikes my heart!
           My stiffened hair stands upright on my head,
           As doe the bristles of a porcupine.

[Enter Coreb, a spirit]

Coreb: Fabel, awake, or I will bear thee hence
           Headlong to hell.
Fabel: Ha, ha,
           Why dost thou wake me? Coreb, is it thou?
Coreb: 'Tis I.
Fabel: I know thee well: I hear the watchful dogs
           With hollow howling tell of thy approach;
           The lights burn dim, affrighted with thy presence;
           And this distempered and tempestuous night
           Tells me the air is troubled with some devil.
Coreb: Come, art thou ready?

---

76. Pact.
77. The actor playing Fabel would almost certainly be 'sleeping' in a curtained space at the back of the stage, intended to represent beds, caves and private spaces and to allow the dramatic 'discovery' of characters as required.
78. Fabel has apparently rigged up a bell to inform him of the expiry of his devilish pact.

Fabel: Whither? Or to what?

Coreb: Why, scholar, the hour my date expires;
                   I must depart, and come to claim my due.

Fabel: Ha, what is thy due?[79]

Coreb: Fabel, thyself.

Fabel: O let not darkness hear thee speak that word,
                   Lest that with force it hurry hence amain,
                   And leave the world to look upon my woe:
                   Yet overwhelm me with this globe of earth,[80]
                   And let a little sparrow with her bill
                   Take but so much as she can bear away,
                   That, every day thus losing of my load,
                   I may again in time yet hope to rise.

Coreb: Didst thou not write thy name in thine own blood,
                   And drewst the formal deed twixt thee and me,
                   And is it not recorded now in hell?

Fabel: Why comst thou in this stern and horrid shape,
                   Not in familiar sort as thou wast wont?

Coreb: Because the date of thy command is out,
                   And I am master of thy skill and thee.

Fabel: Coreb, thou angry and impatient spirit,
                   I have earnest business for a private friend;
                   Reserve me, spirit, until some further time.

Coreb: I will not for the mines of all the earth.[81]

Fabel: Then let me rise, and ere I leave the world,
                   Dispatch some business that I have to do;
                   And in mean time repose thee in that chair.

Coreb: Fabel, I will.

[Coreb sits down]

Fabel: O, that this soul, that cost so great a price
                   As the dear precious blood of her redeemer,
                   Inspired with knowledge, should by that alone
                   Which makes a man so mean unto the powers,[82]

---

79. Surely the magician would know why the bell had rung and what the devil's due was? His confusion must be for dramatic effect.
80. Echoes of Marlowe's *Dr Faustus* (above) are evident in this passage: the plea to be buried in the earth is the strongest (*Faustus*, 'A' text, 5.2.84–8).
81. Not for all the wealth in the mines of the earth.
82. The meaning is not quite clear here: does Fabel say that he has humbled himself (made himself mean) to devils (powers)? Q6 substitutes 'near' for 'mean', which would suggest Fabel is saying that knowledge makes a man close to the powers, presumably God or the gods.

Even lead him down into the depth of hell,
When men in their own pride strive to know more
Than man should know!
For this alone God cast the angels down.
The infinity of arts is like the sea,
Into which, when man will take in hand to sail
Further than reason, which should be his pilot,
Hath skill to guide him, losing once his compass,
He falleth to such deep and dangerous whirlpools,
As he doth lose the very sight of heaven:
The more he strives to come to quiet harbour,
The further still he finds himself from land.
Man, striving still to find the depth of evil,
Seeking to be a God, becomes a devil.

Coreb: Come, Fabel, hast thou done?

Fabel: Yes, yes; come hither.

Coreb: Fabel, I cannot.

Fabel: Cannot? What ails your hollowness?[83]

Coreb: Good Fabel, help me.

Fabel: Alas, where lies your grief? Some *aqua-vitae*![84]
    The devil's very sick, I fear he'll die,
    For he looks very ill.[85]

Coreb: Dar'st thou deride the minister of darkness?
    In Lucifer's dread name Coreb conjures thee
    To set him free.

Fabel: I will not for the mines of all the earth,
    Unless thou give me liberty to see
    Seven years more, before thou seize on me.

Coreb: Fabel, I give it thee.

Fabel: Swear, damned fiend.

Coreb: Unbind me, and by hell I will not touch thee,
    Till seven years from this hour be full expired.

Fabel: Enough, come out.

Coreb: A vengeance take thy art!
    Live and convert all piety to evil:
    Never did man thus overreach the devil.
    No time on earth like Phaetonic flames[86]

---

83. A pun on 'holiness'.
84. Strong spirits known as the 'water of life'.
85. Presumably, very angry.
86. In Greek myth, Phaeton was the son of the sun-god Helios. One day he borrowed his
    father's chariot, in effect presuming to control the sun itself, and tried to drive the sun's

> Can have perpetual being. I'll return
> To my infernal mansion; but be sure,
> Thy seven years done, no trick shall make me tarry,
> But, Coreb, thou to hell shalt Fabel carry. [Exit]

Fabel: Then thus betwixt us two this variance ends,
> Thou to thy fellow fiends, I to my friends. [Exit]

Act 5, Scene 2

After the action of the play, Fabel sums up his worthy role in promoting happiness.

Fabel: Now knights, I enter; now my part begins.
> To end this difference, know, at first I knew
> What you intended, ere your love took flight
> From Old Mounchensey: you, Sir Arthur Clare,
> Were minded to have married this sweet beauty
> To young Frank Jerningham; to cross which match,
> I used some pretty sleights, but I protest
> Such as but sat upon the skirts of art;
> No conjurations, nor such weighty spells
> As tie the soul to their performancy.
> These for his love, who once was my dear pupil,
> Have I effected. Now, me thinks, 'tis strange
> That you, being old in wisdom, should thus knit
> Your forehead on this match;[87] since reason fails,
> No law can curb the lovers' rash attempt;
> Years, in resisting this, are sadly spent.
> Smile, then, upon your daughter and kind son,
> And let our toil to future ages prove,
> The devil of Edmonton did good in love.

Sir Arthur: Well, 'tis in vain to cross the providence:[88]
> Dear son, I take thee up into my heart;
> Rise, daughter, this is a kind father's part.

---

cont.

horses. Inevitably, he failed to control them, came too close to earth and had to be killed by Zeus before he could damage the universe further. Thus he is a symbol of over-confidence and aspiration bringing disaster, and here suggests both Fabel's risky contract with the devil and the burning flames of hell which will reward him if he loses control of this.

87. Frown on this marriage.
88. Despite Fabel's potentially devilish intervention, all is ascribed to God's will.

SEVEN

MAGIC AND MONEY – TWO TRICKSTERS

1. A wise woman

Thomas Heywood, **The Wise Woman of Hogsdon** *(1604?)*[1]

Thomas Heywood (*c.* 1574–1641) probably wrote *The Wise Woman of Hogsdon* in about 1604, when his more famous play *A Woman Killed with Kindness* was enjoying great success in the theatre, but it was not printed until 1638. It is not possible to attribute the play unequivocally to Heywood, but it seems very probable that he is the author, in part because he is identified as such on the title-page of the first edition. Since Heywood once claimed he had had a hand in the writing of over 200 plays, it seems likely that he took at least some part in writing this one.

The play tells the story of some of those people who resort to a cunning woman, a trickster who pretends to supernatural abilities in order to earn a living from her credulous customers. There are very playable scenes involving the cozening of these innocents, which offer a sharp analysis of the methods used by fake magicians and cunning people. But the working out of some of the wisewoman's associates' and clients' love problems shows her nature as a relatively kindly schemer, rather than a detestable witch or a heartless con woman. Like Lyly's rather more talented Mother Bombie,[2] who is mentioned by Heywood in Act Two, Scene One, Heywood's wisewoman is an asset to her community rather than a nuisance to be prosecuted. The play hovers between satire and romance in its treatment of her and the intrigues in which she is involved.

Briefly, she succeeds in bringing about a happy resolution to the problem described at the opening of the play. A young gentlewoman, Luce, has been deserted by her fiancé, a wild young man named Robin Chartley. She disguises herself as a boy to find out what he is doing, and discovers that he has decided to marry another woman named Luce (confusingly known as First Luce

---

1. The text used was published in 1638 and is in the British Library. This edition is indebted also to Michael H. Leonard, ed., *A Critical Edition of The Wise Woman of Hogsdon* (New York and London: Garland, 1980), an original spelling edition containing a full discussion of the text and its context.
2. See the Introduction to *The Merry Devil of Edmonton* above.

because she appears first in the play). Second Luce, Chartley's former love, must prevent the match in order to defend her honour and reclaim her lover. She becomes an assistant to the wisewoman, learning the secrets which enable the trickster to fool her clients, and with her help manages to marry Chartley herself, find a more deserving husband for First Luce and prevent Chartley bigamously marrying yet another woman, Gratiana. The play ends with a triple wedding feast and a speech in praise of the wisewoman, whose spurious wisdom has enabled all to discover their true feelings and marry happily. Heywood celebrates both illusion and female power, ideas closely associated elsewhere with the devil and witches, and in doing so he shows the fascination such ideas exercised over a society which in many ways, and particularly through the prosecution of witchcraft, did its best to stamp them out.

Act 2, Scene 1

[Enter the Wisewoman and her Clients, a Countryman with a urinal, four Women like citizens' wives, Taber, a serving man, and a Chamber Maid[3]]

Wisewoman: Fie, fie, what a toil and a moil it is,
                   For a woman to be wiser than all her neighbours?
                   I pray good people, press not too fast upon me;
                   Though I have two ears, I can hear but one at once.
                   You with the urine.

[Enter Second Luce, and stands aside][4]

Countryman: Here forsooth, Mistress.
Wisewoman: And who distilled this water?
Countryman: My wife's limbeck,[5] if it please you.
Wisewoman: And where doth the pain hold her most?
Countryman: Marry, at her heart forsooth.
Wisewoman: Aye, at her heart; she hath a griping at her heart.
Countryman: You have hit it right.
Wisewoman: Nay, I can see so much in the urine.
Second Luce [aside]:   Just so much as is told her.
Wisewoman: She hath no pain in her head, hath she?
Countryman: No, indeed, I never heard her complain of her head.
Wisewoman: I told you so, her pain lies all at her heart.

---

3. Later described as a kitchen maid.
4. This is Chartley's first love, disguised as a boy in order to serve the wisewoman.
5. An alembic, a vessel used in distilling.

Alas good heart! But how feels she her stomach?

Countryman: Oh, queasy, and sick at stomach.

Wisewoman: Aye, I warrant you, I think I can see as far into a mill-stone as another:[6] you have heard of Mother Nottingham, who for her time was prettily well skilled in casting of waters:[7] and after her, Mother Bomby; and then there is one Hatfield in Pepper Alley,[8] he doth pretty well for a thing that's lost. There's another in Coldharbour, that's skilled in the planets. Mother Sturton in Golden Lane is for forespeaking:[9] Mother Phillips of the Bankside for the weakness of the back: and then there's a very reverend matron on Clerkenwell Green, good at many things: Mistress Mary on the Bankside is for erecting a figure:[10] and one (what do you call her) in Westminster that practiseth the book and the key, and the sieve and the shears:[11] and all do well, according to their talent. For myself, let the world speak: hark you, my friend, you shall take – [she whispers].

Second Luce [aside]:   'Tis strange the ignorant should be thus fooled.
What can this witch, this wizard, or old trot,
Do by enchantment, or by magic spell?
Such as profess that art should be deep scholars.[12]
What reading can this simple woman have?
'Tis palpable gross foolery.

[Exit Countryman]

Wisewoman: Now friend, your business?

Taber: I have stolen out of my master's house, forsooth, with the kitchen maid, and I am come to know of you, whether it be my fortune to have her, or no.

Wisewoman: And what's your suit, lady?

---

6. A proverbial boast, often ironic.
7. Diagnosis by urine.
8. All the places named are streets and districts of London.
9. Bewitchment. Presumably Mother Sturton removes curses from those who have been forespoken.
10. Astrological prediction.
11. Both methods of divination, usually for identifying thieves. Scot explains how the names of suspects were placed in the pipe or shaft of a key, the key placed in the Bible next to the page containing Psalm 49, and the psalm read. Both book and key were expected to fall to the ground, and, after this jolting, the name remaining in the key was thought to be the guilty party. In the second method, shears were stuck into a sieve, which would turn around on the shears when the guilty party was named (Scot, book 12, chapter 17, and book 16, chapter 5).
12. Second Luce's assumption is interesting: magic does exist, but only for the learned to access.

Kitchen Maid: Forsooth, I am come to know whether I be a maid[13] or
no.

Wisewoman: Why, art thou in doubt of that?

Kitchen Maid: It may be I have more reason than all the world knows.

Taber: Nay, if thou comest to know whether thou beest a maid or no, I
had best ask to know whether I be with child or no.

Wisewoman: Withdraw into the parlour there, I'll but talk with this
other gentlewoman, and I'll resolve you presently.

Taber: Come, Sisly, if she cannot resolve thee, I can, and in the case of a
maidenhead do more than she, I warrant thee.

[Exeunt Taber and Kitchen Maid]

Woman: Forsooth I am bold, as they say.

Wisewoman: You are welcome, gentlewoman.

Woman: I would not have it known to my neighbours, that I come to a
wisewoman for any thing, by my truly.

Wisewoman: For should your husband come and find you here –

Woman: My husband, woman? I am a widow.

Wisewoman: Where are my brains? 'Tis true, you are a widow; and you
dwell, let me see, I can never remember that place.

Woman: In Kent Street.

Wisewoman: Kent Street, Kent Street! And I can tell you wherefore you
come.

Woman: Why, and say true?

Wisewoman: You are a wag, you are a wag:[14] why, what do you think
now I would say?

Woman: Perhaps, to know how many husbands I should have.

Wisewoman: And if I should say so, should I say amiss?

Woman: I think you are a witch ...[15]

Second Luce manages to get herself a job as the wisewoman's assistant but no
sooner has she done so than her promise-breaking fiancé, Chartley, bursts
drunkenly into the wisewoman's home demanding that she set up a marriage
for him with First Luce, his new love. He insults the wisewoman grossly, calling
her a sorceress, hag and a dromedary (a thieving rogue). Luckily, First Luce
has other admirers, and the infuriated wisewoman and the wronged Second
Luce resolve, after Chartley has left, to thwart his wedding plans.

---

13. Virgin.
14. A wit, a joker.
15. See note 29 to Thomas Middleton's *The Witch* in Chapter 4 of the present volume.

The next suitor behaves much more politely to the wisewoman, whilst keeping his distance. Reactions to her are often also indications of wisdom or lack of it: those who over-credulously accept her word are fools, those who abuse her are equally foolish. Boyster strikes a moderate note, suggesting Heywood wants us to like him and to accept his view of the wisewoman as a relatively harmless cheat, a clever old woman to whom some respect is due.

[Enter Master Boyster]

Boyster: Morrow.

Wisewoman: Y'are welcome sir.

Boyster: Art wise?

Second Luce: He should be wise, because he speaks few words.[16]

Wisewoman: I am as I am, and there's an end.

Boyster: Can'st conjure?

Wisewoman: Oh that's a foul word! But I can tell you your fortune, as they say; I have some little skill in palmistry, but never had to do with the devil.

Boyster: And had the devil never any thing to do with thee? Thou lookest somewhat like his dam.[17] Look on me: can'st tell what I ail?

Wisewoman: Can you tell yourself? I should guess, you are mad, or not well in your wits.

Boyster: Th'art wise, I am so; men being in love, are mad, and I being in love, am so.

Wisewoman: Nay, if I see your complexion once, I think I can guess as near as another.

Boyster: One Mistress Luce I love; knowest thou her, Grannam?

Wisewoman: As well as the beggar knows his dish. Why, she is one of my daughters.[18]

Boyster: Make her my wife, I'll give thee forty pieces.

Second Luce: Take them, mistress, to be revenged on Chartley.

Wisewoman: A bargain, strike me luck, cease all your sorrow,
Fair Luce shall be your bride betimes[19] tomorrow.

Boyster: Th'art a good Grannam; and, but that thy teeth stand like hedge-stakes in thy head, I'd kiss thee . . .

---

16. A piece of proverbial wisdom, defining Boyster's character for the audience.
17. The devil's mother.
18. Literally, First Luce (referred to here) is the daughter of a goldsmith, but she is one of the wisewoman's favourites.
19. Early.

Witches were thought, particularly by European demonologists, to indulge in orgies with the devil and to kidnap unbaptized children and kill them, afterwards boiling their bodies to make flying ointment: see *The Witch* and *Macbeth* (above) for examples of straightforward dramatization of these ideas. Heywood, contrastingly, offers a prosaic, sordid and resolutely non-magical version of sexual impropriety and of the connection between wisewoman, midwife and infant, which again suggests his resistance to more sensational beliefs about witches. The scene ends with the wisewoman celebrating her talents.

Act 3, Scene 1

Second Luce: ... But Mistress, what mean all these women's pictures, hanged here in your withdrawing rooms?

Wisewoman: I'll tell thee, boy; marry, thou must be secret. When any citizens, or young gentlemen come hither, under a colour to know their fortunes,[20] they look upon these pictures, and which of them they best like, she is ready with a wet finger:[21] here they have all the furniture belonging to a private chamber, bed, bed-fellow and all; but mum,[22] thou knowest my meaning, Jack.

Second Luce: But I see coming and going, maids, or such as go for maids, some of them, as if they were ready to lie down,[23] sometimes two or three delivered in one night; then suddenly leave their brats behind them, and convey themselves into the city again: what becomes of their children?

Wisewoman: Those be kitchen maids, and chamber maids, and sometimes good men's daughters; who having catched a clap,[24] and growing near their time, get leave to see their friends in the country, for a week or so: then hither they come, and for a matter of money, here they are delivered. I have a midwife or two belonging to the house, and one Sir Boniface a deacon, that makes a shift to christen the infants: we have poor, honest and secret neighbours, that stand for common gossips.[25] But dost not thou know this?

Second Luce: Yes, now I do: but what after becomes of the poor infants?

Wisewoman: Why, in the night we send them abroad, and lay one at this man's door, and another at that, such as are able to keep them;

---

20. In the pretence that they want their fortunes told.
21. Without further ado.
22. Keep mum, keep quiet.
23. Lie in and go into labour.
24. Usually, caught a venereal disease, but here meaning to have become pregnant.
25. Godparents, witnesses at the christening.

and what after becomes of them, we inquire not. And this is another string to my bow . . .

Second Luce: . . . but Mistress, are you so
Cunning as you make yourself? You can
Neither write nor read: what do you with those
Books you so often turn over?

Wisewoman: Why, tell the leaves;[26] for to be ignorant, and seem ignorant, what greater folly?

Second Luce: Believe me, this is a cunning woman; neither hath she her name for nothing, who out of her ignorance can fool so many that think themselves wise. But wherefore have you built this little closet close to the door, where sitting, you may hear every word spoken, by all such as ask for you?

Wisewoman: True, and therefore I built it: if any knock, you must to the door and question them, to find what they come about, if to this purpose, or to that. Now they ignorantly telling thee their errand, which I sitting in my closet, overhear, presently come forth, and tell them the cause of their coming, with every word that hath passed betwixt you in private: which they admiring, and thinking it to be miraculous, by their report I become thus famous.

Second Luce: This is no trade, but a mystery . . .[27]

Wisewoman: Let me see, how many trades have I to live by? First, I am a wisewoman, and a fortune teller, and under that I deal in physic and forespeaking, in palmistry, and recovering of things lost. Next, I undertake to cure mad folks. Then I keep gentlewomen lodgers, to furnish such chambers as I let out by the night. Then I am provided for bringing young wenches to bed; and for a need, you see I can play the match maker. She that is but one, and professeth so many, may well be termed a wisewoman, if there be any.

2. A 'chemical cozener' and an astrologer[28]

Ben Jonson, The Alchemist (1610)

Jonson, whose *Masque of Queenes* features in Chapter 4, aimed his satirical plays for the public stage at London society and its ills. Like many satirists, in

---

26. Count the pages.
27. A complex profession.
28. Ben Jonson, *The Alchemist*, 5.5.19. The text used is in Jonson's *Workes* (London, 1616) in the British Library.

portraying tricksters, pimps and whores who preyed on fools and the corrupt, he induced his audience to laugh with the con men against those whom they deceived and robbed. But he also forced viewers to confront their own vices and follies in both sets of characters: greed, dishonesty and hypocrisy being among his favourite targets. In *The Alchemist*, three tricksters have set up shop in the house of a gentleman absent from London because of his fear of catching the plague. His servant, the symbolically named Face, provides a front for the activities of a whore, Doll Common, and an alchemist, Subtle, whose name suggests both skill and sly nature. Subtle, unable to perfect the alchemist's intended conversion of base metals into gold, has turned con man, and fleeces rich clients of vast sums by telling them that he is about to succeed in his experiment, and will give them the full benefit of the gold-making process once it is complete – and also eternal life with the philosopher's stone. His lies, expressed in the jargon of many different pseudo-sciences, perform an alchemy his chemicals cannot: he, Face and Doll turn words into gold. But he offers a range of services alongside his alchemy: here, he pretends to dispense astrological knowledge and magical advice curiously akin to *feng shui* to an aspiring shopkeeper, Abel Drugger:

Act 1, Scene 3

Face: This is my friend Abel, an honest fellow ...

Subtle: He's a fortunate fellow, that I am sure on –

Face: Already, sir, ha' you found it? Lo thee Abel!

Subtle: And, in right way toward riches –

Face: Sir.

Subtle: This summer,
He will be of the clothing of his company:
And, next spring, called to the scarlet. Spend what he can ...[29]

Face: 'Slid, Doctor, how canst thou know this so soon?
I am amused at that!

Subtle: By a rule, Captain,
In metoposcopy, which I do work by,[30]
A certain star i'th'forehead, which you see not.
Your chestnut, or your olive-coloured face
Does never fail: and your long ear doth promise.
I knew't, by certain spots too, in his teeth,

---

29. Abel Drugger, the victim, is a druggist and a member of the Grocer's Company. Subtle promises him advancement to the office of sheriff, meantime trying to induce him to spend money – on Subtle, for example.

30. A type of physiognomy, the study of the face. Ironic, as Subtle has picked up his information about Drugger from Face.

And on the nail of his mercurial finger.

Face: Which finger's that?

Subtle: His little finger. Look.
You're born upon a Wednesday?

Drugger: Yes, indeed, sir.

Subtle: The thumb, in chiromancy,[31] we give Venus;
The forefinger to Jove; the midst, to Saturn;
The ring to Sol; the least, to Mercury:
Who was the lord, sir, of his horoscope,
His house of life being Libra,[32] which foreshowed,
He should be a merchant, and should trade with balance.

Face: Why, this is strange! Is't not, honest Nab?

Subtle: There is a ship now, coming from Ormus,[33]
That shall yield him, such a commodity
Of drugs – This is the west, and this the south?[34]

Drugger: Yes, sir.

Subtle: And those are your two sides?

Drugger: Ay, sir.

Subtle: Make me your door, then, south; your broad side, west:
And, on the east side of your shop, aloft,
Write *Malthai*, *Tarmiel*, and *Baraborat*;
Upon the north part, *Rael*, *Velel*, *Thiel*.[35]
They are the names of those mercurial spirits,
That do fright flies from boxes.

Drugger: Yes, sir.

Subtle: And,
Beneath your threshold, bury me a lodestone[36]
To draw in gallants, that wear spurs ...

Having persuaded Drugger to reward Subtle with a gold coin and leave, Subtle receives his next customer, Sir Epicure Mammon. Mammon, so full of vices himself that he cannot hope to attempt alchemy or the search for the philosopher's stone (it supposedly required a purity of soul, and bodily chastity), is paying Subtle to experiment for him. Subtle uses Mammon's small knowledge of alchemical terms to blind him with science, instructing Face in alchemical theory as well as in the management of the furnace and the

---

31. Palmistry.
32. Venus, not Mercury, was held to govern Libra: but Drugger is unaware of this.
33. Hormuz, in the Persian Gulf.
34. Subtle is mapping the layout of Drugger's shop in his mind.
35. A prescription from Cornelius Agrippa's *De Occulta Philosophia* (Paris (?), 1567).
36. A magnet.

compounds. Unfortunately, these exist only in Mammon's imagination: the room where the experiment is supposedly being secretly conducted is, in fact, empty. Only Surly, Mammon's friend, realizes this and tries to save Mammon from Subtle's clutches. The structure of the verse, where characters' lines run into one another to keep up a steady iambic beat suggests the seamless nature of the tricksters' fluid lies, and the way that clients' desires collaborate with them against their own interests to create a supernatural world of mysticism, infinite possibilities and allure.

Act 2, Scene 3

Subtle: Look well to the register,[37]
              And let your heat, still, lessen by degrees,
              To the aludels.[38]

Face: Yes, sir.

Subtle: Did you look
              O'the bolt's head yet?[39]

Face: Which, on D, sir?[40]

Subtle: Aye.
              What's the complexion?

Face: Whitish.[41]

Subtle: Infuse vinegar,
              To draw his volatile substance, and his tincture:[42]
              And let the water in glass E be filtered,
              And put into the gripe's egg.[43] Lute him well;[44]
              And leave him closed in *balneo*.[45]

Face: I will, sir.

Surly: What a brave language here is? Next to canting?[46]

Subtle: I have another work you never saw, son,
              That, three days since, passed the philosopher's wheel,
              In the lent heat of Athanor; and's become

---

37. Damper.
38. Vessels.
39. A rounded flask.
40. There are supposedly several apparatuses, labelled by letters.
41. Black and white were associated with the early stages of alchemy: red was the desired result.
42. Tincture was the final stage of the alchemical process, elixir. Vinegar is being used to purify the materials here, to move them towards tincture.
43. A pot shaped like a griffin's egg.
44. Seal with clay.
45. A bath of sand or water for gentle heating.
46. The slang of thieves, or the hypocritical terminology of puritans.

Sulphur o' nature.[47]

Mammon: But 'tis for me?

Subtle: What need you?
You have enough, in that is, perfect.

Mammon: O, but –

Subtle: Why, this is covetise!

Mammon: No, I assure you,
I shall employ it all, in pious uses,
Founding of colleges, and grammar schools,
Marrying young virgins,[48] building hospitals,
And now and then a church.

Subtle: How now?

Face: Sir, please you,
Shall I not change the filter?

Subtle: Marry, yes.
And bring me the complexion of glass B . . .
How now? What colour says it?

Face: The ground black, sir . . .

Subtle: No, 'tis not perfect, would it were the crow.[49]
That work wants something.

Surly [aside]:   O, I looked for this.
The hay is a-pitching.[50]

Subtle: Are you sure, you loosed 'hem
I' their own menstrue?[51]

Face: Yes, sir, and then married 'hem,[52]
And put 'hem in a bolt's head, nipped to digestion,[53]
According as you bade me; when I set
The liquor of Mars[54] to circulation,
In the same heat.

---

47. An experiment that has passed through part of the alchemical cycle in the slow fire of an 'athanor' furnace, to become pure sulphur.
48. Mammon means that he will help poor virgins to marry well, but his phrase suggests his own lust.
49. The crow symbolized complete calcination, the first step in alchemy.
50. Surly sees that the tricksters are preparing to ask for more money, and to tell Mammon later that their process has failed: a hay is a snare.
51. Liquid that dissolved metals.
52. Alchemical jargon is full of personifications: the marriage of male (red, Sol/sun or sulphur) and female (white, Luna/moon or mercury) was a favourite conceit, the chemical wedding of the father and mother of all metals. Alchemy linked itself with natural cycles of birth and death, and Christian resurrection, through this idea.
53. Heated to aid maturation.
54. Molten iron.

Subtle: The process, then, was right.

Face: Yes, by the token, sir, the retort broke,
　　　　　　And what was saved, was put into the pelican,
　　　　　　And signed with Hermes' seal.[55]

Subtle: I think 'twas so.
　　　　　　We should have a new amalgama.[56]

Surly [aside]:   O, this ferret
　　　　　　Is rank as any polecat.[57]

Subtle: But I care not.
　　　　　　Let him e'en die; we have enough beside,
　　　　　　In embrion. H has his white shirt on?

Face: Yes, sir,
　　　　　　He's ripe for inceration:[58] he stands warm,
　　　　　　In his ash-fire. I would not, you should let
　　　　　　Any die now, if I might counsel, sir,
　　　　　　For luck's sake to the rest. It is not good.

Mammon: He says right.

Surly: Ay, are you bolted?[59]

Face: Nay, I know't, sir,
　　　　　　I have seen th'ill fortune. What is some three ounces
　　　　　　Of fresh materials?

Mammon: Is't no more?

Face: No more, sir,
　　　　　　Of gold, t'amalgam, with some six of mercury.

Mammon: Away, here's money. What will serve?

Face: Ask him, sir.

Mammon: How much?

Subtle: Give him nine pound: you may gi' him ten.

Surly: Yes, twenty, and be cozened,[60] do.

Mammon: There 'tis.

It is not just Face and Subtle who con clients, however. Like the woman of Hogsdon, Doll Common takes a full part in their schemes, most notably by a pretence to be the fairy queen. A blindfolded client is persuaded to part with his

---

55. The apparatus broke, and the remains were hermetically sealed in a pelican flask. Hermes Trismegistus, supposedly a contemporary of Moses, was the mythical originator of alchemy.
56. Mixture.
57. Metaphorically speaking, Subtle stinks.
58. Waxiness.
59. Stampeded into the snare.
60. Cheated.

purse and jewellery in the belief that his 'aunt' or fairy-godmother will specially bless him, perhaps leaving him her fortune. For this story, as with others, Jonson drew on accounts of actual tricksters' exploits – here probably cunning woman Judith Phillips' legendary bridling and saddling of a gentleman who hoped to meet the fairy queen through this humiliation, detailed in *The Brideling, Sadling, and Ryding, of a Rich Churle* (London, 1595). Jonson's play thus suggests the infinity of 'supernatural' money-making schemes that were possible in a world enchanted by beliefs in witches, fairies, potions and angelic conversations. However, Owen Davies' books on the supposed decline of witchcraft and magic in the eighteenth and nineteenth centuries suggest that this world endured well after prosecutions for maleficent witchcraft ceased officially in the 1730s.

EIGHT

WITCHCRAFT IN AMERICA

The witch trials of inhabitants of the New England town of Salem, Salem Village and surrounding towns, which came to a dramatic climax in 1692, are probably the best known in the history of witchcraft. The story, with its mythic additions, is often retold: the English colonists who had attempted to establish a godly society in the New World believed they were under threat from Satan, and in the early 1690s that threat appeared to manifest itself in a very vivid form. In January or February 1692, two young girls in the house of Salem Village's minister Samuel Parris began to be strangely ill and before long a number of the town's girls and younger women were accusing their neighbours and friends of bewitching them. Tituba Indian, a woman described both as Negro and Indian (that is, Native American, Carib or Amerindian) was among the first to be accused, and she confessed – for reasons which are unclear. Soon others had followed suit, but a significant body of the accused, both women and men, refused to admit guilt. In a legal innovation, those who confessed were (mostly) simply imprisoned, whilst those perceived as obstinate and unrepentant were, when tried and convicted, hanged. As the numbers of accusers and accused grew, so that hundreds of people – some of them among the colony's elite – were either imprisoned or suspected, fears grew that terrible mistakes had been made and that at least some of the convicted were in fact innocent. The court sittings were ended on 29 October and the colonists began a bitter self-searching, which produced some of the defining statements of belief and disbelief in the reality of witchcraft in America and beyond.

Some of the documents on which the trials were based – informations, examinations and indictments – are reproduced here, as well as extracts from the works of three of the key writers on the events of 1692. Relying on personal observation as well as the works of English demonologists, Cotton and Increase Mather and John Hale tried to make sense of events in the months after the trials. The accounts are very different: Cotton Mather's optimistic call to unity against the deceit and divisiveness of the devil, Increase Mather's more boldly stated reservations about spectral evidence, and John Hale's shocked and implicitly self-accusatory reflections on the trial of witchcraft, one of the most bluntly expressed statements of the belief that a great injustice had been done in 1692.

1. Legal documents[1]

Examination of Bridget Bishop

There are two surviving accounts of the examination of Bridget Bishop. The first was written by Samuel Parris, in whose house accusations of witchcraft began. The second was written by church member Ezekiel Cheever, one of those who had complained against Bridget Bishop on 18 April (the day before her examination) and who had been involved in the investigation of suspected witchcraft from the first.

The accounts contrast tellingly, although they do accord in general to give us basic information about Bridget Bishop's examination and they do not contradict each other. They can help us get a sense of the atmosphere, which was clearly very hostile to the suspect, and of Bishop's response: a repeated denial of any crime. Each also confirms some of details in the other: that there were five people 'afflicted' at this stage, that Bishop was caught out in what appeared to be a direct lie, that a cut in her clothing was part of the evidence explored, and so on. If we trust them, the accounts can also fill in some of each other's gaps: some further interventions by the main accusers and others, the assertion that Bishop was accused of killing her husband, and such like. But overall, the impression is that, as with English pre-trial materials and many reports of witchcraft, the writers are selectively setting down ambiguous statements as if they were word-for-word reports of uncontested truths, and they are probably missing out information which the modern observer would regard as vital. Both men show a presumption of the suspect's guilt, and the fact that each account omits much that is in the other leaves the reader wondering what may have been entirely overlooked by both writers. Furthermore, the Salem examinations were public events, with accusers encouraged to interject; a circumstance explicitly condemned by those such as Increase Mather who believed an injustice had been done. It seems likely that the writers were contesting with noise and distraction as well as their own interest in the proceedings, all of which hampered their efforts to give a *verbatim* account of what they saw and heard.

Bridget Bishop was the first of the Salem witches to be tried and executed. She was the first victim because others already examined had confessed, thus (whether they knew it or not) saving themselves from hanging. Bridget Bishop would not confess and, as Bernard Rosenthal argues in *Salem Story*, this may have been because she already had experience of being accused of witchcraft

---

1. All documents are transcribed from the records of the Court of Oyer and Terminer, 1692, property of the Supreme Judicial Court of Massachusetts, Division of Archives and Records Preservation. On deposit at the Phillips Library, Peabody Essex Museum, Salem, Massachusetts and reproduced with their kind permission. Erasures in the documents (omitted from existing transcripts) are indicated by curly brackets.

(in 1679–80) and knew that a suspect should not confess.[2] This court, however, was quite different.

As historians now agree, Bridget Bishop has traditionally been confused with another suspect, Sarah Bishop, and described accordingly as a tavern keeper. This woman was examined by John Hale. But Bridget Bishop was the wife of a sawyer, already twice widowed and known sometimes as Bridget Oliver or Olliver after her second husband. She did, as often cited by historians, wear a red bodice, a most ungodly garment, and probably had a reputation for disorderly life. The Olivers had been successfully prosecuted for fighting with each other in 1670 – incidents in which Bridget was apparently severely hurt – and for name-calling. Bridget reportedly called her husband 'old rogue' and 'old devil' on the sabbath and was sentenced to do public penance for it in 1678. The next year came the witchcraft accusation, and she was also accused of stealing brass in 1688, although no verdict survives. She was clearly a controversial figure, and her reputation must have counted against her when she was examined on 19 April 1692. Rosenthal unpicks the myth of Bridget Bishop and offers a full reading of her case in *Salem Story*, chapter 4, and readers are referred to his book for the best recent account of the case. Also essential for an understanding of the local politics of the accusations (although see Rosenthal for new evidence and corrections) is Paul Boyer and Stephen Nissenbaum's *Salem Possessed: The Social Origins of Witchcraft* (Cambridge, MA and London: Harvard University Press, 1974).

Samuel Parris' version, with record of committal by John Hathorne

The Examination of Bridget Byshop at Salem Village 19. Apr. 1692 By John Hauthorn & Jonath: Corwin Esq'rs.[3]

As soon as she came near all fell into fits[4]

Bridget Byshop, You are now brought before Authority to give acco.[5] of what witchcrafts you are conversant in

I take all this people (turning her head & eyes about) to witness that I am clear.

Hath this woman hurt you speaking to ye afflicted.

Eliz: Hubbard,[6] Ann Putman,[7] Abigail Williams & Mercy Lewes affirmed she had hurt them.[8]

---

2. Bernard Rosenthal, *Salem Story: Reading the Witch Trials of 1692* (Cambridge: Cambridge University Press, 1993), p. 71.
3. Justices of the Peace and members of the legislature, these wealthy merchants were among the most eminent in Salem town.
4. The accusers.
5. Account.
6. This name has been written above an illegible erasure, probably another name.
7. *Sic.* Putnam was the more usual spelling.
8. These girls and young women gave evidence against many of the accused. Elizabeth

You are here accused by 4. or 5. for hurting them, what do you say to it.?

I never saw these persons before; nor I never was in this place before.[9]

Mary Walcot[10] said that her brother Jonathan stroke her appearance[11] & she saw that {he} he had tore her coat in striking, & she heard it tare.

Upon {som} some search in the Court, a rent that seems to answere what was alledged was found.

They say you bewitcht your first husband to death.[12]

If it please your worship I know nothing of it.

She shake her head & the afflicted were tortured.

The like again upon the motion of her head.

Sam: Braybrook[13] affirmed that she told him to day that she had been accounted a Witch these. 10. years, but she was no Witch, the Devil can not hurt her.[14]

I am no Witch.

Why if you have not wrote in the book, yet tell me how far you have gone?[15] Have you not to do with familiar Spirits?

I have no familiarity with the Devil.

How is it then, that your appearance doth hurt these?

I am innocent.

Why you seem to act witchcraft before us, by the motion of your body, which {has in} seems to have influence fluence[16] upon the afflicted.

I know nothing of it. I am innocent to a Witch. I know not what a Witch is.

---

cont.

Hubbard lived with her uncle, the physician Dr William Griggs and was somewhere between 16 and 18 years old; Ann Putnam was the daughter of Thomas and Ann Putnam, and was 12; Abigail Williams was the niece of the recorder, Samuel Parris, and was 11; Mercy Lewis lived with the Putnams as a maid and was 19.

9. Bridget Bishop came from the main town of Salem.

10. Mary lived with the Putnams (Ann was her cousin) and was 18.

11. Jonathan struck the supposed apparition of Bishop.

12. Samuel Wasselbe (see Enders A. Robinson, *The Devil Discovered: Salem Witchcraft 1692* (1991; Prospect Heights, IL: Waveland Press, 2001), p. 307, for Bridget's former names). A full account of documents relating to Bridget Bishop is given in David L. Greene, 'Salem Witchcraft I: Bridget Bishop', *American Genealogist*, vol. 57, no. 3 (July 1981), pp. 129–38, and vol. 58, no. 3 (July 1982), p. 163.

13. Samuel Braybrook gave evidence against several other suspects. It is notable that many of the persons offering evidence against Bishop here were also involved in other cases, with relatively few offering detailed accusations suggesting they had known her well and for a long time.

14. Bishop had first been tried in 1680.

15. This uncontextualized question indicates perhaps the most obvious gap in the record. See Cheever's account for more discussion of the book.

16. Clearly a presumption was made by the writer (and the questioner?) and then withdrawn in favour of '*seems* to have influence'. The text shows stress here with the repeat of 'fluence', not erased, suggesting tension or interruption.

How do you know then that you are not a witch y. {& yet know not what a Witch is?}[17]

I do not {understand} know what you say.

How can you know, you are no Witch, & yet not know what a Witch is.

I am clear: if I were any such person you should know it.

You may threaten, but you can do no more than you are permitted.[18]

I am innocent of a witch.

What do you say of those murders you are charged with?

I hope, I am not guilty of Murder.

Then she turned up her eyes, & they the eyes of the afflicted were turned up

It may be you do not know, that any have confessed to day, who have been examined before you, that they are Witches.[19]

No, I know nothing of it.

John Hutchinson & John Hewes[20] in open Court affirmed that they had told her

Why look you, you are taken now in a flat lye.

I did not hear them.

Note: Sam. Gold saith that after this examination he askt sd. Bridget Byshop if she were not troubled to see the afflicted persons so tormented, said Byshop answered no, she was not troubled for them: Then he ask't her whither she thought they were bewitcht, she said she could not tell what to think about them. Will Good, & John Buxton junr was by, & he supposeth they hear her also.[21]

Salem Village Aprill the. 19th 1692[22] mr Sam'l parris being desired to take into wrighting the Examination of Bridget Bishop, hath delivered it as aforesaid And upon heareing the same, and seeing what wee did then see, togather with the Charge of the afflicted persons then present; Wee Committed the said Bridget Olliver –

John Hathorne.

---

17. It seems likely that this unanswerable question had to be clarified for the suspect (see the next question).
18. Although the questioner takes the suspect's words as a threat, they may equally be an assertion of honesty. Documents cannot record the tone of such a statement.
19. Abigail Hobbs, arrested and questioned at the same time as Bishop, had that day confessed 'I have been very wicked' and admitted to covenanting with the devil.
20. Whilst transcripts read 'Lewis', this is clearly the John Hews who was required, in the original complaint against Bridget Bishop on 18 April, to attend to give evidence against several suspects. John Hutchinson was a relative by marriage of the Putnams.
21. Samuel Gold played no major role in the prosecutions but William Good was the husband of suspect Sarah Good, against whom he gave evidence, whilst John Buxton also accused many other suspects.
22. This paragraph is in a different hand, clearly that of John Hathorne.

Ezekiel Cheever's version

The examination of Bridget Bishop before the Worshipfull John Harthon and Jonathan Curren esqrs

Bridget Bishop being now comeing in to be examined relating to her accusation of suspicon of sundry acts of witchcrafts the afflicted persons are now dreadfully afficted[23] by her as they doe say

(Mr Harthon) Bishop what doe you say you here stand charged with sundry acts of witchcraft by you done or commited upon the bodyes of Mercy Lews and An Putnam and others

(Bishop) I am innocent I know nothing of it I have done no witchcraft

(Mr Har) Looke upon this woman and see if this be the woman that you have seen hurting you Mercy Lewes and An Putnam and others doe doe[24] now charge her to her face with hurting of them

Mr Harthon What doe you say now you see they charge you to your face

(Bish) I never did hurt them in my life I did never see these persons before I am as innocent as the child unborn

(Mr Harth) is not your coate cut

(Bish) answers no but her garment being Looked upon they find it cut or toren two wayes Johnathan walcoate saith that the sword that he strucke[25] goode Bishup[26] was not naked but was within the {scab} scabberd so that[27] rent may very probablie be the very same that mary walcoate {tell} did tell that she had in her coate by Jonathans stricking at her apperance[28]

The afflicted persons charge her, with having hurt them many wayes and by tempting them to sine to the devils Booke at which charge she seemed to be very angrie and shaking her head at them saying it was false they are all greatly tormented (as I conceive) by the shaking of her head

(Mr Har) good Bishop what contract have you made with the devill

(Bish) I have made no contract with the devill I never saw him in my[29] [li]fe. An Putnam sayeth that shee calls the devill her god

[(Mr] Har) what say you to all this that you are charged with can you not find in your [he]art to tell the truth

(Bish) I doe tell the truth I never hurt these persons in [m]y life I never saw them before.

(Mercy Lewes) oh goode Bishop did you not come to our house the Last

---

23. *Sic.*
24. *Sic.*
25. Above the line 'at' is inserted.
26. 'With' inserted above the line.
27. 'The' inserted above the line.
28. This section shows stress in its many minor changes, and was presumably (compare Parris' account) written as a summary of question and answer with and about the Walcots.
29. The page is torn here. Conjectural readings are offered in square brackets.

night and did you not tell me that your master made you tell more then you were willing to tell

(Mr Har) tell us the truth in this matter how comes these persons to be thus tormented and to charge you with doing

(Bish) I am not come here to say I am a witch to take away my life

(M H) who is it that doth it if you doe not they say it is your likenes that comes and torments them and tempts them to write in the booke what Booke is that you tempt them with.

(Bish) I know nothing of it I am innocent.

(Mr Harth) doe you not see how they are tormented you are acting witchcraft before us what doe you say to this why have you not an heart to confese the truth

(Bsh) I am innocent I know nothing of it I am no witch I know not what a witch is.

(Mr H) have not you given consent that some evill spirit should doe this in your Likenes.

(B) no I am innocent of being a witch I know no man woman or child here

(Marshall Herrik)[30] how came you into my bed chamber one morning then and asked me whither I had any curtains to sell shee is by some of the afflicted persons charged with murder

(Mr Harth) what doe you say to these murders you are charged with

(B) I am innocent I know nothing {about} of it

now shee Lifts up her eyes and they are greatly tormented {again}

(Mr Har) what doe you say to these things here horrible acts of witchcraft

(Bish) I know nothing of it I doe not know whither be any witches or no

(Mr Har) no have you not heard that some have confessed.

(Bish) no I did not. two men told her to her face that they had told her here shee is taken in a plain lie now shee is going away they are dreadfully afflicted 5 afflicted persons doe charge this woman to be the very [wo]man that hurts them

[This] is a true account of what I have taken down at her examination according to best [un]derstanding and observation I have also in her examination taken notice that all her actions [hav]e great influence upon the afflicted persons and that have ben torered by her[31]

Ezekiel Cheever

---

30. George Herrick, marshal of Essex County. He had been charged the previous day with bringing in Bishop and others for questioning.

31. Cheever was running out of space to write, which might explain why his account ends abruptly and raggedly.

Indictment of Bridget Bishop for afflicting Mercy Lewis

Anno Regni Regis et Reginae W[illm et][32]
Mariae nunc Angliae &c Quarto:[33]

Essex Ss[34]

The Jurors[35] for our Soveraigne Lord & lady the King & Queen psents that
Bridgett Bishop als[36] Olliver the wife of Edward Bishop of Salem in the
County of Essex Sawyer. the Nyneteenth Day of April in the ffourth Year
of the Reigne of our Sovereigne Lord and Lady William and Mary by the
Grace of God of England Scottland France & Ireland King & Queen
Deffenders of the faith &c: and Divers other Dayes & times aswell before as
after. certaine Detestable Arts {of} called[37] witchcrafts & sorceries, wickedly,
and felloniously {agt} hath used Practised & Exercised, at and within the
Towneship of Salem[38] in the County of Essex aforesd in {and} upon, and
agt one: Mercy Lewis of Salem Village in the County aforsd singlewoman.
by which said wicked Arts the said Mercy Lewis – the sd Nyneteenth Day
of April before as after, was & is hurt Tortured Afflicted {tormented} Pined,
Consumed, wasted: & tormented agt the Peace of our[39] Sovereigne Lord
And Lady the King & Queen and agt the forme of the Statute in that Case
made & provided

Wittnesses
Mercy Lewis
Nathanll Ingersoll[40]
Mr Samll paris
Thomas puttnam Jun'r
Mary Walcott
Ann puttnam Jun'r
Elizabeth Hubbard
Abigail Williams

---

32. The document is torn. Conjectural readings are offered in square brackets.
33. The fourth year of the reign of King William III and Queen Mary II of England; that is, 1692.
34. Sessions.
35. Grand jurors.
36. *Alias*: also known as.
37. 'Of' has been erased and 'called' substituted above the line.
38. A short illegible crossing out here.
39. 'Said' has been omitted and added above the line.
40. Nathaniel Ingersoll and his wife were near neighbours of Samuel Parris and witnesses to fits and accusations.

The bill of indictment was endorsed 'billa vera', a true bill, by the grand jury and so was sent on for consideration by the open court and the petty jury.

Susannah Sheldon, evidence against Bridget Bishop and others

This undated piece of testimony is a good specimen of the more lengthy and lurid kind of claims made about 'spectres' of the suspected witches. It shows the idea of a group or coven of witches fully developed. Susannah Sheldon was not one of the original accusers and Bridget Bishop was not indicted for harming her but for attacking Elizabeth Hubbard, Ann Putnam, Abigail Williams and Mercy Lewis (as above).

Susannah Sheldon, who probably lived with 'Widow' Sheldon, and was 18, joined the group of accusers once a pattern of accusation had been established and accepted, and her claims of spectral assault built on the existing accusations, adding to a weight of evidence. As John Hathorne noted in his addendum to Bridget Bishop's examination (Parris version) several kinds of accepted evidence were converging – accusation, unsatisfactory answers under examination, and apparent witchcraft in court – and Bridget Bishop and Martha Corey were convicted and later executed (10 June and 22 September), whilst Giles Corey was, famously, pressed to death on 19 September for refusing to enter a plea of either guilty or not guilty. Susannah was unoriginal in adding to accusations against these people. The same was true of the others she accused here, but Phillip and Mary English were a wealthy couple who owned the town's largest shipping business, and eventually escaped by fleeing the colony. Their accusation was one of several later charges made against the colony's elite. The mixing in Sheldon's narrative (among others) of persons of very different social status and from different communities suggests the growth of the notions that anyone could be a witch and that there was a witch-conspiracy across the colony at every level. As the ministers' accounts (below) show, the spread of accusation to eminent people was one of the factors that eventually brought the prosecutions to a halt.

on the foarth {a a} day at night[41] Came goody olliver and mrs English and good man Core[42] and a blak man[43] with a hi crouned hatt with books in their hands goody olliver bad mee touch her booke i would not i did not know her name shee told me her name was goody Olliver and bid me touch her booke now I bid her tel mee how long shee had been a witch shee told

---

41. The testimony begins abruptly, a continuation of a longer story. The lack of punctuation and spasmodic capitalization, the careful printing and the erratic, sometimes phonetic, spelling suggest a very different recorder from Parris and Cheever.
42. Note the class distinctions between 'goody' and 'good man' Corey (lower), and 'mistress' English (higher).
43. The devil.

me shee told mee[44] S[45] had been a witch above twenti years then their came a streked snake creeping over her shoulder and crep into her bosom mrs. English had a yelo bird in her bosom and good man Core had two tircels[46] hang to his Coat and hee opened his bosom and put his turcls to his brest and gave them suck then good man core and goody oliver kneeled doune beefour the blak man and went to prayer and then the blak man told mee goody olliver had been a witch twenti years and a{n} half then they all set to biteing mee and so went away the next day Came good man Core mrs English in the morning and told mee i should not eat no vittals i took a spoon and put on spoonful in my mouth and good man Core gave me a blow on the ear and all most choaked mee then he laughed at mee and told mee i would eat when he told mee i should not[47] then he Clenched my hands that they could not be opened for more then a quarter of an our then came phillip english and and[48] told mee if i would touch his book hee would not bit mee but i refused then he did bite mee and went away the sixth day at night Came goody olliver and mrs english good man Core and his wife goodwy[49] Core S profered mee a book i refused it and asked her whear she lived she told mee shee lived in boston prisson then shee puled out her brest and the blak man gave her a thing like a blake pig it had no haire on it and shee put it to her breast and gave it suck and when it had sucked on brest shee put it the other and gave it suck their then shee gave it to the blak man then they went to praier to the blak man then goody olliver told mee that shee had kiled foar women two of them wear the fosters wifes and john trasks wife[50] and did not name the other then they did all bitt mee and went away then the next day Cam goody Core choaked mee and told mee i would not eat when my dame bid mee but now I should eat none

The back of this document also lists evidence against Sarah Buckley and her daughter and 'boston woman' contained in Sheldon's extended story.

---

44. *Sic.*
45. She.
46. Small hawks.
47. He accuses Susannah of wanting to eat when he had told her not to.
48. *Sic.*
49. *Sic.*
50. The Fosters were an Andover family. Christian, wife of John Trask, had committed suicide several years before and *Sarah* Bishop was questioned about her death.

2. Demonologies

Cotton Mather, The Wonders of the Invisible World *(Boston and London, 1693)*

Cotton Mather (1663–1728), the son of Increase Mather (see below) and a fellow-minister, wrote *The Wonders of the Invisible World: Being an Account of the Tryals of Several Witches, Lately Executed in New England* ... as a sincere and passionate engagement with the prosecutions of witches in Salem and other places. It was published in Boston and reprinted in London by John Dunton, and was thus intended to reach a wide audience. Both Mathers included in their work material previously given in sermons.

Cotton's contextualization of the prosecutions and their aftermath is revealing, defining precisely for the reader the motives of those godly New Englanders who accepted most fully the probability that witchcraft was and had been at work. Mather junior, an exceptional linguist and still in his late twenties, has been portrayed as both villain and hero of the Salem trials, although neither representation can explain the complexities of his position. His distance from the centre of events, and his scepticism about the use of so-called spectral evidence, given to the witches' victims by supposed apparitions of the witches themselves, are both clear, and in this he joined his father and other ministers in offering advice to the Governor and Council which should have restrained the court's belief in the less easily substantiated allegations. It was in effect ignored, and although other evidence, such as confession and empirical proof of supernatural ability was sought and sometimes obtained to the satisfaction of the ministers, indictments based almost entirely on spectral evidence convicted most of the Salem witches. One would expect Cotton Mather to be dismayed by this, but his emphasis in *The Wonders of the Invisible World* is firmly on the enormity of the devil's threat to New England and on the consequent justice of several of the convictions of executed witches, where he believed spectral evidence had contributed to correct suspicions based also on other factors. He attended some of these executions and made himself a bad name by justifying them to the crowd, as several accounts relate.

In *Wonders of the Invisible World*, written in the climate of doubt and self-accusation after the trials, Cotton expressed two great fears: that the project of settlement and consolidation in New England would be damaged by ridicule and attack by outsiders, and that internal dissention over the trials would tear the colonies apart. Thus – more so than Increase – he tried to hold together a consensus on witchcraft. He began by saying that 'the World will do New-England a great piece of Injustice, if it acknowledge not a measure of Religion, Loyalty, Honesty, and Industry, in the People there' and added that New England would likely become the subject of scandal because of recent events. However, in censuring the colonists, and losing faith in the successful prosecution of deserving witches, the reader would be contributing to Satan's assaults on the world by damaging the 'New-English Israel'. 'The New-

Englanders', Cotton asserted at once, 'are a People of God settled in those, which were once the Devil's Territories'. Perched on the edge of a continent and embattled by vast rocky woods, which Cotton described as 'a squalid, horrid, American Desart', the colonists had 'richly bespangled' their wilderness with evangelical churches, 'wherein Multitudes are growing ripe for Heaven every day'. Naturally, the devil opposed their pious invasion, and later Cotton enumerated the threats he had sent against the offensive Christians: Indian sorcery, Catholics, crop disease, ague, threats against liberty, massacres, fires, war with the French, and shipwrecks. In this light, the reader was invited to consider both the legitimacy of the colonists' suspicion that the witches were merely Satan's latest affliction, and how their own response to the 1692 crisis of confidence could contribute to Satan's plot. In practice, this tipped the scales against scepticism, obscuring firm reservations about evidence previously expressed by reiterating spectral testimony as part of trial reports of the witches and implying complacency that justice had been done.

It is immediately clear that Cotton Mather was unconvinced by those who claimed, in varying degrees, that the trials had been more of a mistake than a just response to danger.

... An Army of Devils is horribly broke in upon the place which is the Center, and after a sort, the First-born of our English Settlements: and the Houses of the Good People there are fill'd with the doleful Shrieks of their Children and Servants, Tormented by Invisible Hands, with Tortures altogether preternatural. After the Mischiefs there Endeavoured, and since in part Conquered, the terrible Plague, of Evil Angels, hath made its Progress into some other places, where other Persons have been in like manner Diabolically handled. These our poor Afflicted Neighbours, quickly after they become Infected and Infested with these Daemons, arrive to a Capacity of Discerning those which they conceive the Shapes of their Troublers; and notwithstanding the Great and Just Suspicion, that the Daemons might Impose the Shapes of Innocent Persons in their Spectral Exhibitions upon the Sufferers, (which may perhaps prove no small part of the Witch-Plot in the issue) yet many of the Persons thus Represented, being Examined, several of them have been Convicted of a very Damnable Witchcraft: yea, more than One Twenty have Confessed, that they have Signed unto a Book, which the Devil show'd them, and Engaged in his Hellish Design of Bewitching, and Ruining our Land. We know not, at least I know not, how far the Delusions of Satan may be Interwoven into some Circumstances of the Confessions; but one would think, all the Rules of Understanding Humane Affairs are at an end, if after so many most Voluntary Harmonious Confessions, made by Intelligent Persons of all Ages, in sundry Towns, at several Times, we must not Believe the main strokes wherein those Confessions all agree: especially when we have a thousand preternatural Things every day before our eyes, wherein the Confessors do acknowledge their Concernment, and give Demonstration of their being so Concerned. If the Devils now can strike the minds of men with any Poisons of so fine a Composition and Operation, that scores of Innocent People shall Unite, in Confessions of a Crime, which we see actually committed, it is a thing prodigious, beyond the Wonders of former Ages, and it threatens no less than a sort of Dissolution upon the World. Now, by these Confessions 'tis Agreed, That the Devil has made a dreadful Knot of Witches in the Country, and by the help of Witches has dreadfully increased that Knot: That these Witches have driven a Trade of Commissioning their Confederate Spirits, to do all sorts of Mischiefs to the Neighbours, whereupon there have ensued such Mischievous consequences upon the Bodies and Estates of the Neighbourhood, as could not otherwise be accounted for: yea, That at prodigious Witch-Meetings, the Wretches have proceeded so far, as to Concert and Consult the Methods of Rooting out the Christian Religion from this Country, and setting up instead of it, perhaps a more gross Diabolism, than ever the World saw before. And yet it will be a thing little short of Miracle, if in so spread a Business as this, the Devil should not get in some of his Juggles, to confound the Discovery of all the rest.

This reservation allowed Cotton to accommodate the views of those who were most concerned about the rightness of their actions, and he went on to sum up his view of the two 'sides' in the American debate about witchcraft.

On the one side; [Alas, my Pen, must thou write the word, Side in the Business?] There are very worthy Men, who having been call'd by God, when and where this Witchcraft first appeared upon the Stage to encounter it, are earnestly desirous to have it sifted unto the bottom of it. And I pray, which of us all that should live under the continual Impressions of the Tortures, Outcries, and Havocks which Devils confessedly Commissioned by Witches make among their distressed Neighbours, would not have a Biass that way beyond other Men? ... On the other side [if I must again use the word Side, which yet I hope to live to blot out] there are very worthy Men, who are not a little dissatisfied at the Proceedings in the Prosecution of this Witchcraft. And why? Not because they would have any such abominable thing, defended from the Strokes of Impartial Justice ... Only 'tis a most commendable Cautiousness, in those gracious Men, to be very shye lest the Devil get so far into our Faith, as that for the sake of many Truths which we find he tells us, we come at length to believe any Lyes, wherewith he would abuse us ... They would have all due steps taken for the Extinction of Witches; but they would fain have them to be sure ones; nor is it from any thing, but the real and hearty goodness of such Men, that they are loth to surmise ill of other Men, till there be the fullest Evidence for the surmises ... In fine, Have there been faults on any side fallen into? Surely, they have at worst been but the faults of a well-meaning Ignorance.

After the publication of this book, Cotton Mather's zealous desire to sift the matter of witchcraft further led him into controversy when he took the next offered opportunity to try to get to the bottom of the relationship between witches, the devil and evidentiary proof. He began to investigate the accusations of the apparently 'afflicted' Margaret Rule, was attacked in print by fellow-Bostonian Robert Calef, and backed away from a confrontation with him in the courts. The balance of opinion had shifted against demonological experiment, and rather than be caricatured as a callous, credulous witch-monger, Cotton pursued other publishing projects, notably his history of New England, *Magnalia Christi Americana*.

Increase Mather, Cases of Conscience . . . *(Boston and London, 1693)*

Increase Mather (1639–1723) was President of Harvard College, as well as a minister in Boston, when he wrote *Cases of Conscience Concerning Evil Spirits Personating Men; Witchcrafts, Infallible Proofs of Guilt in such as are Accused with that Crime,* and the character of the book reflects his learning. Unlike his son Cotton's *Wonders of the Invisible World*, Increase's text is filled with references to demonological writers. Where Cotton strove for directness and reievance to recent events in America, Increase was providing a contextual reading of those events with reference first to the scriptures, secondly to history and only thirdly to his own experience (as the book's subtitle lists). He expressly stated that he did not dissent from anything written in Cotton's book, but his rhetoric and emphasis are very different. Where Cotton focused excitedly on the threat to New England from a witch-plot, Increase was more concerned with the anxiety that innocents may have been executed, and offered a measured discussion of wider demonological questions to help his readers decide. In this he was consistent with the original advice offered by ministers to the secular authorities and his book served as a rebuke of those who had accepted spectral evidence notwithstanding.

So Odious and Abominable is the Name of a Witch, to the Civilized, much more to the Religious part of Mankind, that it is apt to grow up into a Scandal for any, so much as to enter some sober cautions against the over hasty suspecting, or too precipitant Judging of Persons on this account. But certainly, the more execrable the Crime is, the more critical care is to be used in exposing the Names, Liberties, and Lives of Men (especially of a Godly Conversation)[51] to the imputation of it . . .

    That there are Devils and Witches, the Scripture asserts, and experience confirms, That they are common enemies of Mankind, and set upon mischief, is not to be doubted: That the Devil can (by Divine Permission) and often doth vex men in Body and Estate, without the Instrumentality of Witches, is undeniable: That he often hath, and delights to have the

---

51. Of a godly way of living.

concurrence of Witches, and their consent in harming men, is consonant to his native Malice to Man, and too lamentably exemplified: That Witches, when detected and convinced, ought to be exterminated and cut off, we have God's warrant for, Exod. 22.18. Only the same God who hath said, thou shalt not suffer a Witch to live; hath also said, at the Mouth of two Witnesses, or three Witnesses shall he that is worthy of Death, be put to Death, Deut. 17.6. Much debate is made about what is sufficient Conviction, and some have (in their Zeal) supposed that a less clear evidence ought to pass in this than in other Cases, supposing that else it will be hard (if possible) to bring such to condign Punishment, by reason of the close conveyances that there are between the Devil and Witches; but this is a very dangerous and unjustifiable tenet ... It is therefore exceeding necessary that in such a day as this, men be informed what is Evidence and what is not ...

In the case of Witchcraft we know that the Devil is the immediate Agent of the Mischief done, the consent or compact of the Witch is the thing to be Demonstrated. Among many Arguments to evince this, that which refers to something vulgarly called Spectre Evidence, and a certain sort of Ordeal or trial by the sight and touch. The principal Plea to justifie the convictive Evidence in these, is fetcht from the Consideration of the Wisdom and the Righteousness of God in Governing the World, which they suppose would fail, if such things were permitted to befal an innocent person: but it is certain, that too resolute conclusions drawn from hence, are bold usurpations upon spotless Sovereignty: and tho' some things if suffered to be common, would subvert this Government, and disband, yea mine[52] Humane Society; yet God doth sometimes suffer such things to evene,[53] that we may there by know how much we are beholden to him, for that restraint which he lays upon the Infernal Spirits, who would else reduce a World into a Chaos ...

Increase's summary of his views was signed by 14 clergymen, and he went on to examine the matters on which he had been asked to comment.

The First Case that I am desired to express my Judgement in, is this, Whether it is not Possible for the Devil to impose on the imaginations of Persons Bewitched, and to cause them to Believe that an Innocent, yea, a Pious person does torment them, when the Devil himself doth it; or whether Satan may appear in the Shape of an Innocent and Pious, to Afflict such as suffer by Diabolical Molestations? The Answer to the Question must be Affirmative ... I have my self known several of whom I ought to think that they are now in Heaven, considering that they were of good Conversation and reputed Pious by those that had the greatest Intimacy

52. Undermine.
53. Happen.

with them, of whom nevertheless, some complained that their Shapes appeared to them, and threatned them: Nor is this answered by saying, we do not know but those Persons might be Witches: We are bound by the Rule of Charity to think otherwise: And they that censure any, meerly because such a sad Affliction as their being falsly represented by Satan has befallen them, do not as they would be done by ... And the Devils have of late accused some eminent Persons. It is an awful thing which the Lord has done to convince some amongst us of their Error: This then I declare and testifie, that to take away the Life of any one, meerly because a Spectre or Devil, in a bewitched or possessed Person does accuse them, will bring the Guilt of innocent Blood on the Land, where such a thing shall be done: Mercy forbid that it should, (and I trust that as it has not nor it never will be so) in New-England ...[54]

If one bewitched is struck down at the Look or cast of the Eye of another, and after that recovered again by a Touch from the same person, Is not this an infallible Proof, that the Person suspected and complained of is in League with the Devil? Answer; It must be owned that by such things as these Witchcrafts and Witches have been discovered more than once or twice: And that an ill Fame, or other Circumstances attending the suspected Party, this may be a Ground for Examination; but this alone does not afford sufficient Matter for Conviction ...

Having discussed these two main points, Increase examines what does constitute matter for conviction. He dismisses the swimming test, and other methods he calls pagan and popish. Then he moves on to consider verbal evidence in court, saying

1. That a free and voluntary Confession of the Crime made by the Person suspected and accused after Examination, is a sufficient ground of Conviction. Indeed, if Persons are Distracted, or under the Power of Phrenetick Melancholy, that alters the Case; but the Jurors that examine them, and their Neighbours that know them, may easily determine that Case; if Confession be extorted, the Evidence is not so clear and convictive; but if any Persons out of Remorse of Conscience, or from a Touch of God on their Spirits, confess and shew their Deeds ... nothing can be more clear. Suppose a Man to be suspected for Murder, or for committing a Rape, or the like nefandous[55] Wickedness, if he does freely confess the Accusation, that's ground enough to Condemn him ... It is by some objected, that Persons in Discontent may falsly accuse themselves. I say, if they do so, and it cannot be proved that they are false Accusers of them selves, they ought to

---

54. This is an ambiguous comment. Does the bracketed phrase rule out any suspicion of a miscarriage of justice having already occurred, or not?
55. Atrocious.

dye for their Wickedness, and their Blood will be upon their own Heads; the Jury, the Judges, and the Land is clear ...

2. If two credible Persons shall affirm upon Oath that they have seen the Party accused speaking such words, or doing things which none but such as have Familiarity with the Devil ever did or can do, that's a sufficient Ground for Conviction ... How often have they been seen by others using Inchantments? Conjuring to raise Storms? And have been heard calling up their Familiar Spirits? And have been known to use Spells and Charms? And to shew in a Glass or in a Shew-stone persons absent? And to reveal secrets which could not be discovered but by the Devil? And have not men been seen to do things which are above human Strength, that no man living could do without Diabolical Assistances? ...

Increase's rules of evidence would still have convicted a number of the Salem suspects. For example, George Burroughs' 'unnatural' strength, which Increase heard of at the one Salem trial he did attend, would still have suggested supernatural power. But without a confession or other convincing evidence, it could hardly have been used as a basis for an indictment. Yet both Cotton and Increase defended the execution of the former minister Burroughs and, from the allegations made against him, it seems likely that he was suspected of being a Baptist, and thus in their eyes a misbeliever likely to be tempted by Satan. Rules of evidence were only as effective as the impartiality of those who applied, or ignored, them. But the rules might have saved others, such as Rebecca Nurse and Mary Easty, who were of good reputation and against whom the evidence was of a kind Increase believed might be perverted by the devil. Increase Mather has a final caution for his readers: 'I will add; It were better that ten suspected Witches should escape, than that one innocent Person should be condemned ...' Thus Increase has been mis-remembered simply as a man who spoke out against the prosecution of witches whilst Cotton has been unfairly perceived simply as a rabid supporter of the trials.

John Hale, **A Modest Enquiry Into the Nature of Witchcraft** *(Boston, 1702)*

In 1692 John Hale (1636–1700), another New England minister, was convinced that witchcraft had occurred at Salem, and supported the prosecutions of those suspected until at least early October, when many others were filled with doubt. His church, in the town of Beverley, was only two miles from Salem and so he was closer to the witchcraft events than either of the Mathers. He spoke with suspects, accusers and magistrates, gave evidence against one suspect (Sarah Bishop, not Bridget, as was once thought) and believed that there was strong evidence to examine and convict the accused and to hang them. But as the number of accused grew, and (after the court sittings had been discontinued) Hale's own wife's name was added to the list, he began to suspect that he had been wrong in his initial assessment, and to believe that a dreadful injustice had been done by the devil's help in Salem. *A Modest Enquiry* is his attempt to make amends for the wrong and ensure that it did not recur.

Hale's book shapes many modern accounts of the case, including Arthur Miller's play *The Crucible* through which many people first learn of the Salem trials. Its directness and honest admission of confusion and fallibility are disarming. Hale described in his introduction his reasons for writing. Firstly, it should be obvious to all that something was amiss when those tried later in the sequence of trials were acquitted on evidence no stronger than that which had condemned earlier suspects. Secondly, he had personal knowledge of many of the events and of earlier witch trials. Thirdly, 'I have been from my Youth trained up in the knowledge and belief of most of those principles I here question as unsafe.' Fourthly, he had a deep sense of the irreparable nature of mistakes made, 'and what grief of heart it brings to a tender conscience to have been unwittingly encouraging of the Sufferings of the innocent'. Fifthly, he wrote to prevent disillusion with the very idea of witchcraft from setting in, for Hale still believed that there were witches – most notably, of the kind who could be safely identified as cunning persons by their public practices. Even some of Salem's accused may have been guilty. Picking his way through the same impossible ground as other demonologists, John Hale was no 'Sadducee', but he cited Wier among his arguments for questioning the justice of many convictions, and like many writers of the time it seems likely that he had read or heard the ideas of Scot.

Hale listed some of the reasons which had induced him and others to believe the early witch suspects' confessions, beginning with that of Tituba Indian.

Here were these things rendred her confession credible. (1.) That at this examination she answered every question just as she did at the first. And it was thought that if she had feigned her confession, she could not have remembred her answers so exactly. A lyar we say, had need of a good memory, but truth being always consistent with it self is the same to day as it was yesterday. (2.) She seemed very penitent for her Sin in covenanting with the Devil. (3.) She became a sufferer her self, & as she said for her confession. (4.) Her confession agreed exactly (which was afterwards verified in the other confessors) with the accusations of the afflicted ...

He followed this explanation with an answering list of reasons that induced him to change his mind about many of them.

It may be queried then, How doth it appear that there was a going too far in this affair? A.[56] 1. By the numbers of the persons accused which at length increased to about a hundred, and it cannot be imagined that in a place of so

---

56. Answer.

much knowledge, so many in so small a compass of Land should so abominably leap into the Devils lap at once. 2. The quality of several of the accused was such as did bespeak better things, and things that accompany Salvation … 3. The number of the afflicted by Satan dayly increased, till about Fifty persons were thus vexed by the Devil. This gave just ground to suspect some mistake … 4. It was considerable that Nineteen were Executed, and all denied the Crime to the Death, and some of them were knowing persons, & had before this been accounted blameless Livers … 5. When this prosecution ceased, the Lord so chained up Satan, that the afflicted grew presently well … 6. It sways much with me that I have since heard and read, of the like mistakes in other places …

Hale repeated the well-worn ideas that spectral evidence was unacceptable because Satan could impersonate the spectre of an innocent person, and that the looking and touching test was likewise open to devilish abuse to incriminate good people. He added that he believed the afflicted were demoniacs, and even partly counterfeiting their symptoms, rather than being straighforwardly victimized by witches. He rejected claims that the wounding of a spectre or the tearing of its supposed clothes, which subsequently manifested on the body and clothes of the accused (see Bridget Bishop, above), was reliable evidence, and demolished presumptions of guilt based on prior reputation, family ties to other witches, deathbed accusations, witches' teats, and tests by burning the witches' belongings. Going much further than Increase Mather, he said that it was not enough that a suspect had confessed, especially when that suspect before or after had shown signs of demonic possession or obsession, and he also made some uncomfortably pragmatic observations on confessors' motivation in widening accusations.

I am jealous, and I hope with a godly jealousie, that some by these their accusations of others, hoped to gain time, and get favour from the Rulers. And that some of the inferiour sort of people did ill Offices, by promising them favour thereby more than they had ground to engage. And that some under these temptations regarded not as they should what became of others, so that they could thereby serve their own turns. And I have been credibly informed, that some have since acknowledged so much …

It's probable some being accused, and their own Relations among others, suspecting them, and vehemently urging them to confess themselves guilty, were so surprized and amazed that they confessed that in their haste which they have cause to repent at leisure. And having once accused themselves, they feared to retract it presently lest a worse thing should come upon them …

Yet Hale still believed it unlikely that all the confessors had been innocent.

But there were others, whose Confessions seemed more free and demonstrative of reality, and some who confessed upon real or pretended horrour of Conscience; and these attended with such circumstances, that some will say, there is no believing mankind confessing their guilt of any Crime, if these must not be believed. But I leave the true state of their case, to a farther discovery, when the Lord please, in this life, or when God shall Judge the secrets of men ...

Hale concluded his treatise with sobering reflections.

But to come nigher home, we have cause to be humbled for the mistakes & errors which have been in these Colonies, in their Proceedings against persons for this crime, above fourty years ago and downwards,[57] upon insufficient presumptions and presidents[58] of our Nation whence they came.[59] I do not say, that all those were innocent, that suffered in those times upon this account. But that such grounds were then laid down to proceed upon, which were too slender to evidence the crime they were brought to prove; and thereby a foundation laid to lead into error those that came after ... But I would come yet nearer to our own times, and bewail the errors and mistakes that have been in the year 1692. In the apprehending too many we may believe were innocent, and executing of some, I fear, not to have been condemned ... I would humbly propose whether it be not expedient, that some what more should be publickly done then yet hath, for clearing the good name and reputation of some that have suffered upon this account against whom the evidence of their guilt was more slender, and the grounds for charity for them more convincing ... And this is one end of this present discourse, to take off (so far as a discourse of this nature can) infamy from the names and memory of such sufferers in this kind, as do not deserve the same.

---

57. Accusations of witchcraft had been made in the colonies from the late 1630s: Hale mentions among others the cases of Mary Johnson, Elizabeth Kendall and Alice Lake, executed in the late 1640s, as well as the Parsons of Springfield, Massachusetts, accused in 1651. See David D. Hall, *Witch-Hunting in Seventeenth-Century New England*, 2nd edn (Boston: Northeastern University Press, 1999), for background.
58. Precedents.
59. Hale is criticizing previous interpretations under English law.

NINE

DECLINE AND CHANGE – RESTORATION
TO EIGHTEENTH CENTURY

1. Against the sceptics

Joseph Glanvill, Saducismus Triumphatus *(London, 1681)*

Joseph Glanvill (1636–80), divine and controversialist, wrote his *Saducismus Triumphatus: or Full and Plain Evidence concerning Witches and Apparitions* in order, as he says in his dedication to the Duke of Richmond and Lennox, 'to secure some of the Out-works of Religion'. Thus from the first it is made clear that Glanvill, like many other demonologists, saw belief in witches as a vital part of faith in God. His enemy was not incorrect belief, but downright scepticism, the Sadducism which he saw growing around him (see Scot above for 'the old error of the Sadducees'). The ideas in *Saducismus Triumphatus* had been worked over by Glanvill since his *Philosophical Considerations touching Witches and Witchcraft* of 1668, and his final work was published in London in 1681, with additions by Henry More (1614–87), a fellow clergyman and author of several theological treatises, after Glanvill's death.

Glanvill saw his world in black and white: two parties, eventually crystallizing as Tory and Whig: the one supporting belief in witchcraft as part of allegiance to traditional moral, political and religious values; the other shamelessly abandoning the piety of the past, denying the existence of witches, spirits and – as he saw it – the divine itself. In fact, his chief targets were very diverse radical thinkers. The most hated was perhaps John Webster, author of *The Displaying of Supposed Witchcraft* of 1677, a deeply religious but unorthodox sectarian who responded vigorously to Glanvill's attacks by accusing him of popery. Inevitably, there was also the arch-'Sadducee' Scot, whose thorough-going scepticism had been unmatched since his death some century and a half before Glanvill wrote. Glanvill's most influential targets were philosophers like Thomas Hobbes, who in his *Leviathan* of 1651 doubted the actuality of witches' power (though not their malignity) as part of his wider rethinking of the nature of the human and the divine. The part witchcraft played in such a radical world-view was profoundly disturbing to Glanvill.

The men he saw as the enemy would not naturally have aligned themselves, believing as they did in very different universes, but in the true spirit of party controversy, Glanvill and More tarred them all with the same brush. The Preface to *Saducismus Triumphatus* dismissed them and their followers as possessing 'a mighty confidence grounded upon nothing, that swaggers and huffs and swears there are no Witches', adding for good measure that 'their Opinions came into their Heads by chance'. There was a logic to this linkage of diverse 'Objectors', however: Glanvill saw all such men as presumptuous enthusiasts, each trumpeting his own belief without the humility of recognizing that there was a great deal still to be discovered about the natural and spiritual worlds. As Ian Bostridge shows, he blamed such over-confident theorizing for the sectarian chaos of the Civil War and Commonwealth, and with the Restoration of the monarchy he saw an opportunity to restore traditional religiosity also.[1] The strength of his own opinions was, he felt, tempered by a modest willingness to admit (as he frequently does) that the powers and preferences of God and his spirit world remained unknown.

In fact, Glanvill was so willing to admit his own ignorance that he often damaged his argument. The reader notes his unwillingness to 'affirm' important assumptions, and his refusal to cite specific authorities, or fill in the detail of a knotty point of debate, such as the materiality of the bodies of spirits. A typical abridgement reads: 'there are several considerable Arguments I could alledge to render it exceeding probable. Which things supposed ...', and Glanvill moves on to his next point. Like many other writers of his time, his overriding interest was not in demonology, but in the wider political and theological implications of belief or disbelief in witchcraft – and he expected his audience to forgo the intricacies of proof that it existed in order to preserve what he saw to be greater truths. Glanvill hurled together arguments from earlier British demonologists as well as European writers in a ferment of anxious loathing of the new and the liberal, adding suppositions of his own to patch together a case against atheism. The fragmentary nature of his work suggests a man struggling on all fronts against a tide of scepticism.

From a letter written by Henry More, prefacing *Saducismus Triumphatus*.

... if there were any modesty left in mankind, the Histories of the Bible might abundantly assure men of the existence of Angels and Spirits. But these Wits, as they are taken to be, are so jealous, forsooth, and so sagacious, that whatsoever is offered to them by way of established Religion, is suspected for a piece of politick Circumvention ... And forasmuch as such

---

1. Ian Bostridge, *Witchcraft and Its Transformations c. 1650–c. 1750* (Oxford: Clarendon Press, 1997), p. 75. Bostridge's excellent account of this period provides a detailed discussion of witchcraft beliefs, including those of Hobbes, Glanvill, Hutchinson and Defoe, and their context.

course-grain'd Philosophers as those Hobbians and Spinozians,[2] and the rest of that Rabble, slight Religion and the Scriptures, because there is such express mention of Spirits and Angels in them, things that their dull Souls are so inclinable to conceit[3] to be impossible; I look upon it as a special piece of Providence that there are ever and anon such fresh examples of Apparitions and Witchcrafts as may rub up and awaken their benummed and lethargick Mindes into a suspicion at least, if not assurance that there are other intelligent Beings besides those that are clad in heavy Earth or Clay. In this, I say, methinks the Divine Providence does plainly outwit the Powers of the dark Kingdom, in permitting wicked men and women and vagrant Spirits of that Kingdom to make Leagues or Covenants one with another, the Confession of Witches against their own Lives being so palpable an evidence, (besides the miraculous feats they play) that there are bad Spirits, which will necessarily open a Door to the belief that there are good ones, and lastly that there is a God.

Wherefore let the small Philosophick Sir Foplings of this present Age[4] deride them as much as they will, those that lay out their pains in committing to writing certain well-attested Stories of Witches and Apparitions, do real service to true Religion and sound Philosophy, and the most effectual and accomodate[5] to the confounding of Infidelity and Atheism, even in the Judgement of the Atheists themselves, who are as much afraid of the truth of these stories as an Ape is of a Whip; and therefore force themselves with might and main to disbelieve them by reason of the dreadful consequence of them as to themselves ...

From Joseph Glanvill, Preface to *Saducismus Triumphatus*.

Glanvill begins by attacking his opponents and stating:

That though Philosophical Discourses to justifie the common belief about Witches, are nothing at all to them, or those of their measure; yet they are too seasonable and necessary for our Age, in which Atheism is begun in Sadducism: And those that dare not bluntly say, There is No God, content themselves (for a fair step and Introduction) to deny there are Spirits, or Witches. Which sort of Infidels, though they are not ordinary among the meer vulgar, yet are they numerous in a little higher rank of understandings.

---

2. Thomas Hobbes (1588–1679), whose ideas on the functional regulating influence of political and ecclesiastical authority influenced Baruch Spinoza (1623–77), who denied the immortality of the soul and providence, and privileged human reason over superstition.
3. Conceive.
4. Sir Fopling Flutter, a foolish fashionable gentleman in Sir George Etherege's 1676 comedy *The Man of Mode*.
5. The most effectual and useful service (to the confounding of ... etc.).

And those that know any thing of the world, know, that most of the looser Gentry, and the small pretenders to Philosophy and Wit, are generally deriders of the belief of Witches and Apparitions. And were this a slight or mere speculative mistake, I should not trouble my self or them about it. But I fear this errour hath a Core in it that is worse than Heresie: and therefore how little soever I care what men believe or teach in matters of Opinion, I think I have reason to be concern'd in an affair that toucheth so near upon the greatest interests of Religion. And really I am astonisht sometimes to think into what a kind of Age we are fallen, in which some of the greatest impieties are accounted but Bugs, and terrible Names, invisible Tittles, Peccadillo's, or Chimera's.[6] The sad and greatest instances, are Sacriledge, Rebellion, and Witchcraft ...

Glanvill speaks briefly about sacrilege and rebellion ...

But my business at present is not with these, but the other, Witchcraft, which I am sure was a Sin in elder times; and how comes it about that our Age, which so much outdoes them in all other kinds of wickedness, should be wholly innocent in this? That there May be Witches and Apparitions in our days, notwithstanding the Objections of the modern Sadducee, I believe I have made appear in the Considerations following ...

From 'Some Considerations about Witchcraft in a letter to Robert Hunt, Esq.'[7]

Glanvill puts his opponents' points of view and answers them:

(I.)[8] The Notion of a Spirit is impossible and contradictious, and consequently so is that of Witches, the belief of which is founded on that Doctrine.

To Which Objection I answer, (1) If the notion of a Spirit be absurd as is pretended, that of a God and a Soul distinct from matter, and immortal, are likewise absurdities. And then, that the world was jumbled into this elegant and orderly Fabrick by chance; and that our Souls are onely parts of matter that came together we know not whence nor how, and shall again shortly

---

6. Terrible names (presumably devils, or the names of terrible sins) are believed to be invisible, tiny things of no account (tittles), small sins (peccadillos), mythical beasts (chimeras).

7. Robert Hunt was a Justice of the Peace in Somerset, who sent Glanvill transcripts of his examinations of witches, and the informations of their accusers.

8. Glanvill's numbering of his 'objections' is (unnecessarily) complicated in the original text. Each objector's point is headed with a bracketed number (reproduced here), but, above that, with a section number, which is always one number ahead of the bracketed number because Section I is Glanvill's introduction. To avoid confusion, the numbers of objections have been retained here whilst the section numbers have been removed.

be dissolv'd into those loose Atoms that compound them; That all our conceptions are but the thrusting of one part of matter against another; and the Idea's of our minds mere blind and casual motions. These, and a thousand more the grossest impossibilities and absurdities (consequents of this Proposition, That the notion of a Spirit is absurd) will be sad certainties and demonstrations. And with such Assertors I would cease to discourse about Witches and Apparitions, and address my self to obtain their assent to Truths infinitely more sacred ...

(II.) There Are Actions in most of those Relations ascribed to Witches, which are ridiculous and impossible in the nature of things; such are (1) their flying out of windows, after they have anointed themselves, to remote places. (2) Their transformation into Cats, Hares, and other Creatures. (3) Their feeling all the hurts in their own bodies which they have received in those. (4) Their raising Tempests, by muttering some nonsensical words, or performing ceremonies alike impertinent as ridiculous. And (5) their being suck'd in a certain private place of their bodies by a Familiar. These are presumed to be actions inconsistent with the nature of Spirits, and above the powers of those poor and miserable Agents. And therefore the Objection supposeth them performed onely by the Fancy; and that the whole mystery of Witchcraft is but an illusion of crasie imagination.

To this aggregate Objection I return, (1) In the general, The more absurd and unaccountable these actions seem, the greater confirmation are they to me of the truth of those Relations, and the reality of what the Objectors would destroy. For these circumstances being exceedingly unlikely, judging by the measures of common belief, 'tis the greater probability they are not fictitious: For the contrivers of Fictions use to form them as near as they can conformably to the most unsuspected realities, endeavouring to make them look as like truth as is possible in the main supposals, though withal they make them strange in the circumstance ... This suppos'd impossibility then of these performances, seems to me a probable argument that they are not wilful and designed Forgeries. And if they are Fancies, 'tis somewhat strange that Imagination, which is the most various thing in all the world, should infinitely repeat the same conceit in all times and places.

But again (2) the strange Actions related of Witches, and presumed impossible, are not ascribed to their own powers; but to the Agency of those wicked Confederates they imploy. And to affirm that those evil spirits cannot do that which we conceit impossible, is boldly to stint the powers of creatures, whose natures and faculties we know not; and to measure the world of Spirits by the narrow rules of our own impotent beings. We see among our selves the performances of some out-go the conceits and possibilities of others; and we know many things may be done by the Mathematicks and Mechanick Artifice, which common heads think impossible to be effected by the honest ways of Art and Nature. And doubtless, the subtilties and powers of those mischievous Fiends are as much beyond the reach and activities of the most knowing

Agents among us, as theirs are beyond the wit and ability of the most rustick and illiterate ...

(3) I think there is nothing in the instances mention'd, but may as well be accounted for by the Rules of Reason and Philosophy, as the ordinary affairs of Nature. For in resolving natural Phaenomena, we can onely assign the probable causes, sheing[9] how things may be, not presuming how they are. And in the particulars under our Examen,[10] we may give an account how 'tis possible, and not unlikely, that such things (though somewhat varying from the common road of Nature) may be acted. And if our narrow and contracted minds can furnish us with apprehensions of the way and manner of such performances, though perhaps not the true ones, 'tis an argument that such things may be effected by creatures whose powers and knowledge are so vastly exceeding ours. I shall endeavour therefore briefly to suggest some things that may render the possibility of these performances conceivable, in order to the removal of this Objection, that they are contradictions and impossible.

For the First then, That the confederate Spirit should transport the Witch through the Air to the place of general Rendezvous, there is no difficulty in conceiving it; and if that be true which great Philosophers affirm, concerning the real separability of the Soul from the Body without death, there is yet less; for then 'tis easy to apprehend, that the Soul having left its gross and sluggish body behind it, and being cloath'd onely with its immediate vehicle of Air, or more subtile matter, may be quickly conducted to any place it would be at by those officious[11] Spirits that attend it. And though I adventure to affirm nothing concerning the truth and certainty of this Supposition, yet I must needs say, it doth not seem to me unreasonable ...

(2) The Transformations of Witches into the shapes of other Animals, upon the same supposal is very conceivable, since then 'tis easie enough to imagine, that the power of imagination may form those passive and pliable vehicles into those shapes ...

But then (3) when they feel the hurts in their gross bodies, that they receive in their airy vehicles, they must be supposed to have been really present, at least in these latter; and 'tis no more difficult to apprehend how the hurts of those should be translated upon their other bodies, than how diseases should be inflicted by the imagination, or how the fancy of the Mother should wound the Foetus, as several credible relations do attest.[12]

---

9. Showing? (shewing).
10. Examination.
11. Helpful, facilitating.
12. The imagination and spiritual state of women was thought to affect their unborn babies, sometimes in a very concrete way. Glanvill mentions deformed children and birthmarks, but sometimes women were said to have given birth to money bags or cats as a punishment for sin (see, for examples, David Cressy, *Agnes Bowker's Cat: Travesties and Transgressions in Tudor and Stuart England* (Oxford: Oxford University Press, 2000).

And (4) for their raising Storms and Tempests, They do it not, be sure, by their own, but by the power of the Prince of the Air,[13] their Friend and Allie ...

And (lastly) for their being suck'd by the Familiar, I say (1) we know so little of the nature of Daemons and Spirits, that 'tis no wonder we cannot certainly divine the reason of so strange an action. And yet (2) we may conjecture at some things that may render it less improbable. For some have thought that the Genii (whom both the Platonical and Christian Antiquity thought embodied) are recreated by the reeks and vapours of humane blood, and the spirits that proceed from them:[14] Which supposal (if we grant them bodies) is not unlikely, every thing being refresh'd and nourish'd by its like. And that they are not perfectly abstracted from all body and matter, besides the reverence we owe to the wisest antiquity, there are several considerable Arguments I could alledge to render it exceeding probable. Which things supposed, the Devil's sucking the Sorceress is no great wonder, nor difficult to be accounted for. Or perhaps (3) this may be onely a diabolical Sacrament and Ceremony to confirm the hellish Covenant. To which I add (4) That which to me seems most probable, viz. That the Familiar doth not onely suck the Witch, but in the action infuseth some poysonous ferment into her, which gives her Imagination and Spirits a magical tincture, whereby they become mischievously influential; and the word *venefica*[15] intimates some such matter. Now that the imagination hath a mighty power in operation, is seen in the just now mention'd Signatures[16] and Diseases that it causeth; and that the fancy is modified by the qualities of the blood and the spirits, is too evident to need proof. Which things supposed, 'tis plain to conceive that the evil spirit having breath'd some vile vapour into the body of the Witch, it may taint her blood and spirits with a noxious quality, by which her infected imagination, heightned by melancholy and this worse cause, may do much hurt upon bodies that are impressible by such influences ...

But (III.) I come to another prejudice against the being of Witches, which is, That 'tis very improbable that the Devil, who is a wise and mighty Spirit, should be at the beck of a poor Hag, and have so little to do, as to attend the Errands and impotent Lusts of a silly Old woman.

To which I might answer, (1) That 'tis much more improbable that all the world should be deceiv'd in matters of fact, and circumstances of the clearest evidence and conviction ... In brief, there is nothing more strange in this Objection, than that wickedness is baseness and servility; and that the Devil is at leisure to serve those, he is at leisure to tempt, and industrious to

---

13. The devil.
14. One type of genius (more usually a guiding good or evil spirit) was a spirit propitiated by such festivities.
15. Poisoner, but also (contentiously) witch.
16. Birthmarks.

ruine. And again, (2) I see no necessity to believe that the Devil is always the Witches Confederate; but perhaps it may fitly be considered, whether the Familiar be not some departed humane Spirit, forsaken of God and goodness, and swallowed up by the unsatiable desire of mischief and revenge ... And to this conjecture I'le adventure to subjoyn another, which also hath its probability, viz. (3) That 'tis not impossible but the Familiars of Witches are a vile kind of spirits, of a very inferiour Constitution and nature, and none of those that were once of the highest Hierarchy, now degenerated into the spirits we call Devils ... 'tis very probable that those of the basest and meanest Orders are they, who submit to the mention'd servilities. And thus the sagess and grandeur of the Prince of darkness need not be brought into question.[17]

But (IV.) the opinion of Witches[18] seems to some, to accuse Providence, and to suggest that it hath exposed Innocents to the fury and malice of revengeful Fiends; yea, and supposeth those most obnoxious, for whom we might most reasonably expect a more special tutelary care and protection; most of the cruel practices of those presum'd Instruments of Hell, being upon Children, who as they least deserve to be deserted by that Providence that superintends all things, so they most need its guardian influence.

To this so specious an Objection I have these things to answer. (1) Providence is an unfathomable Depth; and if we should not believe the Phaenomena of our senses, before we can reconcile them to our notions of Providence, we must be grosser Scepticks than ever yet were extant. The miseries of the present life, the unequal distributions of good and evil, the ignorance and barbarity of the greatest part of Mankind, the fatal disadvantages we are all under, and hazard we run of being eternally miserable and undone; these, I say are things that can hardly be made consistent with that Wisdom and Goodness that we are sure hath made and mingled it self with all things. And yet we believe there is a beauty and harmony, and goodness in that Providence, though we cannot unriddle it in particular instances; nor, by reason of our ignorance and imperfection, clear it from contradicting appearances; and consequently, we ought not to deny the being of Witches and Apparitions, because they will create us some difficulties in our notions of Providence ... 'tis likely the mischief is not so often done by the evil spirit immediately, but by the malignant influence of the Sorceress, whose power of hurting consists in the fore-mention'd ferment, which is infused into her by the Familiar. So that I am apt to think there may be a power of real fascination[19] in the Witches eyes and imagination, by which for the most part she acts upon tender bodies ...

---

17. Like many demonologists, Glanvill is unable to suppress an attraction to the idea of the regal and devious devil.
18. The opinion that there *are* witches.
19. Like 'influence', the word 'fascination' is used in a technical sense to imply an almost hypnotic power of bewitchment by eye.

Now in this way of conjecture a good account may be given why Witches are most powerful upon Children and timorous persons, viz. because their spirits and imaginations being weak and passive, are not able to resist the fatal invasion; whereas men of bold minds, who have plenty of strong and vigorous spirits, are secure from the contagion; as in pestilential Airs clean bodies are not so liable to infection as other tempers. Thus we see 'tis likely enough, that very often the Sorceress her self doth the mischief; and we know, *de facto*, that Providence doth not always secure us from one anothers injuries: And yet I must confess, that many times also the evil spirit is the mischievous Agent; though this confession draw on me another Objection, which I next propose.

(V.) Then it may be said, that if wicked spirits can hurt us by the direction, and at the desire of a Witch, one would think they should have the same power to do us injury without instigation or compact; and if this be granted, 'tis a wonder that we are not always annoy'd and infested by them. To which I return, (1) That the Laws, Liberties, and Restraints of the Inhabitants of the other world are to us utterly unknown; and this way we can onely argue ourselves into confessions of our ignorance, which every man must acknowledge that is not as immodest as ignorant. It must be granted by all that own the being, power, and malice of evil Spirits, that the security we enjoy is wonderful, whether they act by Witches or not; and by what Laws they are kept from making us a prey, to speak like Philosophers, we cannot tell; yea, why they should be permitted to tempt and ruine us in our Souls, and restrain'd from touching or hurting us in our Bodies, is a mystery not easily accountable. But yet (2) though we acknowledge their power to vex and torment us in our Bodies also; yet a reason may be given why they are less frequent in this kind of mischief, viz. because their main designs are levell'd against the interest and happiness of our Souls; which they can best promote, when their actions are most sly and secret; whereas did they ordinarily persecute men in their Bodies, their agency and wicked influence would be discover'd ... Thus we may conceive that the security we enjoy may well enough consist with the power and malice of those evil Spirits; and upon this account we may suppose that Laws of their own may prohibit their unlicens'd injuries, not from any goodness there is in their Constitutions, but in order to the more successful carrying on the projects of the dark Kingdom ... And hence (3) we may suppose a Law of permission to hurt us at the instance of the Sorceress, may well stand with the polity of Hell, since by gratifying the wicked person, they encourage her in malice and revenge, and promote thereby the main ends of their black confederacy, which are to propagate wickedness, and to ruine us in our eternal interests.[20] And yet (4) 'tis clear to those that believe the History of

---

20. Glanvill is one of the best examples of how each demonologist conceives of Hell in terms of the world he sees around him: Hell is seen here as a pragmatic polity, with a constitution, laws and institutions such as slavery (see point IX.).

the Gospel, that wicked spirits have vexed the bodies of men, without any instigation that we read of; and at this day 'tis very likely that many of the strange accidents and diseases that befal us, may be the infliction of evil spirits . . .

But (VI.) another prejudice against the belief of Witches, is, a presumption upon the enormous force of melancholy and imagination, which without doubt can do wonderful things, and beget strange perswasions; and to these causes some ascribe the presum'd effects of Sorcery and Witchcraft. To which I reply briefly; and yet I hope sufficiently.

(1) That to resolve all the clear circumstances of Fact, which we find in well-attested and confirm'd Relations of this kind, into the power of deceivable imagination, is to make fancy the greater prodigie; and to suppose, that it can do stranger feats than are believed of any other kind of fascination. And to think that Pins and Nails, for instance, can by the power of imagination be convey'd within the skin; or that imagination should deceive so many as have been witnesses in Objects of sense, in all the circumstances of discovery; this, I say, is to be infinitely more credulous than the assertors of Sorcery and Demoniack Contracts . . . And (2) to deny evidence of act, because their imaginations may deceive the Relators, when we have no reason to think so but a bare presumption that there is no such thing as is related, is quite to destroy the credit of all humane testimony . . . the Reply will be another prejudice against the belief for which I contend, viz.

(VII.) That 'tis a suspicious circumstance that Witchcraft is but a fancy, since the persons that are accused are commonly poor and miserable old women, who are overgrown with discontent and melancholy, which are very imaginative; and the persons said to be bewitch'd are for the most part Children, or people very weak, who are easily imposed upon, and are apt to receive strong impressions from nothing . . .

To which Objection it might perhaps be enough to return (as hath been above suggested) that nothing can be concluded by this and such like arguings, but that the policy and menages of the Instruments of darkness are to us altogether unknown, and as much in the dark as their natures; Mankind being no more acquainted with the reasons and methods of action in the other world, than poor Cottagers and Mechanicks are with the Intrigues of Governments, and Reasons of State. Yea peradventure (2) 'tis one of the great designs, as 'tis certainly the interest of those wicked Agents and Machinators, industriously to hide from us their influences, and ways of acting, and to work, as near as is possible, *incognito*: upon which supposal 'tis easie to conceive a reason, why they most commonly work by, and upon the weak and the ignorant, who can make no cunning observations, or tell credible tales to detect their artifice. Besides (3) 'tis likely a strong imagination, that cannot be weaken'd or disturb'd by a busie and subtile ratiocination,[21] is a necessary requisite to those wicked performances; and without doubt an

---

21. Reasoning, logical argument.

heightened and obstinate fancy hath a great influence upon impressible spirits; yea, and as I have conjectur'd before, on the more passive and susceptible bodies ... And perhaps (4) the Daemon himself useth the imagination of the Witch so qualified for his purpose, even in those actions of mischief which are more properly his; for it is most probable, that Spirits act not upon bodies immediately, and by their naked essence, but by means proportionate, and sutable instruments that they use; upon which account likely 'tis so strictly required, that the Sorceress should believe, that so her imagination might be more at the devotion of the mischievous Agent. And for the same reason also Ceremonies are used in Inchantments, viz. for the begetting this diabolical faith, and heightning the fancy to a degree of strength and vigour sufficient to make it a fit instrument for the design'd performance. Those I think are reasons of likelihood and probability, why the hellish Confederates are mostly the ignorant and the melancholick ...

(VIII.) The frequent impostures that are met with in this kind, beget in some a belief, that all such Relations are Forgeries and Tales; and if we urge the evidence of a story for the belief of Witches or Apparitions, they will produce two as seemingly strong and plausible, which shall conclude in mistake or design; inferring thence, that all others are of the same quality and credit. But such arguers may please to consider, (1) That a single relation for an Affirmative, sufficiently confirmed and attested, is worth a thousand tales of forgery and imposture, from whence an universal Negative cannot be concluded. So that, though all the Objectors stories be true, and an hundred times as many more such deceptions; yet one relation, wherein no fallacy or fraud could be suspected for our Affirmative, would spoil any Conclusion could be erected on them. And (2) It seems to me a belief sufficiently bold and precarious, that all these relations of forgery and mistake should be certain, and not one among all those which attest the Affirmative reality ... And I desire such Objectors to consider, (3) Whether it be fair to infer, that because there are some Cheats and Impostures, that therefore there are no Realities ... to conclude, because that an old woman's fancy abused her, or some knavish fellows put tricks upon the ignorant and timorous, that therefore whole Assises have been a thousand times deceived in judgements upon matters of fact, and numbers of sober persons have been forsworn in things wherein perjury could not advantage them; I say, such inferences are as void of reason, as they are of charity and good manners.

But (IX.) it may be suggested further, That it cannot be imagin'd what design the Devil should have in making those solemn compacts, since persons of such debauch'd and irreclaimable dispositions as those with whom he is supposed to confederate, are pretty securely his, antecedently to the bargain, and cannot be more so by it, since they cannot put their Souls out of possibility of the Divine Grace, but by the Sin that is unpardonable;[22] or if they could so dispose and give away themselves, it will to some seem

---

22. See below for this sin, committed against the Holy Ghost.

very unlikely, that such a great and mighty Spirit should oblige himself to such observances, and keep such ado to secure the Soul of a silly Body,[23] which 'twere odds but it would be His, though He put himself to no further trouble than that of his ordinary temptations.

To which suggestions twere enough to say, that 'tis sufficient if the thing be well prov'd, though the design be not known ... But I attempt something more particularly, in order to which I must premise, that the Devil is a name for a Body Politick, in which there are very different Orders and Degrees of Spirits, and perhaps in as much variety of place and state, as among our selves; so that 'tis not one and the same person that makes all the compacts with those abused and seduced Souls, but they are divers, and those 'tis like of the meanest and basest quality in the Kingdom of darkness: which being supposed, I offer this account of the probable design of those wicked Agents, viz. That having none to rule or tyrannize over within the circle of their own nature and government, they affect a proud Empire over us, (the desire of Dominion and Authority being largely spread through the whole circumference of degenerated nature, especially among those, whose pride was their original transgression) every one of these then desires to get him Vassals to pay him homage, and to be employ'd like Slaves in the services of his Lusts and Appetites; to gratifie which desire, 'tis like enough to be provided and allowed by the constitution of their State and Government, that every wicked spirit shall have those Souls as his property, and particular servants and attendants, whom he can catch in such compacts; as those wild Beasts that we can take in hunting, are by the allowance of the Law our own; and those Slaves that a man hath purchas'd, are his peculiar Goods, and the Vassals of his will. Or rather those deluding Fiends are like the seducing fellows we call Spirits, who inveigle Children by their false and flattering promises, and carry them away to the Plantations of America, to be servilely employed there in the works of their profit and advantage. And as those base Agents will humour and flatter the simple unwary Youth, till they are on Shipboard, and without the reach of those that might rescue them from their hands: In like manner the more mischievous Tempter studies to gratifie, please, and accommodate those he deals with in this kind, till death hath lanch'd[24] them into the Deep, and they are past the danger of Prayers, Repentance, and Endeavours; and then He useth them as pleaseth Him. This account I think is not unreasonable, and 'twill fully answer the Objection. For though the matter be not as I have conjectur'd, yet 'twill suggest a way how it might be conceiv'd; which nulls the pretence, That the Design is unconceivable.

Glanvill moves on to a wider discussion of the spirit world. He asks why so few people are afflicted by witches, suggesting that only those who by wicked living

---

23. An innocent or ignorant body, or person.
24. Launched.

have 'forfeited the tutelary care, and oversight of the better Spirits' can be attacked. He describes a hierarchy of spirits from the gross and evil to the Platonic ideal of the purest disembodied spirit. But in Section XIV, point XII, he returns to the theme of witchcraft with another 'objection'.

(XII.) The belief of Witches, and the wonderful things they are said to perform by the help of the Confederate Daemon, weakens our Faith, and exposeth the World to Infidelity in the great matters of our Religion. For if they by Diabolical assistance, can inflict and cure Diseases, and do things so much beyond the comprehension of our Philosophy, and activity of common Nature; What assurance can we have, that the Miracles that confirm our Gospel were not the effects of a Compact of like nature, and that Devils were not cast out by Beelzebub? If evil Spirits can assume Bodies, and render themselves visible in humane likeness; what security can we have of the reality of the Resurrection of Christ? And if, by their help, Witches can enter Chambers invisibly through Key-holes and little unperceived Crannies, and transform themselves at pleasure; What Arguments of Divinity are there in our Saviour's shewing himself in the midst of his Disciples, when the Doors were shut, and his Transfiguration in the Mount? Miracles are the great inducements of Belief, and how shall we distinguish a Miracle from a lying Wonder; a Testimony from Heaven, from a Trick of the Angels of Hell; if they can perform things that astonish and confound our Reasons, and are beyond all the Possibilities of Human Nature? This Objection is spiteful and mischievous; but thus I endeavour to dispatch it.

(1) The Wonders done by Confederacy with wicked Spirits, cannot derive a suspicion upon Miracles that were wrought by the Author and Promulgers of our Religion, as if they were performed by Diabolical Compact, since their Spirit, Endeavours, and Designs, were notoriously contrary to all the Tendencies, Aims, and Interests of the Kingdom of Darkness ... But besides, I say, (2) That since infinite Wisdom and Goodness rules the World, it cannot be conceived, that they should give up the greatest part of men to unavoidable deception ... And if so, the next Conclusion is, That there is no God that judgeth in the earth; and the best, and most likely Hypothesis will be, That the world is given up to the Government of the Devil ... Now, besides what I have said to the main Objection, I have this to add to the Objectors, That I could wish they would take care of such Suggestions; which, if they overthrow not the Opinion they oppose, will dangerously affront the Religion they would seem to acknowledge. For he that saith, That if there are Witches, there is no way to prove that Christ Jesus was not a Magician, and diabolical Imposter, puts a deadly Weapon into the hands of the Infidel, and is himself next door to the Sin Against The Holy Ghost ...

Glanvill's 'considerations' taper off with a discussion of Scot's arguments on miracles and the alleged silence of the Bible on the subject of witches.

His demonology was forced constantly to return to old arguments to re-legitimate its existence.

2. The 'last word' in scepticism

Francis Hutchinson, An Historical Essay Concerning Witchcraft (London, 1718)

Francis Hutchinson (1660–1739), a clergyman from Bury St Edmunds who was later to become Bishop of Down and Connor, had a wide knowledge of recorded incidents of witchcraft. But of most interest to him were the witchcraft accusations at Boston and Salem, and recent controversial English prosecutions such as that of Jane Wenham (1712), which provoked intense passions and vicious politicking.

Wenham's case was a *cause célèbre*: a cunning woman, in 1712 she had been convicted of witchcraft but reprieved by the judge and subsequently pardoned, despite evidence that in any previous age would have condemned her without further question. Hutchinson visited Wenham and read the pamphlets on her case, and his book sums up the Whig belief that Tory superstition was responsible for condemning her. By 1718 Hutchinson, who had been discouraged from publishing anything contentious after the Wenham affair, was at last convinced that his moment had come and a ready target presented itself: Richard Boulton's *A Compleat History of Magick, Sorcery and Witchcraft* (London, 1715). Boulton was a physician and, like Cotta before him, was arguing that it was possible to tell natural from supernatural diseases. Belief in anything like conventionally defined witchcraft after the Wenham case had begun to look dated and extremist, and Hutchinson wanted to finish it for good.[25]

Although his motivation came partly from party controversy, Hutchinson was part of the beginning of a new way of viewing witchcraft: as an historical curiosity and a matter for careful bibliographical research. His book contains chronological lists of witchcraft events and publications reporting them, and tentative attempts at statistical and cultural analysis of the phenomenon. 'I observe ...' he remarked 'That the Numbers of Witches, and the suppos'd Dealings of Spirits with them increase and decrease, according to the Laws, and Notions, and Principles of the several Times, Places, and Princes'. Moreover, 'a Hebrew Witch, a Pagan Witch, a Lapland Witch, an Indian Witch, a Protestant Witch, and a Popish Witch, are different from one another ...' Hutchinson did not attempt detailed analysis of these differences, but the very fact that he saw witchcraft prosecution as dependent upon political, social and

---

25. See Bostridge for a full account of the Wenham controversy and Hutchinson, pp. 132–6 and 139–54.

cultural factors rather than as a response to an unchanging reality offers a clear indication of the direction writing about witchcraft was to take. It was to focus on culture, politics and human fallibility.

In this sense, although he offers little new evidence Hutchinson's account of witchcraft is thoroughly modern – a history book 'of the moment', with such a strong central thesis that it is content to leave some loose ends. Hutchinson dedicated his book to the Lord Chief Justice, Lord Chief Justice of Common Pleas and Lord Chief Baron of the Exchequer, and his carefully modest appeal for reform of the laws on witchcraft was indeed heeded, although not for a further decade and a half. Meantime, prosecutions ended as a consensus grew among important legal and political figures that witchcraft, as traditionally conceived, did not exist. When Hutchinson died in 1739, it was no longer a crime and the new Witchcraft Act had been in force for four years.

The text below is from the second edition of *An Historical Essay* of 1720.

I think it is a Point very certain, That tho' the sober Belief of good and bad Spirits is an essential Part of every good Christian's Faith, yet imaginary Communications with them, have been the Spring both of the worst Corruptions of Religion, and the greatest Perversions of Justice. How many miserable Creatures have been hang'd or burnt as Witches and Wizzards in other Countries, and former Ages? In our own Nation, ever since the Reformation above a hundred and forty have been executed, if my Book hath any Truth in it,[26] very much upon the Account of one ill translated Text of Scripture.[27] If the same Notions were to prevail again, (and superstition is never far off) no Man's Life would be safe in his own House; for the fantastick Doctrines that support the vulgar Opinions of Witchcraft, rob us of all the Defences that God and Nature have plac'd for our security against false Accusations. for in other Cases, when wicked or mistaken People charge us with Crimes of which we are not guilty, we clear our selves by shewing that at that time we were at home, or in some other Place about our honest Business: But in Prosecutions for witchcraft, that most natural and just Defence is a mere Jest; for if any wicked Person affirms, or any crack'd brain Girl imagines, or any lying Spirit makes her believe, that she sees any old Woman or other Person pursuing her in her Visions, the Defenders of the vulgar Witchcraft tack on an imaginary unprov'd Compact to the Deposition, and hang the accus'd Parties for things that were doing, when they were, perhaps, asleep upon their Beds, or saying their Prayers . . .

---

26. This figure now looks modest: just over 100 witches were executed in the five home counties alone between 1560 and 1700 (see J. A. Sharpe, *Instruments of Darkness: Witchcraft in England 1550–1750*. London: Hamish Hamilton, 1996, p. 111). Patchy survival of records makes it impossible to estimate a nationwide figure.

27. 'Thou shalt not suffer a witch to live'. Like most sceptics, Hutchinson believed that the word 'witch' did not adequately reflect the sense of the Hebrew, Greek and Latin words for soothsayers and/or poisoners.

Hutchinson's emphasis was on accusers as much as witches, for, like Scot, he believed he was combating witchmongers. Although he made use of the traditional explanation of mental illness for witches' self-accusations, he also tried to integrate medical, psychological and 'commonsense' theories of accusation with ominous hints of political manipulation of accusers' stories.

For, tho' a Distemper at first be surprizing, and puts the afflicted Persons beyond their Thoughts of Tricking, yet a little Time makes them familiar with their own Calamity; and when they find themselves to come safe out of strange Fits, and begin to have the Use of their Thoughts while they are in them, and hear what judgements are made of their Case; they manage their Calamity to the serving of their own Interest, or Party, or Passion, or Humour ...

Hutchinson's emphasis on individual liberty, and the possibility that witchcraft belief might regain its credibility, suggest a deep fear of Tory elements in British society. Throughout the *Essay* he was keen to stress the connections he perceived between persecution and Catholicism, and even had an explanation for the unavoidable fact that laws against witchcraft in England were post-Reformation: 'the Government in that Age having been vex'd with continual Plots and bold Attempts ... they found it necessary to shut every Door against them'. Catholic plots and sorceries thus 'explain' Protestant prosecution of witches. Religious enthusiasms of other kinds were, however, also suspect, and Hutchinson explicitly blames the writings of English puritans and the early works of the Mathers for the witchcraft accusations at Salem. Because such elements remained active, he argued that:

I am so far from wishing to see eager Prosecutions of old Women upon the vulgar Notions, and by the common Tryals, that I rather wish there was a Bar put, that they might not break out upon us in any unsettled time. These Doctrines have often been made Party Causes both in our own and other Nations ... Our present Freedom from these Evils are no Security that such a Time may not turn up in one Revolution or another: and it may be worth our Consideration, whether in such a Juncture, the Lives of Men would not be better secur'd under the Fence of a wise and well-consider'd Law, rather than under a superstitious, tho' well meant Statute.

3. Against the devil's party

Daniel Defoe, A System of Magick, or a History of the Black Art (London, 1727)

Daniel Defoe, best known as the author of novels such as *Robinson Crusoe* and *Moll Flanders*, was born in 1660 in Restoration London and died in 1731.

By the time he wrote his two major works on magic, *The History of the Devil* (1726) and *A System of Magick* (1727), he was thus in his mid-sixties, an opinionated and loquacious critic of his own society. His *System of Magick* deals with the failings of those whom Defoe sees as Satan's agents in eighteenth-century England.

Defoe's focus is on the modern world as the culmination of certain historical tendencies, with – to the twenty-first-century reader – surprisingly little attention paid to the medieval and Renaissance flowering of interest in the magical arts. Defoe intended his books to help reform society, and was not really interested in the passions and cruelties of witchcraft accusations. Indeed, his earlier writing had suggested a conventional belief in witchcraft, when it was politically useful to portray it as an enemy of all men, against which they might make common cause to overcome the party factionalism he saw as ruining Britain. By the 1720s, however, after the factional nightmare of the trial of Jane Wenham (see Francis Hutchinson, above), Defoe thought Satan's agents (in the guise of factional politicians as well as religious extremists, experimenters with magic, Catholics and rakes) were triumphant in society and as a solid puritanical citizen, he launched an irritated assault on them. His books show just how much the discussion of witchcraft and magic has changed since the Elizabethan period.

The focus is very much on magic, rather than witchcraft; it is on men, rather than women; and it is on the pretended or metaphorical witch rather than the real one. 'Magic' is used in the widest sense of the word, mutating throughout the text to suit Defoe's antiquarian, satirical or political aims: meaning sometimes specific practices such as incantation, sometimes becoming a metaphor for sin, and even appearing briefly as the embodiment of the true poet's muse. Defoe was intrigued by the Faustian power promised by magical experiment, but appalled by the casual way in which devilish evil was often involved in human affairs. Like others of his time, a decade before the repeal of the Jacobean Witchcraft Act, he believed in the possibility of witchcraft but saw its supposed modern practitioners usually as deluded overreachers, or as tricksters. He believed likewise in the possibility of an 'invisible world', and of communication with the spirits there as part of a rational attempt to learn more, but he was wary of appearing credulous in a field where concrete evidence was hard to find. Like Glanvill, Defoe saw himself as a devout defender of God and moral right – but unlike Glanvill, he was sceptical and radical in his approach to the nature of magic. Often mentioning scientific thinkers such as Newton and Boyle, he sidelined the traditional idea of the witch, and enlarged upon Milton's portrayal of the devil as a creature with explicable, humanlike motives. Both witch and devil become for Defoe inhabitants of the fruitful, disgusting meeting place of human reason, faith and folly.

Defoe's writing was always conditioned by politics. His shifting, multi-targeted satire demonstrates perfectly the much-changed range and concerns of the debate on witchcraft in the eighteenth century. For Defoe, the fight against the devil and the witch was a battle against many forces – political dogma, flirtation with evil, and sin in all its forms.

Preface

... The world has perhaps been imposed upon in nothing more than in their Notions of this dark practice, as well its antient as its modern State. Most People, when they read of the antient Magicians, think they are reading of old Necromancers and Conjurors, when really at first they were very honest Men; and now, when they read of them in their modern Practice, they take them for honest Fellows, when they are, generally speaking, meer Juglers,[28] Cheats, Mountebanks, and Posture-masters; or else, real Wizards and downright Dealers with the Devil.

There is One Sort would fain be called Cunning Men, than which nothing can be a grosser piece of Delusion; and 'tis not their Cunning, but their Clients want of Cunning, that gives them the least appearance of Common Sense in all their Practice. 'Tis a strange Piece of Art where Fools cheat Fools, and the Blind and the Ignorant, are imposed upon by the Blind and the Ignorant ...

I see no great Harm in our present Pretenders to Magick, if the poor People could but keep their Money in their Pockets; and that they should have their Pockets pick'd by such an unperforming, unmeaning, ignorant Crew as these are, is the only Magick that I can find in the whole Science.

The best Course that I think of to cure the People of this Itch of their Brain, the Tarantula[29] of the present Age, in running to Cunning Men, as you call them, and the most likely to have Success, is this, of laughing at them: the Satyr[30] has reform'd the Age of many a Folly, which the Solid and the Solemn could never reach: Even general Vice, would the Men of Wit and Men of Quality join in the attempt, might be hiss'd out of this World, tho' all the Preaching and all the Preachers shou'd prove fruitless and exhausted: Men are to be ridicul'd into good Manners,[31] when they won't be cudgell'd into it ...

... a Magician was no more or less in the ancient Chaldean Times, than a Mathematician, a Man of Science, who stor'd with Knowledge and Learning, as Learning went in those Days, was a kind of walking Dictionary to other People, and instructed the rest of Mankind in any Niceties and Difficulties which occur'd to them, and which they wanted to be inform'd about; and in this Sense we are to be understood when we speak of the Magicians in Egypt, in Persia, in Babylon, &c. ...

Defoe explains that this wisdom of the ancients, originally given by God to Adam and Eve and improved upon by the ingenuity of their descendants, was

---

28. Tricksters.
29. Madness, compulsive movement. The bite of the tarantula spider was thought to cause dance-like convulsions (the tarantella).
30. Satiric.
31. Living a good life.

lost in the Flood, and in the period of wickedness which prompted God to send the deluge. This wickedness provides an opportunity for Defoe to make a rare reference to women as witches – traditionally (see *The Witch of Edmonton* for an earlier example) the allure of women is equated metaphorically with witchcraft, and this allure is described by the knowing author as part of an attack on the corruption of society.

But to return to the Antediluvians:[32] The Old World, I say, as wicked as they were, had some shadow of Good in them, and for some Years, nay some hundreds of Years, they maintain'd the Character of the Sons of God, before they were debauched by the Daughters of Men; that is to say, before they blended the Race with the corrupt Seed of Cain, and mingled Blood with Idolaters. Where, by the way, we have an accurate Description of the Times,[33] I mean in those early Days, of the Race; 'tis evident 'twas just then as 'tis now, the Ladies were the Devils of the Age; the Beauties, the Toasts, the fine Faces were the Baits; the Hell lay concealed in the Smiles of the charming Sex, They were the Magicians, taking the Word in its present Acceptation and its grossest Sense: There lay the Witchcraft, and its Force was so irresistible, that it drew in even the Sons of God, just, in a word, as it does now ...

But even the wise men were not perfect:

The Magi were not always Kings or Emperors; the Wise men and the Southsayers, the Magicians and Astrologers (who by the way were all but one sort of People) were often times in mean Circumstances as to Money, even in those graver Days; they acted for the publick Good indeed, but it was in Conjunction with their own Interest too, they had their Rewards for Southsaying and Divining; and when the King of Syria asked his Servants to go to Elisha the Prophet to enquire for him about his Health, he bad them take a Present in their Hand for the Man of God ... The World, as I have said already, began to be wiser than the Ages before them; the ordinary Magick of the former Ages would not pass any longer for Wisdom; and if the wise Men, as they were called, did not daily produce some new Discoveries, 'twas evident the Price and Rate of Southsaying would come down to nothing.[34]

If this put them upon Stratagem and Art, in order to keep up their Credit, and maintain the Distance between them and the inferior Rank of Men, it is not to be wonder'd at ... At first the Magicians satisfy'd the Curiosity of the People by Juggle and Trick, by framing Artificial Voices and Noises; foretelling strange Events, by mechanical Appearances, and all

---

32. Those who lived before the Flood.
33. Of modern times.
34. The economics of witchcraft are as important to Defoe as its more traditional aspects.

the Cheats which we find put upon the ignorant People to this Day . . . they soon mixt their Religion and their Magick together, their Philosophy and their Idolatry were made Assistant to the general Fraud, and to raise a due Veneration in the Minds of the People ... How strangely does religious Enthusiasm keep its hold of Mankind, and how exactly do past things and present correspond![35] ... How many Popes in particular does History give us an Account of, who have been Sorcerers and Conjurers, and who have dealt with the Devil in the most open and avow'd manner? How has the Romish Church been establisht upon the Artificial Magick of the Clergy? ... And thus we may suppose the World going on for many Ages, till at length, to come nearer our own Times, and indeed nearer to the Practice of our own Times, too, their Mimickry was exhausted; they had no more Tricks to play, the juggling Trade grew stale and dull, the World began to look beyond them, and expected something more; and so the last, I do not say the Church Jugglers, went to the Devil for Help. I had rather tell you that another Generation, who had always been true Magicians, true Practitioners of the Diabolical Part, came in play of course, and succeeded the first, who gradually deposed themselves by their meer Impotency; and just as Darkness is a deprivation of Light, and succeeds it by the meer Consequence of things, so the honest Ignorance of the innocent Magician being unable to keep the Expectation of the People up, and answer the Importunities of the Age, dealing with the Devil succeeded, even by the meer Consequence of things ... The Writers upon this Subject before me seem to have all been at a loss to fix the Original of Magick as an Art Diabolical, and they would fain have us believe it was in Practice in the Antediluvian World. This I have not denied, nor shall I deny it still; but granting the Devil to have a Conquest upon the first Woman, and by her Weakness and Treachery drawing her Husband into the same Snare, we may give up all their Race for as black as Hell could make them ... But my Question has been all along, not what was done before but since the Deluge, and how did Satan introduce himself to the post-diluvian Ages ...

Defoe suggests several biblical figures who might be said to have been Satan's agents after the Flood, concluding that it is 'pretty hard to find out who were the first Magicians'. Nevertheless, he notes the Egyptian magicians who opposed Aaron and Moses as among the first documented. He goes on to trace the development of modern magical practitioners from this 'old Pagan Magick'. The belief that modern magic and witchcraft descended directly from a pagan original was circulating freely and acquiring some of its romantic significance in the eighteenth century.

It may seem a little difficult to bring all the Schemes of Idol or Pagan

---

35. A hit at dissenting sects as well as Catholics.

Worship down to a Level with Witchcraft and Diabolical Magick; and some will tell us, that several Parts of the Pagan Worship, or even Paganism in general, was established upon pure and just Principles, an exact and regular Virtue, the height of Morals, principles of Truth, and of natural Religion, of good Government, and of Dedication to the publick Welfare of Mankind; nay even upon Principles of Piety, and a Homage to be paid to the Divine Being, for all the good attending Human Life; that nothing has been wanting in some Pagans but a Revelation from Heaven, and an opening the Eyes of the Soul by Divine Inspiration, to know the Only True God ... But let us look thro' all this. God for wise Ends did not think fit to accept these little Emanations of Natural Light, or to reveal himself to the Persons; however sincere they may be said to be in the pursuit of Divine Light ... When they had done all, for want of further Illuminations, The Devil was suffer'd to chop in, and confound all their brightest Ideas of Worship, with a horrid Rhapsody of complicated Idolatry. This very Observation is sufficient, or at least it might be expected that it should be sufficient, to crush the Notions which our more Polite Gentlemen now advance, in favour of the study of Magick, as an Art or Science only ... this, they say, duly follow'd, would from the Beginning have made Men be, as the Serpent told them they should be, *viz.* like Gods, knowing Good and Evil. Now these fine-spun Notions or Imaginations, I say, are fully answer'd by taking Notice, that there is apparently no such Infallibility in Man's Judgment, unless assisted by a yet higher and superior degree of Illumination; that is to say, unless God, the Author of all perfect and compleat Illumination, should add to it the Revelation of himself, and of his Mind and Will, giving the Man Rules and Laws for his farther Illumination, and for the Direction of himself ... The Romans were the most civiliz'd Heathens the World ever saw; their Government had in it all the Appearance of Justice and Moderation; they honour'd and rewarded Virtue and Honour, Love to our Country, Courage, Gallantry: How did they crowne those that sav'd a Citizen, give Triumphs to those that had conquer'd their Enemies, give Prizes to those who excell'd in the most commendable Things? How did they honour Chastity in their Vestal Virgins; Temperance, Eloquence, Learning and Philosophy in the Persons of those that excelled, and erect Statues to their Memory when dead?

Yet all this while their Religion was Devil-worship; their Augurs and Southsayers, and the Priests of their Temples and Oracles, were Diviners, Magicians, Wizards, and in the very Letter of it Dealers with the Devil, and that in the worst Sense; all their Sacrifices, and their Institution of Games, for appeasing the angry Gods, were the most horrid and barbarous Pieces of Ignorance, or hellish Cruelty and Brutality, that could be imagin'd, even sometimes to human Sacrifices ... All the while that they erected Temples to Justice, to Honour, to Virtue, and to Peace, they studied all possible ways, by War, and Blood, to amass Treasures, and enlarge their Empire ... Whence was all this, but from the Devil? whose Government of the World had this Magick indeed always in it, that it spread Cruelty and Tyranny in all Parts, founded Dominion in Blood, and made the World a Theatre of Rapin and Violence . . .[36]

Defoe defines what the Black Art has traditionally meant, including the by now usual definition of witchcraft as devil-inspired maleficium, but then returns to the meaning that it has for him.

The brief Definition of what we call the Black Art, that is to say, as I would have it be understood in the rest of my Discourse, is, that it is a new general Term for all the Branches of that Correspondence which Mankind has maintained or does, or can carry on, between himself and the Devil, between this and the Infernal World . . .

Divining, the same as Southsaying.
Observing of Times.
Using Inchantment.
Witchcraft.
Charming, or setting of Spells.
Dealing with Familiar Spirits.
Wizardizing, or Sorcery, thought to be the same as Witchcraft, but mistaken.
Necromancy . . .

4. Witchcraft. This is indeed the blackest part of the Black Art it self: I need not describe it any farther than this, that it is a Power received immediately from the Devil to do Mischief; to gratify Rage, Envy, Malice, Revenge, and the vilest Passions of Men, giving it into their Hands to bewitch Men, Cattle, Places and Things; to burn and destroy, tho' limited, as hinted before in many Particular; the Effects of this Witchcraft we often see, and shall say more in its Place.

    This includes Persons being immediately agitated by an evil Spirit, carried often violently into the Air by the Help of the Devil, and being able to carry away others in the Air also; and not to insist upon all the improbable things said of them, and said to be done by them; yet that the Devil certainly plays his Pranks by those Tools sometimes in a most extravagant manner, I must grant. Why it is generally practis'd by old Women only, is a Point to be consider'd by itself.

    In this Article of Witchcraft is included what we call an Evil Tongue, an evil Eye, Cursing, Blasting, Bewitching, and abundance of Hellish things which those Creatures are permitted to practise, to the Hurt of those that they point their Malice against . . .

---

36. This portrayal of the Roman empire (as a dangerous precedent) had particular significance in eighteenth-century England: many eminent people were idealistically bent on creating a new 'Augustan Age'.

We have also some new Practitioners in Magick among ourselves, who deal with the Devil in a more exalted sublime Way ... We have also some modern Sects of Hellish Divinity not formerly known, no not to the Devil himself ... There remains a Vacancy too for our Friends of the Legend and Calendar ...[37]

In the Grecian and Roman Times, the Minds of Men untaught, and without the Assistance of Divine Illuminations, were easily impos'd upon, given up to strong Delusions, and to believe Lies ... Happy Ignorance! compar'd to our Age, who by their Excess of Knowledge and sense are arriv'd to a degree of Liberty, from the Slavery and Bondage of all Religion; that esteem themselves wise, in having found out a new Happiness for Mankind, freeing him from the Chains of Doctrine and Principle, triumphing in a State of compleat Atheism and Irreligion, and instead of worshipping many Gods, save themselves the trouble of Idolatry, and worship no God at all.

Infernal Spirits Themselves have deify'd,
But Devils nor Men the Being of God deny'd
'Till wiser Ages found new ways to Sin,
And turn'd the Devil out, to let the Atheist in ...

Having, in the last Chapter, brought down this Idol call'd Magick to its true Original, strip'd it of all the Masquerade Dresses, jested a little about it, and at last laid the Bastard at the Devil's Door, who is the true Father of it; One would think so Bare-fac'd an Imposture should be able to appear no longer in the World, that it would be hiss'd of the Stage, and that the very Boys and Girls would throw Stones and Dirt at it in the Street.

But the Case is quite otherwise, and in spight of Contradiction the Devil goes on his own way; if this or that Nation, or Country, or People drop him, and refuse him, he goes to another; like a true Pedlar, if he is answer'd No at one Door, he knocks at the next. If he sells Counterfeits, and is call'd Cheating Knave at one House, he calls himself honest Man at another. The Devil is never baulk'd, but carries on his Game, in spight of all the Repulses he meets with, nay in spite of Heaven itself ...

Defoe's history of the Black Art thus contains a crushing conflation of modern magicians, religious extremists, tricksters, witches and atheists in a way that suggests that magic is both a real, Satanic danger and a metaphor for the ills of human sinfulness and gullibility. Most importantly, though, it is a matter for history in its old sense: a story which may be either truth, fiction or both.

---

37. Catholics.

SELECT BIBLIOGRAPHY AND FURTHER READING

Works reproduced in this book

For further reference, printed editions containing more or less reliable transcripts or facsimiles are cited where they exist: otherwise microfilm reels and websites are given. Readers who have access to Early English Books Online will find many of these titles there.

Acts of Parliament. A. Luders *et al.*, eds, *Statutes of the Realm*. London, 1810.

Anon. *The Merry Devil of Edmonton* (London, 1608). C. F. Tucker-Brooke, ed., *The Shakespeare Apocrypha*. Oxford: Clarendon, 1918.

Anon. *A True and Impartial Relation of the Informations Against Three Witches* (London, 1682). *Witchcraft in Europe and America*, Reel 95. Woodbridge, CT: Research Publications.

Bee, Jesse. *The Most Wonderfull and True Storie of a certaine Witch named Alse Gooderige* (London, 1597), ed. John Denison. *Early English Books 1475–1640*, Reel 1790. Ann Arbor, MI: University Microfilms.

British Library Additional Manuscripts 27402, 32496 and Sloane 972 (see also Fairfax).

Cotta, John. *The Triall of Witch-craft* (London, 1616). *Witchcraft in Europe and America*, Reel 31. Woodbridge, CT: Research Publications.

Defoe, Daniel. *A System of Magick* (London, 1727). Facsimile, ed. Richard Landon. Wakefield: EP Publishing, 1973.

Dekker, Thomas, John Ford and William Rowley. *The Witch of Edmonton* (London, 1658). Available in *The Witch of Edmonton*, Simon Trussler, ed. London: Methuen, 1983, or (best edition) Peter Corbin and Douglas Sedge, eds, *Three Jacobean Witchcraft Plays*. Manchester: Manchester University Press, 1986.

Devon Record Office Chanter MS 855B.

Fairfax, Edward. 'A Discourse of witchcraft ... 1621'. Available as William Grainge, ed., *Daemonologia*. Harrogate, 1882.

Gifford, George. *A Dialogue concerning Witches and Witchcraftes* (London, 1593). Facsimile, ed. Beatrice White. London: Oxford University Press, 1931.

Glanvill, Joseph. *Saducismus Triumphatus* (London, 1681). Facsimile, ed. Bernhard Fabian, Vol. IX of *Collected Works of Joseph Glanvill*. Hildesheim and New York: Georg Olms, 1978.

Hale, John. *A Modest Enquiry Into the Nature of Witchcraft* (Boston, 1702). *Witchcraft in Europe and America*, Reel 48. Woodbridge, CT: Research Publications.

Heywood, Thomas. *The Wise Woman of Hogsdon* (London, 1638). Available as Michael H. Leonard, ed., *A Critical Edition of The Wise Woman of Hogsdon*. New York and London: Garland, 1980.

Hutchinson, Francis. *An Historical Essay Concerning Witchcraft* (London, 1718). *Witchcraft in Europe and America*, Reel 53. Woodbridge, CT: Research Publications.

Jonson, Ben. *The Masque of Queenes* and *The Alchemist* in *Workes* (London, 1616). *The Alchemist* is available in many modern editions, but both texts can be found in C. H. Herford, Percy Simpson and Evelyn Simpson, eds, *Ben Jonson*. 11 vols. Oxford: Clarendon Press, 1925–51.

Marlowe, Christopher. *The Tragical History of Dr Faustus* (London, 1604). Best edition: David Bevington and Eric Rasmussen, eds, *Doctor Faustus: A and B Texts*. Manchester: Manchester University Press, 1993.

Mather, Cotton. *The Wonders of the Invisible World* (Boston and London, 1692). In *Cotton Mather on Witchcraft*. New York: Dorset Press, 1991.

Mather, Increase. *Cases of Conscience . . .* (Boston and London, 1693). *Witchcraft in Europe and America*, Reel 66. Woodbridge, CT: Research Publications.

Middleton, Thomas. *The Witch* (London, 1778). Available in Peter Corbin and Douglas Sedge, eds, *Three Jacobean Witchcraft Plays*. Manchester: Manchester University Press, 1986.

Public Record Office PRO ASSI/35/21/4.

Records of the Court of Oyer and Terminer, 1692, property of the Supreme Judicial Court of Massachusetts, Division of Archives and Records Preservation. On deposit at the Phillips Library, Peabody Essex Museum, Salem, Massachusetts. Available at <etext.virginia.edu/salem/witchcraft/archives/essex/ecca/>.

Scot, Reginald. *The Discoverie of Witchcraft* (London, 1584). Brinsley Nicholson, ed., *Discoverie of Witchcraft*. London, 1886. Or, for an abbreviated version, Montague Summers, ed. New York: Dover Publications, 1972.

Shakespeare, William. *Macbeth* (London, 1623). Best edition: A. R. Braunmuller, ed. Cambridge: Cambridge University Press, 1997.

Spenser, Edmund. *The Faerie Queene* (London, 1590). Best edition: Thomas P. Roche, ed. London: Penguin, 1978.

W.W., *A true and just Recorde, of the Information, Examination and Confession of all the Witches, taken at S. Oses in the countie of Essex* (London, 1582). In Marion Gibson, ed., *Early Modern Witches*. London and New York: Routledge, 2000.

Select further reading on witchcraft in history and literature

These books will provide readers with detailed discussions of the issues introduced by this volume, sometimes in a wider context. The bibliography thereafter is divided into thematic sections, suggesting where readers might most helpfully start pursuing a particular interest, but many books overlap these categories, and individual articles or chapters are cited where they will be most useful.

General discussions of witches and witchcraft in English, European and American history

Ankarloo, Bengt and Gustav Henningsen, eds, *Early Modern European Witchcraft: Centres and Peripheries*. Oxford: Clarendon, 1993.

Barry, Jonathan, Marianne Hester and Gareth Roberts, eds, *Witchcraft in Early Modern Europe*. Cambridge: Cambridge University Press, 1996.

Briggs, Robin. *Witches and Neighbours*. London: HarperCollins, 1996.

Cohn, Norman. *Europe's Inner Demons* (1975). Revised edn. London: Pimlico, 1993.

Easlea, Brian. *The Witch-Hunt in Early Modern Europe*. 2nd edn. Harlow: Longman, 1995.

Ewen, C. L'Estrange. *Witch Hunting and Witch Trials*. London: Kegan Paul, Trench, Trubner, 1929.

Ginzburg, Carlo. *The Night Battles: Witchcraft and Agrarian Cults in the Sixteenth and Seventeenth Centuries*. Trans. John and Anne Tedeschi, 1966. Baltimore: Johns Hopkins University Press, 1983.

Ginzburg, Carlo. *Ecstasies; Deciphering the Witches' Sabbath*. Trans. Raymond Rosenthal. London: Hutchinson Radius, 1990.

Levack, Brian P. *The Witch-hunt in Early Modern Europe* (1987). 2nd edn. London and New York: Longman, 1995.

Oldridge, Darren. *The Witchcraft Reader*. London and New York: Routledge, 2002.

Roper, Lyndal. *Oedipus and the Devil: Witchcraft, Sexuality and Religion in Early Modern Europe*. London and New York: Routledge, 1994.

Scarre, Geoffrey. *Witchcraft and Magic in Sixteenth- and Seventeenth-Century Europe*. Basingstoke and London: Macmillan, 1987.

Sharpe, J. A. *Instruments of Darkness: Witchcraft in England 1550–1750*. London: Hamish Hamilton, 1996.

Thomas, Keith. *Religion and the Decline of Magic* (1971). London: Peregrine, 1978.

Witchcraft in the courts

Further primary reading:

Bernard, Richard. *A Guide to Grand Jury Men*. London, 1627.

Filmer, Robert. *An Advertisement to the Jury-Men of England Touching Witches*. London, 1653.

Secondary reading:

Beattie, J. M. *Crime and the Courts in England 1660–1800*. Oxford: Clarendon, 1986.

Cockburn, J. S. *A History of English Assizes 1558–1714*. Cambridge: Cambridge University Press, 1972.

Gaskill, Malcolm. 'Witches and Witnesses in Old and New England', in Stuart Clark, ed., *Languages of Witchcraft: Narrative, Ideology and Meaning in Early Modern Culture*. Basingstoke: Macmillan, 2001.

Gibson, Marion. 'Witchcraft Trials and a Methodology for Reading Them', in *Reading Witchcraft: Stories of Early English Witches*. London and New York: Routledge, 1999, chapter 2.

Jones, Norman. 'Defining Superstitions: Treasonous Catholics and the Act against Witchcraft of 1563', in Charles Carlton, ed., *State, Sovereigns and Safety in Early Modern England*. Stroud: Sutton Publishing, 1998, pp. 187-200.

Levack, Brian P. 'Possession, Witchcraft and the Law in Jacobean England', *Washington and Lee University Law Review*, 52 (1995), pp. 1613-40.

Rushton, Peter. 'Texts of Authority: Witchcraft Accusations and the Demonstration of Truth in Early Modern England', in Stuart Clark, ed., *Languages of Witchcraft: Narrative, Ideology and Meaning in Early Modern Culture*. Basingstoke: Macmillan, 2001.

Unsworth, C. R, 'Witchcraft Beliefs and Criminal Procedure in Early Modern England', in Thomas Watkin, ed., *Legal Record and Historical Reality*. London: Hambledon, 1989, pp. 71–98.

Elizabethan, Jacobean and pre–Restoration witchcraft

Further primary reading:

A collection of news pamphlets about witchcraft 1566–1621 is Marion Gibson, ed., *Early Modern Witches: Witchcraft Cases in Contemporary Writing*. London and New York: Routledge, 2000.

Anon. *The most strange and admirable discoverie of the three Witches of Warboys*. London, 1593.

Anon. *A Most Certain, Strange and True Discovery of a Witch. Being Taken by Some of the Parliament Forces*. London, 1643.

Hopkins, Matthew. *The Discovery of Witches*. London, 1647.

Secondary reading:

de Windt, Anne Reiber. 'Witchcraft and Conflicting Visions of the Ideal Village Community', *Journal of British Studies*, 34 (1995): pp. 427–63.

Elmer, Peter. 'Towards a Politics of Witchcraft in Early Modern England', in Stuart Clark, ed., *Languages of Witchcraft: Narrative, Ideology and Meaning in Early Modern Culture*. Basingstoke: Macmillan, 2001.

Gaskill, Malcolm. 'Witchcraft and Power in Early Modern England: The Case of Margaret Moore', in Jenny Kermode and Garthine Walker, eds, *Women, Crime and the Courts*. London: UCL, 1994.

Gaskill, Malcolm. 'Witchcraft in Early Modern Kent: Stereotypes and the Background to Accusations', in Jonathan Barry, Marianne Hester and Gareth Roberts, eds, *Witchcraft in Early Modern Europe*. Cambridge: Cambridge University Press, 1996.

Gibson, Joyce. *Hanged for Witchcraft: Elizabeth Lowys and Her Successors*. Canberra: Tudor, 1988.

Gibson, Marion. *Reading Witchcraft: Stories of Early English Witches*. London and New York: Routledge, 1999.

Gregory, Annabel. 'Witchcraft, Politics and Good Neighbourhood in Early Seventeenth-Century Rye', *Past and Present*, 133 (1991), pp. 31–66.

Holmes, Clive. 'Popular Culture? Witches, Magistrates and Divines in Early Modern England', in S. L. Kaplan, ed., *Understanding Popular Culture*. Berlin: Mouton, 1984, pp. 85-111.

Holmes, Clive. 'Women, Witnesses and Witches', *Past and Present*, 140 (1993), pp. 45–78.

Lumby, Jonathan. *The Lancashire Witch-Craze: Jennet Preston and the Lancashire Witches 1612*. Preston: Carnegie, 1995.

Macfarlane, Alan. *Witchcraft in Tudor and Stuart England* (1970). Prospect Heights, IL: Waveland Press, 1991.

Peel, Edgar and Pat Southern. *The Trials of the Lancashire Witches* (1969). Nelson: Hendon, 1994.

Poole, Robert, ed., *The Lancashire Witches: Histories and Stories*. Manchester: Manchester University Press, 2002.

Quaife, G. R. *Godly Zeal and Furious Rage*. London and Sydney: Croom Helm, 1987.

Rosen, Barbara. *Witchcraft in England 1558–1618* (1969). Amherst: University of Massachusetts Press, 1991.

Sharpe, J. A. 'Witchcraft and Women in Seventeenth-Century England: Some Northern Evidence', *Continuity and Change*, 6 (1991), pp. 179–99.

Sharpe, Jim. 'The Devil in East Anglia: The Matthew Hopkins Trials Reconsidered', in Jonathan Barry, Marianne Hester and Gareth Roberts, eds, *Witchcraft in Early Modern Europe*. Cambridge: Cambridge University Press, 1996.

Demonologies and demonologists

Further primary reading:

Cooper, Thomas. *The Mystery of Witch-Craft*. London, 1617.

Gifford, George. *A Discourse of the Subtill Practises of Devilles by Witches and Sorcerers*. London, 1587.

Holland, Henry. *A Treatise Against Witchcraft*. Cambridge, 1590.

James VI and I. *Daemonologie* (1597). London: The Bodley Head, 1924. Available in Normand and Roberts, eds, *Witchcraft in Early Modern Scotland*, below.

Mason, James. *The Anatomy of Sorcerie*. Cambridge, 1612.

Perkins, William. *A Discourse of the Damned Art of Witchcraft*. Cambridge, 1608.

Roberts, Alexander. *A Treatise of Witchcraft*. London, 1616.

Secondary reading:

Anglo, Sydney. 'Reginald Scot's *Discoverie of Witches*: Scepticism and Sadduceeism', in Sydney Anglo, ed., *The Damned Art*. London, Henley and Boston: Routledge Kegan Paul, 1977.

Clark, Stuart. 'King James' *Daemonologie*: Witchcraft and Kingship', in Sydney Anglo, ed., *The Damned Art*. London, Henley and Boston: Routledge Kegan Paul, 1977.

Clark, Stuart. 'The Scientific Status of Demonology', in Brian Vickers, ed., *Occult and Scientific Mentalities in the Renaissance*. Cambridge: Cambridge University Press, 1984.

Clark, Stuart. 'Protestant Demonology: Sin, Superstition and Society (*c.* 1520–*c.* 1630)', in Bengt Ankarloo and Gustav Henningsen, eds, *Early Modern European Witchcraft: Centres and Peripheries*. Oxford: Clarendon, 1993.

Clark, Stuart. *Thinking with Demons: The Idea of Witchcraft in Early Modern Europe*. Oxford: Clarendon, 1997.

Diethelm, O. 'The Medical Teaching of Demonology in the Seventeenth and Eighteenth Centuries', *Journal of the Behavioural Sciences*, 6 (1970), pp. 3–15.

Hitchcock, James. 'George Gifford and Puritan Witch Beliefs', *Archiv fur Reformationsgeschichte*, 58 (1967), pp. 92–4.

Macfarlane, Alan. 'A Tudor Anthropologist: George Gifford's *Discourse* and *Dialogue*', in Sydney Anglo, ed., *The Damned Art*. London, Henley and Boston: Routledge Kegan Paul, 1977.

Wallace, D. 'George Gifford, Puritan Propaganda and Popular Religion in Elizabethan England', *Sixteenth-Century Journal*, 9 (1978), pp. 27–49.

Literary witches

Further primary reading:
Heywood, Thomas and Richard Brome. *The Late Lancashire Witches* (1634).
Lyly, John. *Mother Bombie* (1594).
Marston, John. *Sophonisba* (1604–6).
Shakespeare, William. *The Tempest* (1611).

Secondary reading:

Adelman, Janet. 'Born of Woman: Fantasies of Maternal Power in *Macbeth*', in Marjorie Garber, ed., *Cannibals, Witches and Divorce*. Baltimore: Johns Hopkins University Press, 1987.

Blackburn, Willia. 'Heavenly Words: Marlowe's Faustus as a Renaissance Magician', *English Studies in Canada*, 4 (1978), pp. 1–14.

Callaghan, Dymphna. 'Wicked Women in *Macbeth*: A Study of Power, Ideology and the Production of Motherhood', in Mario A. Di Cesare, ed., *Reconsidering the Renaissance*. Binghampton, NY: Medieval and Renaissance Texts and Studies, 1992.

Clark, Stuart. 'Inversion, Misrule and the Meaning of Witchcraft', *Past and Present*, 87 (1980), pp. 98–127.

Comensoli, Viviana. 'Witchcraft and Domestic Tragedy in *The Witch of Edmonton*', in Jean R. Brink, Allison P. Coudert and Maryanne C. Horowitz, eds, *The Politics of Gender in Early Modern Europe*. Kirksville, MO: Sixteenth-Century Journal Publications, 1989.

Dawson, Anthony B. 'Witchcraft/Bigamy: Cultural Conflict in *The Witch of Edmonton*', *Renaissance Drama*, n.s. 20 (1989), p. 82.

Dolan, Frances. *Dangerous Familiars: Representations of Domestic Crime in England 1550–1700*. Ithaca, NY, and London: Cornell University Press, 1994.

Gibson, Marion. *Reading Witchcraft: Stories of Early English Witches*. London and New York: Routledge, 1999.

Greenblatt, Stephen. 'Shakespeare Bewitched', in Jeffrey N. Cox and Larry J. Reynolds, eds, *New Historical Literary Study*. Princeton, NJ: Princeton University Press, 1993.

Greene, Thomas M. 'Magic and Festivity at the Renaissance Court', *Renaissance Quarterly*, 40:4 (Winter 1987), pp. 636–59.

Grinnell, Richard. 'The Witch, the Transvestite and the Actor: Destabilising Gender and the Renaissance Stage', *Studies in the Humanities*, 23:2 (December 1996), pp. 163–84.

Harris, Anthony. *Night's Black Agents: Witchcraft and Magic in Seventeenth-Century English Drama*. Manchester: Manchester University Press, 1980.

Hattaway, Michael. 'Women and Witchcraft: The Case of *The Witch of Edmonton*', *Trivium*, 20 (May 1985), pp. 49–68.

Keller, James R. 'Middleton's *The Witch*: Witchcraft and the Domestic Female Hero', *Journal of the Fantastic in the Arts*, 4:4 (1991), pp. 37–59.

Lancashire, Anne. '*The Witch*: Stage Flop or Political Mistake?', in Kenneth Friedenreich, ed., *"Accompaninge the Players": Essays Celebrating Thomas Middleton, 1580–1980*. New York: AMS Press, 1983.

Leuschner, Kristin Jeanne. 'Creating the "Known True Story": Sixteenth- and Seventeenth-Century Murder and Witchcraft Pamphlets and Plays'. Thesis, University of California, 1992.

Normand, Lawrence. 'Witchcraft, King James and the *Masque of Queenes*', in Claude J. Summers and Ted-Larry Pebworth, eds, *Representing Women in the English Renaissance*. Columbia: University of Missouri Press, 1997.

Normand, Lawrence and Gareth Roberts, eds, *Witchcraft in Early Modern Scotland*. Exeter: Exeter University Press, 2000.

Orgel, Stephen. *The Jonsonian Masque*. Cambridge, MA: Harvard University Press, 1965.

Orgel, Stephen. '*Macbeth* and the Antic Round', *Shakespeare Survey*, 52 (1999), pp. 143–53.

Purkiss, Diane. *The Witch in History*. London and New York: Routledge, 1996.

Roberts, Gareth. 'Magic and Witchcraft in English Drama and Poetry 1558–1634'. Thesis, University of London, 1976.

Roberts, Gareth. 'The Descendants of Circe: Witches and Renaissance Fictions', in Jonathan Barry, Marianne Hester and Gareth Roberts, eds, *Witchcraft in Early Modern Europe: Studies in Culture and Belief*. Cambridge: Cambridge University Press, 1996.

Roberts, Gareth. 'Necromantic Books: Christopher Marlowe, Dr. Faustus and Agrippa of Nettesheim', in Darryll Grantley and Peter Roberts, eds, *Christopher Marlowe and English Renaissance Culture*. Aldershot: Ashgate, 1996.

Roberts, Gareth. 'Marlowe and the Metaphysics of Magicians', in J. A. Downie and J. T. Parnell, eds, *Constructing Christopher Marlowe*. Cambridge: Cambridge University Press, 2000.

Tetzeli von Rosador, Kurt. 'The Power of Magic from *Endimion* to *the Tempest*', *Shakespeare Survey*, 43 (1991), pp. 1–13.

Willis, Deborah. *Malevolent Nurture: Witch-hunting and Maternal Power in Early Modern England*. Ithaca, NY, and London: Cornell University Press, 1995.

Wills, Garry. *Witches and Jesuits: Shakespeare's* Macbeth. Oxford: Oxford University Press, 1994.

Wynne-Davies, Marion. 'The Queen's Masque: Renaissance Women and the Seventeenth-century Court Masque', in Marion Wynne-Davies and S. P. Cerasano, eds, *Gloriana's Face: Women, Public and Private, in the English Renaissance*. London: Harvester, 1992.

See also 'Magicians, cunning people and tricksters'.

Possession – the devil and the witch

Further primary reading (There are many pamphlet accounts of possessions or obsessions. These are some of the more coherent and informative.)

Anon. *The Disclosing of a Late Counterfeyted Possession by the Devyl of Two Maydens Within the Citie of London*. London, 1574.

Anon. *The Most Strange and Admirable Discoverie of the Three Witches of Warboys*. London, 1593.

Anon. *A True and Most Dreadfull Discourse of a Woman Possessed with the Devill*. London, 1584. Republished as *A Miracle of Miracles*. London, 1614.

Baddeley, Richard. *The Boy of Bilson*. London, 1622.

Darrell, John. *An Apologie, or Defence of the Possession of William Sommers*. Amsterdam (?), 1599.

Darrell, John. *A True Narration of the Strange and Grevous Vexation by the Devil of Seven Persons in Lancashire and William Somers of Nottingham.* n.p., 1600.

Fisher, John. *The Copy of a Letter Describing the Wonderful Woorke of God in Delivering a Mayden Within the City of Chester.* London, 1564.

Harsnet, Samuel. *A Declaration of Egregious Popish Impostures.* London, 1603.

Harsnet, Samuel. *A Discovery of the Fraudulent Practises of John Darrell.* London, 1599.

Nyndge, Edward. *A Booke Declaringe the Fearfull Vexasion of One Alexander Nyndge.* London, 1573.

Secondary reading:

Brownlow, F. W. *Shakespeare, Harsnett and the Devils of Denham.* London and Toronto: Associated University Presses; Newark: University of Delaware Press, 1993.

Connor, Stephen. 'Possessions', in *Dumbstruck: A Cultural History of Ventriloquism.* Oxford: Oxford University Press, 2000, chapters 4–6.

Greenblatt, Stephen. 'Shakespeare and the Exorcists', in *Shakespearean Negotiations.* Oxford: Clarendon, 1988, chapter 4.

MacDonald, Michael, ed., *Witchcraft and Hysteria in Elizabethan London.* London and New York: Tavistock Routledge, 1991.

Rickert, Corinne Holt. *The Case of John Darrell, Minister and Exorcist.* Gainesville: University of Florida Monographs, 1962.

Sharpe, James. *The Bewitching of Anne Gunter.* London: Profile, 1999.

Walker, D. P. *Unclean Spirits.* London: Scolar, 1981.

See also accounts of the Salem witchcraft episode for discussions of demonic possession and obsession.

Magicians, cunning people and tricksters

Further primary reading:

Anon. *The Brideling, Sadling, and Ryding, of a Rich Churle.* London, 1595.

Anon. *A Briefe Description of the Notorious Life of John Lambe, Otherwise Called Doctor Lambe, Together with his Ignominious Death.* London, 1628.

Cotta, John. *A Short Discoverie of the Unobserved Dangers of Severall Sorts of Ignorant and Unconsiderate Practisers of Physicke in England.* London, 1612. Republished as *A True Discovery of the Empiricke with the Fugitive Physition and Quacksalver.* London, 1617.

Coxe, Francis. *A Short Treatise Declarynge the Detestable Wickednesse of Magicall Sciences.* London, 1561.

Dee, John. *A True and Faithfull Relation of What Passed . . . Between Dr. John Dee and Some Spirits.* London, 1659.

Greene, Robert. *Friar Bacon and Friar Bungay* (late 1580s?).

Shakespeare, William. *The Tempest* (1611).

Wier, Johannes. *De praestigiis daemonum* (1563), in *Witches, Devils and Doctors in the Renaissance.* Trans. John Shea, ed. George Mora. Binghampton, NY: Medieval and Renaissance Texts and Studies, 1991.

Secondary reading:

Butler, Elizabeth M. *Ritual Magic* (1949). Stroud: Sutton Publishing, 1998.

Butler, Elizabeth M. *The Fortunes of Faust* (1952). Stroud: Sutton Publishing, 1998.

Couliano, Ioan P. *Eros and Magic in the Renaissance*. Trans. Margaret Cook. Chicago and London: University of Chicago Press, 1987.

Curry, Patrick. *Prophecy and Power: Astrology in Early Modern England*. Princeton, NJ: Princeton University Press, 1989.

Davies, Lindsay. 'Neither Maids Nor Wives in *The Wise Woman of Hogsdon*', in Alvin Vos, ed., *Place and Displacement in the Renaissance*. Binghampton, NY: Medieval and Renaissance Texts and Studies, 1995.

Davies, Owen. 'Healing Charms in Use in England and Wales 1700–1950', *Folklore*, 107 (1996), pp. 19–32.

Davies, Owen. 'Cunning Folk in England and Wales During the Eighteenth and Nineteenth Centuries', *Rural History*, 8 (1997), pp. 91–107.

Easlea, Brian. *Witch Hunting, Magic and the New Philosophy*. Brighton: Harvester, 1980.

French, Peter. *John Dee: The World of an Elizabethan Magus*. London and New York: Routledge, 1972.

Geyer-Kordesch, J. 'Whose Enlightenment? Medicine, Witchcraft, Melancholia and Pathology', in Roy Porter, ed., *Medicine in the Enlightenment*. Amsterdam: Rodopi, 1994.

Harley, David. 'Historians as Demonologists: The Myth of the Midwife-Witch', *Social History of Medicine*, 3:1 (1990), pp. 1–26.

Hill, Christopher. 'Science and Magic in Seventeenth-Century England', in Raphael Samuel and Gareth Stedman Jones, eds, *Culture, Ideology and Politics*. London: Routledge and Kegan Paul, 1982.

Knapp, Peggy A. 'The Work of Alchemy', *Journal of Medieval and Early Modern Studies*, 30:3 (Fall 2000), pp. 575–99.

Levin, Richard. 'Flower Maidens, Wise Women, Witches and the Gendering of Knowledge in English Renaissance Drama', in John Mucciolo *et al.*, eds, *Shakespeare's Universe: Renaissance Ideas and Conventions*. Aldershot: Scolar, 1996.

MacDonald, Michael. *Mystical Bedlam: Madness, Anxiety and Healing in Seventeenth-Century England*. Cambridge: Cambridge University Press, 1981.

MacDonald, Michael, ed., *Witchcraft and Hysteria in Elizabethan London*. London and New York: Routledge, 1991.

Maxwell-Stuart, P. G., ed. and trans., *The Occult in Early Modern Europe: A Documentary History*. Basingstoke: Macmillan, 1999.

Mebane, John S. *Renaissance Magic and the Return of the Golden Age: The Occult Tradition of Marlowe, Jonson and Shakespeare*. Lincoln, NE, and London: University of Nebraska Press, 1989.

Roberts, Gareth. *The Mirror of Alchemy*. London: The British Library, 1994.

Roberts, Gareth. 'The Earliest Tudor Witch in Print: John Walsh', in Mike Pincombe, ed., *The Anatomy of Tudor Literature*. Aldershot: Ashgate, 2001.

Salgado, Gamini. *The Elizabethan Underworld*. London: J. M. Dent, 1977.

Sawyer, Ronald. 'Strangely Handled in all her Lyms: Witchcraft and Healing in Jacobean England', *Journal of Social History*, 22:3 (1989), pp. 461–85.

Shumaker, Wayne. *The Occult Sciences in the Renaissance*. Berkeley: University of California Press, 1972.

Vickers, Brian. *Occult and Scientific Mentalities in the Renaissance*. Cambridge: Cambridge University Press, 1984.

See also 'Literary witches'.

Witchcraft in America

Further primary reading:

Calef, Robert. *More Wonders of the Invisible World*. London, 1700.

Lawson, Deodat. *A Brief and True Narrative of Some Remarkable Passages Relating to Sundry Persons Afflicted by Witchcraft*. Boston, 1692.

Willard, Samuel. *Some Miscellany Observations on Our Present Debates Respecting Witchcrafts*. Philadelphia, 1692.

Secondary reading:

Boyer, Paul and Stephen Nissenbaum. *Salem Possessed: The Social Origins of Witchcraft*. Cambridge, MA, and London: Harvard University Press, 1974.

Breslaw, Elaine G. *Tituba, Reluctant Witch of Salem: Devilish Indians and Puritan Fantasies*. New York and London: New York University Press, 1996.

Gardner, Richard A. *Sex Abuse Hysteria: Salem Witch Trials Revisited.* Cresskill, NJ: Creative Therapeutics, 1991.

Hall, David. *Witch-hunting in Seventeenth-Century New England: A Documentary History 1638–1693*. 2nd edn. Boston: Northeastern University Press, 1999.

Hansen, Chadwick. *Witchcraft at Salem*. New York: George Braziller, 1969.

Harley, David. 'Explaining Salem: Calvinist Psychology and the Diagnosis of Possession', *American Historical Review*, 101 (1996), pp. 307–30.

Hill, Frances. *A Delusion of Satan: The Full Story of the Salem Witch Trials* (1995). New York: Da Capo, 1997.

Hill, Frances, ed., *The Salem Witch Trials Reader*. New York: Da Capo, 2000.

Hoffer, Peter Charles. *The Salem Witchcraft Trials: A Legal History*. Lawrence, KA: University of Kansas Press, 1997.

Karlsen, Carol F. *The Devil in the Shape of a Woman: Witchcraft in Colonial New England*. New York and London: W.W. Norton, 1987.

Kittredge, G. L. *Witchcraft in Old and New England*. Cambridge, MA: Harvard University Press, 1929.

Le Beau, Bryan F. *The Story of the Salem Witch Trials*. Upper Saddle River, NJ: Prentice-Hall, 1998.

Levin, David. 'Did the Mathers Disagree about the Salem Witchcraft Trials?' *Proceedings of the American Antiquarian Society*, 95:1 (1985), pp. 19–37.

Mappen, Mark. *Witches and Historians: Interpretations of Salem*. 2nd edn. Malabar, FL: Krieger Publishing, 1996.

Putnam Demos, John. *Entertaining Satan: Witchcraft and the Culture of Early New England*. Oxford: Oxford University Press, 1982.

Robinson, Enders A. *The Devil Discovered: Salem Witchcraft 1692*. 2nd edn. Prospect Heights, IL: Waveland Press, 2001.

Rosenthal, Bernard. *Salem Story: Reading the Witch Trials of 1692*. Cambridge: Cambridge University Press, 1993.

Smolinski, Reiner. 'Salem Witchcraft and the Hermeneutical Crisis of the Seventeenth Century: Cotton Mather's Response to Thomas Hobbes and the Modern Sadducees', in Winfried Herget, ed., *The Salem Witchcraft Persecutions: Perspectives, Contexts, Representations*. Trier: Wissenschaftlicher, 1994.

Starkey, Marion L. *The Devil in Massachusetts*. New York: Time, 1949.

Thomas, Wyn M. 'Cotton Mather's *Wonders of the Invisible World*: Some Metamorphoses of Salem Witchcraft', in Sydney Anglo, ed., *The Damned Art*.

London, Henley and Boston: Routledge Kegan Paul, 1977.

Trask, Richard B. *The Devil Hath Been Raised: A Documentary History of the Salem Village Witchcraft Outbreak of March 1692*. Revised edn. Danvers, MA: Yeoman Press, 1997.

Weisman, Richard. *Witchcraft, Magic and Religion in Seventeenth-century Massachusetts*. Amherst: University of Massachusetts Press, 1984.

Decline and change: post–Restoration and eighteenth–century witchcraft

Further primary reading:

Anon. *A Tryal of Witches at the Assizes held at Bury St. Edmonds*. London, 1682.

Anon. *The Case of the Hertfordshire Witch Consider'd*. London, 1712.

Anon. *A Full Confutation of Witchcraft*. London, 1712.

Boulton, Richard. *A Compleat History of Magick, Sorcery and Witchcraft*. 2 vols. London, 1715–16.

Boulton, Richard. *The Possibility and Reality of Magick, Sorcery and Witchcraft*. London, 1722.

Bovet, Richard. *Pandaemonium*. London, 1684.

Bragge, Francis. *A Full and Impartial Account of the Discovery of Sorcery and Witchcraft*. London, 1712.

Bragge, Francis. *Witchcraft Farther Display'd Containing . . . An Account of the Witchcraft Practis'd by Jane Wenham . . .* London, 1712.

Bragge, Francis. *A Defense of the Proceedings against Jane Wenham*. London, 1712.

Webster, John. *The Displaying of Supposed Witchcraft*. London, 1677.

Secondary reading:

Bostridge, Ian. 'Witchcraft Repealed', in Jonathan Barry, Marianne Hester and Gareth Roberts, eds, *Witchcraft in Early Modern Europe*. Cambridge: Cambridge University Press, 1996.

Bostridge, Ian. *Witchcraft and Its Transformations c. 1650–c. 1750*. Oxford: Clarendon, 1997.

Davies, Owen. 'Urbanization and the Decline of Witchcraft: An Examination of London', *Journal of Social History*, 30 (1997), pp. 597–617.

Davies, Owen. *Witchcraft, Magic and Culture 1736–1951*. Manchester: Manchester University Press, 1999.

de Blecourt, Willem. 'On the Continuation of Witchcraft', in Jonathan Barry, Marianne Hester and Gareth Roberts, eds, *Witchcraft in Early Modern Europe*. Cambridge: Cambridge University Press, 1996.

Geis, Gilbert and Ivan Bunn. *A Trial of Witches: A Seventeenth-Century Witchcraft Prosecution*. London and New York: Routledge, 1997.

Gijswijt-Hofstra, Marijke, Brian P. Levack and Roy Porter, eds, *Witchcraft and Magic in Europe: The Eighteenth and Nineteenth Centuries*. London: Athlone Press, 1999.

Guskin, P. J. 'The Context of English Witchcraft: The Case of Jane Wenham (1712)', *Eighteenth-Century Studies*, 15 (1981), pp. 48–71.

Jobe, Thomas Harmon. 'The Devil in Restoration Science: The Glanvill–Webster Witchcraft Debate', *Isis*, 72 (1981), pp. 343–56.

INDEX

Note: Many entries relate to witchcraft and witches without specifying these words; works are listed separately from their authors under their titles. An 'n.' following a page number indicates a note.